ALCOHOLISM TREATMENT IN TRANSITION

ALCOHOLISM TREATMENT IN TRANSITION

Edited by
Griffith Edwards and Marcus Grant

UNIVERSITY PARK PRESS BALTIMORE

© 1980 Alcohol Education Research Centre and Addiction Research Unit
Published in North America by
UNIVERSITY PARK PRESS
233 East Redwood Street
Baltimore, Maryland

ISBN 0-8391-4132-7

LC Number: 80-51462

British Library Cataloguing in Publication Data

Alcoholism treatment in transition.
    1. Alcoholism – Treatment – Congresses
    I. Edwards, Griffith II. Grant, Marcus
    III. Alcohol Education Centre IV. University
    of London. *Addiction Research Unit*
    616.8'61'06   RC565

Typeset by Leaper & Gard Ltd, Bristol

Printed and bound in Great Britain

CONTENTS

INTRODUCTION

The purpose of this book is to aid a process of re-thinking alcoholism treatment. Such a process is clearly underway in many parts of the world. A volume such as this can be useful in the modest role of abetting a re-thinking, while it would be far too ambitious for any book at present confidently to say, 'These are now the answers'. Anyone looking for closed and definitive pronouncements, anyone seeking a book which proclaims, 'This is now the way to treat alcoholism', had better quickly go elsewhere.

Alcoholism treatment is very definitely in transition, abandoning old certainties, searching for new syntheses — and that is the only position which we would definitely care to take. These chapters might at best be seen as similar to contributions to one of those seminar series where people feel safe enough to speak their minds and search horizons without striking postures, and where there is a spirit of criticism without nihilistic excess, and a true commitment to a search for understanding. At the end of such a series the participants can sometimes feel that movement and shape can be seen in what was previously a rather amorphous set of ideas. We would hope that those who read this book may enjoy such sense of participation in rewarding adventure.

The contents have been ordered in terms of a number of sections, and the first of these is entitled 'Transition as Challenge'. For any individual, institution, or clinical and scientific endeavour, the experience of transition can be good or bad, handled well or negatively and with fright. It can be characterised by a desperate hanging on to old positions, by a mad flight after new fancies, or it can be just a sort of falling to bits. How transition can be used creatively is the subject of these four chapters.

The second section deals with the question, 'Does Treatment Work?' It is here perhaps that the path between optimism and pessimism is most difficult honestly to steer. The question certainly has to be disarticulated into asking what works for whom, and when. And the third section therefore logically takes as its title 'Towards better questions'.

Whatever the treatment, there is also the treatment system. Study of this system ignores the real material if we are only willing to entertain the assumption that the system is a rationally determined 'health care delivery system', an organisation man's disembodied dream. The organisation of alcoholism treatment is a social happening in its own right, subject to its own evolutionary forces. It is these questions which are here examined.

What though is treatment, and what are we actually treating? Anyone coming into this field from outside might be excused a sharp comment or two on what sometimes looks more like chronic muddle than transition. The debate on what we mean by the key word 'alcoholism' is never ending, but old models of understanding are breaking down and no longer serve us too well. The next section therefore deals with 'Models in Transition'.

The brief final section borrows as its title a phrase which Aubrey Lewis employed to describe the general state of enquiring minds — a state which he saw as being properly characterised as 'Between guesswork and certainty'. This chapter attempts to sum up what others have, as it were, contributed to the seminar.

One issue, not discussed elsewhere in this book, deserves some comment here. The process of re-thinking alcoholism treatment has profound implications for the way we educate and train those whom we expect to do the treating. Most education presumes a happy consensus from which enquiry can logically proceed. The challenge of a subject which is genuinely in transition is that no such consensus is apparent. The excitement is that education itself becomes the process of re-thinking.

There is more to this than giving extra work to the curriculum planners, asking them to develop courses which take account of the changing views of alcohol problems. It cannot be ignored, indeed it is stressed in several of the chapters in this book, that treatment is not a hermetic activity. There is far more to treatment than making sick people well again. A growing part of the treater's responsibility has to do with communicating relevant information to the public at large and in particular to those sections of the public known to be at higher risk. The re-thinking is, therefore, not the prerogative of the treaters. It becomes, through their efforts, part of a larger public debate, which they can stimulate and encourage. Health professionals involved in alcoholism treatment play a crucial role, for example, in the shift we are seeing towards a greater openness to social policy changes, to self-monitoring and to new, pragmatic approaches to treatment.

That openness needs to be reflected in an acceptance in pre- and post-qualification training that the re-thinking involves crossing some traditional boundaries between disciplines. What emerges from this book, above all else, is the imperative need for all those involved in treating alcoholism to become actively and continually involved in developing the skills of themselves and their colleagues. At times of transition, more of us can afford to stand still and watch the patients pass by. Since transition is a process, so too training is best seen not as an end in itself, but as a movement, careful and adventurous, from the guesswork towards the certainty. Thus, education and training become an integral part of the process of re-thinking which this book is seeking to assist.

The general shape of this book was determined by contributions to a conference held at the Institute of Psychiatry in April 1979, jointly organised by the Alcohol Education Centre and the Institute of Psychiatry. Most of the original papers have been substantially revised and some additional material has been added. Generous financial backing was provided by the Department of Health and Social Security (UK), the Addiction Research Foundation (Toronto), the National Institute on Alcoholism and Alcohol Abuse (USA) and the World Health Organisation (Geneva). The planning of the meeting was jointly shared with those organisations and the Royal College of Psychiatrists (London), while the International Council on Alcohol and Addictions helped with publicity for the meeting. The original input of ideas was therefore very international and in particular invited an awareness of the need to make the connections between science, clinical care and governmental concerns.

We would particularly draw attention to the fact that this book contains a discussion of alcoholism treatment in the Third World (Chapter 12). That only one chapter deals directly with the problems of that large segment of the globe might be seen as insufficient, but that chapter at least stands as a reminder that the West does not hold the monopoly of problems, and insensitively exported Western solutions will increasingly be rejected as inept and unwanted. Neither should we indulge in the presumption that Europe and North America are for ever the innovators and teachers. A better world sharing of thinking on what are certainly shared problems, could provide an immensely beneficial corrective to insularity.

Acknowledgements

Our thanks are due to the various national and international organisations already named, and we would like personally to thank Dr Alan Sippert (DHSS), Dr Frederick Glaser (ARF), Dr Robin Murray (Royal College of Psychiatrists), Dr D.L. Davies (AEC) and Dr Lee Towle (NIAA) for a fund of ideas which lay behind the planning of the conference and hence the book.

On the organisational side we must particularly thank Miss Nina Little. Mrs Joyce Oliphant, Mrs Julia Polglaze and Miss Beryl Skinner skilfully undertook the secretarial work. Dr David Hirst kindly provided us with the index.

And finally we wish as editors to thank the contributors to this book who have shown such patience and good nature, and who have, we believe, responded magnificently to the challenge we set them.

Griffith Edwards
Marcus Grant

Part One

TRANSITION AS CHALLENGE

1 THE DOCTOR'S DILEMMA

George E. Vaillant

Introduction

For anyone who both treats alcoholism and engages in related research, there exists a dilemma. Much of the evidence is not there to support his treatment. Confidently to persist, is he a fool, or a knave or a sensible man? How can he retain open-mindedness without losing the confidence to deal with the next patient who is certainly expecting his help? This chapter represents an effort to resolve that dilemma.

Thomas Szasz[1] would have us believe that alcoholism, like the dilemma, is a mythical beast. Unfortunately, sometimes mythical beasts are endowed with real horns. One horn of the dilemma is that Szasz, Al-Anon and the best follow-up research instructs would-be care-givers that they are powerless over alcoholism. To try too hard to *cure* an alcoholic is to break one's heart and follow-up studies suggest that elaborate treatments may be no better than brief sensible advice.[2]

The other horn of the dilemma is the fact that to ignore a chronic malady as painful to the individual, as damaging to his health, as destructive to the family and as refractory to will power, to motivation and to common sense as alcoholism — for doctors to ignore such a malady — is unconscionable. What are we to do?

My own knowledge of this dilemma began ten years ago. I was asked by the relatives of an alcoholic friend for help. The friend, aged 55, was quietly drinking himself to death. He had exhausted the patience of probably the wisest family doctor in Boston; he had frustrated the staff at perhaps Boston's finest teaching hospital; and he had managed to spend several weeks in an excellent Boston psychiatric hospital as a 'bipolar depression' without noticeable improvement. His relatives pointed out that I was considered knowledgeable about addictions. What or whom could I suggest? I called a few very senior colleagues and then reported back that no one on the faculty of my medical school was expert in the treatment of alcoholism and that, as best I knew, modern medicine had little to offer.

The Cambridge-Somerville (CASPAR) Programme

Shortly afterwards, as part of the trend in both America and England to acknowledge the enormity of the alcohol problem, a comprehensive alcohol treatment programme began at the Cambridge-Somerville Mental Health Center. Since Cambridge and her sister city, Somerville, contained an estimated 20,000 alcoholics, the decision was made to redeploy present services so as to offer much less intensive help to many more people. Thus, the single staff member who, by appointment, used to offer therapy and counsel to these 20,000 souls was replaced by a much better staffed walk-in clinic. Caught up in the historical moment and because Boston and Harvard had been found wanting, my friend turned to this public clinic. He found hopeful paraprofessionals who were willing to meet him where he was, who discussed alcoholism *as if* it were a disease — neither a psychological symptom nor some vague unnamed problem waiting to be understood. The clinic staff invited him to groups that they led, in order to discuss his problem with other alcoholics. In part, these groups were designed as stepping stones between a walk-in clinic in a municipal hospital and eventual use of the cheaper, more accessible resources of Alcoholics Anonymous (AA). But my friend had often previously pointed out that for him Alcoholics Anonymous was not a viable alternative. He was no joiner; he rarely went to church; he was an artist; and he was much too sophisticated, both socially and intellectually, to get involved. After two years of clinic contact in the acceptable 'medical' environment of the Cambridge Hospital, my friend found his way into AA. Two years later he became a group chairman and to the best of my knowledge has been sober for the last seven years. His family relationships and health have been gradually restored.

Supported by the generous infusion of government funds into community-based mental health programmes for the treatment of alcoholism, I too was caught in the historical moment. Two years after I had told my friend that I knew of no treatment for alcoholism, I joined the staff at Cambridge-Somerville Mental Health and Retardation Center as a psychiatric consultant to the alcohol programme which had been developed there by Hilma Unterberger, the Center Assistant Director. This programme was designed on a medical model based in a general hospital, with an internist as a director. The programme includes round the clock walk-in counselling to patients and relatives, it includes 'wet' and 'dry' shelters, groups, immediate access to detoxification and to medical and psychiatric consultation. The programme offers alcohol

consultation to the medical, surgical and psychiatric wards, provides
halfway houses for men and women and a comprehensive alcohol
education programme to an entire city school system. At present, we
see 1,000 *new* clients a year, carry out 2,500 detoxifications (50 per
cent directly from the police) and have 20,000 outpatient visits a year.
Annually the programme costs about a million dollars and, including
our education personnel, our staff is around 80. No one is turned away
because of multiple relapses, poor motivation, poverty, criminal history
or skid row membership. At the same time, because skilled and hopeful
consultation is always available, the rich have come as well as the poor.

In joining this programme, I changed too. My training had been at a
famous teaching hospital that from past despair posted an unwritten
sign over the door that read 'Alcoholic Patients Need Not Apply'. I had
then worked for years at a community mental health centre that in
spite of a firm commitment to meet the expressed mental health needs
of the community, ignored alcoholism — which, after all, was untreat-
able and would overwhelm the clinic. At Cambridge Hospital, I learned
how, for the first time, to diagnose the illness and to think of abstinence
in terms of one day at a time. Instead of pondering the sociological and
psychodynamic complexities of alcoholism, while at the bedside I
learned how to keep things simple. (If the over-simplification inherent
in Jellinek's disease model works mischief in research, too much doubt
and vagueness wreaks havoc in the clinic.) My capacity to interview
alcoholics improved. Every time I went, in keeping with clinic policy,
to AA meetings — which was monthly for seven years — I took medical
students and residents along. To me alcoholism became an exciting,
fascinating disease. Students and registrars — if not senior consultants —
were converted to the idea that alcoholics *should* and could be treated
in the general hospital. It seemed perfectly clear to me that by meeting
the immediate individual needs of the alcoholic, by using multi-modality
therapy, by disregarding motivation, by turning to recovering alcoholics
rather than to PhDs for lessons in breaking self-detrimental and more or
less involuntary habits, and by slowly moving patients from the general
hospital into the treatment system of AA, I was working for the most
exciting alcohol programme in the world.

But here is the rub. What alcoholism has failed to borrow is from
medical understanding of chronic relapsing disease — the first principle
of which is to discover the natural history of the disease in question.
Therefore, in our clinic we have continued to follow our first 100 inpatients every year since 1971. (The cost has been less than $2,000 a
year.) Originally the patients had been hospitalised for an average of

eight days. After detoxification these gamma alcoholics (almost all had required 500 mg or more of chlordiazepoxide during withdrawal) were exposed to two or three discussion groups, to educational films, to didactic lectures on alcoholism, and to counselling by staff members, many of whom themselves belong to AA. On discharge they were offered an unlimited invitation to a continuing programme of twice a week staff-led discussion groups. As the years passed, a majority have returned to the clinic for counselling or detoxification or halfway house placement or help with welfare and family counselling. Initially, we created a control group from patients rejected because our beds were full, but after a few months, this seemed pointless. Our treatment network was sufficiently widespread so that, eventually, controls reapplied and were accepted into our treatment system.

Table 1.1 shows our treatment results. After initial discharge only three patients *never* relapsed to at least a brief period of alcoholic drinking and there is compelling evidence that our treatment results are better than the natural history of the disease. The death rate of three per cent a year is appalling and, it might be added, rather inconsistent with a mythical affliction and quite consistent with the metaphor 'disease'. Granted that after seven years the number of abstinents has steadily increased, that 56 per cent have at some point been abstinent for six months and that a small number have returned to social drinking – the financial costs have been considerable. Some of the patients who have continued to drink alcoholically have – over seven years – received as many as 200 detoxifications; 36 per cent have been detoxified at least ten times.

In Table 1.1 the outcome of the CASPAR (Cambridge and Somerville Program for Alcohol Rehabilitation) patients are contrasted with two year follow-ups of [4] treatment programmes that analysed their data in a comparable way and admitted similar patients and[3-6] with three studies of equal duration that purported to offer no formal treatment.[2,7,8] Each treatment population differs, but the studies are relatively comparable; and in the hope of averaging out major sampling differences, the studies have been pooled. Costello,[9] Emerick,[10] and Hill and Blane[11] have reviewed much larger numbers of disparate outcome studies and documented roughly similar proportions of significantly improved and unimproved. Obviously, abstinence or controlled drinking is not the only treatment goal but it is the variable that will be singled out in this chapter.

Our treatment programme was open-ended; a majority of the active drinkers continued to return to our clinical programme, and

Table 1.1: Comparison of Selected Two Year Follow-up Studies

	CASPAR Treatment	Three Pooled 'No Treatment' Studies**	Four 'Treatment' Studies**
N followed original sample	100/106	214/245	685/963
Length of follow-up	2 yr	2-3 yr	2 yr
Abstinent/social drinking	20%	17%	21%
Improved	13%	15%	16%
Trouble/dead	67%	68%	63%

* These are studies by Orford and Edwards,[2] Kendell and Staton[7] and Imber et al.[8] Because at one year there was no difference between Orford and Edwards' treated and control population and because at two years their report did not clearly separate the two populations, all 85 of their subjects on whom they had two year follow-up are included.
** These are the studies by Belasco,[3] Bruun,[4] Robson et al.[5] and van-Dijk-Koffeman.[6]

Table 1.2: Long-term Follow-up of Treated and 'Untreated' Alcoholics

	CASPAR Treatment	Myerson Mayer[15]	Bratfos[12]	Goodwin[16]	Voegtlin[13]	Lundquist[14]
N followed original sample	100/106	100/101	478/1179	93/123	104/?	200/200
Length of follow-up	7 yr	10 yr	10 yr	8 yr	7 yr	9 yr
Abstinent/social drinking	33%	22%	12%	26%	22%	27%
Improved	6%	24%	25%	15%	13%	<20%
Trouble/dead	61%	54%	63%	59%	65%	53%
Dead	25%	20%	14%	5%	?	22.5%
Gamma alcoholics	95%	100%	87%	c75%	?	c 75%

improvement continued.

Therefore in Table 1.2 CASPAR results at seven years are compared with the five rather disparate follow-up studies in the literature which are of similar duration but which looked at very different patient populations. Once again our results parallel the natural history of the disorder. Bratfos,[12] Voegtlin[13] and Lundquist[14] report follow-up of treated middle-class alcoholics. Myerson and Mayer[15] who followed a skid row population and Goodwin *et al.*[16] who followed alcoholic felons report data from essentially untreated populations. Certainly, it is unfortunate that there are *no* more careful long-term (more than six years of follow-up) studies of alcoholism in the world literature, and it can be legitimately argued that there are alternative ways of summarising the findings from each study in Table 1.2. Nevertheless, the similarity of data in Table 1.1 and Table 1.2 are heuristically useful and underscore the fact that over time large numbers of alcoholics remit and that large numbers of those who do not remit die.

The Natural Healing Forces in Alcoholism

In 1976 Gordis[17] editorialised for the *Annals of Internal Medicine* that 'The treatment of alcoholism has not improved in any important way in 25 years and alcoholism is becoming more prevalent . . . Only a minority of patients who enter treatment are helped to long-term recovery. The majority is made up of those who relapse soon and often and those who are lost to follow-up'. Alas, we are forced to agree. The best that can be said for our exciting treatment effort is that we are certainly not interfering with normal recovery process. How can I, a clinician, reconcile my enthusiasm for treatment with such melancholy data?

I must remind you of the second horn of my dilemma. The problem of alcoholism is too immense, the pain it causes too severe and the demands it places on the health care delivery system are too pervasive to tell government bodies that it is useless to fund large scale treatment programmes. It is not a step forward to say that alcoholism is the sole responsibility of families, of the church and of the police. It is not progress for hospitals again to hang out signs that read 'Alcoholics Need Not Apply'. Therefore, if treatment as we currently understand it does not seem more effective than natural healing processes, then we need to understand those healing processes. We need also to study the special role that health care professionals play in facilitating those processes. What alcohol treatment is failing to borrow is the study of medical response to chronic relapsing disease.

Let us look *first* at what the patient brings to his own cure. Consider tuberculosis as an analogy. In 1940 Cecil's[18] well-known textbook of medicine advised 'Since there is no known specific cure for tuberculosis, treatment rests *entirely* on recognition of the factors contributing to the resistance of the patient'. In saying this Cecil's medical textbook did not recommend that the government and doctors get out of the business of treating tuberculosis, nor did it suggest that, because genes and socioeconomic factors were more important than contagion, tuberculosis was really *just* a social problem not a medical disorder. Rather it suggested that doctors learn more about natural healing processes. Let us return to alcoholism.

In concluding an exhaustive review of alcohol treatment programmes, Baekland[19] wrote, 'Over and over we were impressed with the dominant role the patient, as opposed to the kind of treatment used on him, played both in his persistence in treatment and his eventual outcome'. Similarly, Orford and Edwards[2] in introducing their pessimistic control study of treatment wrote, 'In alcoholism treatment, research should increasingly embrace the closer study of "natural" forces which can be captured and exploited by planned, therapeutic intervention'.

In an effort to meet this need, let me describe preliminary results from a naturalistic, longitudinal study of alcoholism. What happens to alcoholics as they occur in nature rather than when they are viewed through the distorting, self-serving lens of the clinic? How do alcoholics get well if left to themselves?[20] A group of 456 inner-city 14 year old youths were selected by chance in 1940 with the important proviso that they *not* be seriously delinquent. In this sense they differ from the prospective studies by Robins[21] and the McCords.[22] These men have been prospectively followed, without significant attrition, until the age of 47. During the course of 35 years of follow-up 110 of these Boston men at some time have developed 4 or more symptoms of alcohol abuse as defined by DSM III.[23] Of these 110 men, 68 could be described as alcohol-dependent, or gamma alcoholics; 69 exhibited seven or more of Cahalan's[24] symptoms of problem drinking. Some were identified as alcoholic by clinicians and others were not. Out of these 110 men with multiple symptoms of alcohol abuse, 49 have achieved at least a year of abstinence and 22 men have been able to return to social drinking. Thus, compared with the studies already reported, the findings of this follow-up study suggest that if we study alcoholics long enough, 10-25 years, a very significant fraction of them — perhaps over half — recover.

Table 1.3 illustrates that very few of the 49 abstainees from this naturalistically derived community sample were initiated during exposure to 'treatment'. Only one abstinence in three began during some kind of formal treatment. Many men claimed to have maintained abstinence without any treatment at all and available clinic records support this assertion. For many men, Alcoholics Anonymous *had* played a significant role. But the path into this organisation was often through friends rather than clinic referral.

Table 1.4 suggests that if we follow the advice of Orford and Edwards,[2] and look at natural healing factors, an interesting pattern emerges. First, in order to facilitate the long-lasting abolition of any

Table 1.3: 'Treatment' Experiences that were Associated with Periods of Abstinence or of Social Drinking of a Year or More

	Abstinent Men N = 49	Returned to Social Drinking Men N = 22
'Professional' Treatment		
Psychotherapy	8%	5%
Antabuse	4%	0%
Halfway house	6%	5%
Alcohol clinic/hospital	30%	0%
Other Treatment		
Effective confrontation	61%	50%
Will-power	49%	23%
Alcoholics Anonymous	37%	0%

Table 1.4: 'Natural' Healing Factors that were Associated with Periods of Abstinence or of Social Drinking of a Year or More

	Abstinent Men N = 49	Returned to Social Drinking Men N = 22
I Substitute Dependence	53%	5%
II Behaviour Modification		
External control	24%	41%
Medical consequences	49%	27%
III Social Rehabilitation		
New love object	32%	18%
IV Increased Hope/Esteem		
Increased religious involvement	12%	5%
Alcoholics Anonymous	37%	0%

enduring habit, it is important to provide a substitute for the proscribed habit. Thus, 53 per cent of the 49 abstinent men found some substitute for alcohol (e.g. food, marijuana, gambling, meditation, three packs/day of cigarettes, compulsive hobbies etc.). Secondly, to change a habit, the individual must be reminded continuously that change is important; thus, in over half of the cases some form of behavioural modification occurred that served repeatedly to remind the men that they were unable to drink. Often they developed an unpleasant medical complaint instantly made worse by alcohol. Thirdly, for reasons not fully understood, it is helpful to replace habitual dependence upon drugs with unambivalent human relationships — not therapy. Thus, a third of the men claimed that their abstinence was facilitated by a new and rewarding personal relationship. Finally, the person's sense of hopelessness and helplessness about the possibility of change must be removed. Thus, more than half of the 49 abstinent men turned to religion or Alcoholics Anonymous for hope and for help. Indeed, Alcoholics Anonymous combines all four of the categories in Table 1.4.

Out of 49 men with a year or more of abstinence, there were 21 men who have experienced sustained community abstinence for more than three years and who are *still* abstinent. If these men are considered separately, then compulsory external control was of no use nor was antabuse or psychotherapy. However, for 71 per cent of these 21 *sustained* abstinences and for 87 per cent of the 15 men who had been gamma alcoholics, either AA *or* two or more of the natural healing factors played a significant role. Such findings suggest that recovery from alcoholism should not be called 'spontaneous' or as resulting from hitting some mysterious 'bottom'. Rather such a profound behavioural change is mediated by forces that can be identified and understood by social scientists and harnessed by health professionals.

In this same naturalistically-identified sample of 110 alcohol abusers, 22 men have returned to social drinking. However, only 4 out of 22 were what Jellinek would call a gamma alcoholic. In contrast 40 of the 49 men who became abstinent were gamma alcoholics. As Table 1.3 suggests, it was easier for those who returned to social drinking to change their drinking patterns than it was for the men who became abstinent. Often effective confrontation and will-power seemed treatment enough. Formal treatment of any kind seemed unnecessary. Table 1.4 suggests that substitute dependencies, fresh self-esteem and new people to care about seemed much less important for the return-to-social-drinking men (who were alcohol abusers) than they were for the abstinent men (who were physiologically dependent). External modification of drinking behaviour patterns, however, was useful, but this modified behaviour often resulted in 'controlled' rather than 'spontaneous' social drinking. For example, these non-gamma alcoholics learned to drink only selected beverages in selected environments during selected time periods. In summary, different factors seem important to recovery at different stages of alcohol dependence.

But what is meant by 'stages of alcoholic dependence'? Obviously, alcoholism is a relative label and represents a continuum. The men I am calling 'alcohol abusers' experienced an average of six of Cahalan's eleven symptoms of problem drinking; the men I call 'gamma alcoholics experienced about nine of Cahalan's symptoms *and* met the DSM III criteria for alcohol dependence. In contrast a heavy social drinker (4-7 ounces of 80 proof liquor daily) would have experienced only two or three of Cahalan's symptoms and be excluded from the compass of this chapter.

What the Therapist Can Add

Let us turn now from the patient's role to the role of the treatment professionals in the recovery process. Throughout history, physicians, faced with the unknown evil of disease they can neither comprehend nor cure, have played archaic but invaluable roles. In his classic monograph *Persuasion and Healing*, Jerome Frank,[25] Professor of Psychiatry at Johns Hopkins University, has offered us a transcultural model for healing that is non-specific for disease or patient; but Frank's model maximises both the relief of suffering and — of special importance in alcoholism — maximises attitude change. Frank acknowledges the paradox that demand for therapy may seem increasingly insatiable at the very time of mounting complaint that such therapy may represent expensive fraud. What feeds such demand is not the patient's need for cure as much as a need to elevate morale. First, alcoholics feel defeated, helpless and unable to change. If their lives are to change, they need hope as much as symptom relief. Secondly, alcoholics often have an ingrained habit that is intractable to reason, threat or will-power. To change a maladaptive habit, be it smoking or getting too little exercise or drinking too much alcohol, we cannot 'treat' or compel or reason with the person. Rather, we must change the person's belief system and then maintain that change. Time and time again, both evangelists and behaviour therapists have demonstrated that if you can but win their hearts and minds, their habits will follow. In other words, if we can but combine the best placebo effects of Lourdes with the best attitude change inherent in the evangelical conversion experience, we may be on our way to an effective alcohol programme. Frank's views will be described in general terms and then illustrated with four relatively successful alcohol programmes.

Jerome Frank's prescription for an effective 'placebo' therapy, for a modern day Lourdes, has as its goal the raising of the patient's expectancy of cure and his reintegration with the group. At Lourdes, pilgrims pray for each other, not for themselves. This stress on service counteracts the patient's morbid self-preoccupation, strengthens his self-esteem by demonstrating that he can do something for others and cements the tie between patient and group. Such therapy involves the sharing of suffering with a sanctioned healer who is willing to talk about the patient's problem in a symbolic way. The sanctioned healer should have status and power and be equipped with an unambiguous conceptual model of the problem which he is willing to explain to the patient. (Within our medical model this is the strategy of Jellinek's disease concept.) Enhancement of the patient's self-esteem and the reduction of anxiety are the inevitable consequence. The common ingredients of such a programme include group acceptance, an emotionally-charged but communally-shared ritual and a shared belief system. Such a ritual should be accompanied by a cognitive learning process that 'explains' the phenomenon of the illness. The point is that if one cannot cure an illness, one wants to make the patient less afraid and overwhelmed by it.

Jerome Frank's prescription for attitude change is initially interrogation by and confession of sins to a high status healer. This process should involve indoctrination, repetition, removal of ambiguity and the opportunity for identification. It has been demonstrated that the patient's active participation in such a process 'increases a person's susceptibility especially if the situation requires him to assume some initiative'[25] for his own attitude change. In the Stanford Heart Disease Prevention Program, internist John Farquhar and his colleagues[26,27] have examined different modes of reducing smoking, altering diet and increasing exercise. In their efforts to reduce thereby coronary risk in large populations of patients, they found that explanation of risk and rational advice by physicians is less useful than systematic indoctrination using mass media and peer support groups. However, as Jerome Frank writes, 'The greatest potential drawback of therapy groups is the tendency not to supply sufficient support, especially in early meetings, to enable members to cope with the stresses they generate'.[25] One of the functions, then, of the medical care system is to facilitate the transition of the isolated patient to group membership. Finally, in order to maintain attitude change, rehearsal of these group rituals and the group support that they engender must be sustained after clinic discharge.

Table 1.5 offers support for Frank's prescription. The table reflects the early treatment results reported by the Shadel[13] clinic using emetine aversion, by the Menninger[28] clinic using antabuse and group therapy, by Beaubrun[29] using an imaginative combination of indigenous paraprofessionals and medically sanctioned Alcoholics Anonymous, and by the Sobells[30] using behaviour modification. Each programme employed the newest method of its decade, was led by competent investigators, and led to results that were clearly superior to those usually reported. Because they were adequately controlled the Wallerstein and the Sobell studies are most convincing. Nevertheless, history has not been kind to these individual treatment methods; and, thus far, none have truly met Mark Sobell's[31] criteria for credibility: 'The foundation of validating successful treatment lies in replication'.

What, then, did emetine aversion conditioning in the 1940s, antabuse coupled with group therapy in a world-famous clinic in the 1950s, the use of AA coupled with indigenous calypso singing, ex-alcoholics in the 1960s and behaviour therapy to return to controlled drinking in the 1970s have in common? They all maximised the placebo effect of

Table 1.5: Two Year Follow-up Results of 'Special' Treatment Programmes Compared with Results from 'Routine' Treatment Programmes

	Four Pooled Treatment Studies*	Emetine Aversion	Antabuse	AA	Behaviour Modif.
		Shadel 1949[13]	Wallerstein 1956[28]	Beaubrun 1967[29]	Sobell 1976[30]
N followed/ original sample	685/963	300/?	40/47	57/57	20/20
Length of follow-up	2 yr	2 yr	2 yr	2 yr	2 yr
Abstinent/ social drinking	21%	60%	53%	37%	35%
Improved	16%	5%		16%	50%
Continued trouble	63%	35%	47%	47%	15%

*   These are the studies cited in Table 1.1[3-6]

medical treatment and effected significant attitude change. As sanctioned powerful healers, each investigator brought hope and provided a rational explanation of mysterious suffering and then created a framework for sharing that suffering with others. In the nineteenth century, Sir William Osler[32] wrote to a friend of his who had been treating tuberculosis, 'That is a fine record . . . I'm afraid there is one element you've not laid proper stress upon — your own personality. Confidence and faith count so much in these cases'. Because the clinicians in Table 1.5 brought the newest techniques of their decade to bear, they not only brought hope but conveyed assurance of their own power to cure. The Menninger Clinic in the 1950s was world renowned and the Sobells' elaborate research unit at Patton State Hospital was an impressive stageset filled with scientific gadgetry. In each programme the illness of alcoholism was carefully explained to each patient and although these explanations differed, they were consistent with the medical knowledge of each era. Although each patient was made responsible for his future involvement, alcoholism was represented as a disorder, not a symptom or as chaos. For example, each of Shadel's[33] patients received ten rules. Rules number 3 and 4 were, 'Do not look on alcoholism as a personal weakness. Remember that alcoholism is an illness . . . sensitivity to alcohol is inborn and you will always have it.' Beaubrun[29] wrote, 'In my culture where gamma alcoholism prevails the most helpful thing which the therapist can say to the alcoholic is that his problem is an illness. There is a world of difference between therapeutic and research orientations in this respect. The therapist knows that the semantic distinction between "addiction" and "disease" can make all the difference to his patient's sobriety. It is the distinction between a criminal and sick person.' Secondly, consistent with altering ingrained behaviour, all four treatments maximised attitude change in an emotionally charged setting. These programmes indoctrinated each patient into a coherent — if differing — ideology.

In each case a daily ritual was prescribed. For example, Wallerstein[28] wrote, 'In maintaining this sober state outside the hospital, the more compulsive the character of the patient and the more he could ritualise the antabuse ceremony itself, the better his prognosis.' Shadel's patients had a sign, 'There is one thing I cannot do' which they were to hang by the mirror while they shaved. Sobell's patients were given a wallet-sized Do's and Don't's card to keep with them at all times and after leaving the hospital. Beaubrun's patients had to continue to go to AA several times a week.

Rather than trying to alter attitude by threat or rational advice, each programme altered attitudes by affecting self-esteem. Sobell's patients highly valued the mastery involved in their return to controlled drinking. They were shown videotapes of themselves drinking in control and out of control. Shadel's[33] rules number 7 and 9 were 'Develop other outlets' and 'Get your strength for living from a desire to help yourself and others and not from the bottle. Help other alcoholics to master their problem.'

As they were encouraged in group activities, a comradeship developed among the patients. Wallerstein's[29] antabuse patients stayed in a psychodynamically-oriented hospital for three months and attended therapy groups as well as took antabuse. Shadel wrote, as each alcoholic came into his clinic environment, 'It is interesting to see how the gang of old patients goes to work on a new patient', and Shadel's patients were encouraged to continue groups after leaving. As Beaubrun[29] put it, 'It was not enough to tell a patient to attend a meeting; someone was sent to bring him to the first few meetings until he got accustomed to the new group.'

The success of Alcoholics Anonymous and its reasonable facsimiles which are continuously being revised, is probably due to the fact that it conforms so well to the natural healing principles that have been outlined earlier in this chapter. First, in AA the continuous hope, the gentle peer support, and the exposure to truly successful people provide a ritualised substitute for drinking, a source of identification and a substitute for lost drinking companions. Like the best behaviour therapy, not only do AA meetings go on daily, especially on weekends and holidays, but like any well-conceived programme of behaviour modification, AA provides strategies to combat unwitting relapse. Obviously, belonging to a group of caring individuals who have found solutions to the typical problems that beset newly sober alcoholics, alleviates social vulnerability. And, finally, the opportunity to identify with helpers who were once equally as disabled and to help others stay sober fits in well with Jerome Frank's general prescription for a therapeutic group process.

Resolution of the Dilemma

Let me now attempt to resolve my dilemma. *First*, recognition of our limited ability to alter the course of alcoholism paradoxically may lead to improved care not chaos. Modern surgery took a giant stride forward when it realised that wound-healing fared best by natural methods, that wound healing could be often slowed but never hastened by surgical intervention. Modern medicine began towards the end of the nineteenth century, it gave up bleeding patients and abandoned virtually its entire pharmacopœia. Today, psychiatry has a lesson to learn from the fact that schizophrenics have a better prognosis in under-developed countries than they do in developed ones.[34] It is important that one of the few conclusions that Emrick[10] drew from his study of 384 alcohol follow-up studies was that it may be easier for improper treatment to retard recovery than for proper treatment to hasten it.

Secondly, I believe that we must remain alert to the limitations of our alcohol treatment programmes. Otherwise national health schemes may suddenly regard as cost ineffective *all* alcohol treatment, rather than just long hospital stays. The 70 per cent improvement rate origin-ally promised in the Rand Report will become dangerous if clinical staff and legislators discover that such hopeful results are a cruel cheat — an illusion produced by attrition, by cross-sectional design and by ignoring the law of initial values. Unless we are careful, doctors and public funding sources may withdraw the support we have grown to expect. Thus, honesty is its own reward. Remembering the first step of Al-Anon, 'And we admitted that we were powerless over alcohol' protects us from maintaining the guilty illusion that if we just try harder and harder, we can cure the alcoholic. Indeed, a major task of my role as psychiatric consultant to an alcohol programme is to remind the staff that they are not to blame for their patients' relapses. As guilt is alleviated, so hope returns.

Thirdly, we have much to learn from how medicine until 1950 learned to cope with tuberculosis. We do not wish to spend either our natural resources nor our own time on just a few alcoholics. Rather, we want to reach as many patients as possible and we never want to ignore the problem. Not surprisingly, the results reported by Kissin and Rosenblatt[35] suggest that openly ignoring alcoholics on a waiting list produced an improvement rate of only four per cent, far worse than naturalistic studies in the literature. As Martin Seligman[36] reminds us, hopelessness kills.

Fourthly, at the same time that Ambroise Paré gave us his humble epigram 'I dressed him, God healed him', he had the wit to invent the surgical ligature to stop haemorrhage. In 1978 the Cambridge-Somerville Mental Health Center provided medical and social assistance to *twice* as many alcoholics as the entire Connecticut Department of Mental Health provided in 1965 to a catchment population that was *ten times* as large. By providing consultation, detoxification, welfare and shelter,

I have no doubt that we stop haemorrhage.

Fifthly, as Table 1.6 illustrates, at Cambridge Hospital if we have not cured all the alcoholics who were first detoxified over seven years ago, we have increased their likelihood of attending Alcoholics Anonymous. The table contrasts our results with those from the naturalistically-derived sample from the same urban area. The comparisons are of the record of our first 106 admissions over seven years with the record of the 110 alcohol abusers in the naturalistically-derived inner-city sample. Of the inner-city sample, 20, or 41 per cent, of the 49 abstinent men became abstinent in part through AA. Each of these 20 men attended an average 300 meetings. After one year of the CASPAR programme, five of our patients achieved an abstinence that had begun through regular attendance in AA. After seven years, 21 patients, or four times as many attained an abstinence that began in part through AA. In the seven years, these 21 patients – 65 per cent of all those stably abstinent – had attended an average of 600 meetings. But in emphasising the belief of *our* programme in AA, I do not wish to suggest that AA is the *best* answer; there are many paths to recovery in alcoholism. We need to understand what is common to all of them. Our treatment programme was designed to respond to the needs of all of the estimated 20,000 alcoholics in our catchment area. We have tried to spread our resources. To concentrate upon 20 or even 200 souls would not do. Therefore, like Dr Blenkinsop in George Bernard Shaw's *Doctor's Dilemma*, we have depended on greengages, as it were. Alcoholics Anonymous is free, readily accessible, consistent with natural healing forces. Our aim was to encourage its use. In that, we succeeded.

Table 1.6: Use of Alcoholics Anonymous Over Time in Treated and 'Naturalistic' Samples

	Inner-city	CASPAR	
N followed/original sample	103/110	106/106	100/106
Length of follow-up	10-25 yr	1 yr	7 yr
Abstinent or social drinking	51%	15%	33%
Improved	17%	19%	6%
Continued trouble or dead	32%	66%	61%
Per cent of those abstinent who became abstinent through AA	41%	31%	65%
Average number of meetings/ abstinent AA attender	300	NA	600

Benjamin Kissin[37] warns us that, 'Perhaps negative results should be reported even more cautiously, since almost everyone tends to view positive ones with a jaundiced eye and to take negative ones at their face value.' If our patients at seven years of follow-up have not fared as well as the inner-city sample at 20 years follow-up, our patients were at a more advanced stage of the disease when they came to us. Besides, the Samaritan role is not to be sneezed at — especially in incurable disease; when large benefits are not forthcoming, patients will be especially grateful for small ones.

Finally, I return to the treatment of alcoholism both with hope and with confidence. I shall continue to hope that our governments and our medical colleagues will continue to regard alcoholism just as worthy of medical treatment and large-scale expenditure of public funds as they regarded tuberculosis in 1940. I would not want to return to the day when due to therapeutic despair great teaching hospitals once again put up signs that read 'Alcoholics Need Not Apply'.

Acknowledgement

This work was supported by the Grant Foundation, Inc., the Spencer Foundation and a research grant (AA-01372) from the National Institute of Alcoholism and Alcohol Abuse.

Notes

1. Szasz, T.S. (1972), 'Bad Habits are Not Diseases', *Lancet*, vol. 2, pp. 83-4.

2. Orford, J. and Edwards, G. (1977), *Alcoholism* (Oxford University Press, Oxford).

3. Belasco, J.A. (1971), 'The Criterion Question Revisited', *British Journal of Addiction*, vol. 66, pp. 39-44.

4. Bruun, K. (1963), 'Outcome of Different Types of Treatment of Alcoholics', *Quarterly Journal of Studies on Alcohol*, vol. 24, pp. 280-8.

5. Robson, R.A., Paulus, I. and Clarke, G.G. (1965), 'An Evaluation of the Effect of a Clinic Treatment Program on the Rehabilitation of Alcoholic Patients', *Quarterly Journal of Studies on Alcohol*, vol. 26, pp. 264-78.

6. van Dijk, W.K. and van Dijk-Koffeman, A. (1973), 'A Follow-up Study of 211 Treated Male Alcoholic Addicts', *British Journal of the Addictions*, vol. 68, pp. 3-24.

7. Kendell, R.E. and Staton, M.C. (1966), 'The Fate of Untreated Alcoholics', *Quarterly Journal of Studies on Alcohol*, vol. 27, pp. 30-41.

8. Imber, S., Schultz, E., Funderburk, F., Allen, R. and Flamer, R. (1976), 'The Fate of the Untreated Alcoholic', *Journal of Nervous and Mental Disease*, vol. 162, pp. 238-47.

9. Costello, R.M. (1975), 'Alcoholism Treatment and Evaluation: In Search of Methods', *International Journal of Addictions*, vol. 10, pp. 251-75.
10. Emrick, C.D. (1975), 'A Review of Psychologically Oriented Treatment of Alcoholism. II. The Relative Effectiveness of Treatment Versus No Treatment', *Journal of Studies in Alcoholism*, vol. 36, pp. 88-109.
11. Hill, M.J. and Blane, H.T. (1966), 'Evaluation of Psychotherapy With Alcoholics: A Critical Review', *Quarterly Journal of Studies on Alcoholism*, vol. 27, pp. 76-104.
12. Bratfos, O. (1974), *The Course of Alcoholism: Drinking, Social Adjustment and Health* (Universitetsforlaget, Oslo).
13. Voegtlin, W.L. and Broz, W.R. (1949), 'The Conditional Reflex Treatment of Chronic Alcoholism. X. An Analysis of 3,125 Admissions Over a Period of Ten and a Half Years', *Annals of International Medicine*, vol. 30, pp. 580-97.
14. Lundquist, G.A.R. (1973), 'Alcohol Dependence', *Acta Psychiatrica Scandinavica*, vol. 49, pp. 322-40.
15. Myerson, D.J. and Mayer, J. (1966), 'Origins, Treatment and Destiny of Skid-row Alcoholic Men', *New England Journal of Medicine*, vol. 275, pp. 419-24.
16. Goodwin, D.W., Crane, J.B. and Guze, S.B. (1971), 'Felons Who Drink: An 8 Year Follow-up', *Quarterly Journal of Studies on Alcohol*, vol. 32, pp. 136-47.
17. Gordis, E. (1976), 'What is Alcoholism Research?' (Editorial), *Annals of International Medicine*, vol. 85, pp. 821-3.
18. Cecil, R. (1940), *Textbook of Medicine* (Saunders, New York).
19. Baekland, F., Lundwall, L. and Kissin, B. (1975), 'Methods for the Treatment of Chronic Alcoholism: A Critical Appraisal', in Gibbons, R.J., Israel, Y., Kalant, H., Popham, R.E., Schmidt, W. and Smart, R.G. (eds.), *Research Advances in Alcohol and Drug Problem*, vol. 2, chapter 7 (John Wiley & Sons, London).
20. Glueck, S. and Glueck, E. (1950), *Unraveling Juvenile Delinquency* (The Commonwealth Fund, New York).
21. Robins, L.N. (1966), *Deviant Children Grown Up: A Sociological and Psychiatric Study of Sociopathic Personality* (Williams and Wilkins, Baltimore).
22. McCord, W. and McCord, J. (1960), *Origins of Alcoholism* (Stanford University Press, Stanford).
23. American Psychiatric Association (1980), *Diagnostic and Statistical Manual of Mental Disorders*, 3rd edn (Washington, D.C., APA, DSM III).
24. Cahalan, D. (1970), *Problem Drinkers: A National Survey* (Jossey-Bass, San Francisco).
25. Frank, J.D. (1961), *Persuasion and Healing: A Comparative Study of Psychotherapy* (Johns Hopkins University Press, Baltimore).
26. Farquhar, J.W., Maccoby, N., Wood, P.D. *et al.* (1977), 'Community Education for Cardiovascular Health', *Lancet*, vol. 1, pp. 1192-5.
27. Farquhar, J. (1978), 'The Community-based Model of Life Style Intervention Trials', *American Journal of Epidemiology*, vol. 108, pp. 103-11.
28. Wallerstein, R.S. (1956), 'Comparative Study of Treatment Methods for Chronic Alcoholism: The Alcohol Research Project at Winter VA Hospital', *American Journal of Psychiatry*, vol. 113, pp. 228-33.
29. Beaubrun, M.H. (1967), 'Treatment of Alcoholism in Trinidad and Tobago, 1956-65', *British Journal of Psychiatry*, vol. 113, pp. 643-58.
30. Sobell, M.B. and Sobell, J.C. (1976), 'Second-year Treatment Outcome of Alcoholics Treated by Individualized Behaviour Therapy: Results', *Behaviour Research and Therapy*, vol. 14, pp. 195-215.
31. Sobell, M.B. and Sobell, L.D. (1973), 'Alcoholics Treated by Individualized Behaviour Therapy: One-year Treatment Outcome', *Behaviour Research and Therapy*, vol. II, pp. 599-618.

32. Cushing, H. (1925), *The Life of Sir William Osler* (Clarendon Press, Oxford).
33. Shadel, C.A. (1944), 'Aversion Treatment of Alcohol Addiction', *Quarterly Journal of Studies on Alcohol*, vol. 5, pp. 216-28.
34. Sartorius, N., Jablensky, A. and Shapiro, R. (1978), 'Cross-cultural Differences in the Short Term Prognosis of Schizophrenic Psychoses', *Schizophrenia Bulletin*, vol. 4, pp. 102-3.
35. Kissin, B., Rosenblatt, S.M. and Machover, S. (1968), 'Prognostic Factors in Alcoholism', *Psychiatric Research Report*, vol. 24, pp. 22-60.
36. Seligman, M.E.P. (1975), *Helplessness: On Depression, Development and Death* (W.H. Freeman, San Francisco).
37. Kissin, B. (1977), 'Comments on Alcoholism: A Controlled Trial of "Treatment" and "Advice" ', *Journal of Studies on Alcohol*, vol. 38, pp. 1804-8.

2   WHAT ALCOHOLISM ISN'T BORROWING

Jerome H. Jaffe

Each spring at a certain medical school, the first year students are given
a one hour lecture on alcoholism as part of their course in psychiatry.
Following the lecture, small groups of medical students gather and each
group (with its own instructors) interviews an individual who has a
problem related to the subject of the lecture. On a recent occasion the
group was taken by a warm and perceptive third year resident in
psychiatry. Arrangements had been made for the students to interview
people affiliated with a local AA group. The instructors and the students were told not to view these individuals as 'patients' but to listen
to their stories about their experiences with alcoholism. The resident
reported that the person who had been interviewed gave a rather clear-
cut history of cyclical mood swings. The resident, a rather conservative
diagnostician, felt certain that this person would meet the criteria for a
mild manic depressive disorder or, at the very least, a cyclothymic
personality. The resident felt that, despite the admonition not to view
these individuals as patients, it would have been inappropriate not to
ask this man whether he had ever taken or heard about the use of
lithium. The answer was that he knew of its use in mood disorders, but
he then added that for him to take lithium would be contrary to the
principles of Alcoholics Anonymous which had proved so helpful to
him in overcoming his alcoholism. The resident was puzzled. How could
it be, he wondered, that an organisation so well respected for its
concern about alcoholics could take such an attitude about lithium,
especially in view of the finding that depression is so common among
alcoholics, and that so many alcoholics will eventually commit suicide?
The young physician said he could understand how an organisation
might take a dim view of the use of drugs that alter mood in a manner
resembling the effects of alcohol, and that a prohibition against the use
of sleeping medicine or anti-anxiety drugs was not entirely unreason-
able. But, since lithium does neither of these, he found the reported AA
view about lithium both puzzling and disturbing.

Some weeks later a physician was seen who was addicted to the use
of meperidine. After reviewing the attempts he had made in the past to
deal with this problem it was concluded that what might be most likely
to help him would be a period of hospitalisation for detoxification and

a stabilisation on the narcotic antagonist naltrexone. A call was made to a colleague in another community who was a chairman of a department of psychiatry which contained within it a very pleasant and well run alcohol treatment unit. He had considerable experience with naltrexone and was using it with several physicians. He said, however, that he would be quite willing to accept this physician-patient onto the general psychiatric unit, but not on the alcohol unit within his own department. He added that the alcohol unit had a fully organised programme that included education about alcoholism, links to AA, and a number of other aspects which made it unlikely that its staff would tolerate a physician addicted to meperidine. He commented, with a note of weariness, 'The political forces in this community are very powerful.'

These two anecdotes suggest that there are influences on the treatment of patients with alcoholism that are not easily explained on the basis of scientific data. The title of this chapter may suggest that there is some monolithic structure which can be designated 'alcoholism'. It would be reckless to assert that this is the case. Certainly, there are many voices and views among those concerned with alcohol and the problems it causes, just as there are about the appropriate response to problems of drug dependence, schizophrenia, and human problems in general. Certainly, within the world of those concerned with alcohol use and alcoholism, there are numerous individuals who see the relevance of issues that may not have been incorporated, as yet, into the mainstream of thinking about treatment. If there is a mainstream, it is not the same from one country to another, or even from one community to another. An experiment in controlled drinking that brings forth cries of outrage from the 'treatment mainstream' in one community may call forth only a quiet scepticism in another. This chapter would be attacking an imaginary target if it focussed upon some stereotyped absolute of 'the alcoholism treatment field today'. Having said that, although there are no stereotypes, there certainly are within particular countries particular favoured fashions.

This chapter will discuss some issues which have not yet had their full impact on those primarily involved with intervention, either because the implications of certain ideas would create major problems for the treating institutions or because the ideas would force us to reorder and complicate familiar notions that are easy to understand and communicate or simply because fashion stands in the way.

The North American Fashion

The overwhelming proportion of formal treatment programmes in the United States, Canada and a number of other Western countries are built solidly around affiliations with Alcoholics Anonymous groups in the surrounding communities. This is true of publicly supported programmes as well as those which are privately supported. This inference can be made from the brochures circulated by private psychiatric hospitals and private alcoholism programmes, as well as descriptions in the literature of the day-to-day activities and the aftercare plans described by a number of programmes which have bothered to write such descriptions. For example, a now prominent programme, as a result of its having treated influential politicians and their relatives, is the programme at the Naval Hospital in Long Beach, California. That programme, as described in 1976,[1] involved primarily ex-alcoholic counsellors, group meetings and extensive integration into the Alcoholics Anonymous programmes in the community. Special Alcoholics Anonymous principles seemed to have been evolved for military personnel.

Treatment programmes that deviate from this general model are the exception. The model involves at least three distinct elements. First, a clear-cut and unequivocal commitment to a specific treatment goal; namely permanent and total abstinence from alcoholic beverages and other substances with similar effects. Secondly, a rationale for that goal: the alcoholic has a 'disease' that is lifelong and involves an inability to use alcohol or similar drugs in moderation. Thirdly, a clear-cut belief that the most effective way for the alcoholic to achieve that goal is through participation in the programmes of Alcoholics Anonymous and that the refusal to accept the need for formal treatment is the equivalent to the denial of 'the problem', and denial is part of the 'disease'. Other treatment approaches are sometimes employed as supplementary to this main thrust or as alternatives for those who find themselves unable to get involved with AA, but there are many who view such approaches as clearly second choice selections. In the United States, the concept of an intervention oriented 'mainstream', is often used interchangeably with the concept of the 'alcoholism constituency', which is active in lobbying governments and industry for more and better treatment for people with alcoholism, and consists of the directors of programmes, alcoholism councils, and a number of prominent individuals who have themselves been successfully treated for a drinking problem.

If this description is overstated, the overstatement applies mainly to the third point. In some places there exists a willingness to concede that some alcoholics can achieve long-term abstinence and improved social function through means other than AA.

There is great controversy surrounding the findings from a number of studies showing that not all problem drinkers who stop and then drink again immediately develop drinking problems.[2-7] This chapter must, however, be limited to noting the outlines of the common or fashionable programme beliefs rather than going into an extended debate on the correctness or otherwise of those beliefs.

What has Alcoholism Borrowed?

The mainstream constituency has borrowed from medicine the concept of 'disease'. Mark Keller[8] has pointed out that the disease concept of alcoholism has not been developed as a recent 'gimmick' to exculpate the person with a drinking problem from assuming responsibility for the neglect of family and social responsibilities. It is a concept that in one form or another has been around for hundreds of years. It implies that when certain individuals interact with alcohol, they lose the capacity to respond appropriately to the demands of their environment. As Edwards[9] has expressed it, at its core, the disease concept involves a 'loss of plasticity'. What the alcoholism mainstream both invented and demonstrated was the role of self-help and spiritual support for people who have developed this loss of plasticity. What the mainstream constituency has not yet accepted is the principle that the concept of 'disease' is always in the process of evolution, and that, in the field of medicine, the concept demands that we remain curious and unsatisfied until we can account for all the varied mechanisms and manifestations of a deviation from health. To label a constellation of signs, symptoms and behaviours as a 'disease' or 'disorder' is only a tentative beginning. We need to find out why they go together. The history of medicine tells us that what appears at first to be 'a disease' often turns out to be a half-dozen or more different disorders with similar manifestations. Indeed, there is hardly a disease which has not in the process of study been further dissected into numerous distinct sub-varieties. Thus, Hippocrates recognised diabetes and named it for the sweetness of the urine associated with the disorder. More than 2,000 years passed before we recognised that this ancient problem that can give rise to sweet urine and eventually to coma and death could be due to disorders in the pancreas, or pituitary gland, or adrenal glands or to cellular receptors for insulin. Two hundred years ago, when in Scotland and the United States, Thomas Trotter and Benjamin Rush were beginning to conceptualise continuous or recurrent heavy alcohol consumption as a disease rather than a moral deficit, their medical colleagues were just beginning to recognise that the ague was not a unitary disease associated with fever but could have many different origins, and that depending on its origins or causes, fever might or might not respond to quinine. The subdivision of fever into specific disorders has shown considerable progress; the recognition that alcoholism may be a manifestation of several interacting disorders has only recently begun.

Resistances to Borrowing

To have borrowed the concept of disease without its intellectual obligations to search further may be to have left behind that which is most valuable.

In a recent review Pattison[10] emphasised the sharp contrast between the exploding knowledge base in the field of alcoholism and the currently used intervention methods, most of which have remained virtually unchanged over the past decade. In looking for an explanation for this paradox, Pattison observed that 'the field of alcoholism has long been manned by paraprofessionals . . . the field of treatment is dominated by paraprofessional values, attitudes and concepts . . . ' He goes on to argue that:

There is a marked difference in the personal approach to alcoholism between the two ideologies. Paraprofessionals often see empirical scientific data as obscure, irrelevant, or contradictory to their personal experiential knowledge of alcoholism. The professional approaches alcoholism from the base of 'academic science' whereas the paraprofessional uses a base of 'folk science'.

Academic science and folk science differ in their objectives:

A folk science is a body of accepted knowledge whose function is not to provide the bases for further advance but to offer comfort and reassurance to some body of believers . . . in an immature field of scientific development there is inevitable conflict which occurs when the results of disciplined scientific inquiry contradict the beliefs of a folk science, usually a popular one which is adopted by the established cultural organs of society. (Ravetz, cited by Pattison [10])

Whatever the motivation, the rapidly-expanding knowledge about the causes of alcohol problems and about their response to social trends and treatment efforts, is penetrating the treatment mainstream with a slowness that suggests barriers which are more than passive.

Some Specific Non-borrowings

In addition to the implications of the disease concept, what else is not being borrowed? There are at least six major areas of research on alcoholism, drug dependence, and related fields where important ideas seem to be gaining acceptance only with great difficulty.

First, and as has already been mentioned, there is a growing awareness that beneath the broad rubric of 'alcoholism', there may be a number of distinct subgroups. From a research point of view, it may be no longer appropriate or adequate to describe an individual as an alcoholic without some further effort at description.

Secondly, it is not enough to subdivide the 'disorder of alcoholism' in terms of different antecedents and concomitant problems. The disorder itself cannot be thought of in terms of presence or absence, as something which is or is not present. Like other varieties of drug dependence as diverse as smoking or heroin addiction, alcoholism must be viewed in multi-dimensional and quantitative terms; it has several dimensions each of which can vary in severity — and, at least theoretically, these dimensions can be major determinants of what treatments are appropriate and how likely they are to alter the behaviour.

Thirdly, the dimensions of the disorders of alcoholism are still not fully explored or understood. A scant decade ago, researchers working with opiate addicts believed that they had a reasonable grasp of the nature of opiate physical dependence. That confidence had dissolved in a wealth of new discoveries of endogenous opioid substances, of new data about normal regulatory processes and of the ways in which chronic opiate use modifies those processes.

Fourthly, a growing body of data indicates that quite apart from any biological vulnerability of psychological problems that the individual drinker may have, the major determinants of the prevalence of alcohol-related problems in a given society are the social arrangements which encourage or discourage alcohol consumption.[7,11,12,13]

Fifthly, the natural history of at least some subgroups of alcoholics is far from the steady and inevitable deterioration depicted in nineteenth century temperance tales, and still accepted as accurate by too many workers in the field of alcoholism treatment. Numerous studies have documented that periods of improvement, and even shifts to total abstinence lasting months or years, are common and can apparently occur in the absence of formal treatment.[3,14,15] Spontaneous and apparently unassisted improvement or 'cure' among people who have smoked cigarettes heavily for years is commonplace; and recent follow-up studies of opiate addicts suggests that they, too, can make changes in drug intake up to and including total abstinence without benefit of formal treatment.[16-19] While we are largely ignorant about the factors or processes that contribute to these periods of improvement, we need to recognise that such processes must exist and for want of a better term we can think of them as 'natural processes of healing'.[20]

Sixthly, the alcoholism syndromes, once developed, appear to be relatively insensitive to changes in intensity of psychological treatment. While treatment often appears to be more effective than no treatment[3,21] and it is occasionally found that the type of treatment makes a difference,[22,23] one looks in vain for evidence that prolonged and intense inpatient or outpatient care is more likely to produce abstinence and good social function than brief and minimally intensive intervention (provided one controls for patient characteristics and the social resources and setting to which the patient returns.)[3,6,7,24-26] We need to do more than recognise that some approaches to treatment are unnecessarily elaborate and expensive (prodigal); we need to be cautious lest our tendencies towards even more prodigal programmes interfere with the 'natural processes of healing'.

Within this chapter there is not the space to deal with all six themes in detail. Important issues come at the beginning and end of that list, and it is the first, second and sixth themes which are taken up more fully below. This is not to ignore the importance of the remaining questions, which would on another occasion certainly repay equally detailed analysis.

Subdividing the Syndrome

It is easy to postulate distinct sub-categories of alcoholism. It is more difficult to disentangle the many threads that seem to lead to comprehensible and clinically useful sub-groups. One scheme for classification is based on clinical diagnosis and places alcoholics into two large groups: primary alcoholics and secondary alcoholics.[27,28] Primary alcoholics have been defined as those individuals in whom there are no other manifestations of diagnosable psychopathology apart from alcoholism or, in whom, if other manifestations are seen, they appeared subsequent to the alcoholism. Two major sub-types of secondary alcoholism are depression-alcoholism and sociopathy-alcoholism.

Shuckit has expressed the view that the natural history of such syndromes is determined largely by the natural history of the primary diagnosis.[27] Classification schemes based on clinical diagnoses are not the only ones proposed or being used and the various schemes based on multivariate or factor analysis of patient characteristics or test scores are not easity integrated.[29]

Even the term 'primary alcoholism' has not been used consistently. In a recent paper which also tried to develop sub-types of alcoholics, Tarter and co-workers[30] divided patients, all of whom fulfilled the criteria for alcoholism of Feighner *et al.*[31] into two sub-groups on the basis of drinking patterns and their subjective response to alcohol. Using a nine point questionnaire, those subjects who reported no known precipitating cause for their excessive drinking, and six or eight characteristics of severe drinking problems or dependence, were assigned to a sub-group labelled 'primary'. If the subjects did not fulfil these criteria, but did fulfil the alcoholism criteria, they were considered 'secondary' alcoholics. Tarter and his colleagues then contrasted the 'primary' with the 'secondary' alcoholics in terms of personal and family drinking history, and history of minimal brain dysfunction (MBD), a concept which is often used in the United States, somewhat interchangeably with the concept of childhood hyperactivity. Primary alcoholics reported almost four times as many symptoms of MBD and began drinking at an earlier age than the secondary alcoholics. Although the family incidence of alcoholism was higher in these 'primary' alcoholics (42 per cent among fathers and only 21 per cent among fathers of 'secondary' alcoholics and 16 per cent among fathers of psychiatric patients), these differences were not statistically significant.

The finding of a sub-group of alcoholics which exhibits many symptoms of childhood hyperactivity or MBD is consistent with findings of several previous studies which showed linkages between alcoholism or sociopathy in the biologic parents of children exhibiting hyperactivity.[32-34] Mendelson *et al.*[35] found that even between the ages of 12 and 16, fifteen per cent of 'hyperactive' children were already demonstrating excessive drinking. The studies indicating that there is at least one sub-category of alcoholics who are not necessarily sociopaths but who exhibit some definable disturbance prior to the onset of alcoholism are of note for several reasons. First, those alcoholics who endorse these MBD items appear to have a more severe form of alcoholism, yet they score lower on six of the ten clinical scales of the MMPI, showing them to be relatively free of psychiatric disturbances other than these specific MBD associate behavioural symptoms.[30] Thus, this group of early-onset, severe alcoholics tends to project a picture of greater psychiatric well-being than either psychiatric patients or late-onset drinkers. At the same time, they report more behavioural disturbance prior to onset of alcoholism. This observation is not inconsistent with the findings of Woodruff *et al.*[36] that there are many alcoholics who meet all the criteria for the alcoholism but who do not seek treatment, although they may have difficulties with school, the police, jobs and marriages, and do not regard themselves as either ill or in need of specialised help. Either these untreated alcoholics do not recognise their alcoholism and social difficulties as problems, or they do not believe that psychiatric attention will be useful. Those alcoholics seeking psychiatric treatment are distinguished from those who do not chiefly by the presence of depression, or by a history of abnormalities of mental content. In contrast to the findings of Tarter *et al.*[30] Woodruff and co-workers[36] found no differences in severity of alcoholism.

Since there may be a relationship between early manifestations of MBD with impulsivity and intolerance of rules, and later delinquency, we are left wondering about the relationship between the primary alcoholics of Tarter and co-workers, and the secondary sociopathic-alcoholics of Winokur and colleagues.[28] The structure of the questionnaires and the descriptions in the written papers do not permit us to know if these are distinct or overlapping sub-categories.

Once considered a childhood syndrome that is outgrown in adolescence, there is increasing evidence that hyperkinesis or MBD is not outgrown, but is simply ignored. A substantial proportion of those with the syndrome continue to have difficulties with concentration and impulsivity.[35,37,38]

The literature on the relationships between alcoholism and depression is too extensive and complex to be compressed into a simple formula. The incidence of diagnosable depression among alcoholics seeking treatment varies from study to study, and ranges from three to 90 per cent, depending on sex ratios, screening techniques, criteria diagnostic instruments, and time of evaluation.[28,39,40,41] The preponderance of studies suggest that it is closer to 40 per cent than to three per cent.[40] That some alcoholics are clinically depressed is not controversial. What is controversial is (1) whether the depressive symptomatology clears spontaneously following detoxification; (2) the degree to which it resembles serious depression in non-alcoholics; and (3) whether it requires and responds to presently available pharmacological or psychological treatments. Some studies have shown considerable spontaneous improvement of depressive symptoms:[27,39] others show that, in the many untreated depressed alcoholics, serious depression may persist for at least a year after initial assessment. Furthermore, those who showed no improvement in terms of depression were more likely to continue drinking.[40] Although the phenomenology of depression appears to be similar in alcoholics and non-alcoholics,[42] there is presently considerable scepticism about the value of tricyclic antidepressants in primary alcoholics who are also depressed.[27,29,43] This scepticism may be inappropriate in light of recent findings on the pharmacokinetics of these drugs. The low doses of tricyclics used in the early studies and even in some recent ones may have been totally inadequate to produce clinically useful blood levels.[44] Furthermore, measures of compliance were often ignored; plasma levels, which are known to vary widely, were never measured. It would be as valid to say that there is no evidence that antidepressants are ineffective as it is to say there is no evidence that they are. In addition, controlled studies of lithium in alcoholics suggest that treated patients experience a decrease in episodes of uncontrolled drinking.[45,46] What is not at all controversial is that alcoholics are far more likely than non-alcoholics to commit suicide.[47]

Further complicating the picture are findings that alcoholics with depression not only resemble the non-depressed alcoholics more than the depressed patients without alcoholism on virtually every measure of family alcoholism and of sociopathy (e.g. fighting before and after age 18, job changes, service demotions, non-alcohol related arrests and imprisonments), but also they exceed the non-depressed alcoholics on each of these measures of sociopathy.[48] Thus, unless there are errors in sampling that are otherwise unapparent, sociopathy with secondary alcoholism seems likely to come to treatment as sociopathy with secondary alcoholism and secondary depression.

What is it, then, that alcoholism under this heading isn't borrowing? To some degree it is not even borrowing from its own research literature the importance of sub-classification. The typical treatment programme is too often content with the simple label of alcoholism. Further, if these observations on depression, sociopathy and MBD are valid, the mainstream rationale and treatment modes, which assume that all was well and will be well again in the absence of alcohol, emphasise sobriety and primarily utilise counselling, may be ignoring important areas of dysfunction in a substantial sub-group of alcoholics, many of whom do not see the dysfunction as a deviation from what they have come to accept as their normality.

It is necessary to underline at this point that we may have, at present, few effective treatments for some of the syndromes that may emerge from research on sub-types of alcoholism. If there are disorders of mood or impulse control or cognition that are causally related to the alcoholism that often occurs in conjunction with sociopathy, MBD and the alcoholism that runs in some families, we have, as yet, no demonstrably effective methods for treatment. Similarly, while tricyclic antidepressants and sometimes amphetamine drugs may be of help with adults who exhibit minimal brain dysfunction, we have little evidence that such treatment alters the pattern of pathologic alcohol consumption in such individuals. Doubts about the benefits of tricyclics in treatment of depression in primary alcoholics have already been mentioned. Yet, it would be most unfortunate if we inferred from this pessimistic assessment of current treatment effectiveness that sub-grouping of alcoholics has no meaning or practical significance. Demonstration of an effective therapy is only one aspect of demonstrating the existence of a specific syndrome that has its own characteristics and natural history in the untreated state. Most of the major psychiatric disorders were well described long before we had demonstrably effective treatments. Indeed, reliable and precise diagnosis is a prerequisite to the development of specific therapy.

Given the foregoing, one would expect to see an interventionist mainstream that pressures researchers to seek better pharmacological treatments for these syndromes. Sadly, this seems not to be the case. Instead, there is a reluctance to use pharmacological treatments in order to avoid substituting one drug for another. The mainstream is not borrowing the research perspective that has led to such substantial advances in general psychiatry.

Prodigal Treatment with Limited Impact Wastes Resources and May Insult the Natural Process

There is in the USA a respected university-affiliated hospital run by staff of the greatest integrity that operates a specialised treatment programme for alcoholism. The hospital is quite proud of the programme which is described as 'eclectic', combining individual psychoanalytically-oriented psychotherapy with group psychotherapy, medication, daily AA meetings and a number of other diverse approaches. The hospital's brochure recommends routinely that a 90 day course of treatment offers the best chance for a full recovery. Treatment costs approximately $300 per day.

By prodigal is not meant expensive. The open heart surgery required to repair a congenital heart defect is expensive, but there are few less expensive alternatives which are comparably effective. By prodigal, is meant treatments that are lavish and expensive beyond the level which can be demonstrated to be necessary by any reasonable scientific standard.

Our concern here is not so much with the sheer waste of resources, but rather with the potential negative consequences of overly expensive programmes. There are several. One possibility is that lavishness feeds the latent belief that 'you get what you pay for', that there are no bargains, and that if something costs more, it must be better. Consumers' groups notwithstanding, cars, perfumes and, ironically, distilled beverages, are still advertised as 'the most expensive' and, by implication, the finest of their genre. To the extent that the public believes that long-term and lavish treatment programmes are equivalent to the best treatment programmes, less elaborate methods consuming less time and offered by less specialised personnel may be seen as 'second class' and may be bypassed by all but the most indigent and most isolated of those with alcohol-related problems. Since treatment outcome is so much determined by the characteristics of patients and by their level of social support, it is predictable that a self-fulfilling pseudo-validation of the value of more elaborate programmes could emerge from any cursory retrospective evaluation of outcome.

From the perspective of a growing body of literature on spontaneous recovery or natural healing, an even more disturbing possibility is that long or lavish programmes will, by their very elaborateness, minimise the importance of the individual's own capacity for positive change, of the role of the family, and of the social support system. Certainly there can be a real advantage in a few days' or weeks' removal from a stressful situation, but to the degree that a worker or a family member is removed from the job or the family over a prolonged period, the supportive network that is vital to long-term adjustment may be weakened.

More than 15 years ago, health economists in the United States were predicting that the country was building too many hospital beds, a prediction based on both population demographics and an assessment of changing medical technology. These predictions were largely ignored. As long as government was willing to finance bright new hospitals, communities lobbied and used political pressure to get the money to build them. Within the last five years, some large cities in the United States have hovered at the brink of bankruptcy. In the case of New York City, not a small element in that near catastrophy was the availability of 4,000 'extra' acute hospital beds, many of them supported by local revenues and by an economic system that created incentives to fill them. These beds were 'extra' within any reasonable definition of the kinds of conditions requiring acute hospitalisation, but they were filled. The resulting cases led to a burdensome and ponderous system of utilisation review which, while paying lip service to the issue of 'quality of treatment', was concerned primarily with making certain that administrators did not fill beds with people who did not require hospitalisation.

There are alarming parallels in the field of alcoholism. Within the past decade there have been at least a half dozen studies showing that for routine situations, prolonged hospitalisation makes little contribution beyond that which can be achieved within a week or two of inpatient treatment. One looks in vain for a single, adequately-controlled study that demonstrates the value of residential or hospital care for an extended period (more than ten days). Despite such findings, and despite the growing public concern about medical expenditure, more hospital beds for the treatment of alcoholism are demanded and most of these are built around treatment programmes lasting from two weeks to ninety days. At the same time, third party payers and employers are being asked to accept alcoholics as employees and to provide them with full medical insurance coverage, including that which may be related to drinking problems. In contrast, the field of drug dependence, which once advocated prolonged residential treatment 'until cured' (often committing unwilling patients to hospitals), now emphasises non-hospital treatment. In a country where physicians were once sent to jail for trying to treat opiate addicts on an outpatient basis, 85 per cent of all treatment (including a substantial proportion of detoxification) is done on an outpatient basis. At any given time, only one per cent of patients in treatment are in hospital beds with another ten per cent residing in therapeutic communities. Recent studies suggest that this outpatient orientation is also feasible in the treatment of alcoholism.

Is it realistic to expect government to pay the costs but to ignore the findings of controlled studies indefinitely? Even if decision-makers were unconcerned, is it fair to recommend to the alcoholic who requests treatment 30 days of inpatient care with its associated costs and loss of income and disruption of family and community ties, if two weeks are adequate? The routine use of hospital beds may be useful in further solidifying the disease model of alcoholism, but it may lead to sharp escalation of burdensome regulations in the future, and, if prodigality runs wild, possibly to a backlash directed against the very concept of treatment. Alcoholism should borrow from the mainstream of medicine the lesson that it is less painful to expand carefully than to contract under adverse conditions.

Cause for Concern

What the six general ideas listed under the 'non-borrowings' heading have in common is that while they are central concerns of the scientific community interested in alcoholism, the implications of these ideas are all too often ignored by the majority of those working directly with individuals with alcohol problems and by many of those who speak to the general public about alcoholism. Others considering the same set of discrepancies between the day-to-day practices and the scientific data base in the field of alcoholism might have selected other areas to highlight or underscore. A longer list would not have required too much additional effort. For the present, the six serve well enough to illustrate a problem that is not unique to alcoholism — the lag between developing knowledge and ongoing practice. To the extent that the lag is greater in the field of alcoholism than in other areas involving human services, there is cause for concern.

Notes

1. Pursch, J.A. (1976), 'From Quonset Hut to Naval Hospital: The Story of an Alcoholism Rehabilitation Service', *Journal of Studies on Alcohol*, vol. 37, pp. 1655-65.

2. Davies, D.L. (1962), 'Normal Drinking in Recovered Alcoholics', *Quarterly Journal of Studies on Alcohol*, vol. 23, pp. 94-104.

3. Armor, D.J., Polich, J.A. and Stambul, H.B. (1976), *Alcoholism and Treatment* (Rand Corporation, Santa Monica, California).

4. Sobell, M.B. and Sobell, L.C. (1976), 'Second-year Treatment Outcome of Alcoholics Treated by Individualized Behaviour Therapy', *Behaviour Research and Therapy*, vol. 14, pp. 195-215.

5. Popham, R.E. and Schmidt, W. (1976), 'Some Factors Affecting the Likelihood of Moderate Drinking in Treated Alcoholics', *Journal of Studies on Alcohol*, vol. 37, pp. 868-82.

6. Edwards, G., Orford, J., Egert, S. *et al.* (1977), 'Alcoholism: A Controlled Trial of "Treatment" and "Advice" ', *Journal of Studies on Alcohol*, vol. 38, pp. 1004-31.

7. Orford, J. and Edwards, G. (1976), *Alcoholism* (Oxford University Press, Oxford).

8. Keller, M. (1976), 'The Disease Concept of Alcoholism Revisited', *Journal of Studies on Alcohol*, vol. 37, pp. 1694-1717.

9. Edwards, G. (1974), 'Drugs, Drug Dependence and the Concept of Plasticity', *Quarterly Journal of Studies on Alcohol*, vol. 35, pp. 176-95.

10. Pattison, E.M. (1977), 'Ten Years of Change in Alcoholism Treatment and Delivery Systems', *American Journal of Psychiatry*, vol. 134, pp. 261-6.

11. Royal College of Psychiatrists (1979), *Alcohol and Alcoholism*, Report of a Special Committee (Tavistock Press, London).

12. Robinson, D. (1977), 'Factors Influencing Alcohol Consumption', in Edwards, G. and Grant, M. (eds.), *Alcoholism: New Knowledge and New Responses* (Croom Helm, London; University Park Press, Baltimore).

13. Schmidt, W. (1977), 'Cirrhosis and Alcohol Consumption: An Epidemiological Perspective', in ibid.

14. Smart, R.G. (1976), 'Spontaneous Recovery in Alcoholics: A Review and Analysis of the Available Research', *Drug and Alcohol Dependence*, vol. 1, pp. 277-85.

15. Gottheil, E., Thornton, C.C., Skoloda, T.E. and Alterman, A.I. (1980), 'Follow-up Study of Alcoholics at 6, 12 and 24 months', *Currents in Alcoholism* (in press).

16. Vaillant, G. (1966), 'A Twelve Year Follow-up of New York Narcotic Addicts. II: The Natural History of a Chronic Disease', *New England Journal of Medicine*, vol. 275, pp. 1281-8.

17. Vaillant, G. (1973), 'A 20 Year Follow-up of New York Narcotic Addicts', *Archives of General Psychiatry*, vol. 29, pp. 237-41.

18. Robins, L.N., Davis, D.H. and Goodwin, D.W. (1974), 'Drug Use by US Army Enlisted Men in Vietnam: A Follow-up on their Return Home', *American Journal of Epidemiology*, vol. 99, pp. 235-49.

19. Stimson, G.V., Oppenheimer, E. and Thorley, A. (1978), 'Seven Year Follow-up of Heroin Addicts: Drug Use and Outcome', *British Medical Journal*, vol. 1, pp. 1190-2.

20. Edwards, G. – To the best of my knowledge the term 'natural processes of healing' was first applied to alcoholism by Edwards.

21. Emrick, C.D. (1975), 'A Review of Psychologically Oriented Treatment of Alcoholism. II. The Relative Effectiveness of Different Treatment Approaches and the Effectiveness of Treatment vs. No Treatment', *Journal of Studies on*

Alcohol, vol. 36, pp. 88-108.
22. Smart, R.G. and Gray, G. (1978), 'Multiple Predictors of Dropout from Alcoholism Treatment', *Archives of General Psychiatry*, vol. 35, pp. 363-7.
23. Bromet, E., Moos, R., Bliss, F. and Wuthmann, C. (1977), 'Post-treatment Functioning of Alcoholic Patients: Its Relation to Program Participation', *Journal of Consulting and Clinical Psychology*, vol. 45, pp. 829-42.
24. Stein, L.I., Newton, R.J. and Bowman, R.S. (1975), 'Duration of Hospitalization for Alcoholism', *Archives of General Psychiatry*, vol. 32, pp. 247-52.
25. Stinson, D.J., Smith, W.G., Amidjaya, I. and Kaplan, J.M. (1976), 'Systems of Care and Treatment Outcomes for Alcoholic Patients', *Archives of General Psychiatry*, vol. 36, pp. 535-9.
26. Clare, A.W. (1977), 'How Good is Treatment?', in Edwards, G. and Grant, M. (eds.), *Alcoholism: New Knowledge and New Responses* (Croom Helm, London; University Park Press, Baltimore).
27. Schuckit, M.A. (1979), 'Treatment of Alcoholism in Office and Outpatient Settings', in Mendelson, J.H. and Mello, N.K. (eds.), *The Diagnosis and Treatment of Alcoholism* (McGraw-Hill, New York).
28. Winokur, G., Rimmer, J. and Reich, T. (1971), 'Alcoholism IV: Is There More than One Type of Alcoholism?', *British Journal of Psychiatry*, vol. 118, pp. 525-31.
29. Pattison, E.M. (1979), 'The Selection of Treatment Modalities for the Alcoholic Patient', in Mendelson, J.H. and Mello, N.K. (eds.), *The Diagnosis and Treatment of Alcoholism* (McGraw-Hill, New York).
30. Tarter, R.E., McBride, H., Buonpane, N. and Schneider, D.U. (1977), 'Differentiation of Alcoholics. Childhood History of Minimal Brain Dysfunction, Family History and Drinking Pattern', *Archives of General Psychiatry*, vol. 34, pp. 761-8.
31. Feighner, J.R., Robins, E., Guze, S. *et al.* (1972), 'Diagnostic Criteria for Use in Psychiatric Research', *Archives of General Psychiatry*, vol. 26, pp. 57-63.
32. Cantwell, D.P. (1972), 'Psychiatric Illness in the Families of Hyperactive Children', *Archives of General Psychiatry*, vol. 27, pp. 414-17.
33. Morrison, J.R. and Stewart, M.A. (1971), 'A Family Study of the Hyperactive Child Syndrome', *Biological Psychiatry*, vol. 3, pp. 189-95.
34. Goodwin, D.W., Schulsinger, F., Hermansen, L. *et al.* (1975), 'Alcoholism and the Hyperactive Child Syndrome', *Journal of Nervous and Mental Disorders*, vol. 160, pp. 349-53.
35. Mendelson, W., Johnson, N. and Stewart, M.A. (1971), 'Hyperactive Children as Teenagers: A Follow-up Study', *Journal of Nervous and Mental Disorders*, vol. 153, pp. 273-9.
36. Woodruff, R.A., Jr., Guze, S. and Clayton, P.J. (1973), 'Alcoholics Who See a Psychiatrist Compared with Those Who Do Not', *Quarterly Journal of Studies on Alcohol*, vol. 34, pp. 1162-71.
37. Wood, D.R., Beimherr, F.W., Wender, P.H. *et al.* (1976), 'Diagnosis and Treatment of Minimal Brain Dysfunction in Adults. A preliminary report', *Archives of General Psychiatry*, vol. 33, pp. 1453-60.
38. Blouin, A.G., Bornstein, R.A. and Trites, R.L. (1978), 'Teenage Alcohol Use Among Hyperactive Children: A Five Year Follow-up Study', *Journal of Pediatric Psychology*, vol. 3, pp. 188-94.
39. Shaw, J.A., Donley, P., Morgan, D.W. *et al.* (1975), 'Treatment of Depression in Alcoholics', *American Journal of Psychiatry*, vol. 132, pp. 614-44.
40. Pottenger, M., McKernon, J., Patrie, L.E. *et al.* (1978), 'The Frequency and Persistence of Depressive Symptoms in the Alcohol Abuser', *Journal of Nervous and Mental Diseases*, vol. 166, pp. 562-70.
41. Keeler, H.M., Taylor, C.I. and Miller, W.C. (1979), 'Are All Recently

Detoxified Alcoholics Depressed?', *American Journal of Psychiatry*, vol. 136, pp. 586-8.

42. Weissman, M.M., Pottenger, M., Kleber, H. *et al.* (1977), 'Symptom Patterns in Primary and Secondary Depression: A Comparison of Primary Depressives with Depressed Opiate Addicts, Alcoholics and Schizophrenics', *Archives of General Psychiatry*, vol. 34, pp. 854-62.

43. Viamontes, J.A. (1972), 'Review of Drug Effectiveness in the Treatment of Alcoholism', *American Journal of Psychiatry*, vol. 128, pp. 1570-1.

44. Glassman, A.H. and Perel, J.M. (1978), 'Tricyclic Blood Levels and Clinical Outcome: A Review of the Art', in Lipton, M.A., Dimascio, A. and Killam, K.F., *Psychopharmacology: A Generation of Progress* (Raven Press, New York).

45. Kline, N.S., Wren, J.C., Cooper, T.B. *et al.* (1974), 'Evaluation of Lithium Therapy in Chronic and Periodic Alcoholism', *American Journal of Medical Science*, vol. 268, pp. 15-22.

46. Merry, J., Reynolds, C., Bailey, J. *et al.* (1976), 'Prophylactic Treatment of Alcoholism by Lithium Carbonate: A Controlled Study', *Lancet*, vol. 2, pp. 481-2.

47. Miles, C.P. (1977), 'Conditions Predisposing to Suicide, A Review', *Journal of Nervous and Mental Diseases*, vol. 164, pp. 231-46.

48. Woodruff, R.A., Guze, S., Clayton, P.J. *et al.* (1973), 'Alcoholism and Depression', *Archives of General Psychiatry*, vol. 28, pp. 97-100.

3 CHALLENGING OUR CONFUSIONS

Marcus Grant and Anthony Clare

There was one particular afternoon session which took place at the conference which relates to this book but which did not involve the presentation of scientific papers. To turn live conference discussion, however stimulating it may have seemed at the time, into material for a book is notoriously difficult. Important issues were, though, raised during that session which are central to the general debate about the directions currently being followed in alcoholism treatment. Working, therefore, from a transcript of that remarkable and stormy session, an attempt has been made first to describe the issues which occupied the energies of the meeting.

A brief description of what actually took place will assist the reader in understanding the form of the occasion. The session was chaired by Dr Anthony Clare (Institute of Psychiatry, University of London) and began with the presentation on videotape of two cases illustrating very different kinds of alcohol problems. Watching these cases was a treatment panel consisting of Dr Sheila B. Blume (New York State Division of Alcoholism), Mr W.H. Kenyon (Merseyside, Lancashire and Cheshire Council on Alcoholism), Dr A.C.R. Skynner (Institute of Psychiatry, London) and Dr Mark Sobell (Vanderbilt University, Tennessee). This panel was invited to comment upon each case in terms of how they would actually treat that individual if he or she happened to present at their clinic. There was also a small non-clinical panel consisting of Mr Marcus Grant (Alcohol Education Centre, London) and Dr Robin Room (School of Public Health, Berkeley, California), empowered to interrupt the treatment panel and discuss assumptions which the clinicians were making. The patients in the videotapes were professional actors whilst the therapists (representing a psychiatrist and a social worker) were alcoholism specialists who had been briefed to concentrate upon eliciting information from the patients rather than offering advice or treatment. In the latter part of the afternoon, there was a general floor discussion in which all those attending the conference were able to express views about the decisions of the clinicians, the doubts raised by the non-clinicians and, most importantly, to contribute to the debate from their own experience and understanding. The way in which the whole occasion was contrived, and the very sensitive acting in

videos, was remarkably successful in stimulating discussion and in
bringing sharply into contact the work-a-day problems of the clinical
world.

The Video Cases

The two cases which were presented as video vignettes had been
scripted so as to present problems at either end of the spectrum of
treatment-seeking individuals. One showed a lady who, although
manifesting early signs of alcohol problems and being, for a variety of
reasons, in a vulnerable position, offered little in the way of specific
areas of damage which were severe enough or sufficiently clearly
alcohol-related to give clinicians a sense of where best to begin and how
best to proceed. The other case showed a man so severely damaged by
alcohol in so many different areas of his life and with such an appall-
ingly bad track record of not responding to previous treatment, that it
was difficult for clinicians to see what more they could offer him or
why he would be likely to improve.

Case 1 (The Barmaid)

The subject is a woman in her mid-thirties. She does not want to stop
drinking and sees no particular reason why she should. She has always
liked a drink and cannot really imagine what life would be like without
it. She works as a barmaid, a job which she has had for the last ten
years or so.

For the last two years she has found that things have been beginning
to oppress her a bit, but feels that this really does not have much to do
with her drinking. Instead, she blames it on trouble at home to do with
her husband whom she has never really liked but who has recently
left her. She also explains that her mother died some three years
previously and it is clear that she still feels considerable grief. She was
further upset by a burglary at her house just a few months ago. These
she says are much more important reasons for her present feelings of
confusion and lack of confidence.

It is true that she has occasionally been drunk on the job and that
she has begun to let her appearance go a little. On the other hand, she
can, if she wants to, go without drink for a whole weekend and has
indeed done so on a number of occasions. She has sometimes wakened
up in the mornings feeling sick and occasionally has actually vomited
but this is not something which occurs every day. Similarly, she

sometimes finds that if people are watching her her hands will be unsteady as she pours drinks early in the day but this only seems to affect her from time to time. Some years ago, she was convicted of driving under the influence of alcohol, her blood alcohol level at the time of the offence being 180 mg%.

She did go to a clinic a year ago on the advice of her doctor. At the clinic, they told her that she must stop drinking because she was an alcoholic. She asked what that meant and they told her about loss of control. She found it therefore impossible to accept the diagnosis of alcoholism because she knew she could control her drinking.

She now has a new relationship with a man who she thinks is good for her. She met him in the pub and recognises that he is himself quite a heavy drinker. She wants to continue her job in the pub but the licensee, who is himself an AA member, has told her that she must never drink again and that if he sees her drinking he will take this to be an infringement of their agreement. He wants her to go back to a clinic to receive more treatment, but she does not believe this is really necessary.

This woman's drinking obviously has a considerable amount to do with environmental pressures relating to her job. She states, probably quite correctly, that many of her customers drink more than she does. She has no really serious underlying psychiatric illnesses and appears to be able still to control many aspects of her life.

She enjoys her job as a barmaid and sees no reason why her drinking should interfere with it. On the other hand, she is not so imperceptive as to fail to recognise that maybe from time to time she does drink a little bit more than is good for her. What really she cannot accept is the notion that the word 'alcoholism' could be applied to her. She has seen people whom she would describe as alcoholics, and knows that she is not like them.

Case 2 (The Derelict)

This subject is a man in his early fifties who presents a rough and unrewarding picture. He is unwilling to talk at length and tends to agree with everything that is suggested to him. Nevertheless, he continues drinking and is desperately dependent upon alcohol. Although he is always wanting to receive treatment, he is often refused it or reacts badly to it. Meek and submissive when sober, he is violent when drunk.

While being interviewed, he does not appear to understand what is being said to him, although he does in fact make the odd incisive remark about himself which is ignored by those who are interviewing him, who have become used to his lack of insight. He is unemployed and has, throughout most of his life, only had casual work. He has been in and out of hospital and in and out of prison. He shows a pattern of repeated DTs when drunk, is withdrawn and has for many years found it necessary to have a drink before getting up in the morning. He exhibits considerable physical damage, complains and shows signs of significant memory lapse. Gradually throughout his life he has been banned from more and more places — initially from pubs because of his fighting, then subsequently from hospitals and eventually even from hostels. His case note file is composed of letters from agencies which all suggest sending him further down the line. At the time of the interview he has just been released from prison and wants to go into a hostel and is sober. The hostel warden has indicated that it is not their policy to accept people straight from prison, but that he can attend groups in the afternoon but must live elsewhere for a period of four weeks. He is therefore sleeping rough and recognises that he is likely to start drinking again very soon. He is out of touch with his family.

He now drinks four or five large bottles of cider a day, together with as much cheap wine as he can lay his hands on. He has no history of periods of sobriety (other than when in prison or in hospital) of longer than a few days. He appears very moody and depressed. Indeed there is evidence that at some point in his past he has received ECT for his presumed depression.

The General Responses to the Videos

As anticipated, the two case vignettes raised different questions. The first focussed attention on the question of the relationship between problem drinking and alcoholism. Some appeared to feel that the decision as to which category the barmaid belonged might well influence the sort of treatment offered to her. The majority, however, felt such diagnostic niceties were clinically irrelevant — she was exhibiting certain early signs and symptoms of a problem involving alcohol. There was a reluctance, particularly expressed by a number of participants from the audience, to concentrate on her problems involving alcohol for fear of neglecting her psychological and social problems. On the one hand, responses concentrated on such features as her drinking at work, morning nausea, occasional tremors, and her high risk occupation of barmaid. On the other hand, the dissenting voices doubted the general practitioner's original referral to an alcoholism clinic, noted the employment pressure on her to seek treatment on this occasion, expressed uncertainty concerning the extent of her involvement with alcohol and in turn emphasised the 'unworked through' quality of her grief concerning her mother's death, her divorce and current relationship and the lack of social activities outside drinking.

However, much of the uncertainty concerning the accuracy of the diagnosis in relation to this case appeared to be related in part to a real uncertainty concerning the best form of treatment response to be made to her. In so far as any consensus emerged, it related to using the clinic opportunity as one in which some facts concerning alcohol and alcohol abuse could be put to the woman in an unthreatening and unemotional fashion. Thus, for example, confusion over the precise meaning of the word 'alcoholism' could be removed. It has to be said that such removal appeared unlikely, in view of the fact that nothing remotely approaching a consensus emerged at the meeting as to what 'alcoholism' does actually mean.

Summarising the first case, it does seem that while the alcoholism literature is replete with regret that patients/clients do not come into contact with counselling and treatment agencies early enough and/or are not identified promptly enough as high-risk individuals, there is a remarkable degree of uncertainty as to how best to proceed when one is confronted with someone who is drinking in a manner which may indicate problems but which is also similar to many people in the community, people who ordinarily would not consider that they had problems and who might not be considered to have problems by anyone else.

The second case, on the other hand, raised less diagnostic disagreement, though even here there was some. The question 'How would you treat this man?' provoked responses ranging from the administration of alcohol in circumscribed and controlled situations, through a monitored programme of abstinence involving the supervised use of antabuse, to no treatment at all on the grounds that such cases represent the terminal stages of alcohol dependence and are analogous to cases of terminal cancer for whom relief may be offered but active treatment avoided.

There was general criticism of the lack of appropriate therapeutic or management facilities for this type of client. But it was far from clear what participants meant by appropriate facilities. On the one hand, there seemed regret at the disappearance of facilities which made minimal demands on such clients, which allowed them overtly or covertly to drink to a limited extent, supplied basic requirements such as food and shelter and did not wrap it up under a therapeutic blanket. On the other hand, there was considerable anxiety that such a minimal approach would be seen as a form of collusion and more active therapists seemed willing to persevere, generally on an outpatient basis, with attempts founded on antabuse and directed towards a goal of abstinence.

Forced by the chairman to indicate which of the two cases would receive the investment of their time and energies in a situation where these were insufficient to cover both, the participants retreated in disarray. The second case was perceived as a clear-cut, highly dependent alcoholic — but was he treatable? The first case was seen as a potential client for an educational approach — but would she respond and, anyway, was her main problem actually alcohol?

Inevitably, the discussion ended with appeals for more research, for studies of sub-categories of alcohol abusers, for more detailed assessments of drinking histories, etc. Clinicians reminded each other, however, that while such research was imperative, people like the two individuals on video were coming into contact with various facilities right now. How were they to be dealt with in the light of current knowledge?

Some Specific Issues Emerging from the Debate

Treatability

These two cases, which were intended to focus discussion on the process of treatment, in fact provoked a rather more basic reaction. As well as discussing how to treat them, the audience spent a great deal of time debating whether it is possible to treat such cases at all. Certainly, the cases were constructed so as to illustrate two ends of the spectrum, the barmaid showing a cluster of clear, though not particularly severe, indicators, whilst the derelict displayed a considerable range of intransigent problems with social, physical and mental disturbance occurring almost throughout his life. Neither represented the most extreme example of an early case or a late case, but it might have seemed, had they not been shown as a pair at an international conference on alcoholism, that their differences were more important than their common ground.

Indeed, so much was this apparent from the discussion, that it seemed the audience was splitting into opposing camps: those who would treat the barmaid and those who would treat the derelict. The implication certainly was that those, or quite a high proportion of those, who chose to treat the derelict would choose not to treat the barmaid and, to a somewhat lesser extent, vice versa. The issue had much to do with whether the barmaid had a condition that was sufficiently advanced to be susceptible to what is generally thought of as treatment. Several people recognised the danger in this line of thinking and pointed out how very close it came to sending her away, telling her to come back when she was 'a real alcoholic'.

In fact, this issue actually brought into sharp focus some fundamental differences within the audience in terms of the treatment model being used. Those who operated with a fairly restricted notion of treatment seemed prepared to offer it to the derelict, despite the fact that all agreed that the prognosis was grim. At the same time, they appeared doubtful of the appropriateness of offering it to the barmaid, since she did not meet the criteria of illness. Those who held such a model, which did exhibit many of the characteristics of the oft-quoted yet rarely defined 'medical model', emphasised the undoubted illness of the derelict, not merely the illness of his clear-cut physical dependence on alcohol but also the illness known to accompany such long-term abuse, in particular brain damage. They readily acknowledged the massive nature of the task of treatment but disputed any suggestion by others that the man might not be treatable.

This suggestion of untreatability, it should be noted, was not put forward by people who doubted the fact that the derelict was ill. Rather, it was advanced as part of an argument to the effect that he was indeed ill but beyond possibility of help. One of the advantages of the medical model, namely its reluctance to give up on even the most hopeless cases, was though illustrated by one speaker who reminded the audience that even hopeless cases sometimes recover.

Indeed, the whole discussion of treatment in relation to the derelict had a distinctly medical aura about it. Issues such as the administration of antabuse, admission to hospital, methods of withdrawal and the need for a thorough assessment of the individual's state of physical health dominated the discussion. The clear assumption seemed to be that treatment was something which therapists did to patients. It appeared to be an active process involving particular skills and even technique.

Not surprisingly, therefore, these medically oriented therapists seemed somewhat at a loss when confronted by the barmaid. She did not appear in the least sick. Indeed, as was pointed out by several participants, to call her an alcoholic, an incipient alcoholic or even an early problem-drinker might well mean that a rather large section of the adult population would find itself sheltering under the same morbid umbrella.

Thus, those who chose to treat the barmaid tended to have a more pragmatic model of alcoholism treatment in which they tried to offer what they thought would fit the circumstances of the patient. The difficulty here, of course, was that it was not always clear what best fitted the circumstances or how it could be best applied. The flexibility of the pragmatic approach, therefore, was contrasted with the extent to which it could be seen as haphazard, depending upon individual skills and good fortune rather than upon a firm understanding of the nature of the problem in a wider context.

This led several discussants to suggest that in the case of the barmaid the time was ripe for giving advice, support or even simple information. Despite the attractiveness of this educational approach, there were many who doubted whether it was likely to prove particularly effective. Also, certainly, there was some doubt as to whether or not it really counted as treatment in the proper sense of the word. Absent from the discussion was any acknowledgement that, since the barmaid might need a response which differed from that required by the derelict, this might well be forthcoming from an agency or agencies which would differ from those working with problems such as the derelict presented. The notion of the all-purpose therapist offering a wide range of therapeutic possibilities to an equally wide range of patients/clients seemed to underpin the discussion.

It was perhaps this melee of models that led one speaker to point out that there was a breakdown in diagnostic terms, in treatment methods, and in treatment goals. He suggested that it would be wise not to let too many people see what was really happening at the meeting unless, of course, we were to take the advice of our patients who say that when you have hit rock bottom, you can only come up.

Diagnostic Indices

Most of the participants were relatively inexperienced in handling a problem such as that posed by the barmaid. It was almost as if the fact that she came so early made them suspicious of the diagnosis. What, they asked, was her general practitioner up to? After all, most general practitioners never spot alcoholism until the patient falls over in the surgery with a blood alcohol level in excess of 200 mg%. What was the barmaid's employer up to? An employer who pressurises his employee to seek treatment for alcoholism must be an authoritarian puritan with an obsession about the evils of alcohol.

However, several people did point out that the barmaid was exhibiting a number of signs and symptoms which research had shown to be indicators of potential risk. She was employed in a high risk occupation; she devoted much of her social life to drinking; she had had a drink-driving offence in the past; she had experienced a significant life event (her husband had left her); she was anxious because of the recent burglary at her house and she appeared depressed over the loss of her mother some years before. Taken individually, such items might not amount to very much. Together, they flashed a warning of greatly increased vulnerability to alcohol problems.

Few people seemed to know how to implement a diagnostic assessment in a case like the barmaid's. The notion of high-risk factors, the model of a powerful psychotropic drug operating in someone undergoing serious psychological and social stress, and the conception of treatment as a process in which the giving of information and advice is a significant, and in certain instances, a dominant feature, all tended to be overshadowed by concern with the appropriateness of the barmaid's inclusion in the sickness-treatment model. One wonders whether a general practitioner, confronted by an overweight, over-working businessman complaining of vague chest pain would worry too much, in the absence of any evidence of established cardiovascular disease, over the illness status of his patient before advising him on the risks involved in his life-style and habits.

Motivation

'I find', said an experienced psychotherapist, 'that in trying to teach family therapists, the main thing I've got to do is to try to cure them of wanting to help people.' As someone not specially involved in the alcoholism treatment world, his surprise was quite evident when he spoke of the active zeal he saw in the audience, which he characterised as 'this enormous urge to treat these people'. In directing attention to the motivation of the therapists, he helped to highlight something which had, at least explicitly, been under-emphasised in much of the preceding discussion, namely the motivation of the patient. There certainly had been the presumption during much of the afternoon that treatment was something therapists did to people. To be reminded that frequently it was the patient who decided to be treated and even how he was going to be treated, was a most useful corrective. It cast into a new light some of the earlier remarks about the barmaid in which there had been heated debate about whether or not she was lying about her symptoms and whether or not she had been forced to attend for interview by her harsh and overbearing employer.

Few admitted that her employer might well be the mildest of men, intent only upon her well-being, and that her ambivalence might proceed less from her unwillingness to accept she needed help than from exasperation at the inappropriateness of the help she was being offered. Similarly, in the case of the derelict, it was suggested that the very fact he was seeking help under duress lessened the chances of his successful acceptance of it. It was recognised that he was genuine in his present concern, but it was suggested that this was more to gain a place in the hostel than to deal with his basic problems. One person suggested that his lack of a stable environment was perhaps his basic problem. This certainly raised the question as to what constituted appropriate motivation. If wanting to keep one's job, or wanting to have a roof over one's head were both suspect then what, one wonders, would such therapists require to convince them of the good intentions of a patient? It is possible that we are indeed back to a religious model of alcoholism in which spiritual desire for salvation is required before the pearly gates of the alcoholism clinic will swing open.

4 CHARTING WHAT HAS CHANGED

Marc A. Schuckit

Introduction

The overall goal of this chapter is to examine whether a transition in treatment has indeed occurred over the last ten years, to document it, and to place it in perspective. Transition must be seen as an inextricable intertwining of social, philosophical and scientific aspects of change. The emphasis will be on alcoholism and its treatment but will occasionally digress to other related scientific topics.

An author of such a chapter does well at the outset to declare the bias of his training and experience. This chapter is written by a psychiatrist with a strong medical identification but with productive experience of interdisciplinary work who would regard goals in treatment as very specific — to return the patient to his normal level of functioning as rapidly as possible with the least cost in money and pain.[1,2] This can best be done by carefully distinguishing between when the doctor 'knows' something and when he is guessing, as these may have profound effects on the risks to which patients are exposed. The views expressed here are strongly influenced by the North American background and many of the comments have their greatest direct relevance to that part of the world, although the general rules have perhaps a more global application.

It is not being implied here that everything is new or in flux, as many aspects of care have not changed much (or at least, subjectively, not enough) in recent years.

We all tend to react to day-to-day problems without developing a global philosophy[3] and too often see the needs of our clients in terms of what our particular centre has to offer, i.e. an 'organisational imperative'.[3] This leads to our emphasis on our personal experience where 'my way is the only way because it worked for me' and a tendency to be closer-minded and fiercely threatened by alternate points of view. Unfortunately, this appears to be as true for the 'scientists' as it does for our colleagues in Alcoholics Anonymous. In fact, treatment evaluations carried out in the 1960s and 1970s have not changed much from what was noted in one of the original syntheses presented by Voegtin and Lemere in 1942.[4-7] We still have a great diversity of programmes and approaches all of which work (or do not work) to about the same degree, pointing out that there is no 'magic cure' and that we have got to continue to look for additional answers.[3-9]

While discussing the transitions that have appeared, neither is it implied that all change is good, as transitions carry some of their own inherent dangers. Our desire for change may lead us to an overly enthusiastic acceptance of the flashy new things — the eye catching fads.[10] This may be a special danger in alcoholism where, for a variety of reasons, good, responsible research has been somewhat lacking with a resulting paucity of anchors other than our own defensiveness to keep us from latching on to the 'miracle' cures such as metronidazole and LSD. This situation is made even more complex by the very variable course of alcoholism and the trend towards spontaneous remission which combine to make a high rate of improvement with time alone.[6,8-12] However, if we are careful and we establish some basic goals and our areas of responsibility to the patient we can go through a period of transition using a realistic appraisal of where we are, testing diverse possibilities for the future, but avoiding general acceptance or emotional commitment until good, hard data have proven that the new approach is worthwhile.

From this general framework, the literature on treatment in the last decade or two has been reviewed looking for signs of transition. The attempt has then been made to synthesise that information to get a global picture.

Social Transitions

Public policy can dictate the definition of a crisis, determine whether long- or short-term goals are deemed most relevant, and allocate the amount of energy and money that can be devoted to handle a problem area. Research and treatment efforts for alcoholism have been affected by a number of important social and political events. In the United States, for example, the Vietnam War diverted efforts from health areas, with the monetary inflation resulting from the war greatly affecting the value of the health care dollar. The recent oil crises along with our inability to decrease gasoline consumption have affected the balance of payments in the United States, Japan, and Western Europe, further feeding inflation and thus decreasing the amount of monies available for research and treatment. The political changes in the 1960s and early 1970s towards a 'new liberalism' resulted in a drive to do something 'now', to divert money from research into treatment (even if treatment efforts are far from ideal), while the increase in patient rights has affected the numbers and types of patients coming into care. We have also witnessed changes in general social values. The result has been the recognition of the importance of various minority and interest groups such as the elderly and racial or ethnic minorities who are now entering treatment in greater numbers. Changes in social values have also called for a new awareness of the rights of women and the young with concomitant decreases in proscriptions against drinking in these sub-populations with apparent resulting increases in intake and alcohol related difficulties.[13, 14] The impact of other strong social changes such as the world-wide trend towards nationalised health care and the resurgence of fundamentalist religious approaches have also been felt.

Another social transition affecting alcoholism treatment and research has been an increased need for accountability, probably reflecting a trend towards decreasing available monies and increasing demands for public disclosure. Public agencies are now more likely to judge alcoholism programmes on various cost/benefit ratios[15] and to demand some proof that any recipient of public monies, including those in alcoholism, prove that their efforts actually work.[16, 17] A related phenomenon is the demand that the people giving treatment meet a minimum standard of competence as measured by some form of licensing.[3, 18]

At the same time, there has been a general social trend in most areas of the world to accept alcoholism as an illness or at least as a problem representing more than a moral weakness. Great changes in public attitudes have occurred in the United States between the 1940s and the 1970s as the general public is beginning to recognise that only rare alcoholics are on skid row.[19] For a variety of reasons a number of important and influential persons ranging from legislators to the wife of an ex-president of the United States have admitted their alcoholism and thus underscored the fact that the alcoholic is not a hopeless and inadequate failure.

Social changes in other areas of the world are just as important as those outlined in North America. Monetary flow and military budgets as well as traditional meanings of drinking and drunkenness probably affect the national statistics and alcohol related energy expenditures in Eastern Europe as well. The less industrialised nations may not have the resources to address alcoholism full-force at present, but still have large problems which will be met in the future. The job can be begun in a limited way taking full advantage of the less formally trained indigenous counsellors. Also, various countries are experimenting with the degree to which the government should control manufacture, distribution, and profits of the liquor industry and the extent to which alcohol-related profits can be used to finance alcoholism treatment and research.

Thus, any changes occurring in the delivery of care for alcohol treatment programmes should not be viewed in a vacuum. Many of the social changes around us affect our ability to treat our patients.

Transitions in Professional Roles and Values

The level of involvement of professionals (arbitrarily defined as those with masters or doctorate level degrees) in the alcoholism field has changed a great deal over the last decade. This has included a series of changes in attitudes towards the alcoholic, shifts in opinions regarding the role and importance of alcoholism treatment, and changes in health care delivery systems.

The attitude of the professional towards alcoholism still suffers from a 'derived stigma' where colleagues are likely to look down upon a professional in this area,[3] but some changes have occurred. This might reflect an influx of money into both research and treatment (even though we all know that there is never enough) and an unrelated explosion in the number of doctorate level psychologists and physicians. There seems to be less of a feeling of lowering one's standards or jeopardising one's career by entering the alcohol areas, although difficulties in recruitment of major leaders in the alcoholism field attest to the fact that the problem has not totally reversed itself. Perhaps the greatest change has occurred in the official positions of professional societies which are now more willing to recognise alcoholism as a disease in need of treatment[3] and is also reflected in the number of professionally oriented books on alcoholism treatment (e.g.[20]). There is even a move within the medical profession for the creation of an alcoholic sub-speciality (for good or bad) and in recent years new alcoholism societies, such as the Research Society on Alcoholism, have grown up. The increasing number of physicians willing to treat alcoholics and hospitals which no longer exclude alcoholics from admission represent an important change from the alarming statistics of the 1940s and 1950s.[21,22] This new awareness has been accompanied by an increase in the number of medical school elective and required courses on alcoholism between 1961 and 1977.[23,24] The shift has not been complete, however, as noted by the continuation of some physicians to refuse to recognise alcoholism in their patients, and the facts that one quarter of medical schools in the United States have five or less hours of teaching on alcoholism, one third have no electives on alcoholism, and 20 per cent have no medical school affiliation with an alcohol treatment programme.[24]

Recent years have also witnessed a trend in professionals towards higher levels of sophistication in the way treatment efforts are viewed. We are more likely to demand more careful definitions of mental health problems, including alcoholism, as evidenced by the Research Diagnostic Criteria, the Washington University Criteria, and the proposed third Diagnostic and Statistical Manual of the American Psychiatric Association.[25-27] There has been a concomitant increase in our understanding of the usual expected course or natural history of disorders including the recognition of the occurrence of 'spontaneous remissions' (or at least responses to non-specific interventions) in alcoholism. An additional phenomenon is the trend towards increasing documentation of the common sense conclusion that there are important sub-types within alcoholism that must be recognised due to their possible unique etiologies, courses, or treatment needs.[28-30] This increased acceptance of the need for documentation and broader understanding has (at least in part) been associated with a slight decrease in the tendency to see things in extremes, a recognition that there are similarities between various approaches at intervention (for example Alcoholics Anonymous and behaviour modification programmes)[3,31] and that it is important to at least consider the relevance of a variety of outcomes as will be discussed in Chapter 5 by Dr Armor and noted in greater detail later in this chapter. These changes have all had an impact on the increasing awareness of professionals that research may have an important impact on future treatment.[16,32,33]

A number of changes in professional attitudes have affected transitions in health care delivery systems and health care research. The last decade has witnessed both the positive and negative aspects of a movement towards community mental health in the United States. One result has been a trend towards increasing the numbers of small inpatient and outpatient programmes within local communities with the resulting increase in the need for non-degreed personnel (often called paraprofessionals). The same movement, however, has resulted in a 'fad' towards closing long-term central facilities with the result that chronically impaired patients now often have no place to go and end up living alone or in impoverished areas in board and care facilities.[34]

A number of changes have also occurred in the style of research. There is a trend (probably a healthy one) towards recognition that many mental health problems, including alcoholism, cut across fields and that interdisciplinary research is sorely needed.[19] Despite major impediments to progress in this area (at least in part as a consequence of university structures which emphasise uni-modal departments, and the reluctance of many of us to share our efforts) there is a trend towards increased funding of interdisciplinary research and the establishment of interdisciplinary institutes. The substantial trend towards centralised records, as noted in Scandinavia for example, has also helped to tie together professionals with diverse approaches.

Researchers in this area are also looking at broader subjects including efforts aimed at attempting to prevent problems such as alcoholism before they begin.[19] This is based on the thought that prevention may be more effective than treatment (using smallpox as a model).[35] However, just as we have no 'magic' cures for alcoholism, no 'magic' modes of prevention have yet been demonstrated and one must guard against creation of new fads.[33,36,37]

Thus, treatment of the alcoholic has been affected by an increased interest and level of sophistication of professionals in a variety of fields. The results of this trend are apparent in the diversity of treatments discussed below.

Transitions in Treatment Programmes

Transitions in treatment have been primarily philosophical, reflecting an increasing tendency towards a realistic appraisal of the state of our art, a trend towards cost-effectiveness, and an increasing desire to question where we are and where we are going. These are all hopeful signs for the future even though one cannot document any major breakthroughs in treatment delivery.[38,39] What is important, however, is that these changes, although minor, lay the groundwork for possible future substantial progress. Some of these studies would have been impossible ten years ago.

Our research has turned to some basic questions including whether treatment, as we now see it, is effective,[9,16] whether education (accepted to be as good and important as motherhood) actually adds an important dimension to rehabilitation programmes[40] and even whether aftercare should be an important part of therapy.[41] The publication in a major alcoholism journal of 'A Controlled Trial of "Treatment" and "Advice" ' by Edwards *et al.*[16] and the relatively supportive and measured responses in the published commentaries following that article[42] indicate that we are ready to question some basic assumptions. Of course, this openness is far from unanimous, but at least it is there.

With the general comments on changes in societal values and professional attitudes in mind, one may then briefly review a number of transitions in alcohol treatment. Note that none of these are black and white changes but rather represent a more subtle evolution in our treatment process.

A Readjustment of the Role of the Professional and Paraprofessional in Alcoholism Treatment

As noted earlier, degreed professionals (masters level, doctorate level and physicians) have not historically shown great interest in the treatment of alcoholism.[19,32] The result has been that the majority of care has been given through self-help groups such as Alcoholics Anonymous (AA) and treatment programmes headed by individuals with practical experience but little formal education (for want of a better word termed 'paraprofessionals'). In the 1960s, the professionals began to recognise the importance of the problem of alcoholism while at the same time increased funding made their participation possible. This was followed by an increased demand for cost-effectiveness with the result, ideally, of programmes mixing professionals and paraprofessionals but with the major clinical care being carried out by the non-degreed staff.

The marriage, however, has not been an easy one.[32] The doctorate level individuals tend to look at health care through a more scientific model requiring data and encouraging modifications of programmes when trends appear. The paraprofessionals, frequently recovering alcoholics, were introduced to the field as a 'craft' learning through a model of apprenticeship emphasising the need for experience and encouraging the replication of the model presented by the leader. In order for these two styles to work together effectively, some level of compromise on both parts will be needed. This becomes especially acute when one asks the question of who will direct the programme — the individual with experience but lower level of formal education or the person following a more scientific model with the advanced degree. This state of flux is still active and can only reach its optimal conclusion regarding the best patient care when it is approached with an open mind.

Of course, many of us find ourselves as craftsmen in one situation and scientists in another. A typical example is the individual who does research in alcoholism (recognising all the frailties of the conclusions that are generally accepted in the area), and then goes off the same day and carries out treatment. The benefit of this arrangement is that the clinician/researcher applies the benefits of his knowledge of the literature and research to the actual clinical setting. The difficulty is that the clear-cut rules used in research must be modified when applied to any specific clinical instance. The fact that many individuals feel comfortable wearing both hats underscores the somewhat arbitrary nature of the proposed dichotomy between scientist and craftsman.

Changes in Populations in Treatment

The increasing awareness of alcohol problems and alcoholism in the general population and the increase in alcohol problem clinics and alcoholism inpatient beds has resulted in an influx of patients with alcohol problems rarely seen in the past. This has been accompanied by an increasing recognition of drinking problems in youth and a trend towards admitting them into treatment,[43] increasing numbers of women entering care,[44] more recognition of alcohol problems in the elderly,[45] increasing participation in treatment of minorities,[46] and an increased recognition of alcohol problems in general medical and surgical patients as well as people in the middle to upper socioeconomic strata.[47] Of course, the specific changes vary in different areas of the world. We have also begun to question whether it is necessary to treat alcoholics and drug addicts in totally separate treatment programmes,[48] a questioning coming at least in part from the recognition of mixed drug dependencies (perhaps reflecting the influx of youth) and a drive towards cost-effectiveness. With these changes in populations, alcohol treatment personnel have found the need to develop flexibility in treatment approaches, although there is little solid evidence that alcoholism runs a different course in these various sub-groups. The increasing complexity of the populations involved, however, does point out the required continued training for people in the field to deal with the unique needs of these groups.

The Trend Towards Outpatient Treatment

A more healthy side of the movement towards community based facilities has been the trend to question whether inpatient alcoholism rehabilitation is needed for every individual and, once this mode of treatment is chosen, how long someone must stay for optimal care. Repeatedly, investigations evaluating longer versus shorter inpatient treatment programmes for the *average* patient have shown the shorter stay to be as effective as longer hospitalisation.[6,49] This line of reasoning led Edwards *et al.*, to question the need for any inpatient care for the average alcoholic.[16] While these studies are of crucial importance for our future growth in the field we must engage in a balanced questioning lest we suffer a worsening of the same scarcity of inpatient beds facing psychiatry. At present, short inpatient stays (perhaps two weeks or less) with follow-up programmes going for a minimum of three months would appear well advised.[39,41] This approach might be especially beneficial to the developing countries where hospital and monetary resources are even more limited.

The Need to Look More Openly at Outcome Criteria

Even when one chooses an alcoholic population, carefully limiting the patients to primary alcoholics (those without evidence of other major pre-existing psychiatric disorders), the level of functioning at outcome can differ greatly from patient to patient and culture to culture. This is not surprising in light of the long-term nature of alcohol problems, the variability in course, and the heavy impact alcoholism has on many life areas.[6,11,12,29] Unfortunately, there is not always a one-to-one relationship between abstinence and improvement in life tenor although the trend is for the level of life functioning to increase when drinking decreases.[29,38] Nonetheless, treatment aimed at helping the individual's entire life style must recognise that even the achievement of abstinence may be associated with a deterioration of the marriage and other interpersonal relationships as rules established to guide the interactions while drinking may fall apart when abstinence is reached.

We are coming to recognise that the 'either-or' criterion of treatment measured only by abstinence is inadequate. Involvement in a treatment programme might be associated with a great change in an individual's life even though that person has not yet achieved permanent abstention from ethanol.[9,29,38] It makes more sense to look at level of functioning in health, emotional adjustment, vocational functioning, and overall life interactions.[29,38]

The Question of 'Controlled' Drinking

One result of our questioning of outcome has been a rapid growth in programmes attempting to evaluate controlled drinking.[50-53] Here, the treatment regimen usually deals with alcoholics who refuse to stop drinking by attempting to teach them how to control their intake and thus drink without problems.

The emergence of this concept has been made by an emotional reaction, especially from those individuals following the Alcoholics Anonymous model. The resulting verbal battles have frequently followed the professional versus paraprofessional lines as the latter point out how often the alcoholic repeatedly tries to control his drinking only to fall 'off the wagon' subsequently, while the former are more attuned to the need for open questioning. Most treatment personnel and researchers, no matter what their level of formal education, do recognise that all viable approaches deserve consideration. The problems come with how experimental the approach should be and whether the results should be released to the general public before carefully controlled investigations are carried out. With adequate trials of programmes aimed at controlled drinking, it will be necessary to determine whether the approach is best for alcoholics or social drinkers with evanescent problems. It will also be important to determine which types of alcoholics respond best to this approach, with preliminary data indicating that those most likely to benefit are those with the best prognoses demonstrating more stable lifestyles and decreased alcohol intake before care.[54,55] At this point in time, the approach is experimental and requires further research before it can be considered clinically applicable.

Changes in the Model of Detoxification

Historically, the goals of detoxification have included offering good medical care, giving patients the option of rehabilitation, and a means of getting the 'down and out' alcoholic off the street. Unfortunately, many programmes have begun to function without specifying which specific goal or goals are involved. One change in the area of detoxification has resulted from the push towards cost-effectiveness and accountability which now mandates that programmes be evaluated in the light of specific goals, which in turn forces the programme to establish clear guidelines.

Most metropolitan areas are beginning to recognise that detoxification is usually not an effective entry into rehabilitation.[56] Rather, the more limited goals of offering good medical care and getting the alcoholic off the street have emerged as the primary reasons for existence for many public detoxification programmes. Most private rehabilitation centres, on the other hand, use the first few days of hospitalisation for detoxification to open the way towards beginning rehabilitation efforts for appropriate patients.

The atmosphere of open questioning of methods and goals accompanied by the need for accountability have resulted in the expansion of at least two alternative approaches to public detoxification in the last decade. The first, as described by Feldman *et al.*, attempts to decrease costs by carrying out detoxification in outpatient facilities.[57] Here patients are carefully screened for medical disorders or signs of serious withdrawal and then, with the help of a resource person such as a spouse, receive their medications (usually brain depressing drugs such as chlordiazepoxide) at home while coming into a 'day hospital' for observation. When used carefully this approach appears to work and functions at a relatively low cost.

A step further in decreasing costs has resulted in the development of what is usually termed a 'social model' of detoxification.[58] The result here is to delete the most expensive aspects of the programme — the need for physicians and registered nurses. Thus, after (ideally) screening patients for signs of serious medical disorders or impending serious withdrawal and sending the relevant individuals to a medical facility, one is left with a majority of patients who do not obviously require medical care. These individuals are allowed to go through their withdrawal in a social environment which helps them to cope with their symptoms. Thus, the cost per patient is greatly lowered and, while some patients are uncomfortable, the prior screening of the seriously ill individuals justifies the withholding of medications. This model is receiving increasing attention in the United States in metropolitan areas functioning under tight fiscal constraints and may have special relevance to nations with more limited numbers of available health care professionals.

Some Other Changes

For many years we have tended to administer almost any kind of medication to the alcoholic. The recent decade has been no exception to the trend but there appears to be a greater tendency now not to accept a medication as effective until it is proven so by controlled studies. For example, we have come to recognise the limited benefits and grave potential damage involved if anti-anxiety drugs and hypnotics are continued beyond the period of detoxification.[59] The pharmacological agents undergoing most active testing in recent years are also somewhat different from those in the past[60] and include lithium,[61] propranalol,[62] and apomorphine.[63] We are learning to postpone routine clinical use of any of these agents until good controlled studies have been carried out.

There have also been some changes in the importance of teaching interpersonal skills within treatment. Much more emphasis is now placed on adjustment to life problems[39] by emphasising family interactions,[64] sexual adjustment,[65] and levels of assertiveness.[66] As noted earlier, more treatment appears to be given within groups, often containing divergent types of patients, sometimes including mixes of alcoholics and drug abusers.[67] Such a mix makes sense in light of fiscal restraints, but has been met with a good deal of resistance by individuals who feel that alcoholics and drug addicts have grossly different problems.

Treatment programmes are now being carried out in a wider variety of settings including industry, based on the premise that they end up saving money for the employer and society by avoiding long-term problems and loss of important personnel.[68] The relevance of screening for alcoholism in general medical and surgical facilities and carrying out treatments in these hospital settings, has also been increasingly recognised as data have been produced to show that alcoholism may be seen in up to one-third of general medical, surgical, or psychiatric patients.[69] The increasing expansion should also be mentioned of behavioural approaches in the treatment of alcoholism including things like relaxation therapy, meditation, and the use of videotape in confrontations,[70] as should the increased interest in prevention of alcohol problems and alcoholism.[71] Consistent with prevention efforts in mental health in general, we need to remind ourselves how little we know about how to prevent and avoid accepting fads in the absence of adequate data.[72]

None of these changes is dramatic. On the other hand, they enable us to evaluate where we are and use controlled studies to test proposed new approaches for their level of efficacy and balance between benefits and risks.

Some Important Transitions in Research

While this is not the main topic of this chapter the opportunity must be taken to note the potential impact of present research efforts on alcoholism treatment. Due to a variety of factors already discussed and perhaps reflecting a healthy scepticism, research findings are rarely implemented overnight and must be viewed from the standpoint of what their potential impact will be over the next decade.

One of the most exciting areas of research has been the recent data on the potential importance of genetics to alcoholism. These studies have consistently noted a higher degree of similarity (i.e. concordance) for alcoholism in one-egg or identical twin pairs than in two-egg twin pairs[73, 74] and shown that the children of alcoholics separated from their parents near birth and reared in separate environments (usually through adoption) have markedly elevated rates of alcoholism, while children of non-alcoholics adopted into the homes of alcoholics have rates of alcoholism approximately equal to the general population.[75, 76] These investigations have led to prospective studies which, preliminarily, indicate that there may be differences between non-alcoholic young men with alcoholic biological parents and those with no alcoholic biological close relatives, with respect to metabolism of alcohol and reaction to a relatively modest dose of the drug.[77, 78] The studies are important because, as has been noted, we do not yet have a powerful cure nor a convincing way of preventing alcoholism. With further refinement one might expect in the next decade to understand more about what is actually being inherited in the genetic predisposition and how alcoholism develops over time, and thus gain insights into how to stop it before it begins and treat it once it appears.

Other great strides have been made in biological areas. We are finally beginning to understand more about the actions of alcohol and the differential vulnerabilities to alcohol-related liver, brain, and other physical and behavioural pathologies in different cultural and ethnic groups.[79, 80] More and more competent investigators are beginning to address this area, producing studies with clearer methodologies and more convincing results.[81] These too may lead to new 'breakthroughs' in our understanding of how alcohol works, the mechanisms of tolerance and physical dependence, possible ways of blocking the effects of alcohol, and perhaps the development of new pharmacological interventions in alcoholism.

Advances in the psychological spheres have also been made, but these studies are much more difficult to carry out than investigations of genetic or biological aspects of alcoholism. Nonetheless, we have developed convincing evidence regarding the complexity of alcohol's effect on emotions, showing that a simplistic reduction of tension does not explain what occurs and reinforcing the view that physiological and psychological mechanisms may be different at raising and decreasing blood alcohol levels. There is increasing evidence to demonstrate that there is no convincing alcoholic personality.

All of these results only begin to touch on the expansion of careful work generated in the last decade. It is here that we should look for the future breakthroughs in our knowledge and treatment of this disorder.

What Do We Do Now?

The alcoholism field is changing. The final results of this flux will come from the balance between our dissatisfactions with our present treatment results and our knowledge of the effects of the drug alcohol and the process of alcoholism on the one hand, and an inertia resisting change from fear of what new problems might lie around the next corner on the other. The required escalation of our level of progress can be maximised by a number of developments. These include:

1. Efforts by those countries with developed treatment and research programmes to help health care providers in newer nations develop their own programmes based on their individual needs.
2. The development of good leadership and spokesmen who can make 'our case' to the general public and to those within the alcoholism field who are reluctant to change.
3. An increased quality of the balance between the craftsman and the scientist in the alcoholism field with the specific ratio varying with the number of available health care providers and the values of that society.
4. A continuation and increasing degree of acceptance of alcoholism as a significant problem worthy of studying.
5. Restraint on any further budget cuts for research and expansion of efforts in all areas of the world. No matter how tight money may be, there is as strong a need for research into alcoholism as for a continuation of present day treatment efforts.
6. An expanded influx of good clinicians and scientists into the alcoholism field and a continued decrease in the trend towards the 'derived stigma'.
7. A careful measured approach to studying alcohol problems avoiding the impulse of doing things quickly and releasing them prematurely.
8. The avoidance of continued in-fighting between groups in the alcohol field.

The major changes will probably come through careful biological and psychological research. Whether this careful step-by-step planning has the desired results or not, it at least opens the door to the possibility of serendipity where we will stumble upon our great 'breakthrough' inadvertently. The affected areas could come from discovering the bases of the actions of alcohol, the mechanisms of development of alcoholism, or finding a more potent and specific treatment (even if we do not know how it works). On the other hand, a potentially significant impact could occur through such mundane things as discovering how to implement those research findings which are already available,[38] or in establishing more realistic guidelines for assigning patients to the type of treatment most effective to them or, in a related manner, more carefully selecting which patient should go to outpatient and which to inpatient type treatments.

Until the advances take place, we are faced with carrying out treatment today. The transitions of the last decade have established a series of guidelines for what the 'ideal' programme might contain. Such a programme will have to function under constraints of cost-effectiveness — carefully defining its population, noting carefully its goals, and routinely following up individuals to make sure that the desired outcome occurs. These constraints will probably result in relatively short inpatient stays which are an optional part of treatment and where the majority of therapeutic interventions occur in an outpatient setting. The patient will probably be treated by a team of individuals of varied disciplines, with most therapeutic interventions occurring in a group setting under the auspices of recovered alcoholics who have received some level of counsellor training and work in conjunction with physicians, psychologists, and social workers. The team will probably establish active liaison with other health professionals attempting to increase referrals by increasing the level of knowledge of the average physician, psychologist and other mental health workers graduating from established programmes. The result will hopefully be an increase in sophistication about alcoholism by health professionals and a decreasing tendency to treat the disorders with inappropriate medications such as the anti-anxiety drugs. This hypothetical treatment programme will constantly evaluate its efforts and question its goals, making sure that it is doing as little harm as possible.

We have progressed in the last 30 years from a lack of recognition of the problem of alcoholism and few treatment facilities, through a period of slow growth with increasing awareness of the problem but interest expressed only by a limited number of dedicated individuals most of whom are themselves recovering alcoholics. The last decade, however, has shown an expansion in public interest and acceptance of the alcohol problem, a slower but nonetheless steady increase in professional interest and acceptance of alcoholism, and a realigning and re-thinking of our present treatment efforts and our desires to increase our knowledge in this area. We are now in a state of flux, We have not accomplished nearly as much as any of us would ideally like, but the changes of the last decade have been more than anyone could have realistically expected in ten years.

Notes

1. Woodruff, R.A., Goodwin, D.W. and Guze, S. (1974), *Psychiatric Diagnosis* (Oxford University Press, New York).
2. Guze, S. (1970), 'The Need for Toughmindedness in Psychiatric Thinking', *Southern Medical Journal*, vol. 63, pp. 662-71.
3. Rossi, J.J. and Filstead, W.J. (1976), ' "Treating" the Treatment Issues: Some General Observations about the Treatment of Alcoholism', in Filstead, W.J., Rossi, J.J. and Keller, M. (eds.), *Alcohol and Alcohol Problems: New Thinking and New Directions* (Ballinger Publishing Company, Cambridge, Mass.).
4. Voegtlin, W. and Lemere, F. (1942), 'The Treatment of Alcohol Addiction: A Review of the Literature', *Quarterly Journal of Studies on Alcohol*, vol. 2, pp. 717-803.
5. Costello, R.M. (1977), 'Alcoholism Treatment Programming: Historical Trends', *Alcoholism: Clinical and Experimental Research*, vol 1, pp. 311-18.
6. Schuckit, M.A. and Cahalan, D. (1976), 'Evaluation of Alcoholism Treatment Programs', in Filstead, W.J., Rossi, J.J. and Keller, M. (eds.), *Alcohol and Alcohol Problems: New Thinking and New Directions* (Ballinger Publishing Company, Cambridge, Mass.).
7. Hill, M.J. and Blane, H.T. (1967), 'Evaluation of Psychotherapy with Alcoholics', *Quarterly Journal of Studies on Alcohol*, vol 28, pp. 76-104.
8. McCance, C. and McCance, P.F. (1969), 'Alcoholism in North-east Scotland: Its Treatment and Outcome', *British Journal of Psychiatry*, vol. 115, pp. 189-98.
9. Emrick, C.D. (1975), 'A Review of Psychologically Oriented Treatment of Alcoholism. II. The Relative Effectiveness of Different Treatment Approaches and the Effectiveness of Treatment vs. No Treatment', *Journal of Studies on Alcohol*, vol 36, pp. 88-108.
10. Straus, R. (1976), 'Problem Drinking in the Perspective of Social Change, 1940-73', in Filstead, W.J., Rossi, J.J. and Keller, M. (eds.), *Alcohol and Alcohol Problems: New Thinking and New Directions* (Ballinger Publishing Company, Cambridge, Mass.).
11. Ludwig, A.M.(1972), 'On and Off the Wagon: Reasons for Drinking and Abstaining by Alcoholics', *Quarterly Journal of Studies on Alcohol*, vol. 33, pp. 91-6.
12. Smart, R.G. (1976), 'Spontaneous Recovery in Alcoholics: A Review and Analysis of the Available Research', *Drug and Alcohol Dependence*, vol. 1, pp. 277-85.
13. Whitehead, P.C. (1976), 'Effects of Liberalizing Alcohol Control Measures',

Addictive Behaviours, vol 1, pp. 197-203.
   14. Schuckit, M.A. and Morrissey, E.R. (1976), 'Alcoholism in Women: Some Clinical and Social Perspectives with an Emphasis on Possible Subtypes', in Greenblatt, M. and Schuckit, M.A. (eds.), *Alcoholism Problems in Women and Children* (Grune & Stratton, New York).
   15. Swint, J.M., Decker, M. and Lairson, D.R. (1978), 'The Economic Returns to Employment-based Alcoholism Programs: A Methodology', *Journal of Studies on Alcohol*, vol. 39, pp. 1633-9.
   16. Edwards, G., Orford, J., Egert, S. *et al.* (1977), 'Alcoholism: A Controlled Trial of "Treatment" and "Advice" ', *Journal of Studies on Alcohol*, vol. 38, pp. 1004-31.
   17. Editorial (1977), 'The Alcoholism Treatment Package', *Lancet*, vol. 2, pp. 488-90.
   18. Blume, S.B. (1978), 'Role of the Recovered Alcoholic in the Treatment of Alcoholism', in Kissin, B. and Bagleiter, H. (eds.), *The Biology of Alcoholism, Vol. 5: Treatment and Rehabilitation of the Chronic Alcoholic* (Plenum Press, New York).
   19. Keller, M. (1976), 'Problems with Alcohol: An Historical Perspective', in Filstead, W.J., Rossi, J.J. and Keller, M. (eds.), *Alcohol and Alcohol Problems: New Thinking and New Directions* (Ballinger Publishing Company, Cambridge, Mass.).
   20. Kissin, B. and Begleiter, H. (eds.) (1978), *The Biology of Alcoholism, Vol. 5: Treatment and Rehabilitation of the Chronic Alcoholic* (Plenum Press, New York).
   21. Mendelsohn, J.H. and Hyde, A.P. (1971), 'Alcoholism Training in Medical Schools: Some Pedagogical and Attitudinal Issues', *Annals of The New York Academy of Science*, vol 178, pp. 66-9.
   22. Norris, J. (1971), 'What AA Can Offer Professional Schools and What It Cannot', *Annals of The New York Academy of Science*, vol. 178, pp. 61-5.
   23. Hirsch, J.M. (1961), 'Alcoholism as a Topic of Teaching in the Undergraduate Medical Curriculum', *Quarterly Journal of Studies on Alcohol*, vol. 22, pp. 135-42.
   24. Pokorny, A.D., Putnam, P. and Fryer, J. (1977), 'Drug Abuse and Alcoholism Teaching in US Medical and Osteopathic Schools, 1975-77', in Galanter, M. (ed.), *Alcohol and Drug Abuse in Medical Education: The State of the Art* (HEW/ADAMHA).
   25. Spitzer, R.L., Endicott, J. and Robins, E. (1975), *Research Diagnostic Criteria (RDC) for a Selected Group of Functional Disorders*, NIMH Clinical Research Branch Collaborative Program on the Psychobiology of Depression, 1 July 1975.
   26. Feighner, J.P., Robins, E., Guze, S. *et al.* (1972), 'Diagnostic Criteria for Use in Psychiatric Research', *Archives of General Psychiatry*, vol. 26, pp. 57-63.
   27. Spitzer, R.L., Endicott, J. and Robins, E. (1975), 'Clinical Criteria for Psychiatric Diagnosis and DSM – III', *American Journal of Psychiatry*, vol. 132, pp. 1187-92.
   28. Kissin, B., Platz, A. and Su, W.H. (1970), 'Social and Psychological Factors in the Treatment of Chronic Alcoholism', *Journal of Psychiatric Research*, vol. 8, pp. 13-27.
   29. Pattison, E.M. (1976), 'A Conceptual Approach to Alcoholism Treatment Goals', *Addictive Behaviours*, vol. 1, pp. 177-92.
   30. Horn, J.L., Wanberg, K.W. and Adams, G. (1974), 'Diagnosis of Alcoholism: Factors of Drinking, Background and Current Conditions in Alcoholics', *Quarterly Journal of Studies on Alcohol*, vol. 35, pp. 147-75.
   31. Burt, D.W. (1975), 'A Behaviourist Looks at Alcoholics Anonymous',

presented at the North American Congress on Alcohol and Drug Problems, 12-18 December, San Francisco.

32. Kalb, M. and Propper, M.S. (1980), 'The Future of Alcohology: Craft or Science?' Santa Clara County Mental Health Alcoholism Division (forthcoming).

33. Edwards, G. (1979), 'British Policies on Opiate Addiction: Ten Years Working of the Revised Response, and Options for the Future', *British Journal of Psychiatry*, vol. 134, pp. 1-13.

34. Lamb, H. (1979), 'The New Asylums in the Community', *Archives of General Psychiatry*, vol. 36, pp. 129-34.

35. Gusfield, J.R. (1976), 'The Prevention of Drinking Problems', in Filstead, W.J., Rossi, J.J. and Keller, M. (eds.), *Alcohol and Alcohol Problems: New Thinking and New Directions* (Ballinger Publishing Company, Cambridge, Mass.).

36. Kalb, M. (1975), 'The Myth of Alcoholism Prevention', *Preventive Medicine*, vol. 4, pp. 404-16.

37. Lamb, H.R. and Zusman, J. (1979), 'Primary Prevention in Perspective', *American Journal of Psychiatry*, vol. 136, pp. 12-17.

38. Pattison, E.M. (1977), 'Ten Years of Change in Alcoholism Treatment and Delivery Systems', *American Journal of Psychiatry*, vol. 134, pp. 261-6.

39. Moore, R.A. (1977), 'Ten Years of Inpatient Programs for Alcoholic Patients', *American Journal of Psychiatry*, vol. 134, pp. 542-5.

40. Uecker, A.E. and Boutilier, L.R. (1976), 'Alcohol Education for Alcoholics Relation to Attitude Changes and Post-treatment Abstinence', *Journal of Studies on Alcohol*, vol. 37, pp. 965-75.

41. Vannicelli, M. (1978), 'Impact of Aftercare in the Treatment of Alcoholics', *Journal of Studies on Alcohol*, vol. 39, pp. 1875-86.

42. Schuckit, M.A. (1977), 'Alcoholism Treatment: Our Need for Open Questioning', *Journal of Studies on Alcohol*, vol. 38, pp. 1813-16.

43. Schuckit, M.A. and Morrissey, E.R. (1978), 'Minor in Possession of Alcohol: What Does It Mean?', in Seixas, F.A. (ed.), *Currents in Alcoholism, Vol. IV: Psychiatric, Psychological, Social and Epidemiological Studies* (Grune & Stretton, Inc., New York).

44. Morrissey, E.R. and Schuckit, M.A. (1978), 'Stressful Life Events and Alcohol Problems Among Women Seen at a Detoxification Center', *Journal of Studies on Alcohol*, vol. 39, pp. 1559-76.

45. Schuckit, M.A. and Miller, P.L. (1976), 'Alcoholism in Elderly Men: A Survey of a General Medical Ward', *Annals of the New York Academy of Science*, vol. 273, pp. 558-71.

46. Zimberg, S. (1974), 'Evaluation of Alcoholism Treatment in Harlem', *Quarterly Journal of Studies on Alcohol*, vol. 35, pp. 550-7.

47. Tamayo, M.B. and Feldman, D.J. (1975), 'Incidence of Alcoholism in Hospital Patients', *Social Work*, vol. 20, pp. 89-91.

48. Baker, S.L., Lorei, T., McKnight, H.A. *et al.* (1977), 'The Veterans' Administration's Comparison Study: Alcoholism and Drug Abuse — Combined and Conventional Treatment Settings', *Alcoholism: Clinical and Experimental Research*, vol. 1, pp. 285-91.

49. Ravensborg, M.R. and Hoffmann, H. (1976), 'Program v. Time: Length of Stay Patterns in Alcoholism', *Drug and Alcohol Dependence*, vol. 1, pp. 51-6.

50. Sobell, M.B. (1978), 'Alternatives to Abstinence: Evidence, Issues and Some Proposals', in Nathan, P.E., Marlatt, G.A. and Loberg, T. (eds.), *Alcoholism: New Directions in Behavioural Research and Treatment* (Plenum Press, New York).

51. Sobell, M.B. and Sobell, L.C. (1976), 'Second-year Treatment Outcome of Alcoholics Treated by Individualized Behavior Therapy: Results', *Behavioural Research and Therapy*, vol. 14, pp. 195-215.

52. Vogler, R.E., Compton, J.V. and Weissbach, T.A. (1975), 'Integrated

Behaviour Change Techniques for Alcoholics', *Journal of Consulting and Clinical Psychology*, vol. 43, pp. 233-43.
    53. Vogler, R.E., Weissbach, T.A. and Compton, J.V. (1977), 'Learning Techniques for Alcohol Abuse', *Behaviour Research and Therapy*, vol. 15, pp. 31-8.
    54. Orford, J., Oppenheimer, E. and Edwards, G. (1976), 'Abstinence or Control: The Outcome for Excessive Drinkers Two Years After Consultation', *Behaviour Research and Therapy*, vol. 14, pp. 409-18.
    55. Popham, R.E. and Schmidt, W. (1976), 'Some Factors Affecting the Likelihood of Moderate Drinking in Treated Alcoholics', *Journal of Studies on Alcohol*, vol. 37, pp. 868-82.
    56. Annis, H.M. and Smart, R.G. (1978), 'Arrests, Readmissions and Treatment Following Release from Detoxification Centers', *Journal of Studies on Alcohol*, vol. 39, pp. 1276-83.
    57. Feldman, D.J., Pattison, E.M., Sobell, L.C. *et al.* (1975), 'Outpatient Alcohol Detoxification: Initial Findings of 564 Patients', *American Journal of Psychiatry*, vol. 132, pp. 407-12.
    58. O'Briant, R., Petersen, M.W. and Heacock, D. (1976-7), 'How Safe is Social Setting Detoxification?', *Alcohol Health and Research World*, vol. 1 (2), pp. 22-7.
    59. Schuckit, M.A., 'Treatment of Alcoholism in Office and Outpatient Settings', in Mendelson, J.H. and Mellow, N.K. (eds.), *Diagnosis and Treatment of Alcoholism* (in press).
    60. Viamontes, J.A. (1972), 'Review of Drug Effectiveness in the Treatment of Alcoholism', *American Journal of Psychiatry*, vol. 128, pp. 1570-1.
    61. Merry, J. (1976), 'Prophylactic Treatment of Alcoholism by Lithium Carbonate', *Lancet*, vol. 2, pp. 481-2.
    62. Carlsson, C. (1976), 'Propranolol in the Treatment of Alcoholism: A Review', *Postgraduate Medical Journal*, vol. 52, pp. 166-7.
    63. Carlsson, C., Johansson, P.R. and Gullberg, B. (1977), 'A Double-blind Cross-over Study: Apomorphine/Placebo in Chronic Alcoholics', *International Journal of Clinical Pharmacology*, vol. 15, pp. 211-13.
    64. Orford, J., Oppenheimer, E., Egert, S. *et al.* (1976), 'The Cohesiveness of Alcoholism Complicated Marriages and its Influence on Treatment Outcome', *British Journal of Psychiatry*, vol. 128, pp. 318-39.
    65. Farkas, G.M. and Rosen, R.C. (1976), 'Effect of Alcohol on Elicited Male Sexual Response', *Journal of Studies on Alcohol*, vol. 37, pp. 265-72.
    66. O'Leary, D.E. and O'Leary, M.R. (1976), 'Social Skill Acquisition and Psychosocial Development of Alcoholics: A Review', *Addictive Behaviours*, vol. 1, pp. 111-20.
    67. Ottenberg, D.J. (1974), 'Combined Treatment of Alcoholics and Drug Addicts: A Progress Report and Discussion From the Eagleville Experience', presented at the North American Congress on Alcohol and Drug Problems, 12-18 December, San Francisco.
    68. Hertzman, M. and Montague, B. (1977), 'Cost-benefit Analysis and Alcoholism', *Journal of Studies on Alcohol*, vol. 38, pp. 1371-85.
    69. Barchha, R., Stewart, M.A. and Guze, S. (1968), 'The Prevalence of Alcoholism Among General Hospital Ward Patients', *American Journal of Psychiatry*, vol. 125, pp. 681-4.
    70. Nathan, P.E. and Lisman, S.A. (1976), 'Behavioral and Motivational Patterns of Chronic Alcoholics', in Tarter, R.E. and Sugerman, A.A. (eds.), *Alcoholism: Interdisciplinary Approaches to an Enduring Problem* (Addison-Wesley, Reading, Mass.).
    71. Centerwall, B.S. and Criqui, M.H. (1978), 'Prevention of the Wernicke-Korsakoff Syndrome', *New England Journal of Medicine*, vol. 299, pp. 285-9.

72. Blane, H.T. (1976), 'Issues in Preventing Alcohol Problems', *Preventive Medicine*, vol. 5, pp. 176-86.

73. Kaij, L. (1960), *Studies on the Etiology and Sequels of Abuse of Alcohol* (Department of Psychiatry, University of Lund).

74. Partanen, J., Bruun, K. and Markkanen, T. (1966), *Inheritance of Drinking Behaviour* (Rutgers University Center of Alcohol Studies, New Brunswick, New Jersey).

75. Goodwin, D. (1976), *Is Alcoholism Hereditary?* (Oxford University Press, New York).

76. Goodwin, D.W., Schulsinger, F., Moller, N. *et al.* (1974), 'Drinking Problems in Adopted and non-Adopted Sons of Alcoholics', *Archives of General Psychiatry*, vol. 31, pp. 164-9.

77. Schuckit, M.A. and Rayses, V. (1979), 'Ethanol Ingestion: Differences in Blood Acetaldehyde Concentrations in Relatives of Alcoholics and Controls', *Science*, vol. 203, pp. 54-5.

78. Schuckit, M.A. (1979), 'Ethanol Intoxication: Differences Between Young Men with Alcoholic Relatives and Controls', submitted to *Journal of Studies on Alcohol*.

79. Blass, J.P. and Gibson, G.E. (1977), 'Abnormality of a Thiamine-requiring Enzyme in Patients with Wernicke-Korsakoff Syndrome', *New England Journal of Medicine*, vol. 297, pp. 1367-70.

80. Kunitz, S.J., Levy, J.E. and Everett, M. (1969), 'Alcoholic Cirrhosis Among the Navaho', *Quarterly Journal of Studies on Alcohol*, vol 30, pp. 672-85.

81. Ellingboe, J. (1978), 'Effects of Alcohol on Neurochemical Processes', in Lipton, M.A., DiMascio, A. and Killam, K.F. (eds.), *Psychopharmacology: A Generation of Progress* (Raven Press, New York).

Part Two

DOES TREATMENT WORK?

5 THE RAND REPORTS AND THE ANALYSIS OF RELAPSE

David J. Armor

In 1976 the Rand report *Alcoholism and Treatment* generated a great deal of controversy over its finding, in a national follow-up study, that some alcoholics returned to 'normal' drinking after treatment.[1,2] While reports of normal or social drinking by some alcoholics are not uncommon,[3,4] several features of the Rand report may have stimulated debate in this instance. The study cohort was itself a point of attention, being a national sample of alcoholics treated in centres sponsored by the newly-created US National Institute on Alcohol Abuse and Alcoholism (NIAAA). Also, the Rand Report found a higher percentage of normal drinkers than most studies, being slightly over one-fifth of the total sample at an 18 month follow-up. Most studies report less than ten per cent of alcoholics drinking in moderate amounts, although the size of the fraction is clearly dependent upon each study's definition of moderate drinking.[5]

The feature of the Rand report that drew the most attention, however, was an analysis of 'relapse'. This analysis was based upon changes in remission status between a six and an 18 month follow-up. The relapse analysis showed that alcoholics who had returned to normal drinking at the earlier follow-up were no more likely to be in relapse at the later follow-up than either short- or long-term abstainers. Despite cautions by the authors, popular and technical discussions of the Rand report nevertheless focussed on this result. For many observers, both lay and professional, a finding that normal drinkers and abstainers have equally good prognosis runs directly counter to 'loss of control' theories of alcoholism. According to classical conceptions, alcoholics by definition cannot control their drinking, and any attempt to drink moderately will be met with unavoidable relapse. Understandably, critics of the Rand report questioned the methodology of the relapse analysis, citing sample sizes, short follow-up periods, and narrow windows of observation as major problems.

Whether one accepts the classical formulation of alcoholism or not, the process of relapse is clearly important in understanding the course of alcoholism. Accordingly, this chapter aims to re-examine the relapse issue with the hope of clarifying certain conceptual and methodological issues and offering stronger evidence on factors that affect relapse rates. First, the conceptual basis for relapse analysis will be restated, showing how it is designed to test various hypotheses derived from classical theories of alcoholism. Secondly, these hypotheses will be tested once again using data from a new Rand follow-up study.[6] This new study avoids some of the methodological problems which constrained the data used in the first report.

Conceptual Issues

In the classical formulations of alcoholism as a disease, a central if not defining role is played by the 'loss of control' phenomenon. According to Jellinek, for the *gamma* alcoholic loss of control marks the 'crucial' phase of physical addiction in which the alcoholic is unable to stop drinking after the first few drinks.[7,8] Other signs of addiction include morning drinking, binges, and eventual withdrawal symptoms, the most common of which is tremor. Once loss of control has been demonstrated, it is commonly believed to be a constitutional factor which does not change even after long periods of abstention. The treatment goal of total abstention flows directly from this formulation of the alcohol dependence syndrome, and it will be referred to in this chapter as abstention theory I.

A great deal of research evidence during the 1960s and early 1970s contradicted this classical conception of instantaneous loss of control. First of all, numerous follow-up studies of treated alcoholics, whose samples meet the addiction requirements of the *gamma* alcoholic, find varying numbers of persons drinking in reduced quantities without serious problems at the time of follow-up.[9] Such was the case with the first Rand report, in which 22 per cent of the sample were classified as normal drinkers.[2] Equally important, a number of experimental studies have not been able to induce the loss of control phenomenon following administration of one or two drinks.[10]

The inability to document instantaneous loss of control for all alcoholics has led to revisions in the classical theory: those by Keller[11] and Ludwig[12] are prominent. One of the treatment professionals reviewing an early draft of the first Rand report objected to the inclusion of normal drinking as a form of remission and cited such a revised theory as the basis for the objection. The reformulation, which may be called abstention theory II, expands the time frame for loss of control so that it is not necessarily instantaneous. Theory II is explained as follows: after abstaining for a period of time, some alcoholics can return to moderate or controlled drinking for a period of time. However, this period of moderate drinking is only a temporary state which cannot be sustained indefinitely; loss of control and a full relapse to alcoholic drinking are inevitable. Since the follow-up study in the first Rand report relied on a 30 day window prior to the interview for evaluating detailed drinking behaviour, abstention theory II anticipates finding some alcoholics drinking in a moderate fashion during this period. According to the argument, however, they should not be classified as remissions, because in truth this group is headed for a total relapse. It should be pointed out that this conception embodies an implicit corollary, which is that abstainers — especially long-term abstainers — are *not* inevitably headed for relapse. Otherwise there would be no clear basis for believing that abstention is the only method for recovering from alcoholism.

The relapse analysis in the first Rand report was designed to test this second and more complex abstention theory. It may not be immediately apparent that a proper test of this theory requires two follow-ups, or at least observations at two separate times following treatment.[13] An interview at admission to treatment is not useful in this regard because nearly all patients are drinking in an alcoholic manner. Rather, the first follow-up is used to establish various hypothesised categories of remission, including long-term abstention and normal or non-problem drinking. The second follow-up is necessary for establishing the relapse rates for each remission category. If a relapse is defined as someone who was in remission at the first follow-up, but who is engaging in alcoholic drinking at the second follow-up, then theory II predicts a high relapse rate for normal drinkers and a low relapse rate for longer-term abstainers. The first Rand study was based primarily on an 18 month follow-up interview, but it also had comparable six month follow-up data on a sub-sample of about 200 subjects. Those two sets of follow-up data made possible a relapse analysis. Using the six month follow-up for the initial classification of remission status, we found no difference in the relapse rates, as observed at 18 months, among three groups: those who abstained for six months before the six month interview; short-term abstainers, who abstained one to five months before the six month interview; and normal drinkers.

Other modifications of abstention theory can also be tested with this type of relapse analysis. For example, some treatment and research professionals have advanced abstention theory III, which embodies a probabilistic conception of the *relative* risk of relapse for moderate or non-problem drinkers.[14] According to this conception some alcoholics can engage in moderate drinking for brief periods, but they run the risk of a full relapse if they do not return to abstention within a short time. In other words, moderate drinking is a riskier venture for alcoholics than abstention, although relapse is not necessarily inevitable. Clearly, theory III significantly weakens the loss of control concept, since it implies that some alcoholics can engage in moderate drinking for short periods, provided they are interspersed within longer periods of abstention. The empirical hypothesis implied by this theory, which can be tested by relapse analysis, is that whatever the overall rates of relapse, moderate or non-problem drinkers distinguished at one point in time should have a higher rate of relapse in the future than abstainers. While this conception abandons the classical notion of loss of control, it nonetheless supports the treatment goal of abstention as the safest path for remission or recovery.

So far the discussion has focussed on alcoholics as a group. More elaborate theories of abstention can be generated which raise the possibility that some formerly addicted alcoholics can successfully return to normal drinking but others cannot. The treatment field has tended to avoid making finer distinctions among those alcoholics who show physical dependence, and indeed the first Rand report could find no factors which differentiated those normal drinkers who relapsed from those who did not. Nevertheless, in view of the complexity of the behaviour and the endless variations in human adaptability, it would not be surprising if factors were ultimately discerned that led to differential relapse rates for abstainers versus moderate drinkers. Of particular interest here is the possibility raised by Edwards[15] that physical dependence can reach a degree of severity that makes re-establishment of moderate drinking very unlikely. Although no specific theories of differential relapse rates have been formulated, relapse analyses should give high priority to examining intervening variables which might affect relapse rates for different types of abstaining or non-problem drinking alcoholics.

A New Relapse Analysis

As we have mentioned, the relapse analysis in the first Rand report was hampered by a number of methodological limitations. Perhaps the two most important problems were a small sample size, which limited the statistical power of tests, and a narrow window of observation that precluded assessment of significant events throughout the entire period between the two follow-ups.

New and improved data for relapse analysis are available from a four year follow-up of the same cohort studied in the 18 month follow-up study. The new study attained a high response rate, examined the validity of self-reports, measured more variables, and broadened the assessment period to cover the entire four years from treatment admission to follow-up.[16] Altogether 475 surviving subjects were available for a relapse analysis covering a much longer period between the 18 month and the four year follow-ups. Moreover, 590 subjects were available for a mortality relapse analysis, in which the relapse criterion is an alcohol-related death.

The basic strategy of the relapse analyses in the four year study was two-fold. First, the number of criteria for studying relapse is expanded from one to several, including alcohol-related mortality and measures over different windows of observation. Secondly, the larger sample size permitted a more detailed examination of factors which might produce differential relapse rates for abstainers and non-problem drinkers.

The four year follow-up study made two significant changes in the definition of remission which should be noted here. In the first study normal drinkers were distinguished from non-remissions by defining limits on both drinking and impairment. Heavy drinkers without impairment were classified as non-remissions, while moderate drinkers with one or two episodes of dependence symptoms (e.g. morning drinking, blackouts) were classified as normal drinkers. In the second study, preliminary analyses showed that even a few dependence symptoms were associated with other significant problems (some of which were unmeasured in the 18 month study), while very heavy drinking without symptoms was not. Accordingly, the new remission definition in the four year study distinguishes between non-problem and problem drinkers, the latter group including anyone with any episodes of dependence symptoms.[17]

A second change occurred in the handling of short-term abstainers (one to five months). For both conceptual and empirical reasons our main remission definition relies on a six month window of observation. This means that short-term abstainers are classified according to their drinking behaviour when they last drank. Since most short-term abstainers turned out to have dependence symptoms (and other problems) during their last drinking period, most short-term abstainers at four years are classified as non-remissions. Compared with the earlier

18 month study, this raises the overall rate of non-remission at four years and it raises the overall rate of relapse whenever a six month window is adopted. The 18 month follow-up has data only on the subject's drinking in the past month. It does not have data sufficient to measure drinking over a six month window. Therefore, in our relapse analysis the 18 month remission definition maintains the classification of long- and short-term abstention, but makes a distinction between problem and non-problem drinking for those who drank in the past month. This approach has the further advantage of highlighting the prognosis of short-term abstention, which turns out to be one of the more interesting findings of the four year relapse analysis. In order to have comparable measures, our first relapse analysis distinguishes the following remission statuses at both the 18 month and four year follow-up assessments:

1. Long-term abstention for six months or more;
2. short-term abstention for one to five months prior to the interview;
3. non-problem drinking in the past month;
4. problem drinking in the past month.[18]

Given the narrow window for measuring drinking behaviour, other relapse criteria which cover longer time periods will also be examined. In addition, analyses will be conducted to investigate the possibility of differential relapse rates among sub-groups in our sample.

Relapse Results

Comparable Status Measures

The first relapse analysis compares the change in status between the two comparable remission definitions at each follow-up. This can be accomplished in a 'turnover' table, which is presented as Table 5.1. If we define relapse to be those cases who were either abstainers or non-problem drinkers at 18 months but who fall into the problem drinking category at four years, then the relapse rates are the first three percentages in the bottom row of Table 5.1. According to this definition, the longer-term abstainers have the lowest rate of relapse, 12 per cent; short-term abstainers have the highest relapse rate, 29 per cent; and non-problem drinkers fall in between with a relapse rate of 22 per cent. The difference between long-term and short-term abstainers is statistically significant at the 0.005 level, but the difference between

Table 5.1: Change in Drinking Status Between 18 Months and Four Years, Using Comparable Status Measures

	Status at 18 months (Per cent Distribution)			
Status at 4 years	Abstained 6 months or more	Abstained 1 to 5 months	Drinking past month— no problems	Drinking past month— problems
Abstained 6+ months	55	35	11	18
Abstained 1-5 months	14	17	14	16
Drinking past month — no problems	19	19	53	12
Drinking past month — problems	12*	Relapses 29*	22*	54
(N)	(115)	(99)	(85)	(175)

* Difference between 6 month abstainers and 1 to 5 month abstainers is statistically at p <0.005 (χ^2 = 8.67, 1 df, corrected for continuity); difference between 6 month abstainers and non-symptom drinkers is significant at the 0.10 level (χ^2 = 2.97, 1 df, corrected for continuity).

the longer-term abstainers and non-problem drinkers is significant at only the 0.10 level.

What we might call 'stable' groups can also be computed from the figure in Table 5.1. A stable group would be those persons who remained in the same status category at both follow-ups. Longer-term abstainers, non-problem drinkers, and problem drinkers have stability rates above 50 per cent, but short-term abstainers have a very low rate of 17 per cent. Short-term abstention seems to be an inherently unstable state, with occupants either relapsing or managing to attain longer-term abstention (35 per cent for the latter). Note, also, that only 11 per cent of the non-problem drinkers become longer-term abstainers. It is not the case that most non-problem drinkers either relapse or adopt long-term abstention, as predicted by abstention theory III.

The higher rates of stability for longer-term abstainers and non-problem drinkers should not be unduly emphasised, since they result in relatively small groups of stable-status persons. Only 13 per cent of the total sample were longer-term abstainers at both follow-ups, and only nine per cent of the sample were non-problem drinkers at both follow-ups. Moreover, if we defined stability as remaining in the same status continuously over the entire four year period, stability rates would be even lower. Only seven per cent of the survivor sample abstained continuously, and while we cannot make a similar calculation for non-problem drinkers, continuous non-problem drinkers probably comprise no more than four or five per cent of the total sample. Long-term, continuous stability of status is clearly rare in our sample, whether it be for abstainers or non-problem drinkers.

Other Relapse Criteria

The relapse analysis in Table 5.1 is not fully satisfactory. First, the window of observation for drinking behaviours is a narrow 30 day period which leaves short-term abstention as a remission category. Secondly, the use of a six month window for defining relapse solves this problem, but we are still left with a great deal of time between the 18 month and four year evaluations. It is quite possible for a person to experience several relapses during this period, with ample time to return to a favourable remission status at four years. Therefore, a proper test of the various revised abstention theories requires additional relapse criteria that give a more complete picture of events taking place between the two follow-ups. The criteria we will use are as follows:

1. Remission status at four years using a six month window;
2. the rate of any problem drinking between 18 months and four years;
3. the number of serious alcohol-related incidents between the 18 month follow-up and the four year follow-up;
4. the rate of alcohol-related mortality during the interval between the 18 month and four year follow-ups.

These additional measures of relapse are summarised in Table 5.2. The first row shows the rate of relapse using our full definition of remission at four years, based on a six month window of observation and including a broader set of problem indicators. The main effect of this change is to raise the overall rate of relapse, which comes about primarily because nearly all short-term abstainers are re-classified as relapses. The absolute difference in relapse rates between longer-term abstainers and non-problem drinkers remains constant at ten per cent, with longer-term abstainers showing a slightly lower relapse rate (which

Table 5.2: Rates for Alternative Relapse Criteria (percentages unless otherwise indicated)

Relapse criterion	Status at 18 months			
	Abstained 6 months or more	Abstained 1-5 months	Drinking past month — no problems	Drinking past month — problems
Problem drinking at 4 years, past 6 months*	30	53	41	73
Problem drinking between 18 months and 4 years**	45	70	55	84
Mean number of serious incidents for problem drinkers, 18 months to 4 years	1.5	1.6	1.3	1.5
(N)	(115)	(99)	(85)	(175)
Alcohol related death between 18 months and 4 years	1.4	8.9	2.9	9.0
(N)	(140)	(124)	(103)	(223)

* Includes adverse consequences in areas of job, health, law, and interpersonal relations.
** Either problem drinking in past 6 months, or any serious incident in areas of job, health, law, and interpersonal relations between 18 months and 4 years.

is not statistically significant). Of the improved groups at 18 months short-term abstention still has the highest rate of relapse.

The absolute rate of relapse rises even further if we expand the window to include any serious alcohol-related incident between 18 months and four years. This broader criterion is shown in the second row. Note, however, that the absolute difference between longer-term abstainers and non-problem drinkers remains at ten per cent, which is not statistically significant. Roughly half of each group remained free of serious problems between the two follow-ups. The average number of serious incidents for problem drinkers is between one and two for all groups, with no significant differences among them.

The final relapse criterion shown in Table 5.2 is based on alcohol-related mortality. We have defined an alcohol-related death to be a death which meets either of the following two conditions:

1. A death certificate with liver disease, alcoholism, or bleeding listed as causes or contributing factors;
2. any other death with a collateral report that the subject was drinking at the time of death (or shortly before), and that alcohol was a factor in the death.

Again, we find the same pattern of relapse: longer-term abstainers have the lowest rate of alcohol-related mortality (1.4 per cent), but it is not significantly lower than the rate for non-problem drinkers (2.9 per cent). Short-term abstainers have a significantly higher rate of alcohol-related mortality (9 per cent) and in fact it is no different from that for non-remissions at 18 months. This result appears to clinch the very poor prognosis of short-term abstention.

Differential Relapse

The relapse analysis so far does not give a great deal of support to those revised abstention theories which posit that non-problem drinkers have a higher risk of relapse than abstainers. In effect, for our sample as a whole, many abstainers are shown to relapse, while many non-problem drinkers do not. The question then becomes whether there are some alcoholics who have a better prognosis if they abstain, while others have a better prognosis if they engage in non-problem drinking.

We examined the possibility of differential relapse rates for a number of background characteristics using multiple regression techniques.[19] We used variables which previous research has shown to be generally related to remission, including severity of alcohol dependence, socioeconomic level, marital and employment status, age, race, and experience with previous treatment. We found that age, severity of dependence, and marital status had statistically significant interactions with abstention versus non-problem drinking in the prediction of relapse at four years.

The regression-based estimated relapse rates for the sub-groups formed by these variables are shown in Table 5.3. First, we note that older men with high severity of dependence symptoms at admission have much lower expected relapse rates if they abstained rather than drank without problems at 18 months, regardless of marital status. On the other hand, for younger men with medium levels of dependence symptoms, the situation was reversed: abstainers have higher expected relapse rates than non-problem drinkers, regardless of marital status. For the other two groups — older men with medium severity and younger men with high severity — the interaction is more complex, with marital status playing an important role. Those who were married

Table 5.3: Estimated Relapse Rates for 6+ Month Abstainers Versus
Non-symptom Drinkers* (Percentages)

Background characteristics at admission	Age under 40		Age 40 or over	
	Abstaining 6+ months at 18 months	Non-symptom drinking at 18 months	Abstaining 6+ months at 18 months	Non-symptom drinking at 18 months
High severity of dependence symptoms				
Married	10	19	6	55
Unmarried	20	8	13	30
Medium severity of dependence symptoms				
Married	18	8	12	31
Unmarried	34	3	23	13

* Based on coefficients from a logistic regression analysis, assuming all other variables at their mean values.

had lower expected relapse rates if they abstained, while the unmarrieds had lower expected relapse rates if they were non-problem drinkers.

One interesting aspect of these interactions is that no one variable plays a commanding role in determining a differential relapse rate. For example, persons with high severity of dependence symptoms generally have a better prognosis if they abstain — with the exception of the younger unmarrieds, for whom predicted relapse is lower if they were non-problem drinkers. Also, those under 40 generally have lower relapse rates if they were non-problem drinkers — with the exception of the high severity marrieds, for whom abstention yields the better prognosis. These findings, if replicated, raise the prospects of a far more complex picture of alcoholic remission and relapse than has been heretofore acknowledged.

Discussion

The results of the relapse analyses are quite consistent regardless of the criteria used. Longer-term abstainers have the lowest rates of relapse, but they are not significantly lower than the relapse rates for non-problem drinkers in most comparisons. As such, neither the classical nor revised versions of abstention theory, based on differing conceptions of the loss of control phenomenon, are strongly supported by our data. The high relapse rate for short-term abstainers raises another potentially important issue. Since an abstainer must pass through an early phase of abstention before reaching the less risky stage of longer-term abstention, it becomes important to determine the risk of relapse during the early stages of abstention. Does the high relapse rate for short-term abstainers in our sample reflect the risk for all early-stage abstainers, or do the short-term abstainers comprise a special group that differs from the long-term abstainers on critical variables? Our analysis could not detect any major differences between these groups at admission characteristics, but the variables available to us at admission do not comprise an exhaustive set. While our data cannot decide between these alternative causal explanations for the difference in relapse between short- and long-term abstainers, this issue clearly deserves further investigation.

The finding of differential relapse rates raises the possibility of more complex theories of alcoholic relapse than are found in classical formulations. It may be that both the classical and revised versions of abstention theory were influenced by samples of alcoholics who in fact could not attain non-problem drinking without relapse. As we accumulate data on the natural history of alcoholism, we may be discovering a broader and more heterogeneous group of alcoholics who differ in their possibilities for remission.

Existing theories of alcoholism offer no ready-made explanation for the specific variables that we have found to intervene in the relapse process. Tentative explanations might be offered which include both physical and environmental factors. On the physical side, our data are consistent with suggestions by Edwards[15] that some alcoholics might reach a certain degree of alcohol dependence beyond which re-establishment of moderate drinking is highly unlikely. Those who are not severely dependent — even though they might qualify as *gamma* alcoholics — may be able to return to non-problem drinking without relapse. Age may also be involved in this relationship by bringing about physiological changes that intensify the effects of dependence.

Both age and marital status raise the possibility of environmental factors that might play a significant role in altering the relapse process. In Ludwig's revisions of the loss of control theory, environmental factors are introduced to explain why loss of control may not be instantaneous.[12] One might extend this reasoning and posit that environmental factors might be strong enough to alter the relapse process entirely. For example, the chances are that younger and unmarried men are likely to find themselves in milieux where frequent drinking is the norm. The attempt by younger or unmarried alcoholics to maintain abstention in a non-supportive environment may induce stress situations which increase the likelihood of relapse. Moreover, married alcoholics may receive considerable support from their spouses when they are abstaining but not when they attempt moderate drinking. Because of the widely held belief that alcoholics cannot return to moderate drinking, spouses of alcoholics who try to do so may view them as failures, setting up a stress situation which eventually contributes to relapse.

Clearly, further research is needed to replicate these relationships and to uncover their explanatory mechanisms. Should these tasks be accomplished, the implications for treatment policy could be very important, especially in light of the high rates of relapse and very low rates of stable status revealed by the four year study. The possibility that different types of alcoholics might be more successfully treated with different treatment goals offers hope for improving remission rates for this stubbornly chronic disorder.

Notes

1. Armor, D.J., Polich, J.M. and Stambul, H.B. (1976), *Alcoholism and Treatment* (The Rand Corporation, Santa Monica, California).
2. Armor, D.J., Polich, J.M. and Stambul, H.B. (1978), *Alcoholism and Treatment* (Wiley, New York).
3. Pattison, E.M., Headley, E.B., Gleser, G.C. and Gottschalk, L.A. (1968), 'Abstinence and Normal Drinking: An Assessment of Changes in Drinking Patterns in Alcoholics After Treatment', *Quarterly Journal of Studies on Alcohol*, vol. 29, pp. 610-33.
4. Richard, L.W., Jr. and Salzbert, H.C. (1975), 'Controlled Social Drinking: An Alternative to Abstinence as a Treatment Goal for Some Alcohol Abusers', *Psychological Bulletin*, vol. 82, pp. 815-42.
5. Some critics of the Rand report pointed out that the Rand definition imposed fairly generous limits on the amount of consumption allowed for normal drinking.
6. Polich, J.M., Armor, D.J. and Braiker, H.B. (1979), *The Course of Alcoholism: Four Years after Treatment* (The Rand Corporation, Santa Monica, California).
7. Jellinek, E.M. (1946), 'Phases in the Drinking History of Alcoholics', *Quarterly Journal of Studies on Alcohol*, vol. 7, pp. 1-88.
8. Jellinek, E.M. (1952), 'Phases of Alcohol Addiction', *Quarterly Journal of Studies on Alcohol*, vol. 13, pp. 673-84.
9. Emrick, C.D. (1974), 'A Review of Psychologically Oriented Treatment of

Alcoholism: I. The Use and Interrelationships of Outcome Criteria and Drinking Behavior Following Treatment', *Quarterly Journal of Studies on Alcohol*, vol. 35, pp. 523-49.

   10. Paredes, A., Hood, W.R., Seymour, H. and Gollob, M. (1973), 'Loss of Control in Alcoholism: An Investigation of the Hypothesis, with Experimental Findings', *Quarterly Journal of Studies on Alcohol*, vol. 34, pp. 1146-61.

   11. Keller, M. (1972), 'On the Loss of Control Phenomenon in Alcoholism', *British Journal of Addiction*, vol. 67, pp. 153-6.

   12. Ludwig, A.M. and Wikler, A. (1974), 'Craving and Relapse to Drink', *Quarterly Journal of Studies on Alcohol*, vol. 35, pp. 108-29.

   13. Instead of two follow-ups one might use retrospective data from a single follow-up about drinking behaviours during two or more distinct time periods. This approach is not as satisfying methodologically, however, given problems of long-term recall and the possibility of halo effects.

   14. Slightly different forms of theory III have been stated by Dr Sheila Blume and Professor John Ewing in private conversations.

   15. Edwards, G. (1976), 'The Alcohol Dependence Syndrome: Usefulness of an Idea', in Edwards, G. and Grant, M. (eds.), *Alcoholism: New Knowledge and New Responses* (University Park Press, Baltimore; Croom Helm, London).

   16. See Polich, J.M., 'Patterns of Remission in Alcoholism', Chapter 6 in this volume, for more detail about the four year follow-up study.

   17. Non-problem drinkers are further distinguished into low and high consumption, but the difference in relapse between the two is not significant in most comparisons.

   18. For reasons of comparability, this measure does not count adverse consequences on job, health, and interpersonal relations. Because of the narrow window and the high correlation between symptoms and consequences, this is not a serious restriction.

   19. See Polich *et al.*, *The Course of Alcoholism: Four Years After Treatment* (The Rand Corporation, Santa Monica, California) for more detail on the analysis of differential relapse rates.

6 PATTERNS OF REMISSION IN ALCOHOLISM

J. Michael Polich

Understanding alcoholic remission is a matter of fundamental importance in treating the alcoholic. Yet, we know relatively little about the nature of remission and its place in the course of alcoholism. Most research evidence on alcoholic remission has come from treatment follow-up studies that characterise a patient's condition at a single time-point.[1] Lacking a time dimension in the analysis of outcomes, such data are ill-adapted to telling us whether a remission state, when observed, is a state of permanent recovery, or merely a temporary phase that will be followed by a relapse into alcoholic drinking. Moreover, what data we have are generally drawn from treated populations; studies on the natural course of alcoholism, in the absence of treatment, are notably sparse.[2]

General understanding of alcoholic remission is also restricted by failure to recognise the variety of forms in which remission appears. The traditional model of alcoholism as a disease, widely disseminated in the work of Jellinek,[3] has been interpreted in many quarters as implying that abstention is a prerequisite for alcoholic remission and recovery. This interpretation does not appear to be consistent with a growing body of empirical evidence, which has shown that some persons once labelled as alcoholics can later be observed to be drinking without manifest problems.[4,5] Nonetheless, the theoretical influence of the traditional model has led many research studies to treat cases of non-problem drinking as lower-grade forms of remission (e.g. 'improved'), or to exclude them outright from consideration as favourable outcomes. The result has been a picture of the course of alcoholism that does not adequately represent the diversity of remission patterns that actually occur.

These issues were important items on the agenda when a research group at The Rand Corporation set out to conduct a four year follow-up study of alcoholics in the USA, in cooperation with the National Institute on Alcohol Abuse and Alcoholism.[6] The principal purpose of the study was to trace the course of alcoholism as it unfolds over time, paying special attention to the nature and stability of different types of remission. This chapter will briefly present some of the study's principal findings on remission. More extensive exposition of background, methodology, and numerous research results not discussed here may be found in the comprehensive study report.[7]

Methodology Of The Four Year Follow-up

Study Design

The four year follow-up study grew out of previous research on a cohort of alcoholics who initially had been associated with Alcoholism Treatment Centers (ATCs) funded by the National Institute on Alcohol Abuse and Alcoholism. The cohort had been the subject of an 18 month follow-up which was reported in earlier Rand volumes.[8,9] One prominent finding of these earlier reports, in keeping with a few other studies,[10,11] was the considerable amount of instability in remission patterns evident at that time. However, the 18 month study was subjected to a number of methodological criticisms, such as the adequacy of its response rate, the validity of self-reports it used, and the appropriateness of its remission measures (which included both abstention and normal-drinking categories). The four year follow-up study set out to collect data relevant to these methodological issues, as well as to address substantive questions on the nature of alcoholic remission.

The four year follow-up sample was drawn from the same cohort as the 18 month study. The principal subject group was a sample of male treatment admissions (N = 758) randomly selected from consecutive admissions in early 1973. In addition to data collected at admission to treatment, quantitative data were recorded on basic aspects of treatment, such as the type of inpatient and outpatient services and the number of days, hours, or visits of each. These treatment data covered both the initial treatment period (usually three to six months) and any later treatment that the patient might receive. A second sample of alcoholics, designated 'contact only', was also included in the study (N = 165). These persons were randomly drawn from the set of individuals who made only a single visit to the facility and who were not admitted to treatment.

Both samples in the cohort were followed up at 18 months and four years after initial contact. Although only about two-thirds of the cohort were successfully located at 18 months, in the four year phase we returned to the original sample and obtained follow-up information on 85 per cent. The basic characteristics of this cohort have been described elsewhere.[8] Like most other alcoholic groups, at admission to treatment the sample as a whole was highly impaired (mean alcohol consumption of 9.3 ounces per day), socially isolated (63 per cent unemployed, 36 per cent separated or divorced), and highly subject to relapse (44 per cent previously treated for alcoholism).

Response Rates and Sample Bias

The high degree of success attained by the four year follow-up — a completion rate of 85 per cent — implied that for this study, the amount of possible bias due to non-response would be very small.[12] However, the study was designed to make use of the 18 month follow-up data, for which the response rate was not as high; and, in any event, the issue of non-response bias is crucial for longitudinal studies in general. Therefore, analysis was conducted to specify the general relationship between response rates and sample bias. Data had been collected on the level of effort required to obtain each subject interview. This permitted an analysis that calculated the characteristics of the sample that would have been obtained had we expended only a given level of effort (implying a particular response rate). The results showed that when response rates are as high as the 60-70 per cent range, bias in the obtained sample is relatively small (five percentage points or less), These findings were consistent across a number of possible outcome measures (abstention, amount of alcohol consumption, alcohol-related problems, etc.) and across a variety of measures of effort. In short, the results suggested that outcome rates are unlikely to be significantly affected by non-response, provided that response rates are in the neighbourhood of 70 per cent or higher.

Validity of Self-reports

Unlike the 18 month study and most other follow-up studies, the four year follow-up did not rely exclusively on interview self-reports. However, it did employ self-reports in most analyses, and the issue of their validity is therefore highly relevant. Two fairly complex substudies were conducted using external criteria to validate interview data: (1) a collateral study, in which other knowledgeable persons ('collaterals') were questioned about the subject's drinking; and (2) a blood alcohol concentration (BAC) study, in which the subject's reported alcohol consumption in the previous 24 hours was compared to his self-reports of consumption. The details of these studies are documented in the comprehensive report.[7]

By and large, the collateral data showed close agreement with subjects' reports for abstention and major events like hospitalisation or arrest (fewer than six per cent of subjects disconfirmed) and low rates of disconfirmation for other self-reports (fewer than 15 per cent for each item, such as alcohol dependence symptoms). However, on some of these latter items about one-third of collaterals were unsure of the subjects' behaviour, leaving room to question the adequacy of the collaterals as a confirming mechanism.

The BAC data also showed that self-reports of abstention are highly valid, with fewer than four per cent of subjects' abstention reports being disconfirmed by the presence of alcohol in the blood. In contrast, about 25 per cent of drinkers consistently under-reported their alcohol consumption, compared to the actual BAC measurement. Nevertheless, most of those persons who under-reported consumption reported other alcohol-related problems that caused them to be classified as problem drinkers in the analysis. The result was that our overall classification of subjects was changed very little by various adjustments for estimated under-reporting. At most, adjustment changed the distribution by four percentage points, even using the most extreme assumptions in the estimating process.[7]

Alcoholic Remission at Four Years

The data collected at the four year follow-up fall into three main categories, each of which is valuable for describing the character of alcoholic remission at the four year point. First, we must consider mortality data. A substantial proportion of subjects had died by the time of the four year follow-up, although, as we shall see, mortality in itself was not necessarily evidence of either remission or non-remission. The second category of data included information on alcohol consumption and drinking problems among survivors. These survivor data constitute our principal source of information for studying alcoholic remission. Finally, the third category of data included measures of *non-drinking* behaviour among survivors; such data, particularly indicators of sociopsychological functioning, are useful for describing the general outlook and character of life among alcoholics who experience various forms of remission.

Mortality

As a number of other studies have shown, mortality rates for alcoholic populations are considerably in excess of those for the general population.[13] Table 6.1 makes it clear that this was also true for the present cohort. About 14 per cent of the initial group admitted to treatment

Table 6.1: Mortality Rates

Cause of death	Actual mortality rate[a] (per cent)	Expected mortality rate[b] (per cent)	Ratio, actual to expected
Deaths from all causes	14.5	5.9	2.5
Deaths from specific causes[c]			
Alcoholism	0.6	0.03	21.0
Suicide	2.3	0.1	20.6
Cirrhosis	1.6	0.2	8.2
Accident	2.0	0.4	5.0
All others	8.0	5.17	1.5
Alcohol-related deaths[d]	8.2	—	—

Notes:

a. Percentage of all subjects alive at admission to treatment (N = 758) who died during the 4.33-year interval from admission to follow-up.

b. Expected rate (percentage) based on age- and race-specific mortality rates for the general US population,[14] standardised on the sample age and race distributions.

c. Underlying causes coded according to the methods of the National Center for Health Statistics.[15]

d. Deaths for which alcoholism, alcohol toxicity, liver disease, or gastrointestinal bleeding was listed as a cause or contributing factor on the official death certificate; or for which a collateral informant reported that the subject was drinking before death and that alcohol was a factor in the death.

had died by the follow-up point. This mortality rate was two-and-one-half times the rate that would be expected from the general male population, after adjusting for the cohort's age and racial distribution.

Information on the official death certificates was also analysed to determine specific causes of death. Table 6.1 indicates the causes whose rates were most elevated compared with expected rates. These causes are among those classically associated with alcoholism, and their rates range from 5 to 21 times the expected rate of death. The results leave little doubt that mortality is a significant outcome to be considered in longitudinal alcoholism studies, even when the cohort is relatively young. (This cohort had a mean age of 45 at admission.)

However, not *every* case of mortality was an indication of a relapse or non-remission before death. Information obtained from several sources, including death certificates and persons who knew the circumstances of the death, showed that in many cases there was no reason to attribute the death to alcohol. For this reason, for certain purposes the four year follow-up study classified mortality according to whether or not the death could be construed as *alcohol-related* (see footnote (d) to Table 6.1). About 8.2 per cent of the baseline sample could be so classified, thus accounting for the same proportion of the sample as the excess of total deaths over expected deaths (14.5 − 5.9 = 8.6). Moreover, the rates of alcohol-related deaths determined by this classification procedure coincided with the excess death rates within a number of different sub-groups, such as those with varying levels of symptomatology reported at the 18 month point. The congruence between the excess death rate and the alcohol-related death rate lends support to the validity of the alcohol-related classification. If one assumes that those who died from alcohol-related causes were definitely not in remission, the importance of including mortality as an indicator of outcome is clear.

Drinking Status Among Survivors

The measurement of alcohol-related behaviour is an essential but complex task for any assessment of alcoholic remission. The complexity arises, first, from the variability of alcohol-related behaviour over time, and secondly, from the multi-dimensional character of the factors contributing to remission and relapse. The first issue, that of time, was addressed by taking the arbitrary period of the six months before the follow-up interview as the time frame of interest. Those who abstained throughout that period were treated simply as abstainers. Those who drank during the period were classified by their drinking-related behaviour and problems, particularly by those occurring during the last drinking period, operationally defined as the 30 days before the last drink. It turned out that reports given by the subjects about this last drinking period were quite representative of their reports about drinking over the entire six month time frame.[16]

For classifying the overall status of such drinkers, we distinguished three types of alcohol-related behaviour:

1. Alcohol Consumption. Each subject interviewed was asked to characterise his typical quantity of alcohol consumption (containers of beer, wine, or distilled liquor, converted to fluid ounces of ethanol[17]) during the 30 days before his last drink if he drank in the past six months. In addition, each subject was asked the number of days during that 30 day period on which he drank as much as an amount equivalent to three ounces of ethanol.

2. *Symptoms of Alcohol Dependence.* Each subject was asked the number of days, during the same 30 day period, on which he experienced specified events that we interpreted as symptoms of the alcohol dependence syndrome.[18] The items included tremors, morning drinking, loss of control, blackouts, missing meals, and continuous drinking (over twelve hours consecutively). These six items were substantially intercorrelated and represented a strong single dimension in factor analysis.

3. *Adverse Consequences of Drinking.* Each subject was asked if he had experienced one or more of the following instances of events that we interpreted as adverse consequences of drinking: (1) health problems, including liver disease, hospitalisation because of drinking, medical advice to stop drinking, and conditions directly related to drinking (pancreatitis, DTs, etc.); (2) law enforcement problems, including arrest or jailing because of drinking; and (3) work and interpersonal problems, including repeated loss of a day's work, inability to work because of drinking, and repeated fights or arguments while drinking.

These measures of alcohol-related problems were used to construct a classification of the subject's overall drinking behaviour, as shown in Table 6.2. At the top of the table are listed categories of abstention segregated by the length of time abstained (for subjects who abstained at least six months before the four year follow-up). Although 28 per cent of the survivor sample had abstained for at least six months, it is notable that only one-quarter of the abstainers — seven per cent of the sample — had abstained throughout the entire period from admission to follow-up.

Among those who drank in the past six months, the table makes a major distinction between *problem drinkers*, those who experienced at least one adverse consequence of drinking or who reported some dependence symptomatology; and *non-problem drinkers*, those who did not experience any such events. Among the non-problem drinkers, it is notable that almost one half — eight per cent of the survivor sample — met the very strict limits for 'low consumption'; these limits were approximately equivalent to four drinks (2 oz of ethanol) on a typical drinking day, combined with the constraint that there were *no* days when consumption was as high as six drinks (3 oz of ethanol). Among the problem drinkers, the difficulties experienced by the great majority are evident. Most of them reported both dependence symptoms *and* adverse consequences.

In general, the data reveal that non-remission, or problem drinking, is the dominant pattern in the cohort at follow-up, including 54 per

Table 6.2: Drinking Status at Four Years (Survivors)

Drinking status at four years	Per cent distribution of cases	
Abstaining		
Abstained from admission to follow-up	7)	
Abstained 1-3 years	14)	28
Abstained 6-11 months	7)	
Non-problem drinking		
Low consumption[a]	8)	18
High consumption[b]	10)	
Problem drinking		
Adverse consequences, no symptoms[c]	6)	
Dependence symptoms, no consequences	12)	54
Symptoms and consequences	36)	
(Total number of cases)	(548)	

Notes:
a. Drank during the six months before the four year follow-up interview; but reported a typical quantity of less than 2 oz of ethanol on drinking days and no days over 3 oz of ethanol during the 30 days before the last drink. (1 oz = 29.57 ml.)
b. Drank during the six months before the follow-up interview, but did not meet both conditions listed in footnote (a).
c. Consequences indicated by one or more occurrences during the six months before the four year follow-up interview; symptoms indicated by one or more occurrences during the 30 days before the last drink (provided the subject drank during the six months before follow-up).

Table 6.3: History of Alcohol Incidents by Status at Four Years

Drinking status category at four year follow-up (1977)	Per cent of category with two or more alcohol incidents* 1973-6	(N)
Abstaining	40	(154)
Non-problem drinking	20	(95)
Problem drinking	52	(288)

* Serious alcohol-related incidents, as reported by subjects at the four year follow-up, including: family disruption (spouse left, physical fights, etc.); serious health problems and accidents; unemployment or loss of promotion; and arrests related to alcohol use.

cent of the survivors. On the other hand, the other 46 per cent appeared to be in a remission state that was stable throughout a six month period. The majority of remissions (28 per cent of the sample) attained that state through abstaining. In addition, some alcoholics (18 per cent of the sample) were found to be drinking without any immediate problems that could be identified from the data. Among these non-problem drinkers, quantities of consumption varied considerably, although in about half of these cases (eight per cent of the sample) consumption was consistently low enough to be considered moderate even in the general population.

It bears emphasis that these remissions during a six month period do not necessarily represent cases of stability over the long-term. Table 6.3 shows one bit of evidence on this point. It tabulates the percentage of each drinking-status category (defined as of the four year follow-up point) who reported multiple alcohol-related incidents during the preceding four year period (excluding incidents at the time of admission to treatment). The table shows that 40 per cent of subjects who were abstaining at the time of the follow-up had a previous history of serious and repetitive difficulties because of alcohol. Indeed, the rate for abstainers is fairly close to the rate for problem drinkers, and it is somewhat higher than the rate for non-problem drinkers. This is one of a number of indications from the longitudinal data base suggesting that many alcoholics in the cohort, including those currently abstaining, have a history of instability when long-term patterns of drinking are considered.

Social and Psychological Status

It is entirely possible for an alcoholic to solve or improve his alcohol-related problems without necessarily improving in other realms of functioning. This observation has been used to attack the use of abstinence as the sole criterion for treatment success,[19] but it applies equally to non-problem drinking. An important aspect of remission, therefore, is the extent to which alcoholics whose drinking problems have abated may also exhibit modes of social and psychological functioning that are more nearly normal than those of the typical alcoholic at admission to treatment. Table 6.4 shows a number of measures of status on such sociopsychological variables, classified by drinking status at four years. Measures (1) to (4) indicate that the two remission groups — abstainers and non-problem drinkers — are considerably more 'normal' than the problem drinkers: they are more likely to be employed full-time, to earn an adequate income, to express general satisfaction with their

Table 6.4: Sociopsychological Behaviour by Drinking Status at Four Years

Drinking status at four years	(1) Employed full-time (per cent)	(2) Earnings past year (median)	(3) Low life satisfaction[a] (per cent)	(4) Frequent psychiatric symptoms[b] (per cent)	(5) Self-concept as 'alcoholic' (per cent)	(6) Traditional alcoholism ideology[c] (per cent)	(N)
Abstaining	58	$ 5,800	14	15	69	61	(156)
Non-problem drinking	57	$ 6,200	14	14	21	31	(99)
Problem drinking	33	$ 1,800	39	49	66	59	(293)
General population norm	88	$ 10,100	10	d	d	d	

Notes:
a. Reported dissatisfied with general life conditions ('not too happy').
b. High score on 5-item self-reported symptom scale, including depression, anhedonia, tension, anxiety, and cognitive impairment.
c. High score on 3-item scale of beliefs about alcoholism, including 'alcoholism is an irreversible disease'; 'once an alcoholic, always an alcoholic'; and 'alcoholics cannot resume moderate drinking'.
d. General-population data not available.

lives, and to be relatively free of reported psychiatric symptoms. Note that there is no systematic difference between abstainers and non-problem drinkers on these factors; the two groups appear about equally well-adjusted in the areas measured. However, it is well worth noting that even the remission groups were quite a bit below the general population norms on social adjustment measures, including employment and earnings. The ATC cohort was substantially impaired on such measures at admission to treatment, and its members generally improved only a little.[20] Social rehabilitation, then, was not a common outcome even for those who were in remission at the four year follow-up.

Although the abstainers and non-problem drinkers are not perceptibly different in measures of adjustment, they are quite far apart in their beliefs, as one might expect. Columns (5) and (6) of Table 6.4 show that abstainers generally describe themselves as 'alcoholic' and endorse statements of traditional alcoholism ideology, whereas non-problem drinkers do the opposite. In fact, abstainers and *problem* drinkers have a common belief system with regard to alcoholism, both in the abstract and in personal frames of reference. This would appear to indicate that simple acceptance of these beliefs is neither necessary nor sufficient to overcome drinking problems. These results suggest that the role of denial in the maintenance of alcoholic drinking may not be as important as is often believed.

Remission and the Extent of Treatment

All of the results shown above were drawn from the cohort of alcoholics who were actually admitted to treatment at the ATCs. The data therefore share in the criticism voiced at the beginning of this chapter: they may represent patterns of remission after treatment, but they are not very enlightening about the 'natural' course of alcoholism in the absence of treatment. And yet, probably the most valuable single datum on alcoholic remission would be an accurate reading of the amount of remission to be expected without treatment.

There are, of course, very good reasons for the paucity of data on natural remission. An important, but only partial, explanation is that alcoholics in treatment make up an easily identifiable group, and one for which research resources are often available. But a more subtle explanation, and one that poses a more difficult problem, lies in the fact that untreated alcoholics are exceedingly difficult to locate. To

Table 6.5: Drinking Status at Four Years by Extent of Treatment

| | Per cent distribution of drinking status at four years | | | |
	Abstaining	Non-problem drinking	Problem drinking	(N)
Extent of treatment	Abstaining	Non-problem drinking	Problem drinking	(N)
Single contact only (not admitted)	16	16	68	(120)
Admitted, low amount	25	16	58	(283)
Admitted, high amount*	32	20	47	(265)

* More than 7 inpatient days, 5 outpatient visits, or 21 days in an intermediate or residential facility.

some extent, this situation flows from the commonly accepted criteria that are employed to define an 'alcoholic': loss of job, family difficulties, physical damage, etc. It may well be that relatively few persons suffer the constellation of problems found in a clinic population, without at some time coming to the attention of a treatment organisation.

To gather some data on an 'untreated' group, the four year follow-up study included a group of subjects who made only a single contact with the treatment centre. Table 6.5 shows their drinking status at the four year follow-up and compares them with two groups of treatment admissions (those who received relatively low and high amounts of treatment, respectively). There is a modest but statistically significant correlation between the amount of treatment received by a patient and his outcome at the four year follow-up. However, because the various groups were not subject to experimental control (in particular, they were not randomly assigned to treatment conditions), this difference should not necessarily be attributed to treatment. It could, for example, be due to self selection, whereby patients with better initial prognosis would be more likely to initiate treatment or to remain longer in treatment.[21]

The direction of the differences in Table 6.5 is interesting in its own right. It suggests that, if anything, the rather pessimistic picture that we have seen for treated alcoholics probably applies at least equally well to those who receive no treatment. It certainly provides little reason to conclude that, with less intervention, alcoholism is likely gradually to ameliorate itself, at least for those alcoholics whose condition has reached the stage where they are apt to come to the attention of a treatment institution.

Prognostic Factors in Alcoholic Remission

The longitudinal data available from the cohort permit much more analysis than simple tabulations of remission status and alcoholic history. In particular, they permit an assessment of the natural history and *prognosis* for various types of alcohol-related behaviour. One can assemble a group of subjects according to their behaviour at one time point and examine their condition later, at a second time point, in order to establish prognosis. The distinctions used in making the definition of status at four years in fact rested on certain analyses of prognosis. Such analyses also reveal important aspects of the process of alcoholic remission. Two such aspects stand out in the findings from the four year follow-up.

The Importance of Alcohol Dependence

The first of these findings is summarised in Table 6.6, which shows four groups of subjects classified according to their drinking at the 18 month follow-up and their rates of various alcohol-related problems *after* the 18 month follow-up. The prognostic importance of dependence symptoms is clear, particularly in columns (2) and (3). Regardless of level of alcohol consumption, those subjects who reported at least one dependence symptom at 18 months were about twice as likely to experience continued symptoms at four years, and about three times as likely to die from an alcohol-related cause. In column (1), the pattern is more complex, since an interaction appears to indicate that only people with both higher consumption levels and dependence symptoms suffer increased risks of later adverse consequences. Nonetheless, the overall pattern strongly suggests that symptoms of alcohol dependence portend serious risks. More detailed analyses also made it clear that even low levels of symptoms, such as one or two events in a 30 day period, are associated with a substantial increase in later problem rates. It is as though a threshold is crossed when an alcoholic moves from being asymptomatic to experiencing even one symptom. These patterns are not explained by other measured variables that might be confounded with symptoms; the relationships in Table 6.6 held up in multi-variate analyses that included a variety of drinking and socio-psychological characteristics. Rather, the presence or absence of alcohol dependence symptoms appears to mark a crucial facet of the alcoholic remission process.

A remarkable aspect of the data is that dependence symptoms appearing at admission to treatment did not play such an important

Table 6.6. Alcohol Problems at Four Years by 18 Month Symptoms and Consumption

Dependence symptoms at 18 months	Typical alcohol consumption at 18 months*	Per cent of 18 month group with alcohol problems at four years			
		(1) Any consequences at 4 years among survivors	(2) Any symptoms at 4 years among survivors	(3) Alcohol-related death 18 months to 4 years	(N)
No symptoms	Less than 2 oz	25	35	3	(66)
No symptoms	2 oz or more	29	32	3	(37)
Symptoms	Less than 2 oz	35	65	10	(30)
Symptoms	2 oz or more	64	72	9	(191)

* Reported quantity of ethanol consumed on a typical drinking day.

role. Partly, this is because relatively few alcoholics were free of such symptoms at that time. Among subjects for whom admission drinking data were available, 90 per cent reported some dependence symptomatology during the month before treatment admission. The frequency of these symptoms, however, was only weakly related to mortality or to drinking behaviour at four years. This may indicate that the alcoholics were almost uniformly in a deteriorated condition before admission, and that they improved at non-uniform rates thereafter. Among those whose dependence re-established itself, even in a tangential or incipient form, the prognosis was relatively poor, whereas among those who drank but managed to avoid the re-establishment of dependence, prognosis was relatively good. These findings call into question the traditional conception of an alcoholic as a unique type of person, for whom 'loss of control' or other symptomatology is the marker indicating a chronic addiction. Instead, they suggest, in conformity with other modern evidence,[18] that alcohol dependence should be viewed as a variable property, differing in degree among alcoholics, and subject to considerable fluctuation over time.

Abstention and Remission

The second finding that has significant implications concerns the stability of long-term versus short-term abstention. Table 6.7 shows

Table 6.7: Alcohol Problems at Four Years by 18 Month Drinking Behaviour

Drinking behaviour at 18 month follow-up	Per cent of 18 month behaviour group with alcohol problems at 4 years			
	Any consequence at 4 years among survivors	Any symptom at 4 years among survivors	Alcohol-related deaths, 18 months to 4 years	(N)
Abstained 6 months	31	23	1	(140)
Abstained 1-5 months	52	43	9	(124)
Drank, no symptoms	27	34	3	(103)
Drank, symptoms	61	71	9	(223)

rates of later alcohol problems for both groups of abstainers and for the drinking groups, defined according to behaviour at the 18 month follow-up. The problem rates for short-term abstainers are considerably higher than those for long-term abstainers or those for non-symptomatic drinkers. Mortality rates, in particular, emphasise the relatively poor prognosis for short-term abstainers.

These findings suggest that short-term abstention is not very promising as a mode of remission. In fact, the data on drinking behaviour during the six months before the four year follow-up showed that, among subjects who were short-term abstainers at the four year point, 85 per cent had experienced either dependence symptoms or adverse consequences of drinking during their last drinking period. The data thus give the impression that many short-term abstainers pursue an unstable path, switching back and forth between remission and alcoholic drinking.[22] The totality of the results, then, implies that short-term abstention, like drinking with even a low level of dependence symptoms, should not be regarded as a form of alcoholic remission.

The differences between short- and long-term abstainers raise important questions about the causal role of stability in alcoholism. Do these results imply that a period of at least six months' abstention is required to indicate a reasonably good prognosis? If so, does the high probability of relapse evidenced by short-term abstainers reflect a general feature of the recovery process, one that applies to all alcoholics who are just beginning a remission period (including non-problem drinkers)? These questions are highly germane to intervention strategies, since affirmative answers might suggest both specific types of treatment goals and the need for interim support procedures. However, our data are insufficient to address the questions properly. What is needed is a more detailed record of the process of alcoholic remission, tracing salient and critical events as well as transition points where abstention or non-problem drinking shifts to another mode (frequently, it appears this shift will be to a mode of resumed alcoholic drinking). In addition, specific information about the individual patient's objectives, motivations, and commitment are needed. At present, we cannot distinguish the committed abstainer who lapses into resumed problem drinking after three months of abstention, from the unstable alcoholic who simply oscillates between drinking bouts and short periods of abstention. One may conjecture about the relative proportion of these two types within the abstention groups we have defined empirically, but a satisfactory model of alcoholic remission awaits data that permit more precise examination of the process over time.

In general, both the data on prognoses and the other evidence presented above point to the *chronic* character of alcoholism. Over the long-term, most members of this sample continued to experience at least some serious problems related to drinking. About 50 per cent were identified as having significant alcohol problems at the four year follow-up point. Only seven per cent abstained throughout the four years, and those who stopped abstaining often appeared to alternate between abstention and serious problem periods. On the other hand, there are some subjects who, from the perspective of four years, appear to be drinking without significant problems, sometimes in quite moderate amounts. The overall pattern for most alcoholics is one of frequent remissions, including both abstaining and non-problem drinking periods. But these remissions are counterbalanced by high rates of individual instability with a high probability of relapse. For many individuals, the chronicity of the alcoholic condition inheres not in its continuous manifestation, but in the brevity and instability of remission periods. A crucial objective of our research efforts should be to uncover the factors that can extend these periods and promote their stability.

Notes

1. Emrick, C. (1974), 'A Review of Psychologically Oriented Treatment of Alcoholism. I. The Use and Interrelationships of Outcome Criteria and Drinking Behaviour Following Treatment', *Quarterly Journal of Studies on Alcohol*, vol. 35, pp. 523-49.
2. Smart, R. (1975), 'Spontaneous Recovery in Alcoholics: A Review and Analysis of the Available Research', *Drug and Alcohol Dependence*, vol. 1, pp. 277-85.
3. Jellinek, E.M. (1960), *The Disease Concept of Alcoholism* (Hillhouse Press, New Brunswick, New Jersey).
4. Pattison, E.M. (1976), 'A Conceptual Approach to Alcoholism Treatment Goals', *Addictive Behaviors*, vol. 1, pp. 177-92.
5. Pomerleau, O., Pertschuk, M. and Stinnet, J. (1976), 'A Critical Examination of Some Current Assumptions in the Treatment of Alcoholism', *Journal of Studies on Alcohol*, vol. 37, pp. 849-67.
6. The study was conducted by The Rand Corporation under Contract ADM-281-76-0006 with NIAAA (Alcohol, Drug Abuse and Mental Health Administration, US Department of Health, Education, and Welfare). I am indebted to my colleagues, David Armor and Harriet Braiker, for collaboration in certain analysis presented in this chapter.
7. Polich, J.M., Armor, D.J. and Braiker, H.B. (1979), *The Course of Alcoholism: Four Years After Treatment* (The Rand Corporation, Santa Monica, California).
8. Armor, D.J., Polich, J.M. and Stambul, H.B. (1978), *Alcoholism and Treatment* (John Wiley, New York).
9. Armor, D.J., Polich, J.M. and Stambul, H.B. (1976), *Alcoholism and Treatment* (The Rand Corporation, Santa Monica, California).
10. Fitzgerald, B., Pasewark, R. and Clark, R. (1971), 'Four Year Follow-up of Alcoholics at a Rural State Hospital', *Quarterly Journal of Studies on Alcohol*, vol. 32, pp. 636-42.
11. Orford, J., Oppenheimer, E. and Edwards, G. (1976), 'Abstinence or Control: The Outcome for Excessive Drinkers Two Years After Consultation', *Behavioral Research and Therapy*, vol. 14, pp. 409-18.
12. Detailed analysis and estimates in the comprehensive report, *The Course of Alcoholism: Four Years After Treatment*, suggest that the distribution of drinking status in the obtained sample is probably affected, at most, by the percentage points as a result of possible biases arising from non-response.
13. National Institute on Alcohol Abuse and Alcoholism (1974), *Alcohol and Health: New Knowledge*, Second Special Report to the US Congress (US Government Printing Office, Washington).
14. National Center for Health Statistics (1975), *United States Life Tables by Causes of Death: 1969-71*, vol. 1, no. 5 (US Government Printing Office, Washington).
15. National Center for Health Statistics (1976), *Vital Statistics Instructions for Classifying the Underlying Cause of Death, 1976-8*, part 2A (Research Triangle Park, North Carolina).
16. In particular, few subjects who reported an absence of alcohol-related problems during the last drinking period reported any problems during the six month period. For example, of the group classified as non-problem drinkers (based mostly on the 30 day period), only five per cent reported even a single occurrence of a symptomatic event (morning drinking, blackouts, etc.) over the six months before the interview.
17. 1 fl oz = 29.57 ml.

18. Edwards, G., Gross, M., Keller, M., Moser, J. and Room, R. (1977), *Alcohol-related Disabilities*, offset publication no. 32 (WHO, Geneva).

19. Baekeland, F. (1977), 'Evaluation of Treatment Methods in Chronic Alcoholism', in Kissin, B. and Begleiter, H. (eds.), *The Biology of Alcoholism, Vol. 5: Treatment and Rehabilitation of the Chronic Alcoholic* (Plenum Press, New York).

20. Both employment rates and constant-dollar family income increased about ten per cent between admission and the four year follow-up.

21. Detailed baseline measures at admission, covering the areas of drinking behaviour, drinking history, and social environment, were available for the low-treatment and high-treatment groups, but statistical adjustments for such variables (using analysis of covariance and various linear and non-linear models) did not affect the correlation of amount of treatment with follow-up status.

22. However, about one-third of the 18 month short-term abstainers did become long-term abstainers at four years.

7 ALCOHOLISM TREATMENT EFFECTIVENESS: SLICING THE OUTCOME VARIANCE PIE

Raymond M. Costello

Those who attended the Liverpool Conference in 1976 may have heard a report of my early work relevant to the present question – 'Determining whether treatment works'. In that address,[1] answers were offered to two simple questions: (1) Do more successful programmes more often report using at least one client-exclusionary criterion than do less successful programmes? and (2) Are certain treatment components more likely to be reported by more successful programmes? The answer to both questions was yes. Further, four essential treatment components were identified to discriminate more from less successful programmes: (a) a 'milieu' or 'therapeutic community' philosophy for residential or inpatient programmes; (b) antabuse; (c) collateral therapy (active involvement of spouses, relatives, friends, employers, etc.) and (d) aggressive follow-through (aftercare, ambulatory care, boosters, or follow-up). Some components (i.e. AA, individual counselling, and group therapy) were reported by the vast majority of programmes and, therefore, could not aid in discrimination. Residential or inpatient treatment without a philosophical orientation which stressed the patient's active involvement in treatment did not discriminate programme quality. Behavioural techniques were few in number (because most behavioural programmes at that time did not follow clients for the required minimum of one year) and, therefore, also did not discriminate programme quality.

The findings were consistent over 80 studies at the one year follow-up point[2] and over 23 studies at the two year follow-up point.[3] Over 200 other studies were omitted because the follow-up length was shorter than one or longer than two years, or because reporting style was so poor that reasonable estimates could not be made about client-exclusionary practices or about outcome.

The original report did not offer a theoretical treatment-outcome model with parameters specified quantitatively on the basis of these historical, empirical observations. This step had to await the tedious process of re-reviewing the pool of outcome studies and indexing each one for client sample characteristics and treatment components. It is this step of the meta-evaluative process that is reported in the present chapter. A treatment-outcome model with quantitative estimates of 'causal' parameters will be presented, as will a normative equation with which actuarial predictions can be made about expected treatment-outcome under various specified circumstances.

Model Specification

What do we need to know to generate such a model? First, prognosis, a characteristic of subjects which influences outcome, must be indexed. To make a very long story very short — all studies in the pool were indexed on each of a number of subject variables by referencing the percentage of subjects reported as possessing various prognostic attributes. Reporting practices regarding such matters have varied tremendously since 1937 (which is the date of the earliest publication in this pool). The greater the number of such attributes which were required of a study to be included in subsequent analyses, the fewer the number of studies that qualified. When the number of variables was reduced to the two which comprised what many investigators called the 'Social Stability Index' (SSI), the number of qualifying studies was maximised. Using this index, 35 studies reporting on 45 groups of subjects were retrieved for the model building.

In an exploratory analysis, a regression line was computed between the Social Stability Index and Success Rate. Eight points (or study groups of subjects) fell well below their predicted value. Studies reporting these groups were reviewed to see if an artifactual circumstance (i.e. non-random error) could be identified to account for the deviation. Non-random error in such instances underestimates the effect of SSI on outcome. These eight points were generated by six studies. Four of these studies reported on single groups of subjects for which the length of the outcome interval was four or more years,[4-7] whereas the large majority of studies reported follow-up at one to three years. Four points were contributed by two studies, both of which attempted 'true' experimental designs comparing drug-treated groups with placebo-groups.[8,9]

It is quite possible that estimation of success at follow-up intervals of more than three years significantly underestimates the success rate achieved over shorter intervals (a result of subject attrition due to loss or mortality, when maintaining the denominator used to calculate success rate fixed at the original N). It is also quite possible that the use of a 'true' experimental procedure with random assignment and blinding of experimental conditions can produce a counter-experimental back-lash or negative feedback which results in poorer outcome than would be the case if no treatment whatever is provided. These possibilities were considered artifactual circumstances sufficient to warrant dropping the studies from final analyses. Therefore, all six studies (eight data points) were eliminated. Thus, the model to be presented specifies outcome expectancies only through three follow-up years, and may not be accurate for studies which do not take into consideration the psychological reactance phenomenon[10] which can result when human subjects in 'true' experimental studies behave in a counter-experimental manner.

The SSI reflects the degree of participation in a social system outside the treatment programme of the programme's clients. High SSI suggests important linkages of clients in a non-treatment setting social network of persons, positions, and roles.[11] The surrogate or summary statement about 'prognosis' of subjects within each group (SSI) was calculated by adding the percentage of subjects reported to be employed to the percentage of subjects reported to be married at the time of enrolment in treatment and dividing this sum by two. The minimum SSI of zero was reported by Myerson in 1956[12] who worked with skid row, homeless men, none of whom was married or employed. The maximum SSI of 96 was reported by Dunne in 1973,[13] who worked with police officers in a counselling section within a police department, all of whom were employed and 91 per cent of whom were married. The average SSI for these studies was 47.3, with a standard deviation of 22.4.

Secondly, a treatment programme index must be identified. Building upon previous work,[1-3,14] each of the 37 treatment groups retained for phase 2 was indexed for 'extensity' of treatment components. Extensity of treatment was defined as a score from zero to three representing the reported availability of 'milieu', 'antabuse', and/or 'collateral' components in the treatment programme. All components were assumed to be equally effective and they were assumed to combine in a unit-weighted additive fashion in effecting outcome. 'Milieu' was credited when a multi-disciplinary, co-ordinated complex of treatments was reported. Clients in such a programme typically were expected to be active participants in a social process. 'Antabuse' was credited whenever it was mentioned as available to clients. Investigators typically did not report average capsule consumption or some other index reflecting degree of exposure to the treatment component. 'Collateral' was credited whenever family members, spouses, friends, relatives, pastors,

employers, business associates, probation or parole officers, etc. were
actively, programmatically-involved in client treatment. It was not
scored when an occasional collateral was involved at the initiative of the
collateral. Nine studies with 10 groups of clients achieved a 'Treatment
Extensity' (TE) score of 0.[15-23] This score reflects either that the
'programmes' offered no treatment whatever (e.g. no treatment or
waiting list control groups; retrospective reviews of cases enrolled but
not returning for treatment), or that the treatment offered (e.g. LSD,
group therapy) did not consist of any of the three 'essential' components. Thirteen studies with 15 groups of clients achieved a score of
one, suggesting that in addition to any other alleged treatments, only
one of the essentials was included in the programme.[12,13,16,19,21,24-31]
Five study groups reported some combinations of two essential components.[32-36] Six studies with seven groups of patients were considered
to have used all three essential components in their treatment programme, perhaps in addition to others not considered essential.[35,37-41]
The average TE was 1.24, with a standard deviation of 1.1.

Thirdly, an active follow-through component (FT) was identified as
a characteristic of the better programmes in previous reviews. Follow-
through was credited whenever programmes reported an aggressive
approach to maintaining contact with clients, irrespective of reported
availability of 'essential' components. Nightly telephone calls, home
visits, telephone calls or postcards to remind clients of appointments
or to check up when appointments were missed, daily or diary-type
homework assignments that were analysed by staff, periodic follow-up
using rating scales and multiple informants, provision of transportation
to facilitate participation in treatment, or other mechanisms which
reinforced mutual contact were scored. Specifically not scored was a
statement that clients were responsible for setting up appointments
and following through on their own initiative as a mechanism to teach
self-management. This variable is not a treatment so much as it is a
stylistic feature describing a programme's approach to maintaining
contact with its clients. When this characteristic is indexed separately
from TE, its statistical importance in effecting outcome can be analysed.
Sixteen studies with 19 groups of clients were credited with an
FT,[12,13,19,25,26,29-33,35,36,38-41] whereas 16 studies with 18 groups of
clients were not.[15-25,27,28,31,34,37]

Outcome, the fourth and final variable of any treatment-outcome
model, is the index of success (OUT). Although outcome can be conceptualised as multi-dimensional, a measure of alcohol drinking status
is obviously necessary. As drinking status has been shown to be

intercorrelated with many other aspects of social functioning,[37] this single dimension was utilised as the outcome index of success. Each group was referenced with regard to the percentage of subjects which could be described as having achieved at the follow-up point a non-problematic status with regard to their consumption of alcohol. Unavoidably, this important score is determined subjectively by the meta-evaluator, as primary investigators have used idiosyncratic rather than standard rating systems. Success was not restricted to categories labelled 'total abstinence', but included other categories such as 'markedly improved', 'abstinent ten of twelve months' and 'controlled drinking with no associated problem as per collateral report'. .

The lowest success rate (seven per cent) was calculated for the study reported by Rhodes and Hudson in 1969.[22] This American team treated skid row clients picked up for treatment when in a tuberculosis sanitorium. Fourteen per cent of their sample was employed, none was married, none of the essential treatment components was used, and follow-through was not available. The highest success rate (80 per cent) was reported by Pfeffer and Berger in 1957.[26] This American team worked in a medical school which had an alcohol treatment programme financed partially and monitored by three large private industries in New York State. All of the subjects were employed and referred by one of the industries, and 58 per cent were married. The only essential treatment component reported for this group was 'collaterals'. Follow-through was also recorded. The average OUT was 40.5, with a standard deviation of 19.3.

Statistical Description and the Notion of Causality

A variance-accumulating statistical approach was used to describe the relationships among variables. A special multiple linear regression technique, path analysis,[42] was used to decompose simple bivariate relationships into a causal component (direct, indirect and joint) and a non-causal component. To make causal statements regarding the inter-relationship of variables, a hypothetical model was constructed prior to data analysis (see Figure 7.1). Causality is suggested when variables covary in a temporally asymmetrical manner, and when the covariation persists when the effects of potential confounds are removed statistically.

The hypothesised linkage between SSI and TE requires comment. A double-headed arrow assumes that as it is not possible to place these

Figure 7.1: Treatment-outcome Model

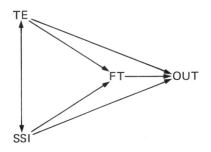

variables into an asymmetrical temporal (i.e. developmental) sequence, the notion of causality cannot be considered. It is true that some programmes are 'designed' at the outset to meet the needs of certain clinical populations. This implies that a variable like SSI occurs prior to TE. It is also true that programmes are opened and simply accept whatever clients show up for treatment. This implies that SSI would be irrelevant to TE. Finally, some programmes are designed to fit the personal preference of the clinician in charge and 'inappropriate' clients are refused treatment. In this case, SSI would be secondary to TE. Thus, the rationale for an *a priori* ordering of SSI and TE was equivocal. FT, however, was considered to be an intermediate variable, following TE in a temporal sequence, filtering effects of prior variables on OUT, and contributing directly to OUT as well.

Within this model, path analysis allows the detection of complex relationships. The analysis describes completely the statistical relationships among variables. The coefficient between one variable and another, with no intervening variables, is the direct causal effect (i.e. standardised partial regression coefficient) attributed to the prior variable on the latter. Indirect effects between variables with one or more intervening variables are calculated by multiplying path coefficients. If more than one indirect path is possible, the total indirect effect is calculated by adding the indirect effects (path coefficient products) along each causal route. Indirect effects are possible, of course, only when intervening variables exist. Bivariate correlations can also possess a spurious, or non-causal, component. This component is an artifactual inflation of the simple relationship because of the influence of a prior variable. Finally, a certain portion of outcome variance can be determined jointly by the correlation between exogenous variables (i.e. SSI and TE) which is not fully analysable.

Results

Figure 7.2 displays the path model with quantitative estimates of causal parameters. The correlation of 0.31 between TE and SSI is a simple correlation because no *a priori* causal hypotheses regarding this relationship were stated. All other path coefficients represent the extents of the direct causal relationship between variables.

Figure 7.2: Treatment-outcome Model with Causal Parameters Specified

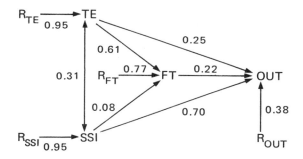

Note that SSI has a powerful direct link to OUT, but a near-zero link to FT. This suggests that the effect of SSI on outcome is primarily direct with a small effect shared with TE along two compound paths. It suggests also, either that treatment programmes, at least with regard to extensity, are built nearly without regard to the social stability of the clients to be treated or that clients do not show a strong tendency to preselect programmes for extensity. Finally, if additions to this basic model are to be made, the near-vanishing SSI-FT link can be omitted without introducing serious measurement error, in order to simplify subsequent models.

The strong direct link between TE and FT (0.64 if SSI-FT is omitted) suggests that it is the treatment programmes with greatest extensity that are most likely to have an aggressive style in maintaining contact with clients. This style pays off in terms of a substantial indirect causal effect of TE on OUT, which complements the modest direct TE-OUT effect. This style also enhances the degree of joint TE-SSI effect on

OUT.

Table 7.1 summarises the decomposition of the simple correlation of each predictor with OUT. Note that the simple SSI-OUT correlation was almost entirely causal (0.70/0.84 = 83 per cent), with a small portion (0.12/0.84 = 14 per cent) shared by the joint effect with TE. The simple correlation of TE-OUT, however, was derived in a very complex manner (41 per cent direct, 0.25/0.61; 25 per cent indirect through FT, 0.14/0.61; 34 per cent joint with SSI, 0.22/0.61). Finally, the simple FT-OUT correlation was modestly direct (38 per cent 0.22/0.56), but was inflated because of the influence of prior predictor, TE (61 per cent, 0.34/0.56).

Table 7.1: Decomposition of Three Bivariate Relationships

Variables	Total correlation	Causal effect			Non-causal effect
		Direct	Indirect	Joint	
SSI-OUT	0.84	0.70	0.02	0.12	none
TE-OUT	0.61	0.25	0.14	0.22	none
FT-OUT	0.56	0.22	none	none	0.34

Table 7.2: Slicing the Outcome Variance Pie

SSI-direct	49%
TE-direct	6%
FT-direct	5%
TE-indirect	15%
SSI-TE-joint	11%
Total	86%

Table 7.2 explains these results in terms of a variance model. The total outcome variance accounted for by each predictor is decomposed into estimates of direct causal, indirect causal, and joint causal components. Thus, the answer to the question 'Determining whether treatment works', when analysed in the manner presented, is a rather complicated yes. An estimate of the amount of outcome variance attributable to treatment programming is 26-37 per cent. This is a respectable figure even relative to the 49-60 per cent effect attributable

to clients' social stability at intake. The actuarial equation which utilises unstandardised coefficients (± 1SE) for each predictor to account for outcome is:

$$0.6 \text{ SSI} + 4.5 \text{ TE} + 8.2 \text{ FT} + 2.3 = \text{OUT}$$
$$\pm .06 \quad \pm 1.57 \quad \pm 3.25$$

Unstandardised coefficients are another means to express the effectiveness of predictors. Thus, a treatment programme with only one essential TE component and no follow-through will succeed with 4.5 per cent of its clients as a direct result of the therapeutic activity. A programme with all three essential components plus follow-through will succeed with 21.7 per cent because of its programming.

Baseline outcome expectancies are generated by the unstandardised coefficient for SSI. It is against these 'spontaneous remission' expectancies that outcome increments attributable to treatment must be measured. For example, a programme with SSI 20 clientele would be expected to achieve a spontaneous remission success rate of 14.3 per cent (12 per cent attributable to SSI, 2.3 per cent attributable to the constant). A programme at the high end of the SSI scale, SSI 80, would be expected to achieve a minimum success rate of 50.3 per cent. Significant downward deviations from these expectancies would suggest a need for an external audit of the programme to identify possible reasons for the deficiency. Significant deviations greater than expected would suggest an external audit to rule out artifactual inflation prior to recommending more widespread use of the method involved.

Discussion

Many questions might be raised subsequent to a research effort of this sort. In the space of this chapter it is not possible to consider many of these questions in depth. The most basic question, of course, is how to evaluate the merit of such an undertaking? A similar attempt to 'meta-analyse' psychotherapy outcome studies[43] has been roundly criticised. The response has ranged from a mild protest that lumping theories into broad 'superclasses' obscures real differences between them,[44] to a much more harsh critique of 'mega-silliness',[45] based on the notion that a low standard of judgement was exercised by Smith and Glass for including reports of undetermined reliability in their analysis — 'garbage-in, garbage-out'. At least two others[46,47] have attacked the conclusions offered by Smith and Glass on methodological grounds. The best position is to accept that the jury is still out. It is too early to determine the true merit of such work. Much more dialogue is required about the basic units of analysis and about methodological assumptions and execution before the approach can be abandoned. This literature represents our archives of accumulated knowledge. To let it lie without serious attempts at distillation of the elements that make it up is simply not responsible.

Many shortcomings were encountered, however, that if outlined may be avoided in the future. As the 'meta-analysis' proceeded, many nodal decision points were reached as a result of deficiences in our previous reporting systems. These were a few of the complications.

First, there are many subject variables which have potential programmatic relevance (i.e. influence the outcome of treatment). Yet in more than 40 years of 'scientific' work on the subject there has been no serious effort to develop a standardised instrument to describe the prognostic class or, obversely, the treatment difficulty presented to a programme by the clients with which it works. Ordinarily, subject variables are itemised with little reference to previous empirical results or theory and a *post hoc* statistical analysis is conducted to search for significant zero-order correlations of such variables with outcome. A preferred approach is to collect information on a standardised, reliable and valid instrument which is generally accepted as the minimal subject descriptive index. Investigators need not be limited to such an instrument, but it should be necessary prior to publication of the study in journals subscribing to the policy.

One hundred and forty five studies of outcome interval of one or more years were examined to find 35 (24 per cent) which described their subjects on, at least, current marital status and current employment status, each variable scored dichotomously, yes or no. Many of the other studies were well-executed and provided broad descriptions of their subjects, but these descriptions were idiosyncratic, thus disallowing any sort of statistical comparison across studies. Many authors recognised the difficulties inherent in cross-study comparisons, and some even seemed to proceed on the assumption that their results, once published, would exist in a vacuum because of these difficulties. It would be much better to proceed on the heuristic basis that comparisons are both possible and necessary, and to report in a manner to facilitate the process.

Secondly, descriptions of treatment programmes have tended to be lean. What constitutes treatment? At least six aspects of treatment should be described in a manner that allows quantification: (1) technical operations, (2) skill of application, (3) therapeutic intent, (4) degree of exposure, (5) ecological context, (6) involvement of subject. The danger now run when studies are pooled on the basis of information available currently has been described as tendency to error due to the 'uniformity assumption myth'.[48] This myth describes the error which results when a reader assumes that a semantic label applied to an operation by various investigators possesses precise denotation. This myth is exploded easily by anyone who reads the literature in question carefully. For example, one of the components rated in the TE index was 'antabuse'. One might think that 'antabuse' as a therapeutic operation could be described without much difficulty. Yet this is not the case. A programme which writes prescriptions for 30 times 500 mg tables with two refills allowed, with no check on how many and which patients actually fill the prescriptions, and how many and which actually take one or more pills, and under what circumstances, is a very different programme than one which requires the patient to report on repeated visits to a specific place to receive one 250 mg pill which is consumed in the presence of others who greet the event with great fanfare. There is no question concerning non-uniformity of application. The meta-evaluator must keep in mind some minimal standard of application when crediting a programme with a particular treatment component. To date, minimal descriptive standards have not been determined.

Thirdly, much more dialogue about application of the experimental laboratory model is necessary to determine its merit in the evaluation of treatment efforts. The concept of 'experimental isolation' basic to the laboratory approach is stretched badly out of shape in the business of treatment evaluation. There are many designs,[49] creative application of which might result in findings of more ecological relevance than those which emanate from a forced attempt at 'true' experimentation. When treatments are described in terms of the six characteristics just mentioned, it becomes obvious that treatment delivered in the context of a research programme is qualitatively different from that delivered in a more natural context of ordinary clinical care. The best approach might be to devise an evaluative strategy which fits the ordinary clinical setting rather than to modify the context to meet demands of experimental rigour.

Finally, the causal parameters estimated in the present study must be considered from the point of heuristic interest, rather than as evaluative standards. Experience with 'effect coefficients', drawn from

Figure 7.3: Plot of Success Rate vs. SSI

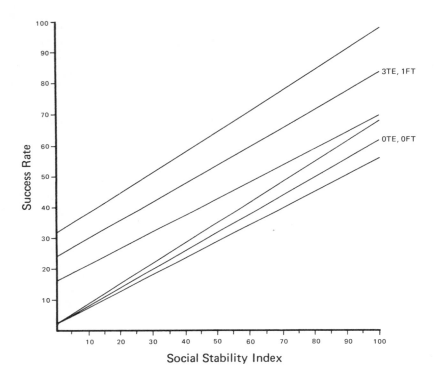

the non-laboratory setting anyway, is one of sample shrinkage, or
unreliability. The statistical axiom to describe this phenomenon is that
of 'bouncing-betas'. If the equation described above is used as one
normative index for evaluation, one must keep in mind that the non-
standardised, 'B' weights are estimates of population parameters, and
are not measured without error. Thus, the regression line fitted by the
equation is actually a fan, narrower at the low SSI end and wider at the
upper SSI end, when the standard error of measurement is considered.
Thus, predictions are made in terms of confidence intervals, rather than
exact points. As the fans, which are descriptive of regressions specific to
various circumstances, overlap, the Type II error of statistical inference
will prove to be a real problem (Figure 7.3).

Notes

1. Costello, R.M. (1977), 'Alcoholism Treatment Programming: Historical Trends', in Madden, J.S., Walker, R. and Kenyon, W.H. (eds.), *Alcoholism and Drug Dependence: A Multi-disciplinary Approach* (Plenum Press, New York).
2. Costello, R.M., Biever, P. and Baillargeon, J.G. (1977), 'Alcoholism Treatment Programming: Historical Trends and Modern Approaches', *Alcoholism: Clinical and Experimental Research*, vol. 1, no. 4, pp. 311-18.
3. Costello, R.M. (1975), 'Alcoholism Treatment and Evaluations: In Search of Methods. II. Collation of Two Year Follow-up Studies', *International Journal of the Addictions*, vol. 10, no. 5, pp. 857-67.
4. Tillotson, K.J. and Fleming, R. (1937), 'Personality and Sociological Factors in Prognosis and Treatment of Chronic Alcoholism', *New England Journal of Medicine*, vol. 217, pp. 611-15.
5. Levinson, T. (1975), 'The Donwood Institute – a Five Year Follow-up Study', presented at the 31st International Congress on Alcoholism and Drug Dependence, Bangkok, Thailand.
6. Selzer, M.L. and Holloway, W.H. (1966), 'A Follow-up of Alcoholics Committed to a State Hospital', *Quarterly Journal of Studies on Alcohol*, vol. 18, pp. 98-120.
7. Kendell, R.E. and Staton, M.C. (1966), 'The Fate of Untreated Alcoholics', *Quarterly Journal of Studies on Alcohol*, vol. 27, pp. 30-41.
8. Charnoff, S.M., Kissin, B. and Reed, J.I. (1963), 'An Evaluation of Various Psychotherapeutic Agents in the Long-term Treatment of Chronic Alcoholism: Results of a Double-blind Study', *American Journal of Medical Science*, vol. 24b, pp. 172-9.
9. Wallace, J.A. (1952), 'A Comparison of Disulfiram Therapy and Routine Therapy in Alcoholism', *Quarterly Journal of Studies on Alcohol*, vol. 13, pp. 397-400.
10. Brehm, J.W. (1972), *Responses to Loss of Freedom: A Theory of Psychological Reactance* (General Learning Press, Morristown, New Jersey).
11. Finlay, D.G. (1978), 'Alcoholism and Systems Theory: Building a Better Mousetrap', *Psychiatry*, vol. 41, no. 3, pp. 272-8.
12. Myerson, D.J. (1956), ' "Skid Row" Problem: Further Observations on a Group of Alcoholic Patients, with Emphasis on Interpersonal Relations and Therapeutic Approach', *New England Journal of Medicine*, vol. 254, pp. 1168-73.
13. Dunne, J.A. (1975), 'Counseling Alcoholic Employees in a Municipal Police Department', *Quarterly Journal of Studies on Alcohol*, vol. 34, no. 2, pp. 423-34.
14. Costello, R.M. (1975), 'Alcoholism Treatment and Evaluation: In Search of Methods', *International Journal of the Addictions*, vol. 10, no. 2, pp. 251-75.
15. Bowen, W.T. and Androes, L. (1968), 'A Follow-up Study of 79 Alcoholic Patients: 1963-5', *Bulletin of the Menninger Clinic*, vol. 32, pp. 26-34.
16. Ellis, A.S. and Krupinski, J. (1964), 'The Evaluation of a Treatment Programme for Alcoholics: A Follow-up Study', *The Medical Journal of Australia*, vol. 1, pp. 8-13.
17. Hyman, M.M. (1976), 'Alcoholics 15 Years Later', *Annals of the New York Academy of Sciences*, vol. 273, pp. 613-23.
18. Imber, S., Schultz, E., Funderburk, F., Allen, R. and Flamer, R. (1976), 'The Fate of the Untreated Alcoholic: Toward a Natural History of the Disorder', *Journal of Nervous and Mental Disease*, vol. 162, no. 4, pp. 238-47.
19. Kanas, T.E., Cleveland, S.E., Pokorny, A.D. and Miller, B.A. (1976), 'Two Contrasting Alcoholism Treatment Programs: A Comparison of Outcomes', *International Journal of the Addictions*, vol. 11, no. 6, pp. 1045-62.

20. Nathan, D.E., Lipson, A.G., Vettraino, A.P. and Soloman, P. (1968), 'The Social Ecology of an Urban Clinic for Alcoholism: Racial Differences in Treatment Entry and Outcome', *International Journal of the Addictions*, vol.3, no. 1, pp. 55-63.

21. Pittman, D.J. and Tate, R.L. (1969), 'A Comparison of Two Treatment Programs for Alcoholics', *Quarterly Journal of Studies on Alcohol*, vol. 30, no. 4, pp. 888-99.

22. Rhodes, R.J. and Hudson, R.M. (1969), 'A Follow-up Study of Tuberculosis Skid Row Alcoholics. I. Social Adjustment and Drinking Behavior', *Quarterly Journal of Studies on Alcohol*, vol. 30, no. 1, pp. 119-28.

23. Wilson, A., White, J. and Lange, D.E. (1978), 'Outcome Evaluation of a Hospital-based Alcoholism Treatment Programme', *British Journal of Psychiatry*, vol. 73, pp. 39-45.

24. Costello, R.M., Giffen, M.B., Schneider, S.L., Edgington, P.W. and Manders, K.R. (1976), 'Comprehensive Alcohol Treatment Planning, Implementation, and Evaluation', *International Journal of the Addictions*, vol. 11, no. 4, pp. 553-70.

25. McCance, C. and McCance, P.F. (1969), 'Alcoholism in North-east Scotland: Its Treatment and Outcome', *British Journal of Psychiatry*, vol. 115, pp. 189-98.

26. Pfeffer, A.Z. and Berger, S. (1957), 'A Follow-up Study of Treated Alcoholics', *Quarterly Journal of Studies on Alcohol*, vol. 18, pp. 624-48.

27. Rae, J.B. (1972), 'The Influence of the Wives on the Treatment Outcome of Alcoholics: A Follow-up Study at Two Years', *British Journal of Psychiatry*, vol. 120, pp. 601-13.

28. Rossi, J.J., Stach, A. and Bradley, N.J. (1963), 'Effects of Treatment of Male Alcoholics in a Mental Hospital: A Follow-up Study', *Quarterly Journal of Studies on Alcohol*, vol. 24, pp. 91-108.

29. Walcott, E.P. and Straus, R. (1952), 'Use of a Hospital Facility in Conjunction with Outpatient Clinics in the Treatment of Alcoholics', *Quarterly Journal of Studies on Alcohol*, vol. 13, pp. 60-77.

30. Wiens, A.N., Montague, J.R., Manaugh, T.S. and English, C.J. (1976), 'Pharmacological Aversive Counterconditioning to Alcohol in a Private Hospital: One Year Follow-up', *Quarterly Journal of Studies on Alcohol*, vol. 37, no. 9, pp. 1320-4.

31. Zimberg, S. (1974), 'Evaluation of Alcoholism Treatment in Harlem', *Quarterly Journal of Studies on Alcohol*, vol. 35, no. 2, pp. 550-7.

32. Davies, D.L., Shepherd, M. and Myers, E. (1956), 'The Two Years' Prognosis of 50 Alcohol Addicts after Treatment in Hospital', *Quarterly Journal of Studies on Alcohol*, vol. 17, pp. 485-502.

33. Ferguson, F.N. (1970), 'A Treatment Program for Navaho Alcoholics: Results After Four Years', *Quarterly Journal of Studies on Alcohol*, vol. 31, pp. 898-919.

34. Maxwell, W.A., Baird, R.L., Wezl, T. and Ferguson, L. (1974), 'Discriminated Aversion Conditioning Within an Alcoholic Treatment Program in the Training of Controlled Drinking', *Behavioral Engineering*, vol. 11, no. 1, pp. 17-19.

35. Ritson, B. (1968), 'The Prognosis of Alcohol Addicts Treated by a Specialized Unit', *British Journal of Psychiatry*, vol. 114, pp. 1019-29.

36. Wilson, L.G. and Short, J.H. (1975), 'Evaluation of a Regional Indian Alcohol Program', *American Journal of Psychiatry*, vol. 132, no. 3, pp. 255-8.

37. Costello, R.M., Baillargeon, J.G., Biever, P. and Bennett, R. (1979), 'Therapeutic Community Treatment for Alcohol Abusers: A One Year Multivariate Outcome Evaluation', *International Journal of the Addictions* (in press).

38. Glatt, M.M. (1961), 'Drinking Habits of English (Middle Class) Alcoholics', *ACTA Psychiatrica Scandinavia*, vol. 37, pp. 88-113.
39. Prothro, W.B. (1961), 'Alcoholics Can be Rehabilitated', *American Journal of Public Health*, vol. 51, no. 3, pp. 450-61.
40. Rathod, N.H., Gregory, E., Blows, P. and Thomas, G.H. (1966), 'A Two Year Follow-up Study of Alcoholic Patients', *British Journal of Psychiatry*, vol. 112, pp. 683-92.
41. Smart, R.G. (1974), 'Employed Alcoholics Treated Voluntarily and Under Constructive Coercion: A Follow-up Study', *Quarterly Journal of Studies on Alcohol*, vol. 35, pp. 196-209.
42. Nie, N.H., Hull, C.H., Jenkins, J.H., Steinbrenner, K. and Bent, D.H. (1975), *Statistical Package for the Social Sciences* (McGraw-Hill, New York).
43. Smith, M.L. and Glass, G.V. (1977), 'Meta-analysis of Psychotherapy Outcome Studies', *American Psychologist*, vol. 32, no. 9, pp. 752-60.
44. Presby, S. (1978), 'Overly Broad Categories Obscure Important Differences Between Therapies', *American Psychologist*, vol. 33, no. 5, pp. 514-15.
45. Eysenck, H.J. (1978), 'An Exercise in Mega-silliness', *American Psychologist*, vol. 33, no. 5, p. 517.
46. Gallo, P.S. (1978), 'Meta-analysis – a Mixed Meta-phor?', *American Psychologist*, vol. 33, no. 5, pp. 515-17.
47. Rimland, B. (1979), 'Death Knell for Psychotherapy?', *American Psychologist*, vol. 34, no. 2, p. 192.
48. Kiesler, D.J. (1966), 'Some Myths of Psychotherapy Research and the Search for a Paradigm', *Psychological Bulletin*, vol. 65, pp. 110-36.
49. Campbell, D.T. and Stanley, J.C. (1963), *Experimental and Quasi-experimental Designs for Research* (Rand McNally & Co., Chicago).

8 TREATMENT OF ALCOHOLIC WOMEN

Helen M. Annis

There has been relatively little serious empirical investigation on the treatment of the woman alcoholic. Perhaps for this reason, one finds that the literature is dominated by rhetoric and speculation. Little of what passes as commonly accepted knowledge in the area is, in fact, founded on a sound empirical basis. What is lacking in evidence, however, is more than compensated for by myth. The area fairly abounds in a myriad of myths and speculative pronouncements. A major task facing the serious student of the woman alcoholic is that of distilling fact from fancy.

This chapter will therefore attempt this task with regard to the question of what is known about the treatment of the woman alcoholic. The presentation will be primarily concerned with examining, in a critical vein, one of the prominent clichés in the area. That is the claim that women alcoholics are harder to treat and have poorer prognosis than male alcoholics. It is this particular cliché that has led to a call for the provision of separate facilities and programming for women alcoholics, women self-help groups and variably for androgynous therapy and feminist counselling. But, before considering these or other possible alternative treatment strategies for the female alcoholic, let us first examine the strength of the evidence for the claim that women under traditional programming are more likely than men to be treatment failures.

Comparison of Male and Female Treatment Outcome

Evidence on this issue will be drawn from a major review of the relevant literature recently completed at the Addiction Research Foundation, Ontario.[1] This review involved a search of all English language reports published between 1950 and 1978 for sex-related outcome results on the treatment of alcoholics. The results of this search are summarised in Table 8.1.

Most notable is the very small number of reports (23) that were found to contain sex-related outcome information. This number contrasts sharply with the hundreds of outcome studies that have been

128

Table 8.1 Sex Differences in Treatment-outcome

Author	Year	Country
(a) *Studies Showing 'No Difference'* (N = 15)		
Davies, Shepherd and Myers[2]	1956	England
Selzer and Holloway[3]	1957	USA
Gerard and Saenger[4]	1966	USA
Pemberton[5]	1967	Scotland
Blake[6]	1967	Scotland
Ritson[7]	1968	Scotland
Bell and Levinson[8]	1971	Canada
Fitzgerald, Pasewark and Clark[9]	1971	USA
Bateman and Petersen[10]	1972	USA
Gillies, Laverty, Smart and Aharan[11]	1974	Canada
Blaney, Radford and MacKenzie[12]	1975	Ireland
Crawford[13]	1976	New Zealand
Browne-Mayers, Seelye and Sillman[14]	1976	USA
Glover and McCue[15]	1977	Scotland
McLachlan[16]	1978	Canada
(b) *Studies Showing Women More Improved* (N = 5)		
Fox and Smith[17]	1959	USA
Davis[18]	1966	USA
Dahlgren[19]	1975	Sweden
Ruggels, Mothershead, Ryszka, Loebel and Lotridge[20]	1977	USA
Kammeier[21]	1977	USA
(c) *Studies Showing Men More Improved* (N = 3)		
Hoff and McKeown[22]	1953	USA
Glatt[23]	1955	England
Glatt[24]	1961	England

published on the male alcoholic. Furthermore, it should be noted that in almost half of these reports (i.e. ten studies) the authors did not analyse for sex differences in outcome rates, but fortunately did provide within their reports sufficient raw data to allow us to perform the necessary statistical tests. Hence, the actual number of studies in which the authors directly tested for sex differences was very small indeed (13 studies). Comment might also be made on the distribution of studies over time. Only one report could be found with sex-related data presentation prior to 1955, whereas eight reports originated within the most recent three year period reviewed (i.e. 1975-8). Given that the alcoholism treatment research literature in general has exploded in recent years, the size of the increase in sex-related data presentation is very modest. This remains a seriously under-researched area. The great majority of outcome reports continue to focus on male-only samples, or include females in largely male samples with no attention to possible sex differences in treatment-outcome results.

Within the small number of available published reports, do female alcoholics have poorer outcome than male alcoholics? The empirical evidence appears to question the validity of this commonly-held belief. Fifteen reports failed to find differences in remission rates for male and female alcoholics following treatment; five studies provided evidence of better improvement rates among females; while three studies supported the contention of better prognosis following treatment among males. It is interesting to note that all three of the studies showing greater male improvement were very early reports (1953, 1955 and 1961), while the literature of the last fifteen years has either failed to find evidence of sex differences in outcome or has found women to be significantly more improved. The clinic populations involved have been drawn widely from England, Ireland, Scotland, New Zealand, Sweden, Canada and the United States.

Accounting for Divergent Outcome Results: Treatment Findings

The studies were examined to determine whether treatment-related factors or differences in study methodology might account for the divergent outcome results observed. With regard to treatment variables, the findings were as follows:

Treatment Setting. The literature reviewed was concerned almost entirely with the effects of hospital inpatient treatment. The great majority of the studies (20 out of 23) involved the effects of inpatient hospital treatment either alone or in conjunction with an outpatient aftercare component. Studies within the discrepant outcome groups were very similar on this dimension. Hence, type of treatment setting could not account for the observed sex differences in treatment outcome.

Length of Programme. Study groups also showed little difference in terms of the length of inpatient or outpatient treatment given and there was no consistent trend for studies finding greater improvement for females to be based on treatment intervention programmes of a long or short duration.

Treatment Modalities. All studies reviewed involved the evaluation of multi-modal treatment packages rather than specific individual treatment techniques. However, considerable variation existed in the components of the treatment packages between studies. No evidence was found that particular therapy modalities characterised programmes in which women showed higher success rates.

It has frequently been argued that individual counselling programmes may be better suited to the needs of the woman alcoholic than group-based techniques.[25,26,5] The present analysis of outcome results provides no support for this proposition. Group therapy characterised four of the five studies reporting better outcome results for females than males, and in one of these studies,[17] group therapy was described as the 'backbone' of the therapeutic programme. In a similar vein, it has been suggested that women may find it more difficult to relate to the group processes and feelings of membership involved in AA.[27] Once again, the present review fails to yield supporting evidence. In one study reporting better outcomes for women,[21] women were found to be more active participants in AA than men and more conscientious followers of the AA programme. With multi-modal treatment packages, it is difficult to attribute change to any particular treatment component. Nevertheless, present evidence fails to provide any basis for concluding the inappropriateness of group techniques for the female alcoholic.

Sex of Therapist. It has frequently been suggested that the female alcoholic may make better progress in therapy with a female therapist.[28,29] Unfortunately, insufficient information is provided in most of the studies reviewed to assess the influence that sex of therapist might have had on the overall outcome results observed. It has been pointed out[28] that the Donwood Institute in Toronto employs a large number of female staff as therapists; in both of the studies conducted at the Donwood,[8,16] no sex difference in treatment outcome was found. Gomberg[26] has noted that the study by Fox and Smith[17] showing women more improved than men, is by two professional women therapists. Only one empirical investigation could be found bearing on this issue.[20] As part of the recent follow-up study of NIAA-funded Alcoholism Treatment Centers in the United States, the relationship of sex of therapist to treatment outcome was examined. Because of the national scope, diversity of patients and treatments, and range of outcome measures employed, this is the most comprehensive alcoholism treatment evaluation undertaken to date. Overall, female patients showed significantly higher remission rates than male patients.

Remission rates for both males and females remained unaffected by the sex of the therapist. However, one caveat should be added. It is not known how many of the female therapists involved in this study were sympathetic to non-sexist counselling techniques or to feminist theories of emotional distress among women. The efficacy of such treatment approaches with the female alcoholic have not yet been submitted to empirical test.

In summary, there was no evidence that the treatment-related factors examined could account for the differential outcome results reported for male and female alcoholics.

Accounting for Divergent Outcome Results: Methodological Factors

Length of Follow-up Period. Most of the outcome studies reviewed involved simple follow-up designs with an absence of randomised control groups. Very little is presently known about possible differences in the natural (i.e. non-treated) course of outcome for male and female alcoholics. Consequently it could be argued that sex-related outcome results observed within any single study might simply be a reflection of differences between the sexes in natural outcome processes. Was there any evidence that women showed more favourable response than men under longer or shorter follow-up periods? The wide range of follow-up intervals (six months to six years) represented across studies permitted an examination of this possibility. However, no evidence was found that sex differences in outcome results were related to length of the follow-up interval. Of course, it is still possible that differences between the sexes in outcome may relate more to non-treatment than treatment factors. More research attention needs to be devoted to the issue of sex differences in the natural course of outcome.

Sex of Patients Lost to Follow-up. There is now considerable evidence that patients lost to follow-up are a serious source of sampling bias.[30,31] For purposes of analysis, such patients are best considered treatment failures.[32-34] When examining sex differences in treatment outcome, this can be an important consideration if more patients of one sex than the other are lost to follow-up. Consequently, the 23 studies under review were searched for information on the sex breakdown within the unsuccessful follow-up group, and in all cases in which such information was provided, outcome statistics were calculated including cases lost to follow-up within the unimproved groups. Studies permitting categorisation on the basis of this calculation were fairly evenly distributed across the three discrepant outcome groups. Therefore, it is unlikely that this factor accounts for the sex-related outcome differences between studies.

Nature of the Outcome Criteria. Divergent study findings may be a function of differences in the outcome criteria employed to measure improvement. Some criteria may be more appropriate measures of success for male than female alcoholics, and vice versa. Were there systematic differences in outcome criteria employed across study groups? In all but two of the 15 studies finding no sex differences, the outcome criterion was drinking behaviour — generally divided into categories such as abstinent/improved/unimproved. A similar criterion applied in the three studies finding a more favourable treatment response in men and in three of the five studies finding women significantly more improved. Such a simple drinking improvement criterion is probably equally appropriate for assessing change in men and women, although multiple indices of adjustment would provide a more sensitive, comprehensive outcome assessment.

It is interesting to note that only two of the studies finding more improvement in males[24, 22] and two finding more improvement in females[18, 20] were based on a drinking-outcome criterion. One study concluding that male alcoholics had better treatment results than female alcoholics,[23] demonstrated significantly more improvement for males only in the area of work adjustment. It is unlikely that this outcome measure is 'sex fair' since many of the female alcoholics studied in England during the early 1950s were probably not in the work force.

The development and refinement of outcome criteria is an underresearched area in the treatment field. Such criteria should be sensitive to change in a wide range of areas and weighted for their importance to functioning for specific groups of alcoholics. For example, outcome measures relating to child care and homemaking would have special relevance to the measurement of improvement in some female alcoholics.[35] If our understanding of sex-related differences in outcome is to be increased, more attention needs to be paid to the appropriateness and sensitivity of the criterion measures employed.

Prognostic Factors

Although most work on patient prognostic factors has focussed on the male alcoholic, some studies have examined good and poor prognostic indicators for the female alcoholic. Housewife status and living with a spouse have been found to be relatively strong prognostic indicators of improvement following treatment, as has age status 45 or over and membership of a club.[10,4,36] Among poor prognostic indicators that have been documented are: alcoholism in parents or siblings; mental illness in primary relatives; psychopathy; early involvement in regular, excessive drinking; abuse of other drugs; and alcohol-related physical complications.[37,38,24] The evidence on positive prognostic indicators, particularly, suggests that the home situation as well as social ties outside the home are of great importance in treatment outcome for the female alcoholic. This agrees with reported clinical observation that women living alone make comparatively poor response to treatment, and that successful female patients typically modify the structure of their familial group to establish for themselves a personally satisfying role within it.[5]

Table 8.2: Female Detoxification Sample: Self-identified Treatment Needs (%)

Residential (e.g. halfway house)	46
In-hospital care	15
Outpatient clinic	16
AA	41
Individual counselling	39
Group counselling	60
female only	16
mixed male and female	15
no choice	28
Sex of therapist	
male	2
female	10
no choice	38

Source: Tetu, S. and Shore, D.[39]

Self-identified Treatment Needs

It is also of importance to assess treatment needs as perceived by different groups of female alcoholics. For example, among a female detoxication population in Ontario reported on by Tetu and Shore,[39] residential care outside of a hospital setting was seen as most appropriate (Table 8.2). In addition, group therapy was viewed as somewhat more attractive than individual counselling approaches. This finding is in contrast to the often quoted study by Curlee[25] in which more socially stable women admitted to a private alcoholism rehabilitation facility in the United States ranked individual counselling as more helpful than group techniques. In contrast also to Pemberton's clinical observations,[5] it seems clear that not all types of female alcoholics are looking for individualised one-to-one relationships. Among the majority of women in the detoxification sample[39] who expressed interest in receiving counselling help. there was no consistent preference expressed for a male or female counsellor, and no fixed notions on the desirability of male, female or mixed therapy groups. Systematic study is needed of the role of these factors in treatment outcome for various groups of female alcoholics.

Background Characteristics and Precipitating Causes

Demographic and background characteristics of 200 admissions to the Addiction Research Foundation's Clinical Institute in Toronto were examined. Approximately 25 per cent of these admissions were female. Discriminant analysis indicated that compared to male alcoholics seeking treatment, the female alcoholics: were younger with shorter drinking history and lower lifetime consumption of alcohol; had lower current involvement with alcohol (as measured by the MAST); had more problems with both prescription and illicit drugs; had lower legal income; and had shorter treatment history and higher social stability scores. The latter factor implied that, on the whole, the female alcoholic admissions had more stable living arrangements than the males. Once again the possibility is raised of capitalising on the home situation of the female alcoholic by involving significant others (relatives, spouse or stable companion) in treatment programming.

There is some evidence that female alcoholics are more likely than men to attribute the onset of their problem drinking to a particular life stress or traumatic event.[40,41] Again drawing on data from admissions to the Clinical Institute, more women (44 per cent) than men (25 per cent) gave as their reason for referral a crisis related to their use of alcohol or other drugs. Gomberg[26] has noted that if alcoholism in women is indeed more often a reactive disorder with abrupt onset and precipitating stress, prognosis should be better. The stresses typically defined by female alcoholics tend to be familial and interpersonal.[42,43] Attention needs to be devoted to the adaptation of therapeutic procedures so that they are more directly responsive to the specific nature of the female alcoholic's presenting concerns. For example, since disruption of familial relationships is frequently a major problem for many female alcoholics, family intervention techniques should receive greater research attention. In view of the apparently important role played by situational precipitating events for women alcoholics, various other environmental intervention strategies may also prove to be particularly appropriate.

Conclusion

Empirical evidence is almost totally lacking on effective treatment modalities for the female alcoholic. Unfortunately, the same is largely true for the male alcoholic as well. Current broad-gauged outcome research addressed to sex differences in response to multi-modal treatment packages needs to be redirected. Major methodological and conceptual changes in research approach are indicated.[44-46] What is needed to advance knowledge on the treatment of the female alcoholic is the systematic study of the response of different types of female alcoholics to a range of specific treatment interventions.

Since the female alcoholic population is not homogeneous, it is extremely unlikely that a single form of treatment will be equally efficacious for all. In fact, the typical procedure of pooling results across all female alcoholic patients may obscure significant improvement within sub-groups. A wide variety of prognostic variables, background characteristics, precipitating factors, and presenting problems and needs have been identified among female alcoholics. These could well provide the basis for the development of specific treatment intervention procedures. It is unlikely, for example, that the needs of the female alcoholic in the workforce are the same as those of the teenage alcoholic, the alcoholic housewife, the alcoholic middle age spinster, the 'empty-nest' alcoholic, or the alcoholic female on skid row. Further directions that have been suggested for specifying types of female alcoholics for study include: primary versus affective disorder alcoholics;[47] process versus reactive alcoholics;[26] chronicity, consumption levels and patterns, and situational determinants of drinking;[48] and a variety of personality dimensions.[49,50] Rather than offering the same basic package of help to all, a range of clearly-defined alternative treatment strategies is needed to meet the specific presenting needs of the particular sub-group of female alcoholics being served. Research addressed to these specific patient-treatment combinations should expand our knowledge on how best to design treatment for the individual female alcoholic.

Notes

1. Annis, H.M. and Liban, C. (1979), 'Alcoholism in Women: Treatment Modalities and Outcomes', in Kalant, O. (ed.), *Research Advances in Alcohol and Drug Problems: vol. 5. Alcohol and Drug Problems in Women* (Plenum Press, New York).
2. Davies, D.L., Shepherd, M. and Myers, E. (1956), 'The Two-years' Prognosis of 50 Alcohol Addicts after Treatment in Hospital', *Quarterly Journal of Studies on Alcohol*, vol. 17, pp. 485-502.
3. Selzer, M.L. and Holloway, W.H. (1957), 'A Follow-up of Alcoholics Committed to a State Hospital', *Quarterly Journal of Studies on Alcohol*, vol. 18, pp. 98-120.
4. Gerard, D.L. and Saenger, G. (1966), *Outpatient Treatment of Alcoholism* (University of Toronto Press, Toronto).
5. Pemberton, D.A. (1967), 'A Comparison of the Outcome of Treatment in Female and Male Alcoholics', *British Journal of Psychiatry*, vol. 113, pp. 367-73.
6. Blake, B.G. (1967), 'A Follow-up of Alcoholics Treated by Behaviour Therapy', *Behaviour Research and Therapy*, vol. 5, pp. 89-94.
7. Ritson, B. (1968), 'The Prognosis of Alcohol Addicts Treated by a Specialized Unit', *British Journal of Psychiatry*, vol. 114, pp. 1019-29.
8. Bell, R.G. and Levinson, T. (1971), 'An Evaluation of the Donwood Institute Treatment Program', *Ontario Medical Review*, vol. 38, pp. 219-26.
9. Fitzgerald, B.J., Pasewark, R.A. and Clark, R. (1971), 'Four-year Follow-up of Alcoholics Treated at a Rural State Hospital', *Quarterly Journal of Studies on Alcohol*, vol. 32, pp. 636-42.
10. Bateman, N.I. and Petersen, D.M. (1972), 'Factors Related to Outcome of Treatment for Hospitalized White Male and Female Alcoholics', *Journal of Drug Issues*, vol. 2, pp. 66-74.
11. Gillies, M., Laverty, S.G., Smart, R.G. and Aharan, C.H. (1974), 'Outcome in Treated Alcoholics: Patient and Treatment Characteristics in a One Year Follow-up Study', *Journal of Alcoholism*, vol. 9, pp. 125-34.
12. Blaney, R., Radford, I.S. and MacKenzie, G. (1975), 'A Belfast Study of the Prediction of Outcome in the Treatment of Alcoholism', *British Journal of Addiction*, vol. 70, pp. 41-50.
13. Crawford, R.J.M. (1976), 'Treatment Success in Alcoholism', *New Zealand Medical Journal*, vol. 84, pp. 93-6.
14. Browne-Mayers, A.N., Seelye, E.E. and Sillman, L. (1976), 'Psychosocial Study of Hospitalized Middle-class Alcoholic Women', in Seixas, F.A. and Eggleston, S. (eds.), *Work in Progress on Alcoholism* (Annals of the New York Academy of Sciences, New York), pp. 593-604.
15. Glover, J.H. and McCue, P.A. (1977), 'Electrical Aversion Therapy with Alcoholics: A Comparative Follow-up Study'. *British Journal of Psychiatry*, vol. 130, pp. 279-86.
16. McLachlan, J. (1978), 'Sex Differences in Recovery Rates After One Year', Research Note no. 9 (The Donwood Institute, Toronto).
17. Fox, V. and Smith, M.A. (1959), 'Evaluation of a Chemopsychotherapeutic Program for the Rehabilitation of Alcoholics', *Quarterly Journal of Studies on Alcohol*, vol. 20, pp. 767-80.

18. Davis, H.G. (1966), 'Variables Associated with Recovery in Male and Female Alcoholics Following Hospitalization', doctoral dissertation, Texas Technological College.

19. Dahlgren, L. (1975), 'Special Problems in Female Alcoholism', *British Journal of Addiction*, vol. 70 (Suppl. no. 1), pp. 18-24.

20. Ruggels, W.L., Mothershead, A., Ryszka, R., Loebel, M and Lotridge, J. (1977), 'A Follow-up Study of Clients at Selected Alcoholism Treatment Centers Funded by NIAAA (Supplemental Report)' (Stanford Research Institute, Menlo Park, California).

21. Kammeier, M.L. (1977), 'Alcoholism is the Common Denominator: More Evidence on the Male/Female Question', Hazelden Papers no. 2 (Center City, Minnesota).

22. Hoff, E.C. and McKeown, C.E. (1953), 'An Evaluation of the Use of Tetraethylthiuram Disulfide in the Treatment of 560 Cases of Alcohol Addiction', *American Journal of Psychiatry*, vol. 109, pp. 670-73.

23. Glatt, M.M. (1955), 'A Treatment Centre for Alcoholics in a Public Mental Hospital: Its Establishment and its Working', *British Journal of Addiction*, vol. 52, pp. 55-92.

24. Glatt, M.M. (1961), 'Treatment Results in an English Mental Hospital Alcoholic Unit', *Acta Psychiatrica Scandinavica*, vol. 37, pp. 143-68.

25. Curlee, J. (1971), 'Sex Differences in Patient Attitudes Toward Alcoholism Treatment', *Quarterly Journal of Studies on Alcohol*, vol. 32, pp. 643-50.

26. Gomberg, E.S. (1974), 'Women and Alcoholism', in Franks, V. and Burtle, V. (eds.), *Women in Therapy* (Brunner/Mazel, New York), pp. 169-90.

27. Curlee, J. (1967), 'Alcoholic Women: Some Considerations for Further Research', *Bulletin of the Menninger Clinic*, vol. 31, pp. 154-63.

28. Birchmore, D.F. and Walderman, R.L. (1975), 'The Woman Alcoholic: A Review', *The Ontario Psychologist*, vol. 7, pp. 10-16.

29. Calobrisi, A. (1976), 'Treatment Programs in Alcoholic Women', in Greenblatt, M. and Schuckit, M. (eds.), *Alcoholism Problems in Women and Children* (Grune and Stratton Incorporated, New York), pp. 155-62.

30. Baekeland, F., Lundwall, L. and Kissin, B. (1975), 'Methods for the Treatment of Chronic Alcoholism: A Critical Appraisal', in Gibbins, R.J., Israel, Y., Kalant, H., Popham, R.E., Schmidt, W. and Smart, R.E. (eds.), *Research Advances in Alcohol and Drug Problems*, vol. 2 (John Wiley and Sons, Toronto), pp. 247-327.

31. Hill, M.J. and Blane, H.T. (1967), 'Evaluation of Psychotherapy with Alcoholics: A Critical Review', *Quarterly Journal of Studies on Alcohol*, vol. 28, pp. 76-104.

32. Miller, B.A., Pokorny, A.D., Valles, J. and Cleveland, S.E. (1970), 'Biased Sampling in Alcoholism Treatment Research', *Quarterly Journal of Studies on Alcohol*, vol. 31, pp. 97-107.

33. Vannicelli, M., Pfau, B. and Ryback, R.S. (1976), 'Data Attrition in Follow-up Studies of Alcoholics', *Journal of Studies on Alcohol*, vol. 37, pp. 1325-30.

34. Wolff, S. and Holland, L. (1964), 'A Questionnaire Follow-up of Alcoholic Patients', *Quarterly Journal of Studies on Alcohol*, vol. 25, pp. 108-18.

35. Homiller, J.D. (1978), 'Sex Bias in Alcoholism Research: Marked Absence of Female-specific Data', *Focus on Alcohol and Drug Issues*, vol. 1, no. 4, p. 11.

36. Bromet, E. and Moos, R.H. (1977), 'Environmental Resources and the Post-treatment Functioning of Alcoholic Patients', *Journal of Health and Social Behaviour*, vol. 18, pp. 326-38.

37. Thomas, D.A. (1971), 'A Study of Selected Factors on Successfully and Unsuccessfully Treated Alcoholic Women', doctoral dissertation, Michigan State

University.
38. Schuckit, M.A. and Winokur, G. (1972), 'A Short-term Follow-up of Women Alcoholics'. *Diseases of the Nervous System*, vol. 33, pp. 672-8.
39. Tetu, S. and Shore, D. (1977), 'A Survey of Treatment Needs of Women with Drug-Related Problems', unpublished manuscript, Ottawa.
40. Lolli, G. (1953), 'Alcoholism in Women', *Connecticut Review on Alcoholism*, vol. 5, pp. 9-11.
41. Lisansky, E.S. (1957), 'Alcoholism in Women: Social and Psychological Concomitants. I. Social History Data', *Quarterly Journal of Studies on Alcohol*, vol. 18, pp. 588-623.
42. Edwards, G., Hensman, C. and Peto, J. (1972), 'Drinking in a London Suburb. III. Comparison of Drinking Troubles among Men and Women', *Quarterly Journal of Studies on Alcohol*, Supplement no. 6, pp. 120-8.
43. Sclare, A.B. (1970), 'The Female Alcoholic', *British Journal of Addiction*, vol. 65, pp. 99-107.
44. Annis, H. (1973), 'Directions in Treatment Research', *Addictions*, vol. 20, pp. 50-9.
45. Glaser, F.B. (1977), 'Comment on "Alcoholism: A Controlled Trial of 'Treatment' and 'Advice' " ', *Journal of Studies on Alcohol*, vol. 38, pp. 1819-27.
46. Kissin, B. (1977), 'Comment on "Alcoholism: A Controlled Trial of 'Treatment' and 'Advice' " ', *Journal of Studies on Alcohol*, vol. 38, pp. 1804-8.
47. Schuckit, M., Pitts, F.N., Jr., Reich, T., King, L.T. and Winokur, G. (1969), 'Alcoholism. I. Two Types of Alcoholism in Women', *Archives of General Psychiatry*, vol. 20, pp. 301-6.
48. Marlatt, G.A. (1975), 'The Drinking Profile: A Questionnaire for the Behavioural Assessment of Alcoholism', in Marsh, E.J. and Terdal, L.G. (eds.), *Behaviour Therapy Assessment: Diagnosis and Evaluation* (Springer, New York).
49. Waller, S. and Lorch, B. (1978), 'Social and Psychological Characteristics of Alcoholics: A Male-female Comparison', *International Journal of the Addictions*, vol. 13, pp. 201-12.
50. Skinner, H.A., Jackson, D.N. and Hoffmann, H. (1974), 'Alcoholic Personality Types: Identification and Correlates', *Journal of Abnormal Psychology*, vol. 83, pp. 658-66.

Part Three

TOWARDS BETTER QUESTIONS AND BETTER METHODOLOGIES

9 UNDERSTANDING TREATMENT: CONTROLLED TRIALS AND OTHER STRATEGIES

Jim Orford

An Illustration of the Strengths and Weaknesses of a Controlled Trial

The trial which will be used here to illustrate some of the problems with this method is the comparison of treatment and advice given to two groups of married men with drinking problems, and their wives, carried out at the Addiction Research Unit, London. The main findings have been reported elsewhere.[1,2] The basic design of that trial is shown in Figure 9.1. Twelve months after assignments to either treatment or advice, there were no differences between the two groups in terms of drinking behaviour, drinking-related problems, assessment of improvement, or social adjustment − either by the husbands' or their wives' accounts. A number of useful criticisms of this study appeared in the *Journal of Studies on Alcohol*[3,4,5] after these findings were first reported there, and this chapter will draw upon these criticisms in speaking of the strengths and weaknesses of such a research design.

Most of those who have commented upon this trial, either critically or otherwise, have taken its findings seriously. It is after all one of the very few studies which has randomly assigned people with serious drinking problems to groups receiving treatment of differing intensities, the more minimal being so minimal that it begins to approach 'no treatment'. The bold, and in our view inappropriately uncautious, conclusion is that treatment for alcoholism does not work. Criticisms of this study can be subsumed under four headings. These four aspects − the clients, the therapists, the treatments, and the outcome − constitute the meat upon which clinical researchers chew when struggling with the design of a treatment trial, and which critics examine minutely during the post-mortem. They are, of course, the very same issues which preoccupy those concerned with the parallel but wider subject of psychotherapy research.[6,7]

Taking the *clients* first, there is one general point to be made and three subsidiary points. The general point about which everyone is in agreement in theory, although it is not always acted upon in practice, is that the clients must be described as fully as is possible. As well as reporting basic demographic details, which should be but is not always

Figure 9.1: Design of the Study of 100 Couples

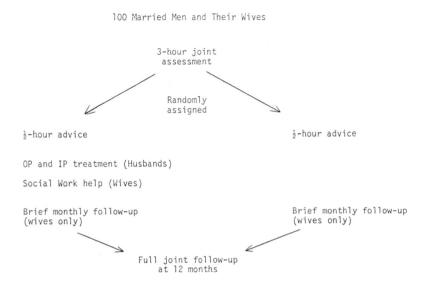

100 Married Men and Their Wives

3-hour joint
assessment

Randomly
assigned

½-hour advice

½-hour advice

OP and IP treatment (Husbands)

Social Work help (Wives)

Brief monthly follow-up
(wives only)

Brief monthly follow-up
(wives only)

Full joint follow-up
at 12 months

a matter of routine, studies in the area of alcohol problems should describe the drinking behaviour, drink-related problems, other problems, history of problems and help-seeking, and the social circumstances of their clients.

The first subsidiary point about clients concerns what Campbell and Stanley[8] in their seminal analysis of experimental design and its alternatives, called a study's 'external validity'. They distinguished between the internal validity of a study, which concerns the degree to which valid conclusions can be drawn about the effectiveness of different treatments for this particular client group in the particular circumstances of this particular study, and its external validity, which is the extent to which these conclusions can be generalised to other client groups in other circumstances. The strength of the experimental design, and in its clinical form the randomised controlled trial, lies particularly in its internal validity. We can be more confident with a controlled trial, although even then by no means certain, that different outcomes are the result of different treatments rather than to differences in client characteristics, to the passage of time, or to some unintended and unmeasured difference in experience. On the other hand the controlled trial can lay no greater claim to external validity than can any other design. This was certainly one of the grounds upon which the 'study of a hundred couples' was quite legitimately criticised. The most obvious limitation of our sample was that it was confined to couples who had intact marriages at the time, although it must be pointed out that the quality and stability of those marriages were very variable indeed. Nevertheless, it is quite reasonable to argue that the results cannot confidently be generalised to apply to samples of unmarried clients, or indeed to married women with drinking problems and their husbands. There are surely many other respects in addition in which our sample was special. This merely argues for the need to replicate a study with different samples, if the original findings are thought to be important enough to warrant it.

The second subsidiary point about clients has to do with the homo-geneity of the sample. The need for homogeneous samples in treatment research has been strongly put many times, for example by Bergin[9] in the *Handbook of Psychotherapy and Behaviour Change*. It is of par-ticular concern in the wider field of psychotherapy research because samples are frequently so very heterogeneous, often covering a range of traditional psychiatric diagnoses, people with drinking problems being one of the few groups regularly omitted. A point made by several commentators on the study of 100 couples was that we were unable to detect the real differences that may exist in outcome after treatment and advice because of the heterogeneity of our sample. There is certainly logic in the argument that, with the exception of the variables sex and marital status, our sample was as varied as our referral agents made it, and that the detection of main or interactional effects requires a much larger heterogeneous sample, or alternatively a much more restricted homogeneous sample. Some of us may now feel that we know the parameters in terms of which to restrict treatment samples – degree of dependence might be a strong candidate, for example.[10] Although it might at first appear otherwise, homogeneity could improve external validity. We might be in a position to argue with greater confidence that our results can be generalised to other samples restricted in the same way as our own.

The third point about clients begins to take us away from issues that are strictly methodological and on to broader issues to do with the very nature of alcohol problems and their treatment. Many of us have been brought up in a school of thinking that can be broadly designated 'clinical'. The bias of our teachers was towards viewing an alcohol problem as the property of an individual, if not as a disease. Hence we continue to persevere with the notion that it is things about the individual — demographic features, drinking pattern and history, personality — which are most important for defining the sample, for increasing homogeneity, and for giving us the best chance of increasing the proportion of outcome variance which we can explain. Moos and his colleagues have argued for the need to assess the extent and quality of clients' environmental resources. For example, Bromet and Moos[11] have confirmed what many others have found, namely that the presence of marital and occupational resources confers a favourable prognosis, and furthermore, that when such resources exist, the perceived quality of these environments has predictive significance. The lower the degree of marital conflict and, for unmarried clients, the greater the degree of job commitment and peer cohesion at work, the better the outcome of the drinking problem. The finding for marital conflict is very parallel to one of our findings from the study of 100 couples, namely that higher levels of marital cohesion predicted a better outcome.[12] Although Bromet and Moos found that quality of the work environment was only important for unmarried subjects, several of our clients at the end of the study attributed improvement to finding more satisfying or higher status jobs.

The distinction here is that between a thorough-going clinical or psychotherapeutic orientation and a thorough-going community or environmental modification orientation.[13,14] Hunt and Azrin's[15] 'community-reinforcement' approach is the only documented example of an approach to the treatment of alcohol problems, known to this author, which attempts to break away from the predominantly clinical or psychotherapeutic model (using the term psychotherapeutic to include all psychological forms of therapy including behaviour therapy and behaviour modification). Their approach was certainly a clinical-cum-community compromise, because their clients were identified patients, rather than a whole community, and their rationale was a behaviour modification one — making improved resources contingent upon modified drinking behaviour. It seems likely that the effective ingredient was the improved quality of life that they were able to bring about for some of their clients by helping them find jobs and putting them in touch with substitute family and friends. One hypothesis which makes sense of the findings of the study of 100 couples, and of much other research besides, is that excessive drinking comes and goes in response to life events and circumstances beside which formal treatment has little impact.

So much for clients; what about *therapists*? The therapist is a much
neglected variable in alcoholism treatment research. Much more attention has been paid to the therapist as a variable in psychotherapy
research, with much more emphasis on the importance of the therapist
in verbal psychotherapy studies than in studies of behaviour therapy.[16]
Strangely enough none of those who commented upon the study of
100 couples appears to have commented upon what seems to us a far
more serious limitation upon external validity than that imposed by
limiting the sample to married men and their wives. We were only able
to study one particular hospital setting with its own peculiarities of
referral system, induction and reputation, and we were only able to
include a small handful of staff people including, for example, only two
psychiatrists, one of whom was responsible for the care of three-
quarters of the patients. Therapists and settings were sampled far less
adequately than clients, and if the findings of the study are important
at all, it needs replicating in different places and with different personnel. In general, authors of research reports have surely as much
reponsibility to describe therapists — their age, sex, socioeconomic
status, training, experience and orientation, for example — as they do
the characteristics of their clients.

There is relatively less need to say much about *treatment* itself, as
relatively much space is always devoted to describing the nature of
treatment in research reports. There are three points to be made here
however. They concern treatment quality control, the cost of treatment, and the client's perception of treatment. Quality control is
particularly important in any controlled trial which involves different
treatments of different intensity or prestige. Clients receiving treatments of lesser intensity or prestige may experience lowered morale
or expectation of good outcome if they know of the existence of
treatments of higher prestige or greater intensity. Indeed it was this
very factor which Emrick[17] concluded was responsible for the findings
of those very few alcoholism treatment studies reported up to 1973
which involved random assignment or adequate matching of clients in
different treatment groups and which produced significant differences
in outcome between groups. Although this was not a problem in the
study of 100 couples, we faced a related problem, that of maintaining
the essential intended difference between two treatments of different
intensities. We had to do all we could to prevent the naturally occurring
processes whereby brief treatment becomes prolonged because of
clients' demands and clinicians' sensitivities, and treatment intended to

be relatively lengthy becomes less so on account of the reluctance of both clients and therapists. We would like to think that we presented enough evidence to show that we were sufficiently successful in repressing those natural tendencies to maintain two distinct treatment groups.

Those who report treatment research rarely make a serious attempt to cost their treatments. It seems quite clear that our 'advice' approach was considerably less costly than our 'treatment' approach. Miller's[18] study is another recent example of an alcoholism treatment investigation demonstrating little difference in outcome between treatments differing in cost. Clients were randomly assigned to one of three behavioural treatments, one of which turned out to be no more effective than the others despite requiring four times more therapist-client contact than the others. The argument that financial cost is a dirty consideration and will be seized upon by administrators eager to save money by cutting resources for people with drinking problems, cuts little ice. It is our responsibility to press for continued and increased resources if we think these are required and our position is surely strengthened rather than weakened by being able to demonstrate that we can do more with the same amount of money.

Lastly, under the treatment heading, there remains a nagging doubt about the real nature of the treatment enterprise. We are good at reporting what we meant to do and what we did in theory, but is that always the same as what we did do, or what our clients thought we did? We know, to take just two fairly concrete examples, that patients very often do not take the medicines which they are prescribed, or in the way advised, and that information doctors give to patients is often given in too complex a form so that patients fail to comprehend and remember, let alone act upon, much advice that they are given.[19] How much more room there is in a complex psychotherapeutic encounter for differences in perception between therapists and clients about what is going on, and how much more scope there is for types of impact which are quite unintended in theory.

There is little that is more fraught in the study of alcoholism treatment than the question of *outcome* assessment. Several of our critics pointed out the lack of the proper double-blind procedures which have become the hallmark of adequate drug trials.[5] Although we can point out that most of the initial assessments were carried out prior to, and therefore without knowledge of, random assignment to groups, that the same set of staff were involved in both 'treatment' and 'advice', and that the final assessment was carried out by a team of three people one of whom was not involved in the treatment or advice itself, nevertheless none of these points fully answers the criticism. The final assessment in such a study could conceivably be carried out by an investigator ignorant about the study, its hypotheses, or treatment group membership; such a procedure has been employed by Vogler and his colleagues[20, 21] in their studies of treatment for hospital and community problem drinkers. It is more difficult to see how the actual administration of treatments could be carried out to satisfy double-blind requirements.

Secondly there is the question of reliability of drinking outcome measures. The study of 100 couples can be criticised for its excessive reliance upon husbands' and wives' recall of past events. The few apparently more objective alternatives which are available — breath tests, taste tests, and operant tasks[22] — do not convincingly offer a more reliable alternative, but there is certainly a need to bolster the client's self-report with the report of a well informed collateral as in the study of 100 couples and Sobell and Sobell's[23] study. However there is certainly room for more studies such as that of McCrady *et al.*[24] reporting upon the degree of consensus between client and collateral. Given that the two are positively but imperfectly matched, there then arises the problem of putting together two discrepant pieces of information if one wishes to make a statement about the outcome of a particular person. For part of the analysis of the study of 100 couples we adopted the unsatisfactory procedure of consigning some couples to an 'equivocal' outcome category on the basis of a disagreement between husband and wife, although we were all well aware that this group contained some people who in truth had done extremely badly and perhaps others who in truth had done extremely well.

Self-accounts, as well as accounts about spouses, are of course extremely 'reactive' measures, to use the term employed by Smith and Glass[7] in their comprehensive analysis of psychotherapy outcome studies. The reactivity of the measures employed in the various studies they examined was just one factor which was examined alongside others in a multiple regression analysis. The importance of reactivity of outcome measures is illustrated by their comparison of verbal and behavioural psychotherapy, a comparison which was a particular focus of their analysis. Over all studies combined, behavioural psychotherapy showed a very modest lead over verbal forms of therapy, but this lead shrank to minute proportions when account was taken of the fact that behavioural studies tended to use more reactive measures (and incidentally to assess a shorter follow-up period — another factor influencing outcome results).

The bigger question about the assessment of outcome remains the old and thorny one of criteria for success. It is now some time since Pattison[25] warned us of the dangers of relying upon abstinence from alcohol as the sole criterion, and his warning has probably now been heeded by most of us. This matter, which has preoccupied psychotherapy researchers for as long as there has been psychotherapy research will not be discussed here any further. Outcome assessment in the study of 100 couples relied largely, although not exclusively, upon data concerning the husband's drinking. Assessment in this area is something which alcohologists are particularly preoccupied with and like to think they are particularly good at, and probably most of us pay less heed to other areas of life adjustment. Suffice it so say that much depends upon the location and orientation of the therapy researcher. Most of us are specialists working in specialist settings and this conditions our preoccupation with drinking. But most people with drinking problems are not helped in specialist settings, and workers in non-specialist settings are much more reluctant to focus so exclusively upon drinking.

Alternatives to Experimental Group Design

Most of the matters discussed so far, under the four headings, are difficulties rather than weaknesses of controlled trials; they would apply with equal if not greater force to any alternative research design. One of the inherent weaknesses of controlled trials, in comparison with other designs, has however been hinted at when discussing the need for treatment quality control. Emrick's[17] view that positive findings from alcoholism treatment controlled trials were often due to knowledge of the existence of another treatment group receiving what was thought to be a better treatment has already been referred to. Ethical requirements for research have been tightened up considerably in recent years, and quite rightly so. Guidelines issued by such bodies as the British Psychological Society and the Medical Research Council (UK) follow the principle of 'informed consent'. Although this term is difficult to define precisely, it may well be that controlled trials in this field, particularly when treatments are of differing intensities or prestige, will soon become a thing of the past.

Ethical considerations as well as the logistical problems involved in conducting a controlled trial, have of course always put many people off, and much thought has been given to the inventing of alternative

Figure 9.2: A Quasi-experimental Design: Time Series With Comparison Group

Experimental group	M M M M	TM M M M M
Comparison group	M M M M	M M M M M

M — Measurement   T — Treatment

designs which preserve as much as possible of the controlled trial's internal validity. Campbell and Stanley[8] outlined a variety of alternative group designs — what they called *quasi-experimental designs*. One of the most robust and generally applicable is depicted in Figure 9.2. This is the 'time series with comparison group' design. Although it clearly lacks the control which the fully fledged experimental design achieves by random assignment, it improves vastly upon totally uncontrolled clinical treatment practice by insisting upon repeated measurement of criterion variable(s) both after and before the introduction of the experimental treatment, and by requiring parallel measurement of members of a 'comparison group'. The comparison group need not be closely matched to the treated group, but the more closely it resembles the treatment group the stronger the design. As with all designs, including a controlled trial, it is the responsibility of the researchers to describe their design in full and to point out its strengths and weaknesses, and its limitations in terms of both internal and external validity.

A quite different design is 'regression discontinuity'. Hypothetical results from a study using such a design are shown in Figure 9.3. In such a study the experimental treatment is given selectively, not to a randomly chosen half of a sample, but rather to a half deliberately chosen because of their scores on some relevant variable which is known to be related to treatment outcome. The effectiveness of the treatment intervention is then hopefully apparent when, as in Figure 9.3, initial pre-treatment scores on this predictor variable are plotted against scores on an outcome post-treatment criterion variable. The break in the regression line provides this indication. This design should be quite feasible in alcoholism treatment research, for example using pre- and post-treatment drinking amount as the predictor and criterion variables respectively. The choice would have to be made, of course, whether treatment was to be selectively given to those drinking most prior to treatment (on the grounds of greatest need), or to those drinking least (on the grounds of better treatment prospects).

Figure 9.3: Hypothetical Results from a Study Using Regression-discontinuity Analysis

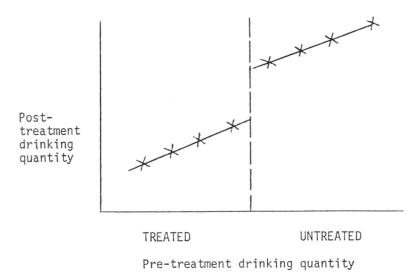

Post-
treatment
drinking
quantity
TREATED
UNTREATED
Pre-treatment drinking quantity

Figure 9.4: Examples of Within Subject Designs

ABAB design	M	TM	M	TM
Multiple-baseline design	M_1	$T_1 M_1$	M_1	M_1
	M_2	M_2	$T_2 M_2$	M_2
	M_3	M_3	M_3	$T_3 M_3$

M — Measurement
M_1 — Measurement of problem 1
M_2 — Measurement of problem 2
M_3 — Measurement of problem 3

T — Treatment
T_1 — Treatment for problem 1
T_2 — Treatment for problem 2
T_3 — Treatment for problem 3

Alternative pre-treatment predictor variables which might be employed in such a design are degree of alcohol dependence and degree of social stability.

The foregoing are both group designs, and like the controlled trial group design are open to the criticism which is often made, namely that the study of groups obscures knowledge of individual process. For this very reason there has been a growing interest in single case or *within-subject designs.*[16,26] Figure 9.4 depicts just two such designs for use with single subjects. Like a time series group design, each relies heavily upon time as a variable. In the ABAB design one looks to find changes in the criterion variable when and only when the experimental treatment is introduced. And in the multiple baseline design one looks to find changes in each of a number of criterion variables only when the treatment relevant to that criterion is introduced. These designs have largely arisen in the context of behavioural analysis and modification experiments. Sadly, they depend upon a number of assumptions which almost certainly do not hold for the treatment of alcohol problems. The multiple baseline design, for example, assumes the independence of different criterion or problem behaviours, and the ABAB design assumes that treatment can be initiated, discontinued, and continued again without the effects of any one of these conditions carrying over too much to the next. Indeed the successful use of an ABAB design would demonstrate failure to achieve the very thing which most therapists aim for, namely maintenance of treatment effects once the treatment itself has been discontinued.

Although such designs for the scientific analysis of individual behaviour seem unsuited to the study of treatment in the natural environment for alcohol problems, which by their very nature seem so very difficult to disentangle from other aspects of a person's behaviour, and which respond to treatment so uncertainly and uncleanly, the idea of within-subject analysis continues to be intuitively very appealing. Much more thought needs to be given to developing an adequate single case methodology for the study of alcoholism treatment processes. We are not short of assessment techniques. As well as the various inventories and behavioural measures of drinking with which we are familiar, we should look for example in the direction of personal questionnaires developed by clinical psychologists,[27] and towards the use of diaries and other methods for obtaining self-accounts in sociology. There is no reason why within-subject analyses should not be combined with some sort of experimental or quasi-experimental group design in the same study, although it is difficult to recall an example where this has been done. The research literature on alcoholism treatment appears to be dominated by, on the one hand, rigorous experiments of the controlled trial type which largely ignore individual process, and on the other hand, treatment accounts which lack the controls necessary for drawing more than minimal conclusions. The scope for invention here is considerable.

Assumptions On The Nature of Treatment

I intend to turn to account the study of 100 couples as a vehicle for
raising questions both about methodology and about our conceptions
regarding the very nature of the treatment of alcohol problems. It
is to the latter that the discussion will now turn. Recall that in the
study we were able to produce quite reasonable results (59 per cent
of husbands reporting definite improvement, and 39 per cent of wives
reporting definite improvement) after a single approximately four hour
session of assessment and brief advice followed by the passage of twelve
months during which a research worker called to see each wife only
(husbands were not seen) once a month in order to complete a fairly
brief research inventory. The results were no better for the group who
received conventional hospital psychiatric and social work treatment.
During these twelve months, as Figure 9.5 shows, an ever-increasing
proportion of clients contravened our advice not to drink, and an

Figure 9.5: Cumulative 'Relapse' Curves of 95 Men for Two Years
Following Intake

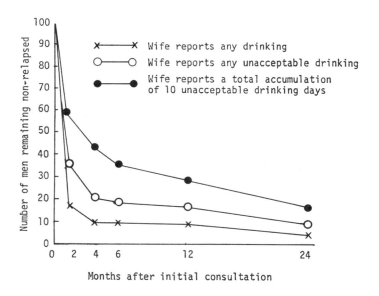

Months after initial consultation

increasing proportion returned to more or less regular excessive drinking. The shape of the relapse curve corresponds to those which Hunt and his colleagues[28] have drawn for smokers, people with drinking problems, and heroin addicts after treatment. Although there is the ever-present danger of obscuring individual processes by constructing such curves based upon group data, they do demonstrate both the high frequency of relapse for habit or excessive behaviour problems, and the particularly high rate of relapse in the first weeks following treatment or advice.

Hunt's view has been that such curves suggest the operation of two types of process: gradual extinction of learning that has taken place during treatment — shown in the early steeper part of the curve; and some kind of decision-making process which establishes the permanence of new behaviour and renders it resistant to extinction — shown by the fact that the curve flattens out well above zero (the fact that the lowest curve in Figure 9.5 drops near to zero is misleading, as this is based on the overly-strict and unfair criterion of total abstinence).

My own model of what is going on when someone with a drinking problem seeks help is along similar lines, and in particular makes use of

Figure 9.6: A Decision Model of Drinking Behaviour Change

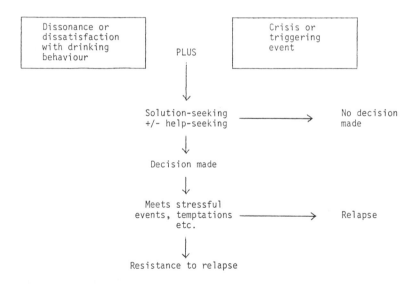

the notion of decision-making. A simple outline of the model is shown in Figure 9.6. It assumes, first of all, that when a person seeks help because of drinking, his drinking account is 'in the red' — there have been more recent debits than credits, losses have overtaken gains, and harm done by drinking has exceeded the pleasure. This of course is an over-simplification. No doubt different people have different levels of tolerance for being in the red, and we know that some people seek help more on account of the motivation of others than of themselves. Nevertheless, some state of dissatisfaction with ongoing drinking behaviour, either on the part of the drinker him/herself or within a social system of which he/she is a part, can be assumed. Secondly, the model supposes some sort of crisis which finally tips the scales, and which finally provokes the excessive drinker or someone close to take action. We now know that this action need not take the form of seeking help from a professional agency, as many people leave the class of problem drinker without receiving treatment.[29] In some cases professional help is sought however, and the model proposes that it is people in such a predicament who enter alcoholism treatment and treatment studies such as the study of 100 couples.

At this stage, the model continues, the individual concerned is sensitised to the possibility of new solutions. These solutions may already be easily to hand, and may not require any prompting from a professional. After all, 'going on the wagon', becoming 'tt', are as much a part of our cultural heritage as are rules and regulations about how to drink in the first place. Maybe 'recognising you are an alcoholic' or 'looking up Alcoholics Anonymous in the phone book' are now part of our heritage too. In other instances hearing from an expert, credible source that you should abstain (accompanied by a persuasive medical or other justification for abstinence), or being persuaded that controlled drinking is possible provided you follow a carefully worked out drinking 'diet', may be required. One way or another, with professional help or without, with friendly advice from uncle or neighbour or without it, with constant nagging from wife or husband or without it, the individual, sensitised to the need for a new solution, makes a decision. The language of crisis intervention theory may be apt for describing this type of process. The latter theory speaks of the capacity for change and growth which occurs in crisis, and it has been suggested[30] that our advice, rather than being a pale shadow of alcoholism treatment, was in fact rather appropriate and expert crisis intervention work.

New resolutions are vulnerable to reversal, and the model goes on to presume that the majority of new drinking decisions, taken in a crisis, are not consolidated in the following weeks and months, and in the natural course of events fall foul of the pressures exerted by stressful life events, unpleasant feelings, and social pressures, of one sort or another. Hence the typical group relapse curve. Some decisions, on the other hand, remain firm. The intriguing question then is why some and not others?

Perhaps it depends on the state of the drinking account at the time of crisis — with those whose account is most in the red having the greatest need to take a firm decision — or maybe some personalities are better than others at taking firm decisions. There is no obvious evidence that would support either of those propositions.

Perhaps the best explanation of successful drinking decision-making is based upon a combination of level of dependence and environmental resources. This would suppose that a decision to discontinue or moderate drinking is made in the face of some level of alcohol dependence, and that the higher this level the greater the opposition to carrying through a new decision. Other things being equal, highly dependent people will fail to carry through their decision, and people with a low level of dependence will succeed. Equally, if not more, important are environmental resources,[11] and this for two reasons. First, environmental resources provide incentives for new decisions. If resources such as a valued family life and a valued job exist then the expected utility, to use social learning terms, of a new decision is high. Secondly, without such resources one would hypothesise that life is fuller of life stresses and bad feelings — the chief enemies of resolution — and emptier of those satisfactions and pleasures that make a newly organised life worth living.

This model is admittedly extremely crude, but something along these lines seems to me necessary in order to make sense of the main facts. It makes sense of the fact that many people do consult both professional and non-professional agencies on account of drinking problems; that when they do, some make very dramatic changes in quite long-standing patterns of behaviour, whilst many others do not — relapsing sooner rather than later back into old behaviour patterns so that it seems to matter relatively little what those agencies do or for how long they do it — and that many people seem to make dramatic changes without consulting such agencies at all. The model puts the emphasis upon naturally occurring processes of decision-making and behaviour change, and in addition places a great deal of emphasis upon environmental resources which may sustain new decision-making, and correspondingly it gives a much more peripheral role to formal treatment. It stands in marked contrast to the implicit model upon which most of our past endeavours have been based — a model which views a drinking problem as some kind of disease or behaviour disorder which requires for its remediation some kind of external intervention, preferably from a professional person with training, for example, in psychology, psychiatry or social work, who has special techniques and skills to bring to bear. Perhaps one could go so far as to argue that there is no such thing as 'treatment', as such, for alcohol problems, merely the possibility of advice or encouragement. This way of looking at things is surely much more akin to the way the average person views tobacco smoking: his first thought about a dissonant smoker would surely be that the latter needs to make a decision about smoking, not that 'treatment' is required. It is no accident that the model outlined here owes more than a little to the model of decision-making and behaviour change outlined by Janis and Mann,[31] who had smokers particularly in mind.

Conclusion

The brief of this chapter was to discuss methodology, and controlled trials in particular. Although it has strayed well away from that focus, methodology is never far out of sight. If there is anything at all in the model which has been outlined, then we need to employ research methods designed to test theories and hypotheses derived from it. If we are to continue with controlled trials, they need to manipulate relevant rather than irrelevant variables. Two such variables are central to a trial which my colleague, Alistair Keddie, and I have presently under way in Exeter (see Figure 9.7). The first is whether people who consult with drinking problems are advised to abstain, or are advised that they can control their drinking. This will enable us to address the question whether there are circumstances in which the one course of action is better advised than the other. The second variable, which concerns only those advised to control their drinking, corresponds to a fair degree with the advice versus treatment variable in the study of 100 couples. This will enable us to begin to test the opinion which is now abroad that, whereas abstinence can sometimes be expected after no treatment at all, controlled drinking is a different matter and requires intensive technique-oriented treatment.

Far more than this is needed however if we are fully to comprehend the change process. Our principal need now is for a shift in the direction of new research designs which are capable of examining simultaneously naturally occurring processes such as decision-making, the advice or treatment input, and environmental support and pressures which affect the outcome. And this is a tall order.

Figure 9.7: Design of the Exeter Study

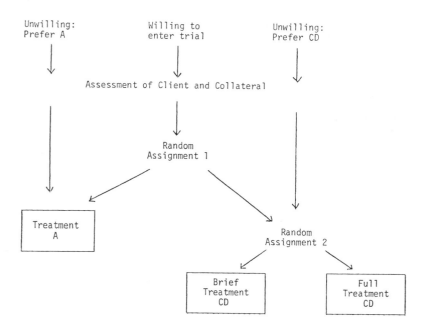

A - Abstinence   CD - Controlled Drinking

Notes

1. Edwards, G., Orford, J., Egert, S., Guthrie, S., Hawker, A., Hensman, M., Oppenheimer, E. and Taylor, C. (1977), 'Alcoholism: A Controlled Trial of "Treatment" and "Advice" ', *Journal of Studies on Alcohol*, vol. 38, pp. 1004-31.

2. Orford, J. and Edwards, G. (1977), *Alcoholism: A Comparison of Treatment and Advice, With a Study of the Influence of Marriage* (Oxford University Press, Oxford).

3. Tuchfield, B.S. (1977), 'Comments on "Alcoholism: A Controlled Trial of 'Treatment' and 'Advice' " ', *Journal of Studies on Alcohol*, vol. 38, pp. 1808-13.

4. Glaser, F.B. (1977), 'Comments on "Alcoholism: A Controlled Trial of 'Treatment' and 'Advice' " ', *Journal of Studies on Alcohol*, vol. 38, pp. 1810-27.

5. Hingson, R. and Day, N. (1977), 'Comments on "Alcoholism: A Controlled Trial of 'Treatment' and 'Advice' " ', *Journal of Studies on Alcohol*, vol. 38, pp. 2206-11.

6. Lambert, M.J. (1976), 'Spontaneous Remission in Adult Neurotic Disorders: A Revision and Summary', *Psychological Bulletin*, vol. 83, pp. 107-19.

7. Smith, M.L. and Glass, G.V. (1977), 'Meta-analysis of Psychotherapy Outcome Studies', *American Psychologist*, vol. 32, pp. 752-60.

8. Campbell, D.T. and Stanley, J.C. (1966), *Experimental and Quasi-Experimental Designs for Research* (Rand McNally, Chicago).

9. Bergin, A.E. (1971), 'The Evaluation of Therapeutic Outcomes', in Bergin, A. and Garfield, S. (eds.), *Handbook of Psychotherapy and Behaviour Change* (John Wiley, New York).

10. Hodgson, R., Stockwell, T., Rankin, H. and Edwards, G. (1978), 'Alcohol Dependence: The Concept, its Utility and Measurement', *British Journal of Addiction*, vol. 73, pp. 339-42.

11. Bromet, E. and Moos, R.H. (1977), 'Environmental Resources and the Post-treatment Functioning of Alcoholic Patients', *Journal of Health and Social Behaviour*, vol. 18, pp. 326-38.

12. Orford, J., Oppenheimer, E., Egert, S., Hensman, C. and Guthrie, S. (1976), 'The Cohesiveness of Alcoholism Complicated Marriages and its Influence on Treatment Outcome', *British Journal of Psychiatry*, vol. 128, pp. 318-39.

13. Zax, N. and Specter, G.A. (1974), *An Introduction to Community Psychology* (John Wiley, New York).

14. Orford, J. (1979), 'Teaching Community Psychology to Undergraduate and Postgraduate Psychology Students', *Bulletin of the British Psychological Society*, vol. 32, pp. 75-9.

15. Hunt, G.M. and Azrin, N.H. (1973), 'The Community-Reinforcement Approach to Alcoholism', *Behaviour Research and Therapy*, vol. 11, pp. 91-104.

16. Jeffrey, D.B. (1975), 'Treatment Evaluation Issues in Research on Addictive Behaviours', *Addictive Behaviors*, vol. 1, pp. 23-36.

17. Emrick, C.D. (1975), 'A Review of Psychologically Oriented Treatment of Alcoholism. II. The Relative Effectiveness of Different Treatment Approaches and the Effectiveness of Treatment vs No Treatment', *Journal of Studies on Alcohol*, vol. 36, pp. 88-108.

18. Miller, W.R. (1978), 'Behavioural Treatment of Problem Drinkers: A Comparative Outcome Study of Three Controlled Drinking Therapies', *Journal of Consulting and Clinical Psychology*, vol. 46, pp. 74-86.

19. Ley, P., Bradshaw, P.W., Kincey, J.A. and Atherton, S.A. (1976), 'Increasing Patients' Satisfaction with Communications', *British Journal of Social and Clinical Psychology*, vol. 15, pp. 403-13.

20. Vogler, R.E., Compton, J.V. and Weissbach, T.A. (1975), 'Integrated Behaviour Change Techniques for Alcoholics', *Journal of Consulting and Clinical Psychology*, vol. 43, pp. 233-43.

21. Vogler, R.E., Weissback, T.A., Compton, J.V. and Martin, G.T. (1977), 'Integrated Behaviour Change Techniques for Problem Drinkers in the Community', *Journal of Consulting and Clinical Psychology*, vol. 45, pp. 267-79.

22. Nathan, P.E. and Briddell, D.W. (1978), 'Behavioural Assessment and Treatment of Alcoholism', in Kissin, B. and Begleiter, H. (eds.) *The Biology of Alcoholism, Vol. 5* (Plenum, New York), pp. 301-49.

23. Sobell, M.B. and Sobell, L.C. (1978), *Behavioural Treatment of Alcohol Problems: Individualised Therapy and Controlled Drinking* (Plenum, New York).

24. McCrady, B.S., Paolino, T.J. and Longabaugh, R. (1978), 'Correspondence Between Reports of Problem Drinkers and Spouses on Drinking Behaviour and

Impairment', *Journal of Studies on Alcohol*, vol. 39, pp. 1252-7.
   25. Pattison, E.M. (1966), 'A Critique of Alcoholism Treatment Concepts with Special Reference to Abstinence', *Quarterly Journal of Studies on Alcohol*, vol. 27, pp. 49-71.
   26. Hersen, M. and Barlow, D.H. (1976), *Single Case Experimental Designs: Strategies for Studying Behaviour Change* (Pergamon Press, New York).
   27. Mulhall, D.J. (1976), 'Systematic Self-Assessment by PQRST (Personal Questionnaire Rapid Scaling Technique)', *Psychological Medicine*, vol. 6, pp. 591-7.
   28. Hunt, W.A. and Matarazzo, J.D. (1970), 'Habit Mechanisms in Smoking', in Hunt, W.A. (ed.), *Learning Mechanisms in Smoking* (Aldine, Chicago).
   29. Clark, W.B. and Cahalan, D. (1976), 'Changes in Problem Drinking Over a Four-Year Span', *Addictive Behaviours*, vol. 1, pp. 251-9.
   30. Hunt, L. (1979), personal communication.
   31. Janis, I. and Mann, L. (1968), 'A Conflict Theory Approach to Attitude Change and Decision-Making', in Greenwald, A.C., Brock, T.C. and Ostrom, T.M. (eds.), *Psychological Foundations of Attitudes* (Academic Press, New York), Chapter 13.

10 TREATMENT STRATEGIES FOR THE EARLY PROBLEM DRINKER

Ray J. Hodgson

The label 'early problem drinker' is not entirely satisfactory although it is used by many people in the alcoholism field to convey the impression that here we have a drinking problem which cannot yet be given the label 'alcoholic'. In order to clarify the use of the term in this chapter, it will be useful to begin with a discussion of the alcohol dependence syndrome.[1,2] According to Edwards and Gross, the severely dependent alcoholic differs from the less dependent subject along a number of partially correlated dimensions. First there is a *narrowing of drinking repertoires*. The severely dependent person does not usually drink two bottles of spirits on Wednesday, a couple of double whiskies on Thursday, ten pints on Friday and one bottle of spirits on Saturday. His drinking tends to be less variable from day to day. The severely dependent alcoholic is characterised by the *salience of drink-seeking behaviour*. Drinking takes pride of place over alternative activities. Adverse consequences are disregarded, responsibilities are neglected, and the wishes of family and friends are ignored. Increasing levels of consumption lead on to increasing levels of *tolerance and withdrawal symptoms*. There is drinking to *relieve and allay withdrawal symptoms*. There is a subjective awareness of a strong *compulsion to drink* and, finally, the syndrome can readily be *reinstated* if the severely dependent alcoholic starts to drink again after a period of abstinence.

According to this view, physical dependence represents the biological substrate of the alcohol dependence syndrome for two reasons. First, it is an indication that there is already severe psychological dependence. The person who consumes sufficient alcohol to become physically dependent is usually someone whose drinking is already strongly influenced by an array of psychological cues. Secondly, the abstinence syndrome is clearly a very unpleasant psychological state which has to be avoided. The severely dependent alcoholic who wakes up 'the morning after the night before' suffering from sweats and shakes can put himself right and even feel elated after a couple of stiff drinks. This is the kind of avoidance conditioning paradigm which can hardly fail to produce a second type of psychological dependence, i.e. a compulsion to drink when exposed to those cognitive and physiological cues associated with withdrawal. So physical dependence is the *sign* of one kind of psychological dependence and the *cause* of another kind of psychological dependence.

One of the distinguishing characteristics of differences in dependence is the set of cues which influence drinking and lead to compulsive drinking. Prior to the development of physical dependence, the problem drinker is strongly influenced by psychological and situational cues, by anger and anxiety, social anxiety, social pressure from others, feelings of helplessness and depression, failure, boredom and numerous idiosyncratic thoughts, feelings and situations. There is now a wealth of data, derived from questionnaire and experimental studies, which support such a broad analysis of the most salient cues.[3-7] When the problem drinker gradually experiences more frequent and more intense withdrawal symptoms, then the second phase of conditioning begins. His drinking gradually comes under the influence of cues associated with withdrawal symptoms, e.g. minimal withdrawal symptoms and expected withdrawal symptoms. Of course, the various phases of alcohol dependence are continuous and overlapping, but we can be sure that severe dependence is characterised by drinking behaviour which is strongly influenced by the cognitive and physiological cues associated with withdrawal.

Although Edwards and his World Health Organisation colleagues speak of the alcohol dependence *syndrome*, they do not seem to be implying a disease state, but simply some covariance between a number of behavioural, physiological and subjective phenomena which are, to some extent, learned or conditioned. To quote Edwards and Gross:

> The learning process is very incompletely understood, but dependence should perhaps be seen as being in the same group of disorders as phobic and obsessional states, with a potent, complicating, biological factor.[1]

Certainly this notion of dependence cannot be reduced to physical dependence. It is an attempt to describe a motivational system which involves both physiological and psychological components.

The question which has now to be asked is whether this concept of alcohol dependence can help us to understand and treat drinking problems. Is it of any use?

The Utility of Alcohol Dependence Assessments

The concept would have some utility if its assessment helped us to interpret ambiguous data and even radically altered the conclusions which could be drawn from experimental results. Two examples demonstrate that the assessment of severity of dependence certainly can alter our interpretations and conclusions.

The first is an experimental test of the notion that some drink can set up a craving for more drink.[8] Volunteer inpatient alcoholics on the Maudsley-Bethlem Alcoholism Treatment Unit assisted in this study. These hospitalised alcoholics were given priming doses in the morning and their craving was tested three hours later, as blood alcohol concentrations were on their way back to zero or near zero levels. We tested the hypothesis that three double vodkas (approximately) would set up more craving than either a low dose (one single vodka) or no dose, using speed of drinking as a measure of craving. Speed of drinking has face validity as a measure of craving or disposition to drink; it is perfectly reasonable to suggest that somebody who craves a drink will consume his drink much faster than someone who does not. However, we also have other experimental evidence that this is a valid measure of craving.[9] When we looked at mean scores, for all 20 subjects, we found absolutely no evidence of any significant effect of the priming dose on drinking times and had we left the matter there, this would be good evidence against the hypothesis that a few drinks can prime craving. Fortunately, we had taken the precaution of obtaining ratings of severity of dependence. These ratings were supplied by a psychiatrist with many years of experience in the alcoholism field, namely Griffith Edwards and, furthermore, they had proven validity.[9] Figure 10.1 shows what happens to the craving measure when this group of hospitalised alcoholics was split into severely dependent and moderately dependent sub-groups.

A significant priming effect is now to be seen after the high dose condition, but only for the severely dependent subjects. The effect is totally washed out when the sub-groups are combined because of the opposite trend in the moderately dependent group – a trend which is actually not significant.

The other evidence which supports the utility of severity of dependence assessments comes from a follow-up investigation of 65 alcoholics treated at the Maudsley Hospital. Twenty-one were considered to be functioning well throughout a two year follow-up period, eleven being totally abstinent and ten being controlled drinkers. This would seem to

Figure 10.1: Time Taken to Consume the First Drink in Afternoon Following a Morning Primer. The two groups are severely dependent (broken line: N = 11) and moderately dependent (solid line: N = 9) hospitalised alcoholics.[8]

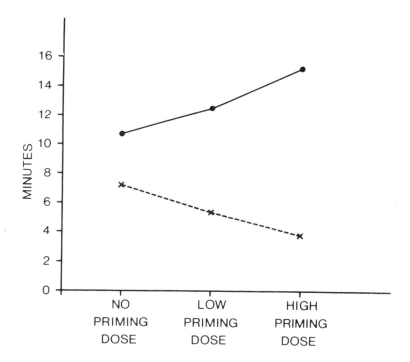

be evidence which contradicts the traditional view that total abstinence is the only possible goal. It would appear from these results that abstinence advice cannot be justified since controlled drinking is an equally likely result. Such a clear-cut conclusion must be modified a little when severity of dependence assessment is taken into account. It turns out that the moderately dependent tend to be the ones who can achieve a controlled drinking goal, whereas the severely dependent tend to be either abstinent or totally uncontrolled.

These two pieces of evidence fit well together. They support the hypothesis that the severely dependent alcoholic is sensitive to minimal withdrawal symptoms, that a few drinks can increase his disposition to drink and that he therefore has great difficulty achieving a controlled drinking goal. It is not being suggested that controlled drinking is impossible for the severely dependent but simply that, in the above study, the less severely dependent were more likely to achieve it. It is apparent that the dimension of dependence described by Edwards and Gross has some predictive validity in process and treatment-outcome research. If different treatment strategies are necessary when dealing with different levels of dependence, then we urgently need research into methods of assessing the dimension[10,11] as well as the prognostic significance of degrees of dependence for different treatment approaches.

Treatment Strategies for the Moderately Dependent Problem Drinker

The first point to note from both a theoretical and an empirical point of view is that controlled drinking appears to be an acceptable goal for the early problem drinker, or moderately dependent alcoholic. It has already been noted that controlled drinking is a more likely outcome for the moderately dependent alcoholic than it is for the severely dependent. Also, data from the Sobells' study[12] strongly suggests that controlled drinking is an attainable goal for the moderately dependent. In this study a group of 40 alcoholics was considered to be suitable for a controlled drinking goal. Clients were thought to be eligible for controlled drinking if they expressed a strong preference for such a goal and if there was good evidence of controlled drinking during the past few years. Almost certainly these criteria would define a group of moderately dependent alcoholics. For this type of person the Sobells provide some evidence that behaviour therapy towards a controlled drinking goal is more effective than traditional therapy towards an abstinence goal.

If controlled drinking stands a reasonable chance of success, then it certainly should be tried. A total abstinence goal has always been considered to be a method of arresting an irreversible disease process. A controlled drinking goal, on the other hand, is based upon the assumption that learned or conditioned behaviour can actually be reversed or unlearned. If this can be achieved then, of course, it is the most desirable outcome. Controlled drinking would therefore appear to be the most appropriate goal for the moderately dependent drinker who is just beginning to experience withdrawal symptoms but is not yet hooked on 'withdrawal-relief' drinking. Certainly, there is no reason to coerce or bamboozle him into accepting an abstinence goal.

There are a number of specific treatment strategies that should now be tested. There are two reasons for concentrating here on the early problem drinker. First, prevention is better than cure. If we cannot prevent drinking problems, then perhaps we can prevent the development of severe dependence once a drinking problem is recognised and admitted. Secondly, by concentrating on the early problem drinker it is reasonable to permit extrapolation from a proven method of helping people to change other addictive and compulsive behaviours such as overeating, smoking and even obsessive-compulsive complaints.

Early problem drinking, like many other excessive behaviours, is influenced by cues and consequences. To be more accurate, it is influenced by subjective cues and expected consequences. Can we help people to change their behaviour by changing cues and consequences or, at least, the way that clients construe them? There is now a rapidly expanding literature on 'the peculiar business of edging people into changing their behaviour'. This chapter will discuss a few examples drawn from various areas which are data-based.

Persuasive Communication

The simplest method of attempting to edge people into changing their behaviour is by way of persuasive communication from a person held in high regard, such as a doctor. A recent study of advice against smoking carried out by Dr Michael Russell and his colleagues[13] suggests that such advice given by a medical practitioner can be a simple and yet effective method of changing behaviour. Almost 2,000 smokers were involved in this study and 73 per cent of them were seen at one year follow-up. The results indicated that spontaneous remission over a one year period was only 0.3 per cent, whereas two minutes of advice from a general practitioner plus a leaflet on giving up smoking, as well as the message that the doctor was interested in seeing the patient later, produced a cessation rate of five per cent at one year.

This may appear to be a trivial effect, but actually it is not. Consider for example, the following facts. There are more than 20,000 GPs in Britain, 90 per cent of adults attend at least once a year over a five year period and the average consultation rate is approximately three per adult per year. There can be no doubt that GPs, in the course of their routine work, see a large proportion of the 20 million smokers in Britain. The results of Russell's study indicate that any GP who routinely told all his cigarette smoking patients to stop, gave them a smoking information leaflet and questioned them on their progress whenever he saw them again, could expect to have about 25 long-term successes per year. If every GP were to adopt this procedure, the national yield could be more than half a million ex-smokers over the course of a year, a target that could only be matched if specialised withdrawal clinics were increased from the present number of around 50 to around 10,000.

As you might expect in a study of this kind, the smokers who were most strongly influenced tended to be the less dependent, and so we can at least entertain the hypothesis that the less dependent drinker might also be influenced by firm advice from his GP. Of course, there are major differences between smoking and drinking which may influence the extent to which simple advice can be effective. It is more difficult to identify the early problem drinker, more difficult to specify a dangerous level of consumption and not possible to advise total abstinence for all. Nevertheless, now is the time to carry out a well controlled study of GP advice, especially in the light of the recent British Department of Health and Social Security Report on 'The Pattern and Range of Services for the Problem Drinker' which argues strongly for more active intervention at the primary level.

Even if advice from a GP is proved to have a significant impact on drinking in the long-term, there will undoubtedly be a large number of GPs who are not willing or who cannot find the time to discuss drinking problems, and also a large number of problem drinkers who do not or cannot heed their doctor's advice.

Faith and Hope

What *simple* procedures can a counsellor use to enhance his effectiveness in helping the early problem drinker? Investigations of specific techniques have always paid lip service to non-specific factors such as faith in the therapist, faith in the treatment, and the warmth, empathy and authenticity displayed by the therapist. In fact, because these factors are turning out to be so important it is becoming increasingly obvious that the label 'non-specific' should be dropped. The non-specifics must be transformed into clearly defined specifics. As an example one may study the rapid smoking technique for modifying smoking behaviour. The rapid smoking procedure, hailed in some quarters as a new method of modifying smoking, involves the client puffing a cigarette every six seconds until he can take no more and usually feels slightly sick. The study in question[14] randomly assigned 36 smokers to two levels of encouragement. One group were told that the purpose of the experiment was to test the effectiveness of the treatment and that its effectiveness was totally unknown. The rapid smoking procedure was conducted rather mechanically by a cold but efficient therapist who gave no reinforcement to those clients who successfully abstained between sessions. In the other group, the relationship between the therapist and the client was warm and friendly, the therapist talked about his own experiences of giving up and his success with rapid smoking. He communicated his enthusiasm for the treatment and the clients were strongly reinforced for abstinence. At each session, the client's progress was charted on a blackboard.

So here we have the same treatment, i.e. rapid smoking, administered in two different ways. The differences in outcome were rather startling. At the three month follow-up the abstinence rates were six per cent for the cold therapist and 72 per cent for the encouraging therapist.

It would appear that the strong encouragement given by the successful therapist is not just a 'non-specific' factor, but a method of counselling which we should work hard to develop. How can we be encouraging and enthusiastic without telling our clients a pack of lies and sounding more like an encyclopaedia salesman than a member of the helping professions? First we must ask ourselves the soul-searching question, 'Why do I think that I might be able to help this client?' The answer may be based upon good data from our own or other alcoholism treatment trials, but that is doubtful. If it is based upon our past experiences of helping people with drinking problems then it may be helpful to describe these to our new client. Perhaps we should be following the lead given by Alcoholics Anonymous and various slimming clubs and have successful clients actually giving a talk to new clients about their experiences. If we have been influenced by research into the treatment of other problems such as overeating or compulsive handwashing, then we owe it to our clients to communicate our reasons for believing that similar methods might help the problem drinker. It is not being suggested that we should start to gush like an inexperienced infant teacher, but simply that, by first convincing ourselves of our usefulness, we will be able naturally to communicate faith and hope, rather than despair.

Proximal Goal Setting

Another rather simple approach is derived from the work of Albert Bandura[15] on self-monitoring and self-regulation. According to Bandura, intentional control of behaviour operates principally through two cognitively based sources of motivation. The first is a capacity to represent future consequences in thought. The second operates through planning or goal setting and self-evaluating reactions to one's own performance. We must differentiate between general intentions and explicitly defined goals. We must also distinguish between end goals and sub-goals. It is argued that immediate goals rather than end goals can strongly mobilise effort and direct our actions in the here and now. In order to test this hypothesis, Bandura and his colleagues[16] studied the influence of proximal goals and distal goals on overeating. All subjects, except those in a control condition, were told that by recording and reducing the number of mouthfuls of food and beverage consumed, they would be able to regain control over their eating habits. Subjects used a wrist counter to keep a tally of the number of mouthfuls. One group of subjects were told to keep a cumulative record of mouthfuls per week and then aim for a weekly reduction of ten per cent over a four week period. Another group recorded intake during four periods each day and were then set the goal of reducing intake by ten per cent in each of these four periods. Actually, this is an experimental test of the AA principle 'one day at a time', except that the day is further subdivided. It was found that those subjects who were focussing upon proximal goals were the only subjects to lose weight, and subjects focussing upon a change in their weekly intake did no better than a control group.

In the same paper, Bandura and Simon also describe an individual case study in which an overweight lady successfully used 'proximal goal setting' as a short-term coping strategy at various times during a period of 76 weeks, in order to reverse any weight increases.

Helping a client to translate long-term goals into short-term sub-goals is a strategy worth trying with problem drinkers, and this applies not only to drinking behaviour but to any other behaviour changes that a client thinks he should make in order to reduce the probability of excessive drinking. He could be helped to increase the amount of exercise that he takes, or to study for an exam. It would seem that the AA advice to concentrate on one day at a time is a basic principle of self-control. Under pressure, it may be necessary to focus on one hour at a time.

Self-control Procedures

Consider next a rather more complicated approach which has been variously labelled 'problem solving', 'self management' or 'self control'.[17-20] Central to this approach is the functional analysis, an attempt to understand drinking behaviour in terms of antecedent cues and actual or expected consequences. Treatment possibilities flow from the individualised functional analysis since it may be possible to work out ways of changing life styles, coping behaviours, or cognitive coping strategies in order to reduce the influence of potent drinking cues. *This approach does not specify a set of techniques but a strategy for generating hypotheses.* To take a clinical example, a writer came for help because he would frequently get very drunk, but was not severely dependent. The main cues for his drinking were experiences of frustration, rejection and failure. He would often have a strong desire to drink heavily when his writing did not flow easily, especially around lunchtime when his custom was to have a glass of wine with a meal. Whenever his plans were thwarted, he began to feel irritated and his thoughts would turn to drink. One drinking binge started after an unsuccessful attempt to meet up with an old friend who was passing through Heathrow airport on his way to Buenos Aires. Another binge started when his wife wrongly interpreted a phone call that he received from an old flame.

The essence of self-control training is to identify cues or cue complexes and then generate a number of possible coping strategies for each cue. From the various strategies the best is selected and then tested out. The coping strategies can be attempts to avoid cues arising or they could be methods of coping with unavoidable cues. For example, the client mentioned above made good use of relaxation exercises to avoid a build-up of tension. He has also worked out a plan of campaign to deal with lunchtime craving when it arises; first he goes for a swim and then he goes to the British Museum to continue his writing there. He views this as a method of altering his physiological state and also his work environment in order to get rid of drinking cues. Of course, there are many situations when it is impossible to dash off for a swim and so he is also successfully using a cognitive strategy. Whenever he feels the urge to drink, he imagines the awful consequences of drinking heavily and also the pleasant consequences of remaining sober. He has two very specific images which appear to help him ensure that long-term consequences are influencing his present behaviour.

Is there any evidence that self-control training works? This type of training was central to the Sobells' successful attempt to help clients achieve a controlled drinking goal. However, they deliberately included a whole gamut of techniques including videotaped feedback of drunken behaviour and repeated practice of controlled drinking in a simulated bar situation. And so we cannot be certain that the complex self-control procedures were crucial.

However, this rather commonsense model has been applied exten-
sively to other excessive behaviours such as overeating. In fact, the best
controlled studies of this approach have been with the overweight, and
it is worthwhile therefore to look at two of these studies which may
have implications for the treatment of other excessive behaviours. The
first was reported by Kingsley and Wilson[21] of Rutgers University.
They compared self-control training carried out individually or in
groups with a social pressure control group. The *social pressure* group
were told that the critical factor in weight loss is the motivational one
and that group pressure is a very strong motivation for most people. In
the social pressure group individuals losing weight successfully were
given a yellow star badge to wear during the meeting, those remaining
at the same weight were given a green turtle, and those gaining weight
were given a red pig to wear. The *self-control* subjects were taught to
identify cues and work out alternative ways of coping. Figure 10.2
shows the weight loss quotients for the three groups. Both of the

Figure 10.2: Mean Weight Reduction Quotients of the Three Treatment
Groups Across Treatments and Follow-ups. The group behaviour
therapy involved self-control or self-management procedures.[21]

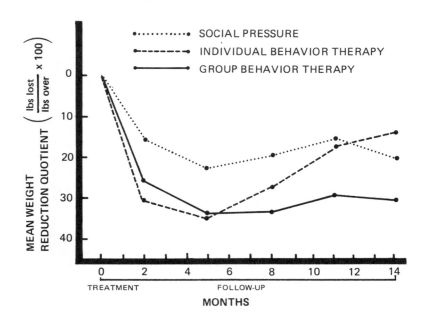

self-control treatments (i.e. group and individual) were effective, but note the significantly greater weight gain during follow-up for clients who had been treated individually. Does this mean that there is something to be achieved by carrying out self-control training in groups? Since group treatment is more cost-effective than individual treatments, it would seem that the answer could be yes. Perhaps groups generate a high level of motivation, a greater number of modelling experiences, greater self-esteem and support. AA members would agree that this is so. Incidentally, the study also demonstrated that booster sessions during the one year follow-up period had a significantly beneficial effect.

The second study of self-control procedures was carried out by research workers at Brown University[22] and adds yet another factor to be considered when planning treatments for early problem drinkers. Subjects in this study were all married and were asked if their spouse would be willing to attend all training sessions. They were then divided into three groups. The first was a group whose spouses refused to attend. The second was a group whose spouses were co-operative, but who were told that an excessive number of applicants necessitated treating some subjects without their spouses, and the third was formed from clients whose spouses were co-operative and attended all sessions, to learn about self-control procedures. They also promised to help in recording eating behaviour and devising alternative coping strategies. All groups lost weight, and there was a significantly greater weight loss, especially at six month follow-up, for clients whose spouses had also learned self-control procedures. This group showed a mean weight loss of 30 lb.

Whether the training of couples is more effective than individual counselling with moderately dependent drinkers is an open question, but these data suggest that the possibility is certainly worth testing. It should be remembered that a mean weight loss of 30 lb over a three month period with no sign of relapse at six months is an amazing result.

Social Skills Training and Community Reinforcement

Self-control training, if at all effective, should lead on to a change in the meaning or significances of cues since antecedent events are no longer considered to be danger signals if the drinker has confidence in his ability to cope. Consider the analogous experience of a learner driver approaching Piccadilly Circus. He will feel very apprehensive because, in his own estimation, he does not have sufficient control over his future well-being. As he develops his driving skills his view of Piccadilly Circus gradually changes and it is no longer a cue for anxiety. The same applies to the control of drinking and drinking cues.

There is very good evidence that many heavy drinkers are particularly influenced by social cues[3-5] and it has been suggested that this is an area in which the significance of a cue can be altered through the development of social competence in a wide variety of situations.[25,27,28] Social skills training[23] or personal effectiveness training[24] has been shown to be effective with some groups, although the supportive evidence has sometimes been over-rated and the approach oversold.

Typically, social skills training involves the identification of specific deficits followed by the repeated practice of graded tasks with the aim of gaining important skills. Sessions involve the role playing of person to person situations such as conversations, being firm with subordinates, job interviews, expressing affection to a loved one and expressing annoyance without being insulting. Feedback (sometimes videotaped) is given after each interaction and the therapist makes suggestions about eye contact, the content of communications etc., usually emphasising positive feedback and encouraging every small improvement. Graded real-life assignments between treatment sessions are an essential component of these training methods.

The problem drinker often reports that not only does he lack a broad range of social skills, but that he does not have a ready answer when drink is offered in a number of situations. The finding that a large proportion of treated alcoholics give as their reason for relapse the social pressure exerted by others to get them to take a drink has stimulated a number of therapists to advocate that the problem drinker should be taught how to 'say no' effectively.

Since some people with drinking problems are unemployed, and furthermore have a feeling of helplessness about their job finding abilities, the attention of counsellors must be directed to a very interesting report on a job finding club.[26] Job finding was viewed as an activity requiring a number of complex skills which could be developed in a structured learning situation. The programme assisted the jobseeker in every area that was believed to be influential in obtaining a job, emphasis being placed upon mutual assistance among job seekers, encouragement of family support, sharing job leads and role-playing of interviews and telephone conversations. Within two months, 90 per cent of the counselled job seekers (not necessarily problem drinkers) had obtained employment, compared with 55 per cent of a control group; furthermore, the average salary was one-third higher for the counselled group.

It has been argued that if the problem drinker is interacting well within his community, then sobriety will be reinforced and excessive drinking will be curtailed.[27] Two trials have been completed which suggest that increasing social and job finding skills and improving marital relationships can have a strong beneficial effect on drinking.[27,28]

Cue Exposure

A recent advance in the treatment of compulsive rituals[29-31] may suggest that a similar approach might be effective in helping to treat the early problem drinker.[32] The treatment, which goes under a number of labels such as flooding, exposure, participant modelling and response prevention, is based upon the simple notion that the strong urge to carry out a compulsion will go away if the urge is resisted. The therapy involves a functional analysis to identify the relevant cues and then exercises designed to produce exposure to these cues along with strong encouragement to resist the compulsion. A person experiencing a strong urge to wash after walking past a hospital will be repeatedly encouraged to visit hospitals and then resist his compulsion. There is now no doubt at all that after such treatment a strong initial urge to wash gradually tends to disappear. Is it possible that such cue exposure practice along with coping skills training might be the best way to extinguish the compulsion to drink once and for all? We are at the moment investigating this notion, and no strong evidence to support it can yet be presented. However, models of compulsions and addictions overlap to such an extent that one must at least entertain the idea that a method that has revolutionised the treatment of obsessional-compulsive complaints might be applicable to drinking compulsions as well.

Although self-control training, social skills training and cue exposure may appear to be simple approaches, in practice they turn out to be rather complicated. The individual functional analysis requires a great deal of probing detective work and also a good knowledge of drinking problems. Asking the right questions and building up a clear and accurate picture of one person's drinking is a creative problem-solving exercise and not a mechanical assessment procedure.

Treatment must focus to some extent on drinking and related behaviour, but the basic aim must be to alter the cognitive as well as the behavioural and physiological components. Recent cognitive approaches[33] have not yet been systematically applied to compulsive and addictive problems, but there is now enough evidence[34,35] to suggest that we should be busily testing their efficacy.

In conclusion, there are now a whole range of cognitive-behavioural approaches which are supported by some investigations of their efficacy with people who overeat, smoke too much or wash their hands compulsively. There is now an obvious need for a series of related studies from different therapists and institutions to assess the value of these methods for people who drink too much, and especially for people who are *beginning* to drink too much.

Notes

1. Edwards, G. and Gross, M.M. (1976), 'Alcohol Dependence: Provisional Description of a Clinical Syndrome', *British Medical Journal*, vol. 1, pp. 1058-61.
2. Edwards, G. (1977), in Edwards, G. and Grant, M. (eds.), *Alcoholism: New Knowledge and New Responses* (Croom Helm, London; University Park Press, Baltimore).
3. Litman, G.K., Eiser, J.R., Rawson, N.S.B. and Oppenheim, A.N. (1977), 'Towards a Typology of Relapse: A Preliminary Report', *Drug and Alcohol Dependence*, vol. 2, pp. 157-62.
4. Higgins, R.L. and Marlatt, G.A. (1975), 'Fear of Personal Evaluations as a Determinant of Alcohol Consumption in Male Social Drinkers', *Journal of Abnormal Psychology*, vol. 84, pp. 644-51.
5. Miller, P.M., Hersen, M., Eisler, P.M. and Hilsman, G. (1974), 'Effects of Social Stress on Operant Drinking of Alcoholics and Social Drinkers', *Behaviour Research and Therapy*, vol. 12, pp. 67-72.
6. Edwards, G., Hensman, C., Chandler, J. and Peto, J. (1972), 'Motivation for Drinking Among Men: Survey of a London Suburb', *Psychological Medicine*, vol. 2, pp. 260-71.
7. Strickler, D.P., Tomaszewski, R., Maxwell, W.A. and Suib, M.R. (1979), 'The Effects of Relaxation Instructions on Drinking Behaviour in the Presence of Stress', *Behaviour Research and Therapy*, vol. 17, pp. 45-51.
8. Hodgson, R.J., Rankin, H.J. and Stockwell, T. (1979), 'Alcohol Dependence and the Priming Effect', *Behaviour Research and Therapy*, vol. 17, pp. 379-87.
9. Rankin, H., Hodgson, R. and Stockwell, T. (1979), 'The Concept of Craving and Its Measurement', *Behaviour Research and Therapy*, vol.17, pp. 389-96.
10. Hodgson, R., Stockwell, T., Rankin, H. and Edwards, G. (1978), 'Alcohol Dependence: The Concept, Its Utility and Measurement', *British Journal of Addiction*, vol. 73, pp. 339-42.
11. Stockwell, T., Hodgson, R., Edwards, G. and Rankin, H. (1979), 'The Development of a Questionnaire to Measure Severity of Alcohol Dependence', *British Journal of Addiction*, vol. 74, pp. 79-87.
12. Sobell, M.B. and Sobell, L.C. (1976), 'Second-year Treatment Outcome of Alcoholics Treated by Individualised Behaviour Therapy: Results', *Behaviour Research and Therapy*, vol. 14, pp. 195-215.
13. Russell, M.A.H., Wilson, C., Taylor, C. and Banker, C.D. (1979), 'The Effect of General Practitioners' Advice Against Smoking' (forthcoming).
14. Harris, D.E. and Lichtenstein, E. (1971), 'The Contribution of Nonspecific Social Variables to a Successful Behavioural Treatment of Smoking', unpublished paper read to the US Western Psychological Association.

15. Bandura, A. (1977), *Social Learning Theory* (Prentice Hall Inc., New Jersey).
16. Bandura, A. and Simon, K.M. (1977), 'The Role of Proximal Intensions in Self-regulation of Refractory Behaviour', *Cognitive Therapy and Research*, vol. 1, no. 3, pp. 177-93.
17. Stuart, R.B. (1977), *Behavioral Self-Management* (Brunner/Mazel, New York).
18. Mahoney, M.J. and Arnkoff, D. (1971), 'Cognitive and Self-Control Therapies', in Garfield, S.L. and Bergin, A.E. (eds.), *Handbook of Psychotherapy and Behavior Change* (John Wiley, New York).
19. Sobell, M.B. and Sobell, L.C. (1978), *Behavioral Treatment of Alcohol Problems* (Plenum Press, New York).
20. Goldfried, M.R. and Davison, G.C. (1976), *Clinical Behavior Therapy* (Holt, Rinehart and Winston, New York).
21. Kingsley, R.G. and Wilson, G.T. (1977), 'Behavior Therapy for Obesity: A Comparative Investigation of Long-term Efficacy', *Journal of Consulting and Clinical Psychology*, vol. 45, no. 2, pp. 288-98.
22. Brownell, K.D., Heckerman, C.L., Westlake, R.J., Hayes, S.C. and Monti, P.M. (1978), 'The Effects of Couples Training and Partner Cooperativeness in the Behavioural Treatment of Obesity', *Behaviour Research and Therapy*, vol. 16, pp. 323-33.
23. Argyle, M., Bryant, B., Trower, P. and Marzillier, J. (1977), *Social Skills and Mental Health* (Methuen, London).
24. Liberman, R.P., King, L.W., DeRisi, W.J. and McCann, M. (1975), *Personal Effectiveness* (Research Press, Champaign, Illinois).
25. Miller, P.M. and Mastria, M.A. (1977), *Alternatives to Alcohol Abuse* (Research Press, Champaign, Illinois).
26. Azrin, N.H., Flores, T. and Kaplan, S.J. (1975), 'Job-Finding Club: A Group Assisted Program for Obtaining Employment', *Behaviour Research and Therapy*, vol. 13, pp. 17-27.
27. Hunt, G.M. and Azrin, N.H. (1973), 'The Community Reinforcement Approach to Alcoholism', *Behaviour Research and Therapy*, vol. 11, pp. 91-104.
28. Azrin, N.H. (1976), 'Improvements in the Community Reinforcement Approach to Alcoholism', *Behaviour Research and Therapy*, vol. 14, pp. 339-48.
29. Rachman, S., Hodgson, R. and Marks, I.M. (1971), 'Treatment of Chronic Obsessive-compulsive Neurosis', *Behaviour Research and Therapy*, vol. 9, pp. 237-47.
30. Marks, I.M., Hodgson, R. and Rachman, S. (1975), 'Treatment of Chronic Obsessive-compulsive Neurosis by *in-vivo* Exposure', *British Journal of Psychiatry*, vol. 127, pp. 349-64.
31. Rachman, S. and Hodgson, R. (1979), *Obsessions and Compulsions* (Prentice Hall, New Jersey).
32. Hodgson, R. and Rankin, H. (1976), 'Modification of Excessive Drinking by Cue Exposure', *Behaviour Research and Therapy*, vol. 14, pp. 305-7.
33. Beck, A.T. (1976), *Cognitive Therapy and the Emotional Disorders* (International Universities Press Inc., New York).
34. Rush, A.J., Beck, A.T., Kovacs, M. and Hollon, S. (1977), 'Comparative Efficacy of Cognitive Therapy and Pharmacotherapy in the Treatment of Depressed Outpatients', *Cognitive Therapy and Research*, vol. 1, no. 1, pp. 17-37.
35. Meichenbaum, D. (1977), *Cognitive-Behaviour Modification* (Plenum Press, New York).

11 ANYBODY GOT A MATCH? TREATMENT RESEARCH AND THE MATCHING HYPOTHESIS

Frederick B. Glaser

That it is the course of wisdom to assure the greatest degree of complementarity between particular problems and the means employed to remedy them is, at first glance, neither a novel nor a radical idea. Medicine, in large measure, is built upon the principle of differential diagnosis followed by differential treatment. So, too are built many other bodies of applied knowledge which deal with human behaviour.

Nevertheless, as is the case with so many other sound ideas, the notion of suiting the remedy to the problem is often more honoured in the breach than in the observance. The simplicity, convenience, and indeed glory of possessing, or more usually believing that one possesses, a single remedy suitable for all problems, often proves in practice to be too tempting to avoid. In what follows, some general aspects of the attempt to find specific ways to deal with specific problems related to the consumption of alcohol will be discussed.

The Matching Hypothesis: General Considerations

A judicious analysis of human nature holds that 'Every man is in certain respects (a) like all other men, (b) like some other men, and (c) like no other man'.[1] Most interventions designed to alter (and usually to ameliorate) human behaviour take their point of departure from the first two of these assertions.[2] Therefore, the question narrows to whether all persons manifesting a given type of behaviour are to be dealt with in the same way, or whether they are to be divided on some basis into groups and each group dealt with in a different way. The question is not whether similarities and differences between individuals exist — they both do — but which is prepotent in determining the outcome of treatment.

Dissatisfaction with Uniform Treatment Approaches

In most circumstances at the present time, the similarities between individuals are assumed to be prepotent, and hence all individuals presenting are dealt with in the same way. Thus all students in a given school, all offenders in a given correctional facility, and all patients in a given treatment setting for psychological problems, drug dependence problems, alcohol problems, and even medical problems, tend to be dealt with in exactly the same manner. There is something to be said for this. Since everyone gets the same thing, the delivery of service is far less complicated. In addition, a few of the problems which beset people, even those with protean manifestations (syphilis and tuberculosis are examples in the medical area) do have an underlying single aetiology and can be effectively dealt with using a restricted range of interventions. But whether this is generally true is another matter.

Definitive evidence on the efficacy of interventions is not plentiful, which is perhaps why the matching hypothesis in most fields remains an hypothesis. Yet in certain instances, such as with respect to alcohol problems, controlled experimentation has suggested that the results of uniform intervention applied across the board are no better than those achieved with minimal interventions.[3] Such work as this gives weight to a growing consensus that the *differences* between groups of people are of the greatest importance in terms of the outcome of various kinds of interventions, and hence that those interventions ought not to be uniform. Material culled from many fields bears witness to this point, for example, medicine,[4] education,[5] corrections,[6] psychology[7] and drug problems.[8] In the field of alcohol problems one finds similar opinions:

> . . . most studies consider alcoholics as a unitary group, thereby tacitly assuming within-group homogeneity. If a group average personality profile does not adequately represent most patients classified as alcoholics, then analyses using a group profile could wash out meaningful individual variances . . . Certainly, the most important finding in this study is that there are many distinct types of alcoholic patients widely differing in personality and psychopathology . . . this . . . may prove useful during hospital intake for classifying and then channeling patients into optimal treatment programmes.[9]

The population of persons with alcohol problems is multivariant. Correspondingly, treatment services should be diverse, emphasizing the development of a variety of services, with determination of which treatments, delivered in which contexts, are most effective for which persons and which types of problems.[10]

Although work on the matching of clients and interventions is further advanced in some fields (medicine, education, corrections) than in others, it is evident that similar principles apply across fields and that a matching approach is seen as generally promising. Conversely, accompanying the prevalence of uniform approaches in each area is a general pessimism regarding the efficacy of human therapeutics. Teachers, counsellors, correction officers, physicians, and indeed all those who can broadly be defined as clinicians or human service workers, tend to 'burn-out' after several years of practice, frustrated in their efforts to induce significant changes in the great majority of those entrusted to their care. Uniform approaches to complex problems rarely produce satisfactory results in more than a small proportion of cases. A larger proportion will either be unchanged or actually worsen. This general phenomenon has been informally enshrined as the Rule of One Third.[11]

In addition to being generally ineffective, uniform approaches to complex problems may compound therapeutic pessimism by disguising or obscuring significant interactions between particular sub-groups and the treatment being provided. It is more than coincidental that, when two or more interventions are compared with each other, the most common result is a tie.[3, 12-14] While the theoretical possibility exists that this may reflect unrecognised but common effective factors in all interventions,[15-17] a more likely explanation is that the assumed homogeneity of the target population is illusory. If the population being treated is in fact heterogeneous, but is dealt with as if it were homogeneous, those variables which are critical for successful client-treatment interactions for both forms of intervention will tend to be uniformly distributed in the differing conditions of the experiment, and the results in each condition will be the same for that reason.[11]

Even in studies which do not end in a tie, but which appear to demonstrate the superiority of one form of treatment over another, considering the population homogeneous may lead to an incorrect interpretation of results. In this regard an excellent example was a carefully controlled, double-blind study which initially appeared to find that depressed patients responded better to a major tranquilliser than to a tricyclic antidepressant. The authors showed that on closer analysis a very different interpretation had to be put on the results, involving highly specific interactions between definite sub-groups within the study population and the two pharmacological agents utilised.[18] Careful matching of clients and interventions, as suggested by this and many other studies, may produce superior results and hence have the potential for reversing the 'burn-out' and therapeutic pessimism which arises from largely unsuccessful attempts at uniform treatment.

Variations of the Matching Hypothesis

At least three major variants of the matching hypothesis may be identified, each concerned with different aspects of the therapeutic
situation.[19] Much work has been done on the match between *attributes
of clients and attributes of therapists*, and has dealt with such matters
as the personalities and moral values of the patients involved.[20-24] A
humorous example of this, though it represents an unintentional
match, is the so-called Yavis syndrome, an acronymic designation
suggesting a tendency of psychotherapists to select for treatment those
clients who are young, attractive, verbal, intelligent and successful.[25]
This type of match tends to downplay the specificity of the therapy
and to emphasise the specificity of the therapist.

A third type of match is between *attributes of clients and treatment goals*. Such a match may be unintentional, in that it may be
found upon retrospective examination of outcome data that certain
types of clients achieved one goal (such as controlled drinking) more
regularly, even though this was not an explicit aim of therapy.[26,27] On
the other hand, the same treatment may be deliberately utilised to
achieve different goals for different clients, such as in experimental
work now in progress at the Addiction Research Foundation in
Toronto which utilises a cognitive restructuring approach to achieve
either a goal of abstinence or of controlled drinking. Perhaps more
commonly, treatments and goals are assumed to be inextricably linked
together; thus, the only drinking behaviour goal which Alcoholics
Anonymous envisages for its members is total lifetime abstinence. This
type of match tends to downplay the specificity of the therapy and to
emphasise the specificity of the goal.

A third approach to matching seeks complementarity between
problems of clients and specific capabilities of treatments. The most
obvious examples here derive from chemotherapy, in which specific
antiobiotics may be matched against specific invading organisms, or
specific antidepressant agents may be matched against specific types or
degrees of depression.[18,28-30] Some non-drug therapies, such as family
therapy and marital therapy, are targeted upon clients with specific
problems. Others are not so targeted, since they are presumed to be
useful for all clients. For example, in the treatment of alcohol problems,
'group psychotherapy seems to stand supreme in the modes of treatment, even though it has never been proved or disproved that this
necessarily is the best type of treatment to offer alcoholic patients.'[31]

Nor has the particular type of problem addressed by group psycho-therapy been clearly specified. Nevertheless, it is possible to conceptualise group psychotherapy and other allegedly useful therapies as in fact addressing specific client problems, and hence to test them within the context of this variant of the matching hypothesis.[32] This type of match emphasises the specificity of the therapy.

All three variants of the matching hypothesis are unquestionably important and worthy of further study. Indeed, there has been some tendency to examine them all simultaneously, in the hope that specific therapists using specific methods on specific clients might achieve specific goals. While this is doubtless a desirable final goal, such inter-actions in practice may prove to be rather complicated, and it may be wiser to examine only a single kind of match at a time. In this regard the third variant seems somewhat more practical than the other two. Developing specific interventions which effectively deal with specific problems when deployed across a variety of interveners assures a broader applicability of treatment. Although in the past it has occasionally been possible to hire treatment staff whose personal atrributes matched those of specific elements of the client population (e.g.[6]), this seems less feasible in an area of militant fair employment practices.

The Need for Specificity

Irrespective of the type of match under study, it is clear that matching experiments require the *specification* of clients, therapists, interventions and goals, at least along those dimensions which are considered crucial to outcome. Unless this is done, it is difficult to know whether a match has occurred. For obvious reasons, particularly that of replication by other investigators, the simpler and more objective the specification of the variables, the better. An instructive example is the evolution of increased precision in specifying the A-B therapist match in psycho-therapy.[20]

Much has been accomplished in the development of appropriate means of specifying client populations. Similar measures to those applied to clients may be utilised to specify therapists. The goals of treatment are not unusually difficult to specify, though this is all too infrequently done. It is likely that specification of the intervention employed may prove to be the most difficult problem of all. But some means will have to be developed to permit others to understand very clearly and to replicate with precision an intervention under investi-gation in a given experiment.[33]

Directions for the Future

As is hopefully illustrated by the foregoing discussion, a picture
emerges from past experience to guide future exploration of the matching hypothesis. In order to enhance the probability that a given
experiment tests the hypothesis, sound theoretical reasons for supposing
that a match exists should be explicated and, if possible, existing
empirical data bearing upon the match should be brought forward to
support its cogency. Provision should be made for all of the elements of
the match, including clients, therapists, interventions and goals, to be
clearly, objectively, reliably and if possible readily specified. It will
frequently be the case that the matching criteria will exclude from the
experiment all but a small proportion of the clients who are seeking
treatment. Thus provision should be made for screening a very large
population in order to find those clients relevant to given research
efforts. At the same time it is ethically mandatory to provide for the
alternative management of those clients who are selected out, or who
drop out, of treatment.

Once the treatment-seeking population is properly screened, characterised and classified, it should be randomly distributed among the
conditions of the experiment. One of these should usually involve what
may be termed minimal care. This is at once a more practical and a
more ethical control condition than a no-care group, and it also
provides a basis for cost-effectiveness studies. Sufficient time should be
permitted for follow-up subsequent to treatment. Experiments will be
more convincing if at least two client samples, an original sample and a
replication sample, are used. Consideration may also be given to shar-
pening the specification of the match following the initial analysis of
data, and then replicating the experiment to see whether superior
results can be achieved with more refined selection criteria.[34]

The Matching Hypothesis: Evidence from Alcohol Studies

The notion of matching problems with treatments is virtually co-
extensive with the scientific study of alcohol problems. In the course
of an exhaustive review of what was then known about the treatment
of patients, Bowman and Jellinek observed almost four decades ago that:

> . . . the only possibility (of improving treatment for alcoholism) is
> to bring greater order into psychotherapeutic procedures. By this we
> mean that a definite effort has to be made to establish criteria for

the suitability of any given method to a given patient; the criteria so
far established are definitely superficial.[35]

But the matching hypothesis remains hypothetical. However promising it may be, it is as yet unproven. One major inhibiting factor may be
the prevalent conviction (e.g.[36]) that client-outcomes are largely
explicable in terms of pretreatment client characteristics. If this were
so, attempting to match clients to the right treatment would be irrelevant. However, the *amount* of variance in client-outcome explained by
pretreatment client characteristics is not great. In a recent careful study
of 429 clients seen at five different treatment facilities in the same
geographic area, it was found that client characteristics accounted for
only 15 per cent to 33 per cent of the variance.[37] Further analysis of
this data base suggested that the preponderant role often attributed to
pretreatment client characteristics may in considerable measure be an
artifact of the statistical methods used to analyse the data. More
sophisticated methods, which are able to account for the indirect
effects of variables (i.e. those effects which are mediated by other
variables), suggest that a much larger proportion of variance in outcome
is in fact due to programme factors. The authors feel that 'perhaps the
most important conclusion to be derived from these results is that
alcoholism treatment programmes may have more substantial differential
effects on outcome than previous literature has suggested . . . some of
these effects are probably related to patient-programme selection and
congruence . . .'.[38]

With this in mind, let us examine the evidence. Very few direct tests
of the matching hypothesis have been undertaken in the field of alcohol
problem treatment. In what follows, four examples of experimental
treatment research in this field will be explored for what light they can
shed on the matching hypothesis. Although they are inconclusive, it is
hoped that the promise which they hold for the future will be evident.

On 1 January 1950, an experiment was begun at Winter Veterans
Administration Hospital in Topeka, Kansas. It addressed the differential
treatment of chronic alcoholism. As described by the principal investigator, Dr Robert S. Wallerstein,[39,40] it had two major purposes. The
first was to see 'whether any of the offered treatment programs should
be the one of choice'.[39] In particular, the drug disulfiram (antabuse)
had just entered the therapeutic lists with glowing endorsements, and
the researchers wished to examine its effect, as well as to study other
treatment interventions which had either received similarly positive
reports (e.g. conditioned reflex therapy) or which they themselves

found interesting and thought might be effective (e.g. group hypno-therapy). But what was described as 'a second major set of hypotheses'[39] had to do with differential treatment indications. Not surprisingly, in view of the presence and influence in Topeka of the prestigious Menninger Clinic, a psychoanalytically oriented treatment institution, the specification of the 'match' was couched in psychodynamic terms.[40] Consequently, the investigators principally looked at the results of the interaction between psychiatric diagnosis and treatment modality. As noted above, antabuse, conditioned reflex therapy, and group hypnotherapy were three of the treatments which were explored. The fourth was milieu therapy; it was originally intended to be a control condition for the other three treatments, but demonstrated to the investigator's satisfaction that it had a distinct therapeutic character of its own. A total of 178 male inpatients were randomly assigned to the four conditions of the experiment, treated, and followed.

Although it will be appreciated from the foregoing description, as well as from other critiques of the study (e.g.[36]), that methodological problems existed, the results were nevertheless quite instructive. No single treatment proved to be the treatment of choice.[40] There was a scatter of improvement rates across psychiatric diagnoses that is at least suggestive of matching effects (Table 11.1). For both conditioned reflex therapy and milieu therapy, it proved possible to revise the classification scheme for patients in such a way that more precise matches were revealed. It was found, for example, that a *post hoc* combination of several of the diagnostic categories into a bipartite classification of 'less aggressive' and 'more aggressive' revealed a marked discrimination in improvement rates in conditioned reflex therapy, the more aggressive patients showing much less improvement (Table 11.1). Similarly, when the use of psychiatric diagnoses gave little promise of predicting outcome in milieu therapy, patients were reclassified according to a three factor index based upon marital status, work adjustment, and sexual adjustment. The resultant 'attachment factor' was highly correlated with improvement in milieu therapy (Table 11.2).

Of course, such retrospective restructuring of data may be somewhat suspect. But it at least represents a high degree of confidence in the cogency of matching clients to treatments, which seems to have been generated by the study. In addition, and most importantly for progress in the field, the investigators showed a willingness to re-examine their original hypotheses regarding matching in the light of actual data. This did not stop with the type of restructuring outlined above; Dr Wallerstein

Table 11.1: Restructured Outcome Data on Conditioned Reflex
Therapy by Level of Aggression

Level of Aggression	Improved	Unimproved
Less aggressive	8	1
More aggressive	4	16
Total	12	17

Source: Wallerstein study.[40]

Table 11.2: Outcome Data on Milieu Therapy by Attachment Factor

Attachment Factor	Improved	Unimproved
Positive	10	5
Negative	1	10
Total	11	15

Source: Wallerstein study.[40]

and his colleagues intended to push on to further experimentation.[40]
Unfortunately, the successor project was never mounted, though this
was not related to a lack of confidence on the part of the investigators
in its general conclusions.[41]

Another major study of the treatment of alcoholism was launched
about two decades later. Though of relatively recent date, it has already
achieved a measure of fame and currency throughout the world. While
its considerable merits richly deserve this fate, its far-flung reputation
may in part be an instance of the right thing happening for the wrong
reason. Despite the rigorous precautions its authors took to avoid it, the
study of 100 married male alcoholics in treatment by Dr Griffith
Edwards, Dr Jim Orford and several colleagues[3] has widely been
understood to have proved, at long last, what everyone always 'knew':
that the treatment of alcohol problems does not work.

Essentially, the 100 or so married male clients in this study were
randomly assigned to a control and an experimental condition. The
experimental group received what is referred to as an 'average package
of help', thought by the authors to be congruent with a relatively good
level of the standard sort of treatment generally available to alcoholics
in the Western world. The overall outcome for those who received
treatment was no better than for those who received advice.

In discussing these results, the authors did not interpret the study as reflecting negatively upon treatment. Rather, they felt that it illustrated 'a need for development of new treatment techniques and their rigorous testing'.[3] 'The implications of this study', they cautioned, 'must not be seen as nihilistic. In an area of health care so much in the need of development it would be sad indeed if a research report were misread as evidence that the treatment of alcoholism must forever be a worthless enterprise.'[3] And they specifically noted that 'a reservation which should properly attach to any too absolute interpretation of a clinical trial is that conclusions based on the averaging process and simple comparisons of group means may fail to bring out important patient type — treatment modality interactions.'[3]

On reflection, the most appropriate interpretation of this study would appear to be *not* that treatment is no more effective than advice, which seems to be the way in which it is commonly understood; but rather that, if the *same* treatment is indiscriminately applied to all patients, the results on balance do not improve upon the results achieved by advice. An inspection of *two* year follow-up data on clients from the same study[27] strongly underscores this possibility. While the numbers involved are quite small, it appears that there were clear-cut differential results for different kinds of clients in the two conditions of the study. Those diagnosed as dependent or *gamma* alcoholics achieved much better results in the treatment group, while those otherwise diagnosed tended to do much better in the advice group (Table 11.3). In addition, there was an interaction between the types of clients and the goals they achieved, with the gamma alcoholics achieving good results through abstention and the others tending to achieve good results through controlled drinking (Table 11.4).

Had the study population been matched to treatments and/or to goals in this way, it is difficult to see how the results could have failed to be superior. A replication of this study is very much in order. By providing so promising a lead to additional experimentation, and by providing a further elaboration of the implications of their 'advice' group,[42] the authors have convincingly underscored their assertion that there is 'a need for the development of new treatment techniques and their rigorous testing'.[3]

Another recent experimental study[29,30] in the treatment of alcohol problems both supports the cogency of the matching hypothesis and illustrates the tyranny of the mean. Patients hospitalised in a regional alcoholic unit in England were administered the Back depression inventory, with those scoring 15 or more (when free of drugs and/or

Table 11.3: Outcome Data by Jellinek Classification of Clients

	Advice	Treatment
Non-dependent alcoholics	11*	6*
Dependent (*gamma*) alcoholics	0**	9**

*p <.01;   **p <.01
Source: Orford *et al.*[27]

Table 11.4: Outcome Data by Goal Achieved

	Number of abstainers	Number of controlled drinkers
Non-dependent alcoholics	5	10
Dependent (*gamma*) alcoholics	6*	0*

*p <0.025
Source: Orford *et al.*[27]

alcohol) being classified as depressed alcoholics. All patients, whether depressed or not, were then randomly assigned to either a placebo condition or to treatment with a sustained release form of lithium carbonate. Both patients and therapists were blind to diagnostic category and treatment. Results in patients continuing in the study for an average of 41 weeks on one of the outcome criteria, mean number of days spent drinking, are reported in Table 11.5.

Those patients who received lithium spent less than half the number of days drinking than did patients who received the placebo. Though this difference was not statistically significant, an embattled family might well appreciate an extra 11.2 days per year free of drinking behaviour. Given such considerations, and categorical statements from the prior literature to the effect that 'lithium appears to have a marked and statistically significant beneficial effect on chronic alcoholics',[43] the uncritical acceptance of the mean data from this study might have resulted in the widespread dosing of alcoholics with lithium.

The balance of the data, however, illustrates the fallacy in this approach, and the cogency of matching the use of lithium to the objectively determined degree of depression. In patients who were depressed according to the criterion employed in this study, there was a highly significant reduction (37 fold!) in the number of days spent drinking. Non-depressed patients actually spent a *greater* number of days drinking when on lithium.[44] Thus the favourable results achieved by lithium in this study can be entirely explained by its effects in depressed alcoholics. Its administration to non-depressed alcoholics appears to make matters worse, and its widespread use in unselected alcoholic clients is presumably contraindicated.

Finally, a set of studies which provide a fascinating illustration of matching will be explored. The theoretical ideas underlying the matching of clients and treatments upon which they are based involve the notion of Conceptual Level. As explained by MacLachlan,

> Conceptual level may be described as a blend of the cognitive and motivational aspects of personality orientation ranging from low to high. Persons lowest in CL are seen as being poorly socialized, egocentric, impulsive and cognitively simple. At the next stage, they are dependent on authority, compliant and concerned with rules. At the third level, they are independent, questioning and self-assertive. Finally, persons highest in CL are interdependent, empathic, and cognitively complex.[24]

The postulated match is of unstructured individuals (i.e. those with a low Conceptual Level) with structured treatments, and vice versa; in this sense, it is an inverse match. Application of this paradigm to treatment was based on prior observations suggesting that therapists with lower CLs provided highly structured therapy, while therapists with higher CLs provided non-directive or at least less structured therapy. Aftercare following therapy could also be characterised in this manner; clients who were residents of the city in which the study was mounted took part in a highly structured aftercare programme; while

Table 11.5: Outcome Data (Mean Number of Days Spent Drinking) by Type of Treatment and Level of Depression

	All patients (N = 38)	Non-depressed patients (N = 22)	Depressed patients (N = 16)
Placebo	20.7	0.77	48.1*
Lithium	9.5	15.5	1.3*

* p > 0.01
Source: Merry *et al.*[29] and Reynolds *et al.*[30]

Table 11.6: Outcome by Degrees of Match for 94 Clients

Matching paradigm	Recovery rate (%) of	
	Clients matched	Clients mis-matched
To structure of therapy	70	50
To structure of aftercare	71	49
To both	77	38

Source: McLachlan[23,24]

clients who resided in other areas were kept in contact but were provided with no programme. Thus aftercare for out-of-town clients could be viewed as relatively unstructured. Consequently, in this study one could examine the outcomes of clients matched to therapy, to aftercare, or to both.

Results for 94 clients (Table 11.6) were significant beyond what might have been expected by chance; that is, clients who were matched either to therapy or to aftercare did significantly better than clients who were not. Of particular interest is the fact that clients who were matched to therapy alone or to aftercare alone did about equally well in comparison with mis-matched clients; but clients who were matched to *both* therapy and aftercare had a slightly higher overall recovery rate than those matched only to one condition, and the gap between these clients and those who were mis-matched to both conditions of treatment was a great deal wider.

An overall inference favourable to the matching hypothesis can with justice be drawn collectively from the four experimental studies reviewed above. They do not definitively prove that matching is effective in the treatment of alcohol problems. But they would certainly appear to demonstrate that there is much potential merit in the undertaking of further investigation of the matching hypothesis by treatment researchers. In the final section, a systematic way of approaching treatment research which it is hoped will facilitate its conduct will be described.

A System to Facilitate Treatment Research

Treatment research is usually imposed upon existing treatment services from without. This creates enormous difficulties for all concerned, which may be the reason that so few major treatment research studies are done. An alternative is to build a system, or to restructure an existing non-system, in such a way that there is a close interaction between treatment and research. The Clinical Institute of the Addiction Research Foundation in Toronto, Canada, which deals with approximately 2,400 new cases of alcohol and drug dependence per year, has been engaged in designing, testing and implementing such a system for some time.

Several descriptions of the system are extant.[45-53] Hence this description will be brief. Studies are carried out in parallel with active treatment programmes providing many potential interventions to which the client may be directed as alternatives to research interventions. All clients enter the system through a single point, which quite readily allows their initial contact to be with a primary care worker. This individual has overall responsibility for the management of the client's care. He or she will provide a basic level of supportive care to the client as needed, and will assure continuity of care with whatever speciality interventions may be indicated. Should a client enter a research project, the primary care worker will recede into the background; but if the client should drop out of the research project, or if the research project should terminate, the primary care worker will re-emerge, to look after the client's needs. By this means the system satisfies the contemporary ethical requirement that, notwithstanding the need for research, each client must be provided with at least a basic level of care.[54, 55]

Concern that such primary care may be a confounding variable in experimental studies, and that a no-treatment group might be preferable, is understandable if short-sighted. Ethical considerations aside, no-treatment controls have many practical problems. Especially in countries where some form of universal health insurance obtains, such as in Canada and the United Kingdom, clients seeking treatment who are given one are quite likely to go elsewhere. Since there is then no control over what interventions they may receive, clients being seen by primary care workers may paradoxically represent less of a confound than those placed in an alleged no-treatment group. In addition, they and the record of their care remain within the ambit of the treatment system, making it easier to specify what happens to them over time than if they leave the system. Finally, since the primary care workers and the research belong to the same system, precise specification of the activities of the primary care workers can be agreed upon in advance and confirmed by supervision. And, of course, when the time comes to follow the clients up, those who remain in contact with their primary care workers will be much easier to find. Thus, on balance, it appears that the primary care component of the system greatly facilitates research.

It is highly desirable to have the capability of screening many clients prior to treatment, so that all those eligible for research may be diverted to it and large number of subjects thereby generated. It should be possible to screen these clients on a large number of variables, both standard and experimental in nature. All of this work should be performed 'blind' by personnel not involved in treatment.

Such requirements are met by the Clinical Institute system. A well-staffed Assessment Unit is supervised and managed by highly trained personnel. Clients are routinely referred to this unit following their initial primary care contact or contacts, rather than being referred to treatment programmes. Indeed, access to treatment programmes, as well as to research experiments, is contingent upon assessment. Clients refusing assessment (approximately 15 per cent of the treatment-seeking population) are provided only with primary care, on the ground that specialised or definitive treatment without appropriate assessment is indefensible. Since virtually all data are gathered at a single point, both in space and time, their collection, collation and processing are facilitated. Computerised print-outs of the assessment data on all clients have been routinely available for some time, and rapid progress in the direction of on-line testing of clients and automated scoring of test results is being made.

Finally, there is the issue of providing adequate follow-up. In many treatment research studies, an entire follow-up team must be assembled from scratch, trained, and used to perform a single study of a single programme. This is a manifest inefficiency. In the Clinical Institute system, a permanent, full-time Follow-up Unit which can provide these services to all research projects requiring them has been established.

To summarise, the Clinical Institute treatment research system provides reliable and consistent basic services of primary care, assessment, and follow-up to all investigators. Any investigator whose protocol passes rigorous scientific, ethical, and administrative review may utilise these services. Experienced research administrators are available to provide advice on how this might best be done. The system is designed to facilitate pre-test and post-test experimental designs (it places all interventions automatically within this context) and, in particular, it facilitates treatment research experiments involving the matching hypothesis.

To date, emphasis has necessarily been upon the construction of this system. Its use in experimental treatment research is largely a matter for the future. But there is reason to think that it will avoid many of the difficulties of the past by bringing treatment and research together within the same operational context and permitting them to work synergistically. Hopefully this will allow the concerted, incessant, long-term effort required to assure that effective and efficient treatment will emerge in the long-run with the least possible damage to the spirits and wills of investigators, therapists and clients. For all that has been said, written, and done about the treatment of alcohol problems, we still appear to be at the beginning of the beginning. One thinks of the portrayal of the 'connoisseur of chaos' by Wallace Stevens.

The squirming facts exceed the squamous mind,
If one may say so. And yet relation appears,
A small relation expanding like the shade
Of a cloud on sand, a shape on the side of a hill.[56]

Acknowledgements

The author wishes to acknowledge the assistance of Drs Helen Annis, Griffith Edwards, Chad Emrick, Yady Israel, John McLachlan, Alan Ogborne and Robert Wallerstein in the preparation of this manuscript. Responsibility for the opinions herein, however, rests solely with him. Thanks are also due to Mrs Olive Lewis for assuming the inordinate secretarial burden engendered by the manuscript.

Notes

1. Kluckhohn, C. and Murray, H.A. (1971), 'Personality Formation: The Determinants', in Kluckhohn, C. and Murray, H.A. (eds.), *Personality in Nature, Society and Culture*, 2nd edn (Alfred A. Knopf, New York).
2. From an instrumental point of view, the elaboration of a *totally* novel and unique intervention for each individual, which would seem to follow logically from the third assertion, is a practical impossibility under most circumstances. Preconceived interventions in which practitioners have received at least a modicum of training are required for a timely response.
3. Edwards, G., Orford, J., Egert, S., Guthrie, S., Hawker, A., Hensman, C., Mitcheson, M., Oppenheimer, E. and Taylor, C. (1977), 'Alcoholism: A Controlled Trial of "Treatment" and "Advice" ', *Journal of Studies on Alcohol*, vol. 38, pp. 1004-31.
4. Fries, J.F. (1976), 'A Data Bank for the Clinician?', *New England Journal of Medicine*, vol. 294, pp. 1400-2.
5. Hunt, D.E. (1971), *Matching Models in Education: The Coordination of Teaching Models with Student Characteristics*, Monograph Series 10 (Ontario Institute for Studies in Education, Toronto).
6. Warren, M.Q. (1969), 'The Case for Differential Treatment of Delinquents',

Annals of the American Academy of Politics and Social Science, vol. 381, pp. 47-59.

7. Kiesler, D.J. (1966), 'Some Myths of Psychotherapy Research and the Search for a Paradigm', *Psychological Bulletin*, vol. 65, pp. 110-36.

8. Freedman, A.M. (1966), 'Drug Addiction: An Eclectic View', *Journal of the American Medical Association*, vol. 197, pp. 878-82.

9. Skinner, H.A., Jackson, D.N. and Hoffmann, H. (1974), 'Alcoholic Personality Types: Identification and Correlates', *Journal of Abnormal Psychology*, vol. 83, pp. 658-66.

10. Pattison, E.M., Sobell, M.B. and Sobell, L.C. (1977), *Emerging Concepts of Alcohol Dependence* (Springer Publishing Company, New York).

11. Glaser, F.B. (1978), 'Selecting Patients for Treatment: An Heuristic Model', in Glaser, F.B., *The Phase Zero Report of the Core-Shell Treatment System Project: Early Working Papers* (Addiction Research Foundation, Toronto).

12. Luborsky, L., Singer, B. and Luborsky, L. (1975), 'Comparative Studies of Psychotherapies: Is it True that "Everyone Has Won and All Must Have Prizes?" ', *Archives of General Psychiatry*, vol. 32, pp. 995-1008.

13. Emrick, C.D. (1975), 'A Review of Psychologically Oriented Treatment of Alcoholism. II. The Relative Effectiveness of Different Treatment Approaches and the Effectiveness of Treatment vs No Treatment', *Journal of Studies on Alcohol*, vol. 36, pp. 88-108.

14. Emrick, C.D. (1978), 'Relative Effectiveness of Alcohol Abuse Treatment', manuscript prepared for the National Institute on Alcohol Abuse and Alcoholism.

15. Rosenzweig, S. (1936), 'Some Implicit Common Factors in Diverse Methods of Psychotherapy', *American Journal of Orthopsychiatry*, vol. 6, pp. 412-15.

16. Frank, J.D. (1959), 'The Dynamics of the Psychotherapeutic Relationship: Determinants and Effects of the Therapist's Influence', *Psychiatry*, vol. 11, pp. 17-39.

17. Truax, C.B. and Wargo, D.G. (1966), 'Psychotherapeutic Encounters that Change Behavior: For Better or Worse', *American Journal of Psychotherapy*, vol. 20, pp. 499-520.

18. Overall, J.E., Hollister, L.E., Johnson, M. and Pennington, V. (1966), 'Nosology of Depression and Differential Response to Drugs', *Journal of the American Medical Association*, vol. 195, pp. 946-8.

19. It is not implied that the possibilities discussed here exhaust the types of matches which may require investigation. They are only those most commonly investigated to date. If one asks what potential matches may be studied, the possibilities seem rich for future investigation.

20. Razin, A.M. (1971), 'A-B Variable in Psychotherapy: A Critical Review', *Psychological Bulletin*, vol. 75, pp. 1-21.

21. Martini, J.L. (1976), 'Patient-therapist Value Congruence: Interpersonal Attraction and Outcome in Marathon Group Therapy with Alcoholics', Sub-study no. 776 (Addiction Research Foundation, Toronto).

22. Peretz, M. and Glaser, F.B. (1974), 'Value Change in Drug Education: The Role of Encounter Groups', *International Journal of Addictions*, vol. 9, pp. 637-52.

23. McLachlan, J.F.C. (1972), 'Benefit from Group Therapy as a Function of Patient-therapist Match on Conceptual Level', *Psychotherapy, Theory, Research and Practice*, vol. 9, pp. 317-23.

24. McLachlan, J.F.C. (1974), 'Therapy Strategies, Personality Orientation, and Recovery from Alcoholism', *Canadian Psychiatric Association Journal*, vol. 19, pp. 25-30.

25. Schofield, W. (1964), *Psychotherapy: The Purchase of Friendship* (Prentice-Hall Inc., New Jersey).

26. Popham, R.E. and Schmidt, W. (1976), 'Some Factors Affecting the Likelihood of Moderate Drinking by Treated Alcoholics', *Journal of Studies on Alcohol*, vol. 37, pp. 868-82.

27. Orford, J., Oppenheimer, E. and Edwards, G. (1976), 'Abstinence or Control: The Outcome for Excessive Drinkers Two Years After Consultation', *Behavioural Research and Therapy*, vol. 14, pp. 409-18.

28. Paykel, E.S. (1972), 'Depressive Typologies and Response to Amitriptyline', *British Journal of Psychiatry*, vol. 120, pp. 147-56.

29. Merry, J., Reynolds, C.M., Bailey, J. and Coppen, A. (1976), 'Prophylactic Treatment of Alcoholism by Lithium Carbonate: A Controlled Study', *Lancet*, vol. 2, pp. 481-2.

30. Reynolds, C.M., Merry, J. and Coppen, A. (1977), 'Prophylactic Treatment of Alcoholism by Lithium Carbonate: An Initial Report', *Alcoholism: Clinical and Experimental Research*, vol. 1, pp. 109-11.

31. Rathod, N. (1976), 'Making Treatment Better', in Edwards, G. and Grant, M. (eds.), *Alcoholism: New Knowledge and New Responses* (Croom Helm, London; University Park Press, Baltimore).

32. Glaser, F.B. (1978), 'Problem-Indicator-Intervention Matrix: An Attempt', in Glaser, F.B., *The Phase Zero Report of the Core-Shell Treatment System Project: Early Working Papers* (Addiction Research Foundation, Toronto).

33. Glaser, F.B. (1978), 'Specifying the Shell', in Glaser, F.B., *The Phase Zero Report of the Core-Shell Treatment System Project: Early Working Papers* (Addiction Research Foundation, Toronto).

34. This strategy reflects the general view that an incremental accretion of knowledge, built up over a series of experiments, may be far more fruitful in the long run than any dramatic attempt to transfigure a given field with the blinding insights derived from a single brilliant experiment. Episodes of this sort belong more to the realm of fiction than science.

35. Bowman, K.M. and Jellinek, M.E. (1941), 'Alcohol Addiction and its Treatment', *Quarterly Journal of Studies on Alcohol*, vol. 2, pp. 98-176.

36. Ogborne, A.C. (1978), 'Patient Characteristics as Predictors of Treatment Outcome for Alcohol and Drug Abusers', in Israel, Y., Glaser, F.B., Kalant, H., Popham, R.E., Schmidt, W. and Smart, R. (eds.), *Research Advances in Alcohol and Drug Problems, Vol. 4* (Plenum Press, New York).

37. Bromet, E., Moos, R., Bliss, F. and Wuthmann, C. (1977), 'Post-treatment Functioning of Alcoholic Patients: Its Relation to Program Participation', *Journal of Consulting and Clinical Psychology*, vol. 45, pp. 829-42.

38. Cronkite, R.C. and Moos, R.H. (1978), 'Evaluating Alcoholism Treatment Programs: An Integrated Approach', *Journal of Consulting and Clinical Psychology*, vol. 46, pp. 1005-19.

39. Wallerstein, R.S. (1956), 'Comparative Study of Treatment Methods for Chronic Alcoholism: The Alcoholism Research Project at Winter VA Hospital', *American Journal of Psychiatry*, vol. 113, pp. 228-33.

40. Wallerstein, R.S. (1957), *Hospital Treatment of Alcoholics: A Comparative Experimental Study* (Basic Books, New York).

41. Wallerstein, R.S. (1979), personal communication.

42. Edwards, G. and Orford, J. (1977), 'A Plain Treatment for Alcoholism', *Proceedings of the Royal Society of Medicine*, vol. 70, pp. 344-8.

43. Kline, N.S., Wren, J.C., Cooper, T.B., Varga, E. and Canal, O. (1974), 'Evaluation of Lithium Therapy in Chronic and Periodic Alcoholism', *American Journal of Medical Science*, vol. 268, pp. 15-22.

44. Data for non-depressed alcoholics on this criterion are not provided in the study as published. However, the means for the non-depressed patients can readily be calculated. Unfortunately, insufficient data are provided to test the difference between the two means (lithium and placebo) for significance; by estimate, it

approaches significance. No explanation for this unusual finding was provided.

45. Adler, F., Moffett, A.D., Glaser, F.B., Ball, J.C. and Horvitz, D. (1974), *A Systems Approach to Drug Treatment* (Dorrance & Co., Philadelphia).

46. Glaser, F.B., Greenberg, S.W. and Barrett, M. (1978), *A Systems Approach to Alcohol Treatment* (ARF Books, Toronto).

47. Glaser, F.B. (1974), 'The Treatment of Drug Abuse in the Rural South: Application of the Core-Shell Treatment System Model', *Southern Medical Journal*, vol. 67, pp. 580-6.

48. Glaser, F.B. (1978), *The Phase Zero Report of the Core-Shell Treatment System: Early Working Papers* (Addiction Research Foundation, Toronto).

49. Staff of the Core-Shell System, *The Phase I Pilot Test of the Core-Shell Treatment System* (Addiction Research Foundation, Toronto, in press).

50. Staff of the Core-Shell System (1977), *The Phase II Pilot Test of the Core-Shell Treatment System*, Sub-study no. 962 (Addiction Research Foundation, Toronto).

51. Staff of the Core-Shell System (1978), *The Phase III Pilot Test of the Core-Shell Treatment System*, Sub-study no. 1035 (Addiction Research Foundation, Toronto).

52. Staff of the Core-Shell System (1977), *An Overview of the Core-Shell Treatment System*, Sub-study no. 840 (Addiction Research Foundation, Toronto).

53. Glaser, F.B., Annis, H.M., Pearlman, S., Segal, R.L. and Skinner, H.A. (1979), 'The Differential Therapy of Alcoholism: A Systems Approach', in Masserman, J. (ed.), *Current Psychiatric Therapies* (Grune & Stratton, New York).

54. Fried, C. (1975), 'Rights and Health Care – Beyond Equity and Efficiency', *New England Journal of Medicine*, vol. 293, pp. 241-5.

55. Fried, C. (1975), 'Equality and Rights in Medical Care: Analysis and Critical Proposals', in Perpich, J.G. (ed.), *The Implications of Guaranteeing Medical Care* (Institute of Medicine, Washington).

56. Stevens, W. (1954), 'Connoisseur in Chaos', in Williams, O. (ed.), *The Pocket Book of Modern Verse* (Pocket Books Inc., New York).

Part Four

TREATMENT SYSTEM AS CASE FOR STUDY

12 THE MEANING OF 'TREATMENT SERVICES FOR ALCOHOL-RELATED PROBLEMS' IN DEVELOPING COUNTRIES

David V. Hawks

There is a hospital in a 'developing' country where the wards are built around shaded courtyards and where each courtyard is adorned by a fountain, where the doctors and nurses dress in impeccable white and where the research staff, if necessary, can converse in any one of three European languages. Such is the attention given to individual admissions, the careful working up of their histories and the innumerable examinations to which they are subjected that patients can only be admitted one day a week.

Immediately outside the hospital hundreds of patients and their relatives sit on their haunches in the shade of trees or in the sun waiting for public transport, transport that at best comes once or twice a day and which is so inadequate in its coverage of the city as to deposit most of them miles from their homes.

The relatively few patients who are admitted to this hospital for alcohol-related problems will receive intensive treatment while they are in hospital. Their charts will be decorated with the results of innumerable tests, no body fluid will be left unexamined and the results of such examinations will be summarised in research papers, reports of which will be sent to scores of foreign collaborators.

How Relevant is Treatment?

And what, it may be asked, has been the impact of such treatment on the alcohol-related problems of that country? The answer is 'very little'. Patients, once discharged, will not be followed-up, they will inevitably return to the same impoverished circumstances, the same unemployment, the same subsistence diet, the same overcrowding and, just as inevitably, will return to the same dependence on alcohol as the only means, however maladaptive, of escaping that reality.

If the meaning of treatment for alcohol problems in the developing world is to be discussed, one must say at the outset that treatment has *no meaning* except in the context of prevention in the developing world and probably in the developed world as well. What is perhaps advantageous about the situation in some developing countries is that the virtual non-existence of treatment facilities for alcohol-related problems allows that the horse, for once, may be put in front of the cart rather than, as characterises the developed countries, prevention being thought of only when the impracticality of treatment becomes apparent.

Let us be clear, lest there be any misunderstanding, that the argument here is not against treatment for alcoholism, only against the belief that treatment is a practical possibility in the absence of any attempt to prevent alcoholism. Alcoholism is a condition so pervasive and so liable to relapse that treatment only makes any sort of sense when every effort has been made to prevent its occurrence in the first place. Except when the probability of its occurrence has been, or is being reduced, those responsible for maintaining treatment services are confronted with the fact that they stand at the end of a conveyor belt catching every tenth or hundredth casualty, conscious both of the fact that they can never cope with all those presently requiring their services and at the same time aware that the processes guaranteeing the 'production' of further casualties continue unabated. There can be few, if any, more unsatisfying roles.

Glaser[1] argues that the principal implication of his systems analysis of alcohol treatment is that there must be a significant expansion of treatment capability, but acknowledges the fact 'that expansion of treatment to cover even those who wish to be treated, let alone those who need to be treated, is most probably a manifest impossibility. Even if the will were there, the fiscal resources would not be'.

There will always be a moral imperative to treat those who seek treatment for alcoholism, even while acknowledging that they constitute only an unrepresentative and small minority of those requiring treatment. Such essentially moral gestures, however, must surely only make sense in the context of a much larger investment of effort in discerning the intricacies of prevention.

If 'adequate' resources for the treatment of alcohol-related problems, as they have been conventionally described, were ever seriously contemplated, their cost would be so enormous it would be immediately apparent that they could not be entertained. We are able to maintain our belief in the need for further treatment facilities only because the realisation of those beliefs is never even a serious possibility.

In any situation with the scarcity of resources which characterises the developing world, there can be no sense, or justification, in the deployment of those resources in the treatment of problems so prevalent and so recurrent as those associated with alcohol. If one needed to be further persuaded, one only has to consider the uncertainty of outcome which characterises even those, so called, optional treatment methods in use in the developed world.

Principles of Treatment in Developing Countries

Assuming, however, that it is agreed that treatment cannot be justified in the absence of a deliberate policy and programme to prevent alcohol-related problems, what can be said about the necessary principles of treatment in developing countries?

First of all, they must be relevant to the setting in which they are carried out. Relevance must be defined partly in the dynamic sense, in that treatment must reflect an understanding of the development and maintenance of the problems in that setting. Relevance must also mean an acknowledgement of the constraints of the situation. Included among these constraints will be the absence of specialised staff and inpatient facilities. The principles of treatment espoused will therefore need to be accessible to staff with perhaps only primary school education. They will need to be simply expressed, perhaps in the form of diagnostic flow charts and decision matrices.[2]

Such principles will also need to be applied by a wide variety of staff having contact with alcohol-related problems. At least three different levels of application can be envisaged.

The Treatment of Alcohol-related Emergencies. Even in those countries in which there is no attempt formally to treat alcohol-related problems, such problems present in acute or emergency forms and so dictate that some form of treatment be administered. In such situations it is likely that those engaged in treatment will have no specific training in the recognition and treatment of alcohol-related problems. In these circumstances it is clearly necessary to develop assessment and treatment guidelines for incorporation into the training of such staff.

The Recognition and Treatment of Alcohol-related Problems by Primary Health Care Staff. It is abundantly clear that in developing countries the majority of alcohol-related problems will be identified and managed, if at all, by non-specialist staff. It would seem, therefore, that there is a pressing need to develop guidelines for the use of such non-specialised staff.

The Training of Specialised Staff. While the recognition and management of alcohol-related problems will remain the responsibility of
primary health care personnel it will probably be necessary to establish
in each developing country a nucleus of specialist expertise, if only to
provide input into the training programme of primary health care
workers.

Treatment of alcohol-related problems in developing countries will
need to acknowledge the importance of community support for moderation and community inducement to intemperance. Those involved in
treating these problems will need to enlist the co-operation of those
who have traditionally exercised influence in this area, rather than seek
to make such persons redundant.

But, most of all, treatment will need to be applied in the context of
a national policy on prevention.

Importance of Social Context

Most of us would allow that part of the fascination of this field lies in
the embeddedness of alcohol and of alcohol-related problems in the
social context — their interest, in part at least, stems from the fact that
they symbolise a more pervasive social malaise. They are the outward
expression, in part at least, of an unworkable society and an intolerable
existence. Concern with these problems inevitably involves us in an
analysis of that society.

If alcoholism is ever a resort from a meaningless existence, then in
the end those of us who are concerned with these problems must be
concerned with the meaninglessness of that existence. A treatment or
prevention policy which pretends that alcohol-related problems are not
related to wider social and economic issues is doomed to failure.
Discerning the nature of that relationship is difficult and intervening
in it even more difficult and contentious. The only possible consideration which justifies the undertaking of so difficult a task is the
inefficacy of the alternative — not to acknowledge the relevance of
these factors.

Alcohol-related problems, if they are to be addressed with the force
which their pervasiveness and seriousness warrant, must be seen to be
related in developing countries to such diverse matters as land policy,
educational policy, trade and fiscal policy. To pretend otherwise is to
render our efforts useless. To be convinced of this we need only to
consider the ineffectuality and hypocrisy of many programmes in the

developed West which at the same time that they advocate the education of the young in responsible drinking practices also tolerate an adult model of irresponsible drinking; which pretend it is enough to provide some information as to the dangers of excessive drinking while allowing an overwhelming commercial inducement to drinking; which while complaining of the high economic cost of alcoholism nevertheless do nothing which would significantly reduce consumption and therefore the revenue earned from drinking.

There can be no effective management of alcohol-related problems in the developing world until it is recognised that such problems may be inherent in the very process of development itself and steps taken to alleviate the worst consequences of this process.

While alcohol problems have the same basic type of medical, psychiatric and social impact whatever the country, evidence now emerging suggests that countries in a state of rapid socioeconomic development may, in addition, be especially vulnerable. The very fact of rapid development brings about sociocultural changes which loosen formal or informal control. New wealth becomes available and industrial technologies of liquor production and the activities of multi-national breweries supplant traditional methods of brewing and distribution and greatly increase the supply of alcohol.

In many such countries, individuals are subject to new forms of demand and stress at a time when old forms of family and community support become less available. Drinking may become a symbol of prestige and success as well as a ready tranquilliser.

The consequences in such countries can also be partly understood in terms of the special vulnerability of particular groups. A cluster of circumstances make emergent professional and managerial sectors one such group. Young people caught in a situation in which old values are being eroded are another, while women exposed to the possibility of drinking in cultures which previously forbade this, are also especially vulnerable. Prevalence also appears to be particularly high in the shanty towns surrounding urban centres in developing countries where a large number of rural dwellers have chosen to migrate and where the way of life found is very different from that experienced before.

If alcohol-related problems are to be addressed with any kind of effectiveness a broad perspective will need to be adopted, the interrelationship of the several sectors, economic, social and personal, will need to be acknowledged, and planning will need to be holistic rather than piecemeal.

It might be reasonably asked whether it demands too much of

alcohol policy that it consider the ramifications of so many processes, whether it is reasonable to regard alcoholism as a reflection of the quality of a society's human relationships. On the other hand, it could be argued that these demands are necessary and legitimate, and that it is only when the profundity of the issues involved is faced that there is any hope of addressing them.

Acknowledgements

A number of the ideas expressed in this chapter were developed during discussions with Griffith Edwards and Joy Moser. While not wishing to imply that they agree with the particular form in which these ideas have been expressed here, the author would nevertheless wish to acknowledge their origin.

Notes

1. Glaser, F.B., Greenberg, S.W. and Barrett, M. (1978), *A Systems Approach to Alcohol Treatment* (Addiction Research Foundation, Toronto).
2. Essex, B. (1979), 'Diagnostic Flow Charts for Use by Primary Health Workers in Developing Countries' (forthcoming).

TREATMENT-SEEKING POPULATIONS AND
LARGER REALITIES

Robin Room

At least in the United States, everyone who has worked in the epidemiology of alcohol problems must at one time or another have been asked the question, 'but how many alcoholics are there in the population?' It is, in fact, a source of considerable frustration to such researchers that this seems to be the only question that seriously interests policy-makers in their work. And it is a source of even greater frustration to policy-makers that the researchers often decline to come back with a single concrete figure.[1]

The present chapter is about this issue of numbers and the other issues that it raises, and more generally about the relation between a treatment system and those who might need its services. It will draw mostly on US experience. But this parochial approach may still have relevance for other societies, for there are a number of ways in which the US experience is instructive. Not the least of these is to examine what may happen if the issue of numbers is taken seriously by a society. For, albeit in a halting and half-conscious way, the US has tried over the last 35 years to do just this, to patch together a treatment system that is capable of treating alcoholism wherever it is found in the population. Whatever its shortcomings and peculiarities, there is now in the US a very large treatment system for alcoholism, and this represents an astonishing social change in a relatively short period of time. Although the figures in Table 13.1 are rough and incomplete, they give a concrete sense of the magnitude of the change in the US in the space of one generation: an increase of at least 20-fold in the caseload treated for alcoholism in what may be broadly construed as health institutions.

The Alcoholism Movement and the Treatment Establishment

This change did not come about by accident or inadvertence, but because of the efforts of a sustained social movement, the alcoholism movement, which has dominated thought and action about alcohol problems in the United States since the early 1940s. When we think of this movement, we normally think in terms of its governing image,[2] the

Table 13.1 Alcoholism Treatment Caseload in the US, 1942 and 1976 (partial and approximate figures)

	1942		1976
State mental hospitals	10,461[a]		106,615[c]
Private mental hospitals	4,754[b]		10,827[c]
Public and other general hospitals	22,147[b]		481,000[c,d]
Special institutions for alcoholics	6,689	federally-funded alcoholism programmes (except CMHCs and drinking driver)	308,929
Veterans Administration hospitals	3,886		95,000
Small numbers for Alcoholics Anonymous, outpatient programmes, non-medical institutions (missions, rehabilitation farms, etc.)		Community mental health centres	121,300[c]
		Drinking driver programmes	49,472[c]
		Military programmes	40,000
		Indian hospitals	137,000
		Halfway houses	36,000
		Alcoholics Anonymous	320,000
Total US resident population	133 m		214 m

Notes:
a. 1940.
b. Incomplete returns.
c. 1975.
d. Apparently does not include 89,057 psychiatric caseloads in general hospital services.

> Sources: 1942: Corwin, E.H.L. and Cunningham, E.V., 'Institutional Facilities for the Treatment of Alcoholism', *Quarterly Journal of Studies on Alcohol, vol. 5,* (1944).
>   1976: Mental Hospitals: 'President's Commission on Mental Health', Appendix, vol. II (1978), p. 102; all other figures: 'PCMH', Appendix, vol. IV (1978), p. 2096.

classic disease concept of alcoholism, as initially reshaped from available cultural materials by Alcoholics Anonymous[3,4] for the fellowship's own internal therapeutic purposes, and later translated into scholarly terminology by Jellinek[5,6] and others. In accordance with this governing image, all alcohol problems, or at least all problems of concern to public health policy, could be subsumed under and regarded as symptoms or manifestations of a single disease entity characterised by the experience of loss of control over drinking.

But the alcoholism movement came to have not only a governing image but also a plan of action that extended beyond the self-help efforts and personal proselytism of the Alcoholics Anonymous fellowship. In the early 1940s a few recovered alcoholics with public relations expertise, aided by the scholar-entrepreneurs of the Yale Center of Alcohol Studies, set out on a programme to establish alcoholism as a public health concern of the society. The disease concept, in their view, carried implications beyond its therapeutic utility for individual alcoholics:

> Sickness implies the possibility of treatment. It also implies that, to some extent at least, the individual is not responsible for his condition. It further implies that it is worthwhile to try to help the sick ones. Lastly, it follows from all this that the problem is a responsibility of the medical profession, of the constituted health authorities, and of the public in general.[7]

While Alcoholics Anonymous emphasised self-help and declined external assistance or alliances, this outward-directed face of the movement adopted a very different programme. Its major strategy for social action very early became focussed on the classic public health approach to the problem: the involvement of the state in alcoholism treatment. Under the movement's impetus, by 1952, 38 states had 'passed laws recognising alcoholism as a public health problem and creating boards or commissions to establish programs'.[8] In the 1960s the focus turned to the federal level, resulting eventually in the creation of the National Institute on Alcohol Abuse and Alcoholism in 1970, with a system of incentives that also forced the establishment of a 'single state agency' to handle alcoholism in every state.

The thought and work of the alcoholism movement thus largely underlie the persistent question, 'How many alcoholics are there in the population?', with which this chapter started. The movement's governing image of alcohol problems as a single disease entity, 'alcoholism', leads to a focus on a single figure which will represent the number of 'alcoholics'. The movement's emphasis on state action has resulted in the attention to the overall size of the problem as a system planning need, and indeed has created the alcoholism agency bureaucrat who is asking the question.

General Population Studies and the Issue of Numbers

While the question of the number of alcoholics arose early, those studying drinking patterns and problems in the general population were long shielded from having it posed to them by the popularity of answers in terms of simply-derived indirect estimates, notably in terms of the Jellinek formula. But as the news of the untenability of that formula's assumptions percolated out in the late 1950s and 1960s, the questioning of those engaged in general population studies of drinking became more frequent and indeed insistent. At the federal level, the most formal expression of this to date resulted from a Congressional mandate to build a 'needs' estimate into the formula for allocating federal alcoholism services money between the states, in response to which a survey-derived estimation procedure, developed by the National Center for Health Statistics, was promulgated in federal regulations.[9,10]

When systematic work on studies of drinking practices and problems in the US general population was getting under way around 1960, however, researchers were not under a great deal of pressure to address immediate policy agendas, and thus often felt free to define and measure their variables in their own way. In the eclectic and atheoretical tradition of survey research in general, the common solution was to collect a variegated series of actual and potential problems with drinking, along with measures of drinking behaviour, reasons for drinking and abstaining, and attitudes about drinking. In analysis, researchers would commonly take the plunge toward relevance and identify some summary scale of the items as a 'problem drinking' or 'alcoholism' score.

Although researchers to a greater or lesser extent would tiptoe up to the prevalence of alcoholism question somewhere in their analysis, this was by no means the focus of their analysis, and it was not until the 1970s that any survey-based estimates of the number of alcoholics gained general currency. Meanwhile, the researchers were occupied with the description of drinking behaviours and problems as they found them in the general population.

While the summary measures varied from one study to another, they tended to draw on a common pool of underlying items, which varied only in detail in their expression in individual studies. This was because, with whatever variations a study team found desirable for clarity or originality, the studies, carried out by survey researchers then generally fairly new to the alcohol field, drew on common traditions. For drinking behaviour and reasons for drinking, there was a survey research tradition dating back to Straus and Bacon[11] and Riley and Marden.[12] For drinking problems and 'alcoholism' measures, the source was the disease concept of alcoholism, as interpreted conceptually by Jellinek in the WHO definition or by Keller, and as represented in concrete items by the AA-designed questionnaire and Jellinek's proposed version of it in the 1946 Grapevine Study. Although researchers thus had varying degrees of commitment to the disease concept, they found themselves willy-nilly making their general population measures with items defined in its terms. Often without any systematic intention, the researchers thus found themselves in a position to compare 'symptoms of alcoholism' as manifested in the general population with those manifested by alcoholics in clinics.

General-population Alcohol Problems Versus Clinical Alcoholism

Often by accident, and sometimes without realising the implications of their findings, general-population researchers thus stumbled into several puzzling or provocative discoveries about 'alcoholism' as manifested in the general population, in comparison with alcoholism in clinical populations.

In the first place, the rate of alcohol problems in the general population varied considerably by the indicator chosen, and for most criteria and samples was very much greater than the clinical caseload of 'alcoholics'. Clark[13] neatly demonstrated that the rate could be varied within very wide limits according to the criteria chosen. Furthermore, there was no natural cutting point which distinguished 'normal drinkers' from 'alcoholics': any particular cutting point was thus inherently arbitrary.

The fact that rates shown by general-population measures of drinking problems were higher than the clinical caseload excited little surprise in the US. For one thing, the patchwork quality of the US health services makes an unduplicated count of treated alcoholics impossible to attain. For another, Jellinek formula estimates had established a climate of expectation that general-population rates of 'alcoholism' would be at least three per cent. Most importantly, the finding fitted an already prevalent rhetoric which proposed that 'hidden alcoholics' far outnumbered those identified and treated as alcoholics[14,15] — a rhetoric which was related to the purposeful de-emphasis of skid row as a locus of alcoholism[16] and the assumption, drawn from

AA experience, that alcoholics would deny their problem until they 'hit bottom'.[17]

Despite the political acceptability of the relatively high rates of 'alcoholism' implied by general-population surveys, estimates based on surveys, though they can occasionally be found earlier, did not come into vogue in the US until the 1970s. Discrepancies between estimates based on surveys and other estimates were often regarded in the US as a vague source of embarrassment rather than as a matter for comment and investigation. It was actually British researchers who most systematically drew attention to the differences between survey prevalence estimates and treated prevalence, as measured in reporting agency studies.[18,19] Both Edwards and Wilkins noted that estimates based on questionnaire data showed far higher rates of alcoholism than estimates based on records in reporting-agency studies.

Following this lead, Edwards and co-workers actually empirically measured the overlap between a reporting-agency study and a survey in the same district, and found that only somewhere between one in four and one in nine of those identified as 'problem drinkers' by the survey were known to agencies.[20,21]

In the US, at least, it was the survey researchers themselves who were most acutely uncomfortable when their results were interpreted as prevalence rates of alcoholism. The researchers were too well aware of the arbitrariness of definitions and cutting points involved in any survey-based measure of 'alcoholism'.[22] On a variety of occasions, they pointed out that plausible-sounding definitions could yield 'problem drinker' rates ranging up to one-third of the male population. The usual response of interpreters of their findings was to ignore such inconveniently large estimates.

In the second place, alcohol problems in the general population looked different from the picture in clinical populations. The first systematic report using comparable questions on general and clinical populations was published by Mulford and Wilson.[23] On the basis of data published in this report, it could be seen that the patterns of reponse of hospitalised alcoholics differed from those of general-population samples.[24] Further, a sample of non-institutionalised known alcoholics gave reports different from and intermediate between the clinical and general-population samples — a finding which Mulford and Wilson tended to regard as a methodological difficulty, but which could also be seen as having substantive implications.

In the work in the tradition of Knupfer,[25] Clark[13] and Cahalan[26] the question of the dissimilarity of alcohol problems in clinical and general-population samples was somewhat obscured by the researchers' concomitant argument for a 'drinking problems' perspective rather than an 'alcoholism' perspective. Certainly by the early 1970s, however, the argument was being made very explicitly that alcohol problems in the general population not only did not match the classic disease concept of alcoholism but also did not resemble alcoholism as it empirically appeared in clinical samples.[27]

In general, the picture which emerged in general-population data was of alcohol problems much more diffuse and sporadic than the clinical picture had suggested. While the classical descriptions of the disease concept of alcoholism had presented it as an accumulation of symptoms in a determinate order (a characterisation which overstated the case even for clinical populations[2]), in the general population a particular problem with drinking was only modestly associated with other drinking problems and provided only a modest prediction of future problems.

In part, this finding could be seen as resulting from the criteria for 'problem drinking' or 'alcoholism' used in general population studies. The classical descriptions of alcoholism were conjunctive: alcoholics had symptom A *and* symptom B *and* symptom C. But, although researchers struggled to maintain some element of conjunctivity, the criteria they settled on were largely disjunctive: item A *or* item B *or* item C. The problem with attempting to use a fully conjunctive definition, as Mulford found, was that 'to employ indicators for *all* the descriptions of the species of alcoholism given by Jellinek soon eliminates virtually all cases'.[28]

Again, while it was easy to see this problem as a methodological embarrassment, it also held substantive complications. Perhaps what was being measured as alcoholism or drinking problems in the general population was qualitatively as well as quantitatively different from alcoholism as it appeared in the clinic. Somewhat tentatively, researchers began to think in terms of the 'two worlds of alcohol problems',[29] clinical and general-population.

It might be noted that a similar development occurred in measuring the prevalence of psychiatric disorders in the general-population in the Midtown Manhattan study, researchers concluded that 23 per cent of the population were 'impaired', which was seen as 'analogous to patients in psychiatric therapy'. But later research suggested that such criteria included many cases less 'severe' than the typical clinical case.[30] Again, the diagnostician's tendency to define clinical categories inclusively, so as to avoid all risk of false negatives, seems to have played into the survey researcher's need to have a workable number of 'positive' cases.

But if alcohol problems in general populations look different from clinical samples of alcoholics, the question arises of how many people in the general population resemble those in clinics in their drinking behaviour and problems? This, it might be argued, is the true population of 'hidden alcoholics', and not the much larger number projected from survey drinking-problems scores.

It appears that there are no really satisfactory answers to this question yet, although work under way, for instance on the World Health Organisation study of Community Response to Alcohol-related Problems, will help provide some answers. In a general population study in San Francisco, it was found that the criterion in terms of tangible consequences of drinking has to be made very stringent to yield a general-population sub-group with a distribution on amount of drinking similar to clinical samples of alcoholics. About one per cent of the population met this criterion.[31] A finding in the work of Armor *et al.*[32] provides some corroboration. Their group of 'problem drinkers', identified out of general-population surveys with a criterion partly based on consumption, comprised only about three per cent of the general population, and yet the males reported only about half the daily consumption of alcohol reported by a male sample of clinical alcoholics.

If only about one per cent of the general adult population drink as much as those in treatment for alcoholism this puts the problem of the 'hidden alcoholic' in a new light. With a treatment system for alcoholism in the US that is now serving maybe one million clients in the course of a year,[33] the number of people in the general population who resemble those in clinical populations may be no larger than the number in treatment or recently out of it.

In the third place, problem drinkers in the general population show a different demographic profile from clinical alcoholics. Armor *et al.*'s[32] comparisons show a number of differences in a convenient form; we will zero in here on a couple which seem especially implicative.

(1) The clinical alcoholic population is much more likely to be employed or to be in marginal jobs, and to be divorced or separated. These general characteristics of clinical alcoholics can be found repeated in any number of studies. One-half of all clients in US alcoholism treatment facilities are separated or divorced, and about 60 per cent are currently not employed. These characteristics are not unique to alcoholism treatment populations: similar patterns can be found for other institutionalised populations such as mental hospital patients. The similarities in demography across institutionalised populations suggest that alcoholism treatment may be simply one among a number of

alternative dispositions for spare and awkward people, so that the increase in treatment for alcoholism in the last 40 years in the US needs to be fitted into a larger framework including, for instance, the decline in tuberculosis hospital and mental hospital caseloads in the same period.[34]

To some extent, then, those in treatment for alcoholism differ from problem drinkers in the general population in being 'spare people' individuals who are no longer tied to conventional work and family roles. We may suspect that the process of entering treatment is to some extent a process of extrusion from the general population, that many clients come to treatment after having exhausted their moral credit with employers and families, and seek to gain from the treatment a re-establishment of their moral credit. It should be noted that the moral credit seems to be harder to rehabilitate than the drinking behaviours which presumably resulted in the discrediting. Armor *et al.*[32] found little effect of alcoholism treatment on employment, earnings, or marital status.

(2) The clinical alcoholic population is much older than the general-population problem drinking population, particularly among males. In Armor *et al.*'s[32] data, the clinical population's median age is twelve years older among males, and four years older among females. That heavy drinking[35,36] and all kinds of drinking problems[26,37] are heavily concentrated among young males is one of the best established patterns in general-population data. It was recognised quite early that this pattern differed sharply from the pattern for samples of treated alcoholics, which typically are concentrated in the age range of 35-60.

Again, that treated alcoholics are in their 40s and 50s supports the conception of treatment as the end-point in an often lengthy process of compounding of drinking problems in different life areas. At first glance, that clinical alcoholics are older than general-population problem drinkers also provides some support for the notion that these are simply two stages of the same population: that the general-population problem drinkers of today are the alcoholics in treatment of tomorrow. As it has gradually become clear that drinking problems in the general population are not simply clinical alcoholism writ large, this notion of the relation between the two populations has become widely accepted. The assumption of a close coupling between the two populations has also become a major justification for case-finding and intervention among general-population problem drinkers.

The flaw in these perspectives is that the linkages between the populations are not particularly close. This is especially true for the time linkage among males: the distribution of drinking problems by age in the general population is quite discontinuous with that in the clinical population: one peaks before age 25 and the other in middle age. There is also a great disparity in numbers: as we have noted above, the problem drinking population is very much larger than the population of treated alcoholics. Thus most people reporting drinking problems in the general population never go on to receive treatment for alcoholism. Furthermore, while aggregate rates of drinking problems in the population are relatively stable, there is a great deal of turnover from one year to the next in who is manifesting the problems. Filmore *et al.*[38] have shown this also to be the case over the longer term: experiencing drinking problems as a college student is not a very powerful predictor of drinking problems in middle age. It even seems in this data set that those with the most florid problems as college students are more likely than some other groups to 'mature out' of their problems. All these findings imply that catching and treating young problem drinkers is not likely to be an efficient way of forestalling clinical alcoholism — even if we are convinced we have an effective treatment for youthful drinking problems.

Problems in Defining and Measuring Need for Services

Our general conclusion from these various comparisons of drinking problems in the general population with clinical samples of alcoholics, thus, is that alcohol problems outside the clinic are not simply the projection on to a larger population of alcohol problems inside the clinic. A treatment system that is proposing to move toward active case-finding and tackling alcohol problems in the larger society is therefore going to need not only larger resources but also new strategies and methods of approach. Nevertheless, survey-based estimates of rates of drinking problems in the population are now firmly established in the US as a basis of defining need for services in an area. Thus a paper by Marden[39] describing a simple synthetic estimation procedure which adjusts Cahalan's[26] national rates to a treatment catchment area on the basis of demographic composition, has at times been routinely sent out with application kits for federal treatment grants.

Such an estimation procedure equates two populations, treated alcoholics and general-population problem drinkers, who are in many ways incommensurate. But it seems to me that the problems with such procedures extend beyond this, and beyond their questionable assumption of the invariability of the relation of drinking problems and demographics in different places. A major problem lies in the ambiguous meaning of the word 'need' when we talk of need for services. Who is to define what constitutes a need for service? To base the definition upon existing data is to put it in the hands of a survey researcher who had quite different considerations in mind on constructing the scales and cutting-points. To tie survey criteria more closely to diagnostic standards, as has been the practice of Guze, Robins and co-workers at St Louis or Weissman at New Haven, transfers the definition of need into clinical hands. But this does not bring us any closer to an estimate of the likely queue outside if a clinic opens its door. As mentioned earlier, the clinician in his or her work is properly more concerned about false negatives than false positives, and in the alcohol and mental health areas it is clear that the general population is often tolerant of deviations in behaviour a clinician would regard as needing immediate treatment. Self-definition of need, or definition of need by significant others, are both quite different from a clinician's definition of need — or from definitions of need by other important actors, such as the merchant on whose doorstep the drunk is sitting. Behind the term 'need', thus, lies a whole agenda for investigation rather than assumption about the circumstances in which people come into treatment — as well as important ethical issues about rights to treatment and to non-treatment.

Some Features of the US Treatment System

As noted at the outset, the recent US history of alcoholism programmes is in a way an experiment in what happens when the treatment capacity is greatly expanded in a society. Even at the risk of resorting to the anecdotal and speculative, it seems worth making some observations on what appear to be some results of the experiment.

One obvious result is that many people identified as alcoholics are getting care and assistance who in former times would have received neither. Observers have often commented on the paradox that, while the alcoholism movement emphasised the disease nature of alcoholism the era of the movement's triumph has seen an explosive growth in free-standing alcoholism treatment centres rather than an integration of alcoholism treatment into general health and mental health services. This development did not happen by accident, or indeed often as a first choice. As resources started becoming available for alcoholism treatment, the initial approach, for instance by Loran Archer in California, was to buy a place for the treatment in existing health and mental health systems. The hard experience was that the systems took the money but did not provide the equivalent services: frequently the alcoholic remained underserved and unwanted. As Shaw *et al.*[40] and Robinson[41] have documented in the British health system, along with a formal referral system often goes an informal system of discouragement and disowning. To a considerable extent, the construction of a separate alcoholism treatment system in the US was a gesture of despair about the reorientation of the general health and mental health systems towards providing humane and effective service to alcoholics.

One striking feature of alcoholism treatment services in the US is that, although they are largely government-funded, they operate with a strongly entrepreneurial flavour. Whether the funding is through direct appropriations, grants, or contracts, there is a great deal of explicit competition for resources in the system. This has produced a great emphasis on public relations, on glossy brochures and optimistic reports and evaluations. It has also meant that treatment organisations are very sensitive to the winds of funding change, and many are quite flexible about treating whatever is the policy priority of the moment — teenage alcoholics, pregnant heavy drinkers, battered wives, urban Indians. The administrators of the organisations are, in fact, experts in discovering precisely the niches in their funding and service environment which will be most advantageous to their organisation. Thus the system as a whole can change its character and orientation quite rapidly. In the late 1960s California discovered that a greater leverage on federal funds could be obtained by characterising alcoholism as a vocational disability. As a result, for a while in California, if you didn't have what could qualify as a vocational disability you couldn't be treated for alcoholism.

This adaptability and entrepreneurial orientation has resulted in a considerable differentiation of treatment services for alcohol problems, as treatment organisations discovered opportunities attached to particular institutions or social problems. The funding from a highway safety agency would result in a drunk driver treatment programme, corporate concerns about alcohol-related loss of productivity would result in an industrial alcoholism programme, urban development funds would result in a public inebriate programme, and law enforcement concerns about alcohol and crime would result in a criminal diversion treatment programme.

In the initial stages of this differentiation, the programmes were conceptualised as conventional alcoholism treatment programmes which were simply being carried out in different environments. Often, indeed, the programmes were justified as especially efficient and effective ways of finding and treating alcoholics. But as time has passed, the programmes have responded to the very different populations and circumstances they each encountered, and the hegemony of a unitary disease concept of alcoholism as the definition of what was being treated has begun to fade. Programme managers are gravitating towards a 'disaggregated' model of alcohol problems, where each particular kind of problem is treated in its own terms – a model which originally derives from the survey studies of drinking problems in the general population.

The differentiation of alcohol problem treatment services and the drift towards conceptual disaggregation perhaps also reflects some realities about the client population which emerged, at least as a private knowledge of those in the treatment agencies, as the system expanded. The treatment system began to run short of people to treat – at least people who fit the conventional disease concept of alcoholism. Observers report that people in the agencies use such euphemisms as 'political realities' to refer to the need to undertake active scrounging for new cases to keep the beds full. In the 'private sector' of treatment, primarily funded by job-based group health insurance coverage, programme entrepreneurs are more direct about their basic necessity – it is 'bed-selling'.

Finding the Clients to Fill the Beds

There have been at least four kinds of response to the problem of filling the treatment slots, often pursued in combination with each other. One has been to make the treatment more attractive to the clients. This is a welcome direction for any government-funded health and welfare activity to take, and has resulted in the halting first signs of a consumer satisfaction literature for alcoholism treatment.[42] But often what the clients directly want – for instance, a 'wet hotel' where skid row folk can do their drinking off the street – a government-funded service cannot provide, for moral and ethical reasons. And sometimes the result has been that the treatment service becomes a travesty, as for instance where the main function is as a laundromat for clients.

A second response has been to seek out new 'undeserved' demographic segments of the population and provide special alcoholism treatment services for them. This response has been notably applied for various ethnicities, for women and for youth. Such an approach has undoubtedly broadened the scope and coverage of the treatment system. But to require that clients be from special demographic categories potentially exacerbates the problem of filling the treatment slots. Thus when Chaucey[43] set out to study the 'teenage alcoholics' in the programmes set up in response to a wave of public concern in the last few years, he found himself studying instead how something gets defined as a social problem, when there are essentially no cases which show up for treatment in the programmes designed to meet the problem.

A third response has been diversification into treatment of specific problem areas already mentioned. Orientation of a programme around a specific problem-area potentially draws in a client who could not fit a global 'alcoholism' criterion (although to meet the administrative necessity of maximum inclusiveness such global criteria, as in the NCA criteria, have often been stretched very wide). In fact, as the diversification proceeds, the target group increasingly becomes the whole general-population drinking problems spectrum rather than the classical alcoholic. Depending on the area and case-selection methods involved, special-area treatment populations may come much closer to resembling the general-population problem drinkers than clinical alcoholic samples. This has been a common experience, for instance, with drinking driver treatment programmes. Thus the drinking-driver clients looked so different from the other alcoholism treatment clients in the federal treatment monitoring system that the RAND report analysts dropped the drinking-drivers from their analysis.[32]

A major problem with the trend towards treating particular drinking problems rather than alcoholism is the frequent lack of developed rationales around which to organise the treatment. How, for instance, does one treat a drunk driver for his or her drink-driving problem, if the driver does not fit a classical alcoholism model? Except for some behaviour therapists, few treatment theoreticians or researchers have perhaps faced this general issue.

Roizen[42] found that in the absence of other ideas, and with a strong AA presence on their staff and another ideology, many treatment agencies fall back on a watered-down classical alcoholism treatment strategy even in the most unpromising situations. The first step, as always, is thus to attempt to convince the client that he or she has an alcoholism problem.

A fourth response is the resort to compulsion in one form or another.

This response is perhaps the most pervasive but the least noticed, since the forms of compulsion have diversified beyond the traditional court commitment for treatment or police arrest for public drunkenness. Formally, at least, the client is usually offered a 'choice', though the incentives are often so heavily weighted that the offer cannot rationally be refused. One knowledgeable probation officer in Southern California offered the estimate that 80 per cent of the people in treatment for alcohol-related problems were there under some kind of court coercion. Kindly or other coercion has always played a large part in the process of coming into treatment for alcoholism. Over half of the calls to alcoholism referral agencies are from relatives or other interested parties rather than from the potential client himself or herself; threats and ultimata from worried or fed-up spouses propel many alcoholics in the clinic door. but the growth of resort to coercion as a means of filling the treatment slots has some new and worrisome features to it. And the lack of public discussion of coercion into treatment as an issue has meant that ethical dilemmas involved have not been faced.

Roizen reports that at some alcoholism treatment agencies there is a saying that clients come into treatment because of the 'four Ls' — liver, lover, livelihood and the law. Leaving aside the undoubted truth that many people come into treatment for alcoholism because they feel very sick, and concentrating on the other three Ls, perhaps the most explicit discussions of coercion are in the 'livelihood' area. 'Constructive coercion' or 'confrontation' was explicitly discussed as a technique in industrial alcoholism programmes as early as 1967.[44] The high rate of success claimed for such programmes is often attributed to the effectiveness of the threat being held over the client's head. But in the industrial field, there are some limits on the coercion: there is a general norm that a company should be concerned only with work performance, and not with what employees do in their spare time if it does not affect performance; there are often legal protections of job security imposing due-process requirements; and labour unions frequently act as advocates for the interest of the potentially coerced client. In the area of 'lovers' — family coercion — there are, of course, no such procedural safeguards, nor would most of us desire them. But this offers an open field for the operation of an entrepreneurially-inclined agency seeking to fill its beds. Consider, for instance, the following scenario for the routinised 'intervention' efforts of a corporation offering hospital treatment for alcoholism in a nationwide chain of facilities, usually paid for by health insurance coverage. The spouse — let's say the wife — who has called in response to a brochure arguing that such a call is an act of love is encouraged to come in. After a staff assessment of the problem, she is coached on assembling a bill of facts (rather than judgement) to present to her husband on his problems from drinking, and encouraged to bring other significant parties — the children, and sometimes the employer — to a formal rehearsal where each is coached on the ultimatum they are prepared to give and follow through on if the husband does not enter the treatment programme. The session at which these prepared positions are presented is attended also by the corporation staff person involved.

This scenario is worrying on several counts. No amount of rhetoric about 'tough love' can obscure that the results of this intervention will sometimes break the Hippocratic injunction that treatment should 'do no harm'. The corporation is potentially using the ambiguity of who is the client and the cover of family informality to break the drinker's privacy with regard to his employer. Most problematically, the process of intervention and constructing a coercive situation is a matter of direct economic significance to the treatment staff.

Such routinised and explicit procedures may not exist at directly government-funded treatment facilities in the US. Nevertheless, we may surmise that the general strategy of using the spouse as a coercive technique to fill the beds is not unknown in such environments. The ethical and practical dilemmas of such an approach to case-finding need to be faced and discussed.

The most prominent involvement of 'the laws' in coercion into treatment is for drunk driving. 'Counter-measures' programmes involving one or another method of diversion from criminal penalties or driver's licence removal into alcoholism treatment have grown apace in recent years. Recently, alcoholism treatment systems have been moving also into the area of court diversion for non-alcohol-specific crimes — robbery, assault, etc. Ironically, this latter development occurs just as the winds of neoclassic criminology are eliminating treatment and rehabilitation as an aim of the general penal and probation system, so that it has been said that in California alcohol and drug diversion procedures are the last refuge of a treatment ideology in the criminal law system. In another irony, the development comes just as the 'disinhibition' theory of the action of alcohol, which underlies beliefs that drinking causes crime, has come under attack.[45,46]

Much of the court diversion is done informally and sometimes extralegally, on the initiative of individual judges. Often it is in the form of conditions of probation, which the 'client' can refuse only if he or she is willing to choose a stiff sentence. Routinely, such probation conditions reflect the predilections of the judge about what constitutes an effective cure for alcoholism. For instance, a common condition, besides entry into a treatment programme, is that the 'client' should totally abstain during the term of probation. In American law, there are few limitations on what a judge can choose to impose as a condition of probation.

So far, this trend has been little noted or discussed. Treatment agency staff have paid little attention to the potential conflict between their ethical responsibilities to their client and their institutional responsibilities to the legal system. There is only a scattered literature on the practical and ethical problems of treating alcohol or drug problems under compulsion.[47-50] Those with an interest in a humane and effective alcoholism treatment system should be greatly worried about the long-term effects on the system of the drift towards a clientele there under compulsion.

Too Much Treatment?

A tentative summary of the American experience with expansion of the alcoholism treatment system might be that the treatment-seeking population has turned out to be smaller than the conventional rhetoric of 'hidden alcoholism' might have led one to expect. As the system has nevertheless expanded, it has diversified into a number of specific-problem programmes and moved into more active case-finding and intervention. Some problems have been pointed out with what is usually regarded as a praiseworthy development, and one might ask whether a formal treatment system is the most appropriate, humane and effective method of solving many of the problems now coming in the clinic door. One possible conclusion from the American experience for a society with limited resources to spend on alcoholism treatment was voiced in the US as long ago as 1964:

> It is a safe estimate that in most communities between one-third and one-quarter of all alcoholics (using Jellinek-type estimate) are in contact with and labelled as problem drinkers by one or more of the following: mental hospitals, psychiatric clinics, general hospitals, welfare and social agencies, police departments, prison officials and public health nursing agencies. Clearly just attempting to care for and manage these alcoholics adequately is an immense job. There is more than enough work to be done without spending great effort on

the so-called 'hidden' alcoholics. The known alcoholics in any community generally will be those with the most severe problems, and also those placing the greatest financial drain on the community. In addition, the known alcoholic is more likely to lack familial resources to assist him and his family in coping with his drinking problem and with the social and other damage resulting from it than is the case with the hidden alcoholic. I would also argue that the principal responsibility of a tax-supported program is to serve those persons and families who are least able to provide for themselves. Since public facilities are necessarily limited in their size and scope their primary obligation probably should be to assist persons and families who are in the poorest position to fend for themselves.[51]

Perhaps the most astonishing thing about the American alcoholism treatment system and its social ecology — where its clients come from, under what conditions, and who and what it misses — is how little has been studied. As has been mentioned the discussion given in this chapter has often been based on anecdote or speculation. Under its national alcohol research centre grant from the National Institute on Alcohol Abuse and Alcoholism, the Social Research Group is beginning on the task of filling in the blanks. In association with the World Health Organisation study of Community Response to Alcohol Problems, the Group is undertaking an empirical study of the relation of a passage between general and clinical populations and of the social ecology of the alcoholism treatment system in the US, in a comparative frame with the international study directed by David Hawks.

Notes

1. Room, R. (1977), 'Notes on the Spectrum of Opiate Use', in Rittenhouse, Joan (ed.), *The Epidemiology of Heroin and Other Narcotics*, NIDA monograph 16 (NIDA, Washington).
2. Room, R. (1978), 'Governing Images of Alcohol and Drug Problems', PhD dissertation, Department of Sociology, University of California, Berkeley.
3. Levine, H.G. (1978), 'The Discovery of Addiction', *Journal of Studies on Alcohol*, vol. 39, pp. 143-74.
4. Blumberg, L. (1977), 'The Ideology of a Therapeutic Social Movement: Alcoholics Anonymous', *Journal of Studies on Alcohol*, vol. 38, pp. 2122-43.
5. Jellinek, E.M. (1946), 'Phases in the Drinking History of Alcoholics', *Quarterly Journal of Studies on Alcohol*, vol. 7, pp. 1-88.
6. Jellinek, E.M. (1952), 'Phases of Alcohol Addiction', *Quarterly Journal of Studies on Alcohol*, vol. 13, pp. 673-684.
7. Anderson, D. (1942), 'Alcohol and Public Opinion', *Quarterly Journal of Studies on Alcohol*, vol. 3, pp. 376-92.

8. Henderson, R.M. and Straus, R. (1952), 'Alcoholism in 1941-51. VI. Programs on Alcoholism in the United States, 1952', *Quarterly Journal of Studies on Alcohol*, vol. 13, pp. 472-95.

9. Cahalan, D. (1976), 'Some Background Considerations in Estimating Needs for States' Services Dealing with Alcohol-Related Problems', paper presented at a conference on 'need' methodology for formula grants, Rockville, Maryland, July.

10. Federal Register (1977), 'Grants to States for Alcohol Abuse and Alcoholism Prevention, Treatment and Rehabilitation Services. Allotments to States', *Federal Register*, vol. 227, pp. 60398-403.

11. Straus, R. and Bacon, S. (1953), *Drinking in College* (Yale University Press, New Haven).

12. Riley, J. and Marden, C. (1947), 'The Social Pattern of Alcoholic Drinking', *Quarterly Journal of Studies on Alcohol*, vol. 8, pp. 265-73.

13. Clark, W. (1966), 'Operational Definitions of Drinking Problems and Associated Prevalence Rates', *Quarterly Journal of Studies on Alcohol*, vol. 27, pp. 648-68.

14. O'Hallaren, P. and Wellman, W.M. (1958), 'Hidden Alcoholics', *California Medicine*, vol. 89, pp. 129-31.

15. Henderson, R.M. and Bacon, S.D. (1953), 'Problem Drinking: The Yale Plan for Business and Industry', *Quarterly Journal of Studies on Alcohol*, vol. 14, pp. 247-62.

16. Kurtz, N. and Regier, M. (1975), 'The Uniform Alcoholism and Intoxication Treatment Act', *Journal of Studies on Alcohol*, vol. 36, pp. 1421-41.

17. Rubington, E. (1972), 'The Hidden Alcoholic', *Quarterly Journal of Studies on Alcohol*, vol. 33, pp. 667-83.

18. Edwards, G. (1973), 'Epidemiology Applied to Alcoholism', *Quarterly Journal of Studies on Alcohol*, vol. 34, pp. 28-56.

19. Wilkins, R.H. (1975), *The Hidden Alcoholic in General Practice* (Elek Science, London).

20. Edwards, G. (1973), 'A Community as Case Study', *Proceedings of the Second Annual Alcoholism Conference*, Pub. (HSM) 73-9083 (NIAAA, Washington, D.C.), pp. 116-36.

21. Edwards, G., Hawker, A., Hensman, C., Peto, J. and Williamson, V. (1973), 'Alcoholics Known or Unknown to Agencies', *British Journal of Psychiatry*, vol. 123, pp. 169-83.

22. Bruun, K. (1970), 'Comments', *Drinking and Drug Practices Surveyor*, vol. 1, pp. 6.

23. Mulford, H. and Wilson, R. (1966), *Identifying Problem Drinkers in a Household Health Survey*, National Center for Health Statistics Publication 1,000, series 2, no. 16 (Washington, D.C.).

24. Room, R. (1966), 'Notes on Identifying Problem Drinkers', Social Research Group, Berkeley Working Paper F-10.

25. Knupfer, G. (1967), 'The Epidemiology of Problem Drinking', *American Journal of Public Health*, vol. 57, pp. 973-86.

26. Cahalan, D. (1970), *Problem Drinkers* (Jossey-Bass, San Francisco).

27. Room, R. (1972), 'Notes on Alcohol Policies in the Light of General-Population Surveys', *Drinking and Drug Practices Surveyor*, vol. 6, pp. 10-12.

28. Mulford, H. (1968), ' "Alcoholics", "Alcoholism", and "Problem Drinkers" ', paper presented at the 28th International Congress on Alcohol and Alcoholism, Washington, D.C.

29. Room, R. (1977), 'Measurement and Distribution of Drinking Patterns and Problems in General Populations', in Edwards, G. *et al.* (eds.), *Alcohol Related Disabilities*, Offset Publication 32 (WHO Geneva).

30. Dohrenwend, B.P. (1970), 'Psychiatric Disorder in General Populations: Problem of the Untreated "Case" ', *American Journal of Public Health*, vol. 60,

pp. 1052-64.

31. Room, R. (1968), 'Amount of Drinking and Alcoholism', paper presented at the 28th International Congress on Alcohol and Alcoholism, Washington, D.C.

32. Armor, D.J., Polich, J.M. and Stambul, H.B. (1978), *Alcoholism and Treatment* (John Wiley, New York).

33. Liaison Task Panel on Alcohol-Related Problems (1978), report in *Task Panel Reports Submitted to the President's Commission on Mental Health*, vol. IV (GPO, Washington D.C.), pp. 2078-102.

34. Task Panel on the Nature and Scope of Problems (1978), Report in *Task Panel Reports Submitted to the President's Commission on Mental Health*, vol. II (GPO, Washington, D.C.), pp. 1-138.

35. Knupfer, G. and Room, R. (1964), 'Age, Sex and Social Class as Factors in Amount of Drinking in a Metropolitan Community', *Social Problems*, vol. 12, pp. 224-40.

36. Cahalan, D., Cisin, I. and Crossley, H. (1969), *American Drinking Practices*, Monograph 6 (Rutgers Center of Alcohol Studies, New Brunswick, New Jersey).

37. Cahalan, D. and Room, R. (1974), *Problem Drinking Among American Men*, Monograph 7 (Rutgers Center of Alcohol Studies, New Brunswick, New Jersey).

38. Filmore, K., Bacon, S.D. and Hyman, M. (1979), *The 27-Year Longitudinal Panel Study of Drinking by Students in College, 1947-76*, Final Report, C-22 (Social Research Group, Berkeley).

39. Marden, P. (1974), *A Procedure for Estimating the Potential Clientele of Alcoholism Service Programs* (ADAMHA, Rockville, Maryland).

40. Shaw, S., Cartwright, A., Spratley, T. and Harwin, J. (1978), *Responding to Drinking Problems* (University Park Press, Baltimore; Croom Helm, London).

41. Robinson, D. (1976), *From Drinking to Alcoholism* (John Wiley, London).

42. Roizen, R. (1977), 'Alcoholism Treatment's Goals and Outcome Measures', Social Research Group, Berkeley Working Paper F-61.

43. Chauncey, R. (1978), 'Social Construction of a Social Problem: Teenage Drinking', Department of Sociology, University of California, San Diego, working paper.

44. Roman, P. and Trice, H.M. (1967), 'Alcoholism and Problem Drinking as Social Roles: The Effects of Constructive Coercion', paper presented at the Annual Meeting of the Society for the Study of Social Problems, San Francisco.

45. Pernanen, K. (1976), 'Alcohol and Crimes of Violence', in Kissin, B. and Begleiter, H. (eds.), *The Biology of Alcoholism, Vol. IV: Social Aspects* (Plenum Press, New York and London), pp. 351-444.

46. Aarens, M., Cameron, T., Roizen, J., Roizen, R., Room, R., Schneberk, D. and Wingard, D. (1976), 'Alcohol, Casualties and Crime', Report C-18 (Social Research Group, Berkeley).

47. Christie, N. (1965), 'Temperance Boards and Interinstitutional Dilemmas', *Social Problems*, vol. 12, pp. 415-28.

48. Newman, R. (1971), 'Involuntary Treatment of Drug Addiction', in Bourne, Peter (ed.), *Addiction* (Academic Press, New York).

49. Aiken, R. and Weiner, S. (1974), 'The Interface of Mental Health and Judicial Systems', *Proceedings of the Third Annual Alcoholism Conference* (National Institute on Alcohol Abuse and Alcoholism, Washington, D.C.), pp. 292-300.

50. Wexler, D. (1973), 'Therapeutic Justice', in National Commission on Marijuana and Drug Abuse, *Drug Use in America, Second Report; Technical Papers*, vol. IV (GPO, Washington, D.C.), pp. 450-73.

51. Plaut, T.F.A. (1964), 'The State Alcoholism Program Movement. A Critical Analysis', in *Selected Papers Presented at the Fifteenth Annual Meeting* (NAAAP, Washington, D.C.), pp. 74-93.

14 WHAT CAN MEDICINE PROPERLY TAKE ON?

Klaus Mäkelä

Alcohol Problems: What Kinds of Deviance?

There are two basic types of deviance: disease and bad conduct. The distinction is based on whether we regard the behaviour or condition as dependent or independent of the volition of the individual. Diseases are treated by the medical profession, but bad conduct is dealt with by legal and moral authorities. In the course of the last two centuries or so, an ever-growing number of types of behaviours and conditions have been reclassified as diseases rather than as bad conduct, and the domain of the medical profession has correspondingly been broadened.

The distinction between disease and bad conduct is of fundamental cultural importance, and it also has many practical implications. It should, however, be complemented by another dichotomy. Types of deviance should be classified according to whether or not special professional techniques exist to alter the behaviour or condition independently of the volition of the individual. By professional techniques is meant the treatment skills that may be acquired through vocational training, in contrast to those means of influencing other people's behaviour that are based on everyday wisdom and experience of life.

We can obtain a four-category table as shown in Table 14.1. When looking for an answer to the title question, 'What can medicine properly take on?' we have to consider how alcohol dependence should be placed on this four-fold classification and, moreover, how various types of alcohol problems are related both to dependence and to the typology of deviance.

The simple decision to designate alcoholism or alcohol dependence a disease does not solve the problems raised by the four-fold table. The ideal type of a disease naturally belongs to square A as opposed to the crimes or sins in square E, but such clear-cut cases are not as common as one might expect. Even unequivocally somatic diseases may be placed in different squares. In some cases of allergy, the only cure may be based on the patient's conscious efforts to avoid the allergogenic substance. This case should thus be placed in square B. By contrast, many people may argue that a man has himself to blame if he is foolish

225

Table 14.1 Four-fold Classification of Deviance

	Nature of techniques available to alter or prevent the deviant condition	
	Techniques independent of the volition of subject	Only techniques dependent on the volition of subject
Subject not regarded as morally responsible for his deviance	A	B
Subject regarded as morally responsible for his deviance	C	D

enough to contract a venereal disease, but the effectiveness of the treatment is nonetheless totally independent of his volition. This case thus ends up in square C.

Bad conduct may thus lead to a disease, and some diseases are incurable. In this context, the recent tendency to remove unhealthy conditions into the domain of the moral responsibility of the individual is of special interest. The tremendous increase in health expenditure has given impetus to a revival of health moralism. The late John H. Knowles, a medical doctor and President of the Rockefeller Foundation, left no room for doubt: 'I believe the idea of a "right" to health should be replaced by the idea of an individual moral obligation to preserve one's own health — a public duty if you will'.[1]

To complicate matters further, there are types of bad conduct that do only minimal harm to others as well as diseases that are extremely dangerous to the social environment of the patients. We thus need to complement the four-fold typology of deviance by a third dimension, defined by the principal locus of harm caused by the deviant behaviour or condition. The division of labour between various professions and authorities is clearly affected by whether the deviant individual is seen as mainly harming himself or his environment. Even an incurable contagious disease belongs to the realm of the medical profession, but in some cases the police may be needed to prevent the patient from infecting others.

The somatic examples given have their counterparts in alcoholism debates. The allergy example bears a close resemblance to the notion of alcoholism advocated by the AA movement. Drinking and smoking habits naturally are of special interest to the new health moralists who use 'risk behaviours' and 'self-care' as their key concepts. And the neighbours of a violent alcoholic may call the police irrespective of whether or not they regard him as morally responsible for his behaviour.

Drinking Behaviours, Dependence and Consequences of Drinking

The discomfort to be sensed around the by now classic disease concept of alcoholism is closely related to its all-or-none character, despite all the phases, sub-types, cautions and exceptions formulated by Jellinek and his followers. The classic view looked upon alcoholism as a complex entity, and all kinds of moral, emotional and physical conditions, and adverse life events, as well as drinking behaviours, were conceptualised as symptoms of the disease entity.[2] It is well to remember that the 1952 WHO definition included various bodily and mental consequences of drinking as well as social and economic problems caused by drinking as constituent elements in the very definition of alcoholism. It is also symptomatic that what is given is a definition of an alcoholic, a person suffering from a complex disease entity, not a definition of the disease in itself.

R.E. Kendell, a prominent representative of the medical profession, wrote in a recent article: 'Until we stop regarding alcoholism as a disease, and therefore as a problem to be dealt with by the medical profession, and accept it as an essentially political problem . . . we shall never tackle the problem effectively. The medical profession and the caring professions in general are just as incapable of dealing with the harm and suffering caused by alcoholism as the medical services of the armed forces are incapable of dealing effectively with the harm and suffering caused by war.'[3] This may be true from the perspective of the prevention of alcohol problems or, for that matter, wars, but not too much is achieved by denying alcoholism the status of a disease. Disease or non-disease, somebody has to deal with alcohol related disabilities, and the medical profession probably has to play an important role in this context, anyway.

In this respect, the work presented by a WHO scientific group in 1975 and later incorporated into the ninth revision of the International

Classification of Diseases represents an important step forward.[4] According to the new approach, alcohol dependence should be analytically distinguished from various adverse consequences of drinking or alcohol-related disabilities. The dependence syndrome may in principle be diagnosed independently of the adverse consequences of drinking. Moreover, to quote Griffith Edwards: 'It is possible for a person to be in some degree dependent on alcohol while having sustained no interference with physical or mental health, or social or economic function. Similarly, it is eminently possible for a drinker to be in no way abnormally dependent on alcohol, but to have sustained major disabilities in several dimensions of his life.'[5]

This new approach makes it possible to keep separate, at least on a conceptual level, the social or psychological etiology of excessive drinking, the actual drinking behaviours, the possible dependence on alcohol, and the multifarious consequences of drinking. It thus also provides tools for discussing the division of labour of various professions and authorities in a more detailed fashion than the entity notion of alcoholism.

Instead of asking whether alcoholism is a disease or not we may now discuss the role of medicine in, first, remodelling problematic individual patterns of drinking, secondly, treating alcohol dependence in itself, and thirdly, curing various health ailments related to excessive drinking.

Most somatic consequences of prolonged alcohol use clearly belong to the domain of the medical profession. A broken leg is a broken leg irrespective of whether the accident was caused by drunkenness, and no special wards are required for treating fire burns in alcoholics, whatever the new health moralists might have to say about the public duty of an individual to preserve one's own health. The situation becomes a little more complicated in cases where the patient's drinking behaviour has an impact on the prognosis of the ailment to be treated. A given case of liver cirrhosis may remain essentially the same irrespective of whether alcohol plays a role in its etiology or not, but its treatment may require that the patient discontinues his drinking. To take another example, skid row alcoholics were among the last remaining groups in Finland to suffer from tuberculosis. On the one hand, their living conditions tended to render them especially vulnerable, and, on the other hand, they tended not to follow the treatment instructions. In this example, the condition to be treated is a clearly distinguishable somatic disease, and one would have to stretch the notion of causality very far to even label it as alcohol-related. Nevertheless, the alcohol dependence of the patient is an essential factor affecting the treatment of the disease, and at least in Finland, special wards were instituted for the treatment of alcohol-dependent tuberculotics.

The last two examples also give an indication of the limits of an analytical approach to alcohol problems. Whether alcoholism is an entity or not, in concrete cases it may be a futile exercise to distinguish between the treatment of alcohol-related health ailments and the control of the drinking behaviour and the possibly underlying alcohol dependence.

Even the treatment of clearly identifiable somatic alcohol-related diseases may thus have to be combined with attempts to control the drinking habits of the patient. It is, however, a slightly different matter to discuss the role of medicine in dealing with deviant drinking and alcohol dependence in general.

Locus of Harm and the Role of Medicine

Let us turn back to the four-fold typology and the complementing dimension of locus of harm. Even if we do not morally blame an alcoholic for his drinking, the concern for heavy drinkers is, in many countries, in perhaps the majority of cases motivated by the harm their drinking causes to their families and social environment. This being the case, the medicalisation of alcohol problems only leads to blurring of the social role of the medical system as opposed to those authorities whose explicit task is to maintain social order.

It is especially unfortunate if a medical disguise is given to efforts to control deviant drinking in order to safeguard the environment of the patients. It should not be up to the medical profession to take care of public order and the safety of the drunkard's family, which easily happens when social sanitation is couched in treatment terminology. In Finland, health statistics reveal a number of involuntary commitments to mental hospitals based on the diagnosis of alcoholism. It is very unlikely that all patients have been psychotic in the strict medical and legal sense of the word. Rather it seems that involuntary commitments have been used as a convenient way to solve family crises and social conflicts caused by heavy drinking. It should be borne in mind that a shift of compulsory control of deviant use of alcohol from 'punishment' to 'treatment' often actually means the application of more severe measures.

Drunkenness was decriminalised in Finland in 1969, which means that people are no longer sentenced to fines for drunkenness alone and offenders are no longer subjected to other penalties in lieu of inability to pay, either. Pressure to have public drunkenness brought under control thereafter grew to the extent that in a committee report published in the spring of 1974, the proposal was made that any person arrested three times in a period of two months for drunkenness should be automatically placed in a treatment institution for 30 days. According to the proposal, the regulation would be applied mechanically and without consideration of the special circumstances attending any given case. In the light of the statistics on arrests for drunkenness, it may be calculated that the new regulations would have led to deprivation of a person's freedom considerably more often than the procedure of adjusting fines for drunkenness according to the old law. From the standpoint of getting an alcoholic into a fit condition, again, it is all the same whether he sits against his will for 30 days in prison or in a treatment centre. The whole proposition would merely have meant that a certain problem of maintaining public order would be wrapped up in therapeutic word magic, while persons under arrest would be deprived of the legal protection afforded by due process of law.[6]

The significance of cautions of this type against a medicalisation of alcohol problems clearly depends on the cultural climate, and especially on the prevailing patterns of drinking. They are most consequential in countries where reckless drinking habits cause problems that are not related to alcohol dependence. It is probably in these countries that 'the two worlds of alcohol problems', the problems of the everyday world and those of clinical populations,[7] are most clearly identifiable. One certainly finds this dichotomy in the US and in Scandinavia, but the situation is probably not as clearly demarcated in France or Italy. Correspondingly, the danger that an overall medicalisation of alcohol problems blurs the social functions of the medical system is more acute in North European countries than in Mediterranean countries.

The most important bounds to an overall medicalisation of alcohol problems are, however, set by the non-existence of effective professional techniques to treat alcohol dependence that would radically differ from the techniques of advice, persuasion and conversion used in everyday social interaction. Many people may think that this formulation is too categorical, and undoubtedly it should be qualified in many respects. After all, professional training does help a person to understand the situation of a heavy drinker, and even everyday social skills may be developed by formal courses. Nevertheless, compared to the highly specialised techniques available in somatic medicine, these professional skills are not that different from everyday social competence. This is

among the most important reasons for arguing that the role of medicine
should be discussed in terms of its impact on the cultural climate and
the self-perception of deviant drinkers.

The Medical Model and the Structure of Medical Services

The workings of the medical model are influenced by the overall
structure of medical services in each country. To take one example, it
makes an important difference if the service system in general is concentrated in large hospitals rather than based on a network of general
practitioners or family doctors. Therefore, it should be stressed that
health services present radically different structures even in countries
that have similar economic resources.

One might easily expect that available resources are so decisive for
public health expenditure that all kinds of medical services are positively
correlated with economic development and with each other. However,
an analysis of public health expenditure in OECD countries reveals
important qualitative differences. As a matter of fact, the intercountry
correlation between the annual number of doctor visits per person and
the annual number of hospital days per person is substantial and
negative. Sweden and Finland have a high hospital use ratio but a low
use ratio of outpatient medical services, whereas the situation is
reversed in, for instance, Belgium and Italy. Austria is high while Great
Britain relatively low on both variables.[8] The primary data used in this
analysis refer to medical expenditure in general, but it is not improb-
able that similar differences could be detected within the field of
mental health services. This should remind us of the possibility that a
medicalisation of alcohol problems may signify radically different
organisational arrangements in different countries.

Great care should be taken to avoid all kinds of organisational and
other arrangements that mystify alcoholism treatment and create an
illusion of the existence of specialised techniques. This basic position
has several implications.

First of all, much caution should be taken not to invest too much
money and hopes in inpatient treatment institutions. Also, the goals
of inpatient treatment should not be too ambitious. The most realistic
aim could well be to put the patient in reasonable physical shape rather
than expecting to cure his dependence. Consequently, the treatment
time should be kept very short.

Secondly, it may be wise to avoid too specialised work roles within the treatment organisation. If the special expertise of, for instance, the consulting psychiatrist, is heavily emphasised, this may well paralyse the initiative of the less educated personnel; at least this has been the Finnish experience. In the beginning of the 1970s the newly founded youth clinics for alcohol and drug users adopted a very ambitious treatment ideology, but in some phases they were threatened by complete stand-still or even anarchy, as expert opinion was requested to deal even with the simplest everyday situations between patients and treatment personnel.[9]

Thirdly, no formal barriers should be raised between professionally trained treatment personnel and former alcoholics, whose everyday wisdom and experience should be utilised in full.

Until now, the main emphasis of this discussion has perhaps been on what the medical profession should not take on, and it is about time to say something affirmative. Because of their authority, professional training and life experience medical doctors are in a much better position to inform, advise and blame people in regard to their drinking habits than, for example, are sociologists of alcoholism. And this they should do.

Acknowledgement

This chapter has greatly benefited from discussion with Ron Roizen and Robin Room.

Notes

1. Knowles, J.H. (1977), 'The Responsibility of the Individual', in Knowles, J.H. (ed.), *Doing Better and Feeling Worse: Health in the United States* (W.W. Norton & Co., New York), p. 59.
2. Room, R. (1978), 'Governing Images of Alcohol and Drug Problems: The Structures, Sources and Sequels of Conceptualizations of Interactable Problems', doctoral dissertation, University of California, Berkeley.
3. Kendell, R.E. (1979), 'Alcoholism: A Medical or Political Problem?', *British Medical Journal*, vol. 1, pp. 367-71.
4. Edwards, G., Gross, M.M., Keller, M., Moser, J. and Room, R. (eds.) (1977), *Alcohol-Related Disabilities* (World Health Organisation, Geneva).
5. Edwards, G. and Grant, M. (eds.) (1977), *Alcoholism: New Knowledge and New Responses* (Croom Helm, London; University Park Press, Baltimore), pp. 136-56.
6. Mäkelä, K. (1980), 'Criminalization and Punishment in the Prevention of Alcohol Problems', *Contemporary Drug Problems*, in press.
7. Room, R. (1979), 'Treatment Seeking Populations and Larger Realities',

paper presented at the Conference on Alcoholism Treatment: Finding New Directions, Institute of Psychiatry, London, and see Chapter 13 in this volume.
8. Mäkelä, K. (1977), unpublished analyses of data presented in Public Health Expenditure, OECD, Paris.
9. Siren, P. (1977), 'Nuorisoasema Päihteitä Käyttävien Nuorten Hoitoyhteisönä' ('A Juvenile Clinic as a Therapeutic Community for Youth Using Alcohol and Drugs'), *Report III* (Social Research Institute of Alcohol Studies, Helsinki).

David Robinson and Betsy Ettorre

Introduction

In 1951 a National Health Service (NHS) consultant applied for
nomination to attend a WHO scientific meeting on alcoholism, held in
Copenhagen with E.M. Jellinek as Director in Charge of Studies. He
reports that he was told by the then Ministry of Health that there was
no alcoholism in England and Wales and that the subject hardly merited
the time of a consultant psychiatrist in the National Health Service.[1]
In 1978 the government's Advisory Committee on Alcoholism[2]
suggested that, at a conservative estimate, there are half a million
people in England and Wales with a serious drinking problem and that
a whole multitude of professional and voluntary organisations have a
part to play in the overall pattern and range of services for problem
drinkers.

These two events succinctly bracket some of the major changes
which have taken place over the past quarter of a century: the
increased awareness of the magnitude of 'the alcohol problem'; the shift
from thinking solely of alcoholism to a consideration of the wide range
of problems to which alcohol consumption is a contributory factor; and
the shift from the assumption that it is a matter of psychiatrists treating
alcoholics, to a belief that all health and social service professionals and
many lay people and organisations are quite able to offer help to
problem drinkers. One feature of this period, 1951 to 1978, has been
the establishment of special Alcoholism Treatment Units.

In this chapter we shall begin by outlining the latest official advice
about what should be the place of Alcoholism Treatment Units in the
overall pattern of alcoholism services. We shall then trace the government's changing position on the special units via their official statements
of policy, go on to indicate some key themes and issues which must be
considered in any coherent account of the history, development and
operation of the ATUs and, finally, focus on certain aspects of the early
period before 1962, the date of the first government memorandum to

recommend the establishment of special alcoholism units.

The Latest Advice

The latest advice on the position of the ATUs came in a report on 'The Pattern and Range of Services for Problem Drinkers'[2] produced in September 1978 by the Department of Health and Social Security's Advisory Committee on Alcoholism. This report concluded, among other things: that generalist professional workers – GPs, social workers and so on – either fail to recognise problem drinkers or, if they do recognise them, are hesitant to deal with them 'because they lack the necessary confidence, training and resources' (Section 7.1); that 'the specialist statutory services which do respond are patchily distributed and poorly co-ordinated' and 'could not be expected to cope if the majority of problem drinkers came to them for help' (Section 7.2); and that the voluntary agencies which have expanded in response to unmet needs are 'short of money and their development has been uneven' (Section 7.2).

In the light of this, the committee proposed a community response to alcoholism which should be 'flexible and comprehensive' (Section 7.3). Wherever possible, the committee felt, problem drinkers should be treated 'at the primary level' by GPs, social workers, probation officers, shop front workers, etc., and that, in order for them to do this, 'second level' specialist alcoholism workers in both statutory and voluntary sectors should provide advice, support, training and specialist treatment, care, intensive social support and residential accommodation where necessary.

In this overall pattern and range of services it is proposed that the 32 special Alcoholism Treatment Units 'should no longer act as treatment units for a Regional Health Authority' but merely for the Area or District in which they are located, thus becoming, 'even for the local community, just a part of the total provision of services' (Section 4.25 iiic). The committee recommend that no more ATUs 'of a regional character should be set up' (Section 4.25 iiia).

If the Department of Health accepts and acts on this particular Advisory Committee recommendation, then the special Alcoholism Treatment Units will no longer occupy their current position, as D.L. Davies[3] describes it, at the 'core' of service provision for alcoholics. This, however, is a matter for government and others and for the future. Our concern is with how the ATUs achieved their core position in the first place.

Statement of Official Policy: 1962, 1968 and 1973

There have been three main official policy statements relating to ATUs. The first was memorandum HM(62)43 entitled *Hospital Treatment of Alcoholism*[4] issued by the then Ministry of Health in 1962, which 'commend' to Regional Hospital Boards 'advice on the development of hospital facilities for the treatment of alcoholism'. At that time, 1962, there were three special alcoholism treatment units in operation in the United Kingdom; the first one having been established by Max Glatt at Warlingham Park in 1951.

After pointing out that the arrangements for giving hospital treatment for alcoholism were 'somewhat haphazard', since small numbers of patients were being treated in a wide range of psychiatric and general hospitals, the one-page memorandum recommended 'that treatment for alcoholism and alcoholic psychosis should, as far as possible, be given in specialised units'. In carrying out this recommendation Regional Boards were asked to have regard to the following points:

> The units will normally be situated at psychiatric hospitals or psychiatric units at general hospitals.
> It is suggested that the units should be between 8 and 16 beds. This would be a convenient size for group therapy, which the Advisory Committees regarded as often being a valuable form of treatment.
> It will be necessary for the special units to run outpatient clinics and to co-operate in after care with Alcoholics Anonymous (who have a very important contribution to make) and, where appropriate, with the local health authority or other interested agencies. (Section 4.)

The second memorandum, HM(68)37, this time entitled *Treatment of Alcoholism*[5] rather than 'hospital' treatment of alcoholism, was issued six years later. The main point of this three-and-a-half page memorandum was to reinforce the value of the specialist ATUs but also to stress the importance of outpatient treatment, while mention is made for the first time of 'the community' and research.

> Treatment will frequently involve an initial admission to hospital as in-patient and more than one admission to hospital may be necessary

because of relapse. In-patient treatment can best be undertaken in small specialised hospital units . . . (Para 5.)
    In the views of some experts energetic out-patient care alone will sometimes give as good results. An in-patient may come to rely on the supports of hospital life and their removal when he leaves hospital may present difficulties . . . Out-patient treatment has the general advantage of enabling the patient to retain his job and thus remain in the community; he is also thereby better able to maintain contact with his family . . . Clinical trials are needed to investigate special indications for in-patient and out-patient care. (Para 7.)

By the time the third official statement was issued, in 1973, there were 17 special ATUs in England with a total of 369 beds and work was in progress to establish a further six units in the following two years. Circular 21/73 from the now Department of Health and Social Security was a very different document from the previous two from the Ministry of Health. Entitled 'Community Services for Alcoholics'[6] its main purpose was to provide a framework for the establishment of rehabilitation facilities for homeless and/or offending alcoholics. Following the 1971 report by a Home Office working party on *Habitual Drunken Offenders*[7] and after widespread consultations, it had been decided that departmental responsibility for the provision of facilities for those who are habitually drunk in public places should pass to the DHSS as part of 'a comprehensive treatment and rehabilitation service for all alcoholics'.[6]
    Circular 21/73 went on to place the ATUs firmly within a community response and, further, to suggest that they would be ineffective if they were not so placed:

The hospital treatment services for alcoholics are at present being developed and further guidance to general practitioners on the recognition and treatment of alcoholics is in preparation. Development of treatment facilities alone will however be ineffective without a complementary development of community services. The community health and personal social services needed range across a broad front from those concerned with prevention, through social work support for the alcoholic and perhaps his family, to rehabilitation and, if necessary, residential care. (Para 3.)

The main body of the 16 page circular 21/73 was concerned with outlining the range and role of the various community services, information centres, shop fronts, detoxification centres and hostels and, most important, contained five pages setting out details of the grants available toward both the revenue and capital costs of voluntary rehabilitation hostels for alcoholics.

Amid all this, only two paragraphs (9 and 10) were devoted to hospital treatment facilities and much of these two paragraphs was taken up with noting the variety of hospitals within which alcoholics are treated and with stressing that hospitals should develop relationships with social services departments, voluntary organisations and other rehabilitation and support services in the community. Nevertheless the ATUs were still seen to occupy an important place in the overall scheme:

> The proposed pattern for the future is to develop, as a sub-regional speciality . . . special hospital units for the treatment of alcohol addiction, with at least one unit in each Hospital Region located within reasonable distance of every major centre of population. (Para 9.)

The assumption throughout Circular 21/73 was that 'identification' was the real problem; getting people into the services, together with referring them through to the professional and voluntary specialists, the ATUs, rehabilitation hostels and so on. By contrast, the recent Advisory Committee report on *The Pattern and Range of Services for Problem Drinkers*[2] discards referral to the specialist as the basic, natural response. It proposes that those who identify people with drinking problems at the various 'entry points' to the system – general practice, social work, shop front, counselling service, etc. – should deal with the problem drinker there and then. So rather than community services supporting the 'core' work done by the ATUs it is now proposed that the ATUs and other specialists support the basic services for alcoholics which ought to be provided 'at the primary level'.

Themes and Issues

Official policy statements provide only the barest skeletal account of the developments of the ATUs. A coherent history requires this skeleton to be 'fleshed out' with contextual and related data of various kinds.

No account of the special Alcoholism Treatment Units would be adequate which ignored, for example: the broad changes in medicine over the past 20 years; the growing emphasis on co-ordinated health and social services, primary health care and, lately, prevention or the broad changes in psychiatry; the community and social psychiatry movements, the drug 'revolution' and the 'open door' policy in relation to mental hospitals; the rapid accumulation of epidemiological evidence, both in this country and elsewhere, on the extent of alcohol-related problems of various kinds; the growing awareness and understanding by the general population of the extent of alcohol-related problems and the services provided in response to them; or administrative changes such as the incorporation of the Ministry of Health into the new Department of Health and Social Security, and the widespread reorganisation of local government and health and social services. The list is endless.

Within this broad context of developmental themes there is a range of specific issues to which we shall be paying particular attention. Five are briefly mentioned by way of example.

The World Health Organization, through its publications, meetings and consultants, has exerted considerable influence on the development of ideas about the nature of, extent of and possible responses to alcoholism. This is clearly of interest to us, as is the history of the relationships between WHO and the Ministry, subsequently Department, of Health.

Without subscribing to a great man theory of history, it is nevertheless obvious to anyone familiar with the British response to alcohol problems that certain individuals have had a large measure of direct and indirect influence: Max Glatt to mention just one. This we cannot ignore.

We are particularly interested in the relationships between research and policy. What research basis was there for the various policy recommendations on the ATUs? What contribution did the units themselves make to scientific research? What was the basis of the government's policy on research into treatment and services for problem drinkers?

Fourthly, Alcoholics Anonymous has had its influence right from the beginning; it was mentioned in that first brief memorandum in 1962. Building on a recent study[8] we want to look at the relationship between the growth, philosophy and operation of the fellowship and the activities of the ATUs.

Finally, anyone familiar with alcoholism treatment in the 1960s cannot fail to be struck by the speed with which ATUs were established following the 1962 memorandum. Government departments would be absolutely delighted if even a quarter of their recommendations were taken up so readily. Why did the regions respond in this way?

We are interested in these and many other issues. In the remainder of this short chapter we focus on the question of why that 1962 memorandum was produced in the first place, in response to what, for what purpose, who was involved, in relation to what other developments, and so on.

Prelude to the 1962 Memorandum

We shall be considering a variety of issues in the pre-1962 period. In this chapter we briefly discuss just three of them: the role of WHO, the influence of particular individuals, and broad trends in alcoholism research.

The Role of WHO

WHO has played a significant role in the development of ideas about the nature, extent and management of alcohol-related problems over the past 30 years. The 1951 definition of alcoholism still reverberates round the alcoholism literature. Many of the shifts in rhetoric from alcoholism to alcoholisms to alcohol addiction to alcohol dependence to alcohol-related disabilities, together with the increased attention given to alcohol control policies and the alcohol problems of the developing world cannot be understood without taking into account the role of WHO, its offices, particularly in Geneva and Copenhagen, its publications and its succession of key advisers.

In 1950 the WHO Expert Committee on Mental Health expressed the need for more information on the nature and prevalence of alcoholism in different areas. To obtain this information and to consider other issues an Alcoholism Sub-committee was set up. The first two sessions of the Sub-committee in 1950 and 1951, closely followed by the European Seminar and Lecture Course on Alcoholism, to which our NHS consultant had been given grudging permission to attend, and the European Seminar on Prevention and Treatment in 1954, all helped to clarify ideas on alcoholism at that time.

In their first session the Alcoholism Sub-committee stressed the importance of alcoholism as a disease and a social problem and drew attention to the lack of interest in many countries in the extent of the problem, lack of action on prevention and treatment by health authorities and, in particular, the lack of adequate definitions and of a coherent framework for the discussion of alcohol problems. The sub-committee, in fact, abandoned its original agenda and devoted the session to a discussion of theoretical and other general principles concerning the definition, extent and nature of the problem, treatment facilities, means of treatment, education and information, and the role of voluntary organisations. Jellinek, although he had prepared papers for the meeting and his Estimation Formula was appended to the report,[9] was unable, through illness, to attend. It was decided that a second session be convened as soon as possible. The sub-committee met nine months later in Copenhagen with Jellinek in attendance.

In their second session, the sub-committee set out to consider 'the more practical and specific aspects of the problem of alcoholism'.[10] They were indeed much more clear in their recommendations about who should be treated, when, where, by whom and in what way. Underpinning these recommendations was the conception of alcoholism as a disease and Jellinek's delineation of phases of alcohol addiction. In the light of this, particular treatment packages were linked to the particular addictive phase to which the alcoholic has progressed: early, middle, chronic and, finally, 'alcoholism with apparently irreversible deterioration'.[10] Special inpatient facilities were considered feasible and desirable only for the third and fourth categories. The vast majority of alcoholics, it was suggested, should be given 'ambulatory' or out-patient treatment.

At the beginning of the first session of the sub-committee's deliberations prevention had been closely linked with treatment as the key concern. By the end of the second session it had been very much relegated to secondary significance.

> Without prejudice to the preventive aspects of the programme the sub-committee feels that progress . . . is most feasible only after the large number of alcoholics throughout the world has been considerably diminished through a large-scale rehabilitation effort . . . When the public understands the disease nature of alcoholism, a much greater acceptance of preventive measures may be expected.

This consideration of medical treatment, in isolation from prevention and broad 'control measures', was certainly carried over into the European Seminar and Lecture Course where, as Jellinek, the Course Director, said, the main subject was 'the aetiology and the clinical picture of alcoholism'. He went on to point out that the selection of this aspect 'is in keeping with the interests and competence of the

organisation which conducts this Seminar — namely the WHO'.[11] The
policy of concentrating on mainly medical aspects was certainly adopted
by the Ministry of Health when it, at last, began to show some interest
in the alcohol problem in the early 1960s. It has taken about 15 years
to move from its initial concentration on special units, in the 1962
memorandum, to the hesitant steps toward a rather more comprehensive approach taken by the, recently disbanded, DHSS Advisory
Committee on Alcoholism.

The brief 1962 Memorandum was certainly consistent with the
general tenor of the yearly WHO reports: emphasising special treatment facilities for those people with severe alcoholism and alcohol
psychosis and the importance of group therapy and co-operation with
Alcoholics Anonymous. We know very little, however, about the
relationship between WHO and the Ministry of Health during the pre-
1962 period. No one from England, for instance, was on the
Alcoholism Sub-committee and only one person from England
attended the course in Copenhagen as opposed to five or six each from
Denmark, Yugoslavia, Italy, Switzerland, France and several other
countries. What was the relationship at that time? Was it cool? Was it
indifferent? Was it only in the field of alcoholism that the Ministry
appeared to avoid international deliberations, or was it in all areas, and
how much has this changed in the intervening years, if at all?

Influential Individuals

In the pre-1962 period certain individuals were particularly influential
in the alcoholism field, E.M. Jellinek, clearly, on an international scale
and Max Glatt, certainly, in England.

In 1939, Jellinek, who was then a Research Associate in Applied
Physiology at Yale University, directed a *Study of the Effects of
Alcohol on the Individual*, funded by the Research Council on Problems
of Alcohol. He analysed, with others[12] the existing scientific literature
on alcoholism and revealed that most of it tended to focus upon
isolated aspects of alcoholism rather than on the central problem itself.
In the following years, until his death in 1963, Jellinek played an
enormous part in directing attention to alcoholism, its nature and, via
his formula, its extent and, via his researches and travels, its variations.

From a reading of its reports it appears that Jellinek dominated the
WHO Alcoholism Sub-committee. This may or may not be a gross over-
simplification, and only interviews with other people involved will
reveal that. What Jellinek's influence with the Ministry of Health in
Britain was is unclear. We know, of course, that he visited here in the

early fifties in order to collect statistics for his calculations of prevalence. At that time there was an interest in alcoholism in Britain
but it was not regarded as a big problem. Listen to D.L. Davies's
recollections of that time:

> Everybody said that other countries had their alcohol problems but
> not Britain. Jellinek came here, I think in 1950 or '51, and I
> remember a discussion in Aubrey Lewis's office here at the Institute
> of Psychiatry with Aubrey Lewis and Jellinek, this curious little
> tubby man who looked as if he had stepped out of a cartoon. He
> came along and said to Aubrey Lewis that he thought that we did
> have a problem and he wanted to get statistics, and Aubrey Lewis
> put him in touch with people at the Ministry of Health. I remember
> C.P. Blacker, who was adviser to the Ministry in some aspects of
> epidemiology, saying to me that alcoholism wasn't a problem here
> and he thought that Jellinek was wasting his time. But they gave him
> what statistics they had. It was after that that Jellinek produced
> his prevalence figure of 350,000.[13]

That, in turn, spurred other people in this country to take some
interest in the question of prevalence: people like Parr,[14] Prys-
Williams,[15] and Moss and Beresford-Davies.[1] We have not yet, however,
had a national survey of the type recommended by Jellinek and
conducted, for example, across the Atlantic in the 1960s by Cahalan
and his associates.[16]

At just about the time that Jellinek was collecting his statistics from
the Ministry of Health, Max Glatt was setting up the first NHS special
treatment unit for alcoholics at Warlingham Park under the guidance of
T.P. Rees. It appears at first sight, and it is certainly the conventional
wisdom in this country, that Glatt's work at Warlingham, his experience
and his writings had a direct impact on government policy.[17-19]

We know that in 1961 Glatt's follow-up study of nearly 100 patients
claimed a 30 per cent recovery rate after two to three years.[20] We
also know that although he was not on the committee, Glatt drafted
the Memorandum on Alcoholism of the Joint Committee of the
British Medical Association and the Magistrates Association,[21] which
recommended the establishment of special units.

Soon afterwards the Ministry of Health memorandum appeared,
accepting the advice of the Standing Mental Health Advisory
Committees, recommending establishment of the ATUs and completely
endorsing the Glatt treatment model which he had set out in the

BMA-Magistrates Association report. Yet Glatt was not on the Ministry of Health Advisory Committee and we know that there was opposition on that committee to the idea of special units, from D.L. Davies among others. We also know that Glatt was not asked to present evidence. We need, therefore, to get some idea of what other evidence was available and taken into consideration, what place the Ministry of Health felt ATUs would have in a comprehensive alcoholism service or whether they imagined that the alcoholism problem could simply be tidied away or even solved by establishing a network of special units. All this requires interviews with Max Glatt, of course, together with other people who were involved, and access to contemporary material and committee papers.

Trends in Alcoholism Research

The activities of the WHO Advisory Committee, and individuals like Jellinek and Glatt did not, of course, take place in a vacuum. We are interested also, therefore, in the general background to these events — for instance, the contemporary trends in alcoholism research.

The mid 1930s in America saw the beginning of a broad scientific approach to alcoholism. Joliffe, Bowman, Jellinek and Howard Haggard were in varying degrees involved with the unsuccessful Research Council on Problems of Alcohol, then with the founding of the QJSA in 1940 and the establishment of the Yale Centre of Alcohol Studies.[22] Alcoholics Anonymous was starting to make itself felt, with its own particular view on the nature and treatment of alcoholism.

Examining 'problem drinking' within the perspective of social change, Robert Straus points out that perceptions of the problems associated with excessive drinking changed during the 1940s. In the early 1940s studies were 'limited to the then visible, captive populations of alcoholics in prisons, mental hospitals and on skid row'. By the late 1940s there was a major shift from ideas of 'chronic alcoholism' to those of 'respectable alcoholism'. Straus contends that two factors brought about this transition: the emergence of AA and the development of the community outpatient clinic approach to the treatment of alcoholics. He says that gradually: 'Research studies picked up the emphasis that a majority of alcoholics were not fallen skid row . . . but men and women who were struggling to maintain family and job stability.'[23]

As far as the situation in England was concerned, we must analyse the medical and other literature, to see what were the main research concerns, and whether there was a shift of emphasis similar to that across the Atlantic. We must look for the development of treatment ideas, and, in particular, the notion of specialised inpatient treatment units. We want to uncover the relationship between research concerns and treatment philosophy in that period and the relationship between social research and social policy.

This last point, the impact of alcoholism research on policy and the development of government policy on alcoholism research, is, of course, an important political issue. As David Hawks, in his discussion of drug policy, put it:

> Politicians are . . . not only concerned with what is right or true in the scientific sense but what is expedient or functional in the political sense. In some instances, these two systems of values will coincide; in others, however, they will be in conflict . . . In that political decisions are affected by a multitude of considerations additional to those affecting the conduct and outcome of research, the results of any investigations may be deemed expendable at the time of their eventual publication.[24]

In considering the pre-1962 period we have touched briefly on the role of WHO, the influence of specific individuals and some of the broad trends of alcoholism research. As our own research gets under way we hope to answer a whole multitude of questions in relation to these and other issues in an attempt to account for the establishment of special treatment units for alcoholics.

Conclusions

In this short chapter we have sought to introduce some preliminary ideas from our recently established study of the history and development of policy in relation to the special alcoholism treatment units in England and Wales. This history will be, in a very real sense, a history of the British response to alcohol problems over recent decades, since changes in policy in relation to the ATUs have been symptomatic of broader shifts of concept, emphasis and activity.

Those at the Department of Health, and others with responsibility for the health services, are never short of people telling them what is wrong with their official policies and how they should be changed or developed. On the other hand, much too little attention is given to trying to understand why particular health policies have developed, in response to what, and with what implications. Yet it is only after such questions have been answered that we can hope to get away from the rank *ad hoc*ery that characterises alcohol policy, in so many countries, and begin to construct rational, or at least coherent, or at very least in some way adequate policies in relation to the prevention of alcohol problems and the provision of services for problem drinkers and, in particular, for example, decide whether or not it makes any sense at all to have 'special units for common problems'.

Notes

1. Moss, M.C. and Beresford-Davies, E. (1969) *A Survey of Alcoholism in an English County* (Geigy, London).

2. DHSS (1978), *The Pattern and Range of Services for Problem Drinkers*, Report by the Advisory Committee on Alcoholism (HMSO, London).

3. Davies, D.L. (1979), 'Services for Alcoholics', in Grant, M. and Gwinner, P. (eds.), *Alcoholism in Perspective* (Croom Helm, London; University Park Press, Baltimore).

4. Ministry of Health (1962), *Hospital Treatment of Alcoholism*, Memorandum HM(62)43.

5. Ministry of Health (1968), *Treatment of Alcoholism*, Memorandum HM(68)37.

6. DHSS (1973), *Community Services for Alcoholics*, Circular 21/73.

7. Home Office (1971), *Report of the Working Party on Habitual Drunken Offenders* (HMSO, London).

8. Robinson, D. (1979), *Talking Out of Alcoholism: The Self-Help Process of Alcoholics Anonymous* (Croom Helm, London; University Park Press, Baltimore).

9. WHO Expert Committee on Mental Health (1951), *Report of the First Session of the Alcoholism Sub-committee*, Techn. Rep. Series no. 42 (WHO, Geneva).

10. WHO Expert Committee on Mental Health (1952), *Report of the Second Session of the Alcoholism Sub-committee*, Techn. Rep. no. 48 (WHO, Geneva).

11. WHO (1952) *Report from European Seminar and Lecture Course on Alcoholism* (WHO, Geneva).

12. Jellinek, E.M. (ed.) (1942), *Alcohol Addiction and Chronic Alcoholism*, (Yale University Press, New Haven).

13. Davies, D.L. (1979), Interview in *British Journal of Addiction*, vol. 74, p. 3.

14. Parr, D. (1957), 'Alcoholism in General Practice', *British Journal of Addiction*, vol. 54, no. 1, pp. 25-31.

15. Prys-Williams, G. (1965), *Chronic Alcoholics* (Rowntree Social Science Trust, London).

16. Cahalan, D., Cisin, I.H. and Crossley, M. (1969), *American Drinking Practices: A National Study of Drinking Behaviour and Attitudes* (Rutgers Center of Alcohol Studies, New Brunswick, New Jersey).

17. Glatt, M.M. (1955), 'A Treatment Centre for Alcoholics in a Public Mental Hospital: Its Establishment and its Working', *British Journal of Addiction*, vol. 52, pp. 55-89.

18. Glatt, M.M. (1958), 'Alcoholism, Crime and Juvenile Delinquency', *British Journal of Delinquency*, vol. 9, pp. 84-93.

19. Glatt, M.M. (1961), 'Drinking Habits of English (Middle Class) Alcoholics', *Acta Psychiatrica Scandinavica*, vol. 37, pp. 88-113.

20. Glatt, M.M. (1961), 'Treatment Results in an English Mental Hospital Alcoholic Unit', *Acta Psychiatrica Scandinavica*, vol. 37, pp. 143-68.

21. BMA-Magistrates Association (1961), 'Memorandum on Alcoholism', *British Medical Journal*, vol. 2, supplement, pp. 190-5.

22. Keller, M. (1976), 'Problems with Alcohol: An Historical Perspective', in Filstead, W., Rossi, J.J. and Keller, M. (eds.), *Alcohol and Alcohol Problems* (Ballinger, Cambridge, Mass.).

23. Straus, R. (1976), 'Problem Drinking in the Perspective of Social Change, 1940-73', in Filstead, W.J., Rossi, J.J. and Keller, M. (eds.), *Alcohol and Alcohol Problems* (Ballinger, Cambridge, Mass.).

24. Hawks, D. (1976), 'Social Research as a Determinant of Social Policy', in Edwards, G., Russell, M.A.H., Hawks, D. and MacCafferty, M. (eds.), *Alcohol Dependence and Smoking Behaviour* (D.C. Heath, Farnborough, Hants.).

PROFILES OF TREATMENT-SEEKING
POPULATIONS

Harvey A. Skinner

There is considerable dissatisfaction with the present state of knowledge about alcoholism treatment. Unrest about the effectiveness of
current treatment methods has fuelled a growing urge to find new
directions, to attempt a bold step forward. However, before embarking
on new research ventures it is helpful to synthesise what is already
known about the profiles of clinical alcoholic populations.

This chapter has four specific aims. First, general characteristics of
clinical alcoholic populations are reviewed. For example, what variables
seem to determine whether a client is given outpatient or inpatient
care? Secondly, empirical data are presented from a multivariate
examination of clients assessed at the Clinical Institute of the Addiction
Research Foundation, Toronto. Differences are examined among clients
assigned to either (1) inpatient programmes, (2) outpatient programmes,
or (3) a lower cost basic care alternative. Thirdly, a model of psychopathology is introduced as a framework for integrating previous
research on alcoholic populations who have completed the Minnesota
Multiphasic Personality Inventory (MMPI). Several recent studies from
the alcoholism treatment literature are evaluated using the model.
Finally, directions for future research are summarised. In particular,
there is need for 'technically feasible' evaluations of the 'client type by
treatment interaction' hypothesis.

Literature On Client Characteristics

As an aid for evaluating the literature on clinical alcoholic populations,
it is important to consider the broader context of an alcoholism treatment system. A prototype system has been suggested by Pattison, Coe
and Rhodes[1] where a distinction is made among three classes of
variables (Figure 16.1). Among the client variables, the central question
is whether one may identify relatively homogeneous sub-groups with
distinct syndromes. In brief, are we dealing with one population or are
meaningful sub-populations present? Secondly, although treatment
programmes may be given different names, one must question the

Figure 16.1: Classes of Variables

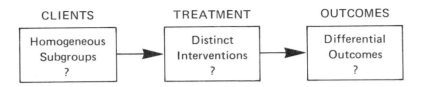

CLIENTS	TREATMENT	OUTCOMES
Homogeneous Subgroups ?	Distinct Interventions ?	Differential Outcomes ?

extent to which many interventions regress to the same basic approach in actual practice. Are they really distinct at the operational level? Often multi-modal packages are offered that make it nearly impossible to determine which component is most effective. Thirdly, to what extent is there evidence for differential outcomes from treatment, or are we dealing with a global unimproved-improved continuum that is used in many studies? Recently, various outcome criteria have been proposed,[2] and there is empirical support for the multivariate assessment of treatment outcome.[3]

Client Types

There is consistent evidence that one may identify distinct sub-groups among alcoholics.[4,5] For example, in a study of male alcoholic patients, Skinner, Jackson and Hoffmann[6] identified eight personality types that replicated across three samples. These types are based on a dimensional classification model. A plot of the two most important typal dimensions is given in Figure 16.2. Clusters of individuals may be located at the poles of each axis. The first dimension contrasts a generalised anxiety syndrome at one pole, with a defensiveness syndrome and blunted affect at the other pole. Similarly, one pole of the second dimension represents a character disorder of rebelliousness and impulse control problems, whereas the other pole is characterised by hypochondriasis and a preoccupation with bodily complaints. Over 37 per cent of the alcoholic samples were classified according to Figure 16.2.

In this study, Skinner *et al.*[6] speculated that aside from the manifest problem of alcohol abuse, 'alcoholic' clients may be little different from other types found in a general psychiatric population. A subsequent study by Skinner, Reed and Jackson[7] evaluated the representatives of these types among psychiatric patients, prison inmates and college students. The two typal dimensions of Figure 16.2 were

Figure 16.2: Two Typal Dimensions Based on the Differential
Personality Inventory

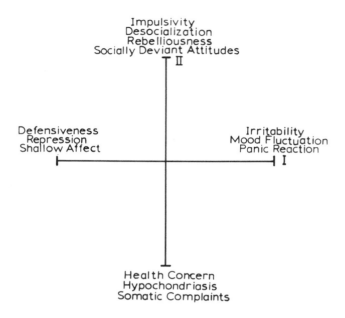

notably pervasive across all samples. Perhaps the treatment of alcoholic
clients who cluster at a given pole should focus more upon the clinical
syndrome and less upon overt evidence of alcohol abuse.

Comparison of Treatment Programmes

Another approach is to compare the characteristics of clients who enter
different programmes. To a great extent, this research only highlights
the process of self-selection by which clients are attracted to different
programmes. For example, Kern, Schmelter and Fanelli[8] compared
(1) inpatients in a public hospital, (2) outpatients voluntarily receiving
psychotherapy and (3) clients who were ordered by the court to
undergo outpatient therapy as a result of two or more arrests for
driving while intoxicated. The most important finding was that the
three groups could be ordered along a *continuum* of problems related
to drinking. The inpatients reported the most severe level of problems,

followed by the voluntary outpatients with the court remanded clients at the lowest end. Possible explanations were that the court remanded clients were denying the extent of their drinking, or that these clients may indeed be at an earlier stage of alcoholism.

Further evidence for a dimensional representation of the differences among programmes is given by Pattison, Coe and Doerr.[9] Clients at four programmes were found to 'demonstrate a continuum of social competence that maintained internal consistency between the various types of data obtained'. A similar conclusion was reached by Bromet, Moos and Bliss[10] and by Cronkite and Moos[11] in their extensive study of five treatment programmes. They found that a composite variable, termed 'social background' (age, sex, marital status, ethnic group, education), was an important determinant of the type of programme a client entered. Also, several studies have found that social class interacts with the treatment programme that alcoholic clients enter.[12,13] Finally, English and Curtin[14] found that clients at three inpatient programmes (VA Hospital, state hospital, halfway house) could be differentiated along two dimensions of anxiety and self-esteem as assessed by the MMPI.

The pervasive finding that clients differ across treatment programmes raises an interesting question. What if they have consistently picked the wrong programme?

A rigorous comparison of client characteristics across different treatment settings is hampered by a host of confounding variables that could potentially account for observed differences. Consequently, another approach is to examine clients who make use of alcoholism treatment services *within* a given community. In this respect, Delahaye studied clients at various treatment agencies in Manchester, England. These agencies ranged from a specialised residential unit for alcoholism, to more general facilities at public and mental hospitals. Although Delahaye identified 'clear differences between the client groups at each separate agency',[15] variations among treatment approaches at each agency were less well defined. If agencies in fact are offering more or less the same treatment package, what factors attract clients to one service versus another?

Client Type By Treatment Interactions

An elusive goal of alcoholism treatment research is to achieve a close match between a client's particular problems and the most effective intervention.[16] To date, this crucial hypothesis has *not* been adequately tested in a scientifically meaningful way. Many treatment services offer only one approach,[17] and there is frequently poor standardisation of procedures or quality control. Furthermore, because of the self selection by clients described above, a given treatment programme deals with a restricted sample. How would one know whether other types of clients would do better in a programme if they are always under-represented?

The recent study by Finney and Moos[18] provides an excellent illustration of issues which bear on matching. Although they examined five treatment programmes, each programme offered a variety of services and there was considerable overlap between services available at each facility. For example, most offered AA meetings and some variant of group therapy. Thus, one must seriously question if these treatment programmes were sufficiently distinct to enable the emergence of a client type by programme interaction. Furthermore, patient types were not systematically distributed across programmes. Low social competence types were more frequent in the Salvation Army, public hospital and halfway house programmes, whereas the high social competence types predominated the milieu oriented and aversion conditioning programmes. Since certain patient types rarely got into a particular programme (e.g. low social competence in the milieu programme), one has scant data on how they would have fared with this method.

Clearly, if one is to have a fair test of the 'matching hypothesis' then treatment interventions must be appreciably distinct and all client types should be equally represented in each programme. In brief, there is no substitute for a controlled study that involves random assignment of client types to interventions. All short-cuts are problematic.

Comparison Of Clients By Treatment Programmes

In this section, an in-depth look is taken at a random sample of clients who were seen during 1977 and 1978 at the Clinical Institute of the Addiction Research Foundation, Toronto. The sample excludes clients that were given emergency care or acute medical services. All clients completed a comprehensive two day assessment programme before being assigned to treatment. Although the population at the Clinical Institute is not entirely representative of all individuals with alcohol-related problems in the metro-Toronto area, this population is reasonably heterogeneous. Thus, the results should have moderate generalisability. Furthermore, this sample is relatively unique both in the range of treatment services offered and in the extent of assessment information collected on all clients. A detailed description of this study is given in Skinner.[19] Only the key findings will be highlighted here.

Subjects

The total sample consisted of 296 clients, of whom 76 per cent were male and 24 per cent female. The average age was 33.7 years (standard deviation = 12.0) with a range from 14 to 66 years. The clients had been drinking for an average of 16.7 years (standard deviation = 10.0), while in the past two months 55 per cent drank daily, 18 per cent in binges, 10 per cent on weekends, 12 per cent occasionally and 5 per cent were abstinent. With respect to substance of abuse, 64 per cent were referred for alcohol-related problems, 18 per cent for drug abuse and 18 per cent for mixed alcohol-drug problems. The largest category for marital status was single (41 per cent), followed by separated (21 per cent), married (20 per cent), divorced (12 per cent) and common law (5 per cent). The majority of clients (63 per cent) had their own apartment or house.

Since the sample size was not sufficient to enable an analysis of each treatment programme, clients were compared across three broad treatment categories:

I. *Inpatient:* consisted of two programmes, a relatively traditional inpatient service for clients with alcohol problems, and a behavioural programme that used group contingency management techniques. The number of clients assigned to inpatient care was 112 or 38.6 per cent.

II. *Outpatient:* seven programmes were offered on an outpatient basis, including relatively traditional modes of psychotherapy such as individual, group, family and marital. A total of 119 clients or 39.2 per cent were assigned to outpatient programmes.

III. *Primary Care:* provided supportive counselling and help with practical details. Primary Care is seen as a lower cost basic level of care that may be offered to all clients.[20] This intervention received 65 clients or 22.2 per cent.

Materials

All clients were tested upon intake as part of a comprehensive two day assessment programme. The instruments were administered by specifically trained assessment workers in the Assessment Unit at the Addiction Research Foundation. The measures used in this study are divided into six content domains, namely (1) alcohol use scales and related measures, (2) demographic variables, (3) response styles ('denial', 'social desirability', and the 'infrequency' scale which measures carelessness and lack of understanding), (4) intellectual abilities and neuropsychological tests, (5) personality characteristics, and (6) psychopathology scales (e.g. anxiety, depression). The measures in this comprehensive battery had been carefully designed, and extensive reliability and validity studies have been carried out.[19]

Analyses

Multiple discriminant analysis[21] was used as the principal technique for comparing clients across the three treatment categories: Inpatient versus Outpatient versus Primary Care. This multivariate procedure derives weighted linear combinations of variables that optimally differentiate among the three treatment groups. An advantage of this method over repeated univariate comparisons is that it takes into account correlations among the dependent variables.

Results

For each of the six content domains, the discriminant function weights, structure coefficients and univariate F tests are given in Skinner.[19] Only the salient findings will be highlighted in this section.

1. *Alcohol Related Measures.* The first dimension ordered the three groups according to symptoms of general alcoholism. That is, clients assigned to the inpatient programmes had more skid row characteristics, tended to experience more severe withdrawal symptoms, drank in a compulsive style, reported loss of control when drinking, had a greater daily consumption of alcohol, and had more often sought help for drinking problems. Primary care clients were at an intermediate level along this discriminant function, whereas the outpatient clients anchored the lower end.

2. *Assessment Validity Scales.* Some interesting differences were evident with respect to the assessment validity scales. First, the primary care clients exhibited a stronger tendency to be defensive and minimise

problem areas. An implication is that primary care clients had been screened from the most costly interventions at least in part because they were less open about describing symptoms or admitting to drinking problems. Secondly, the outpatient group was higher on social desirability, that is, a tendency to present an overly favourable picture of oneself.

3. *Demographic Variables.* The outpatient group was higher on social stability which is a composite index that considers present accommodation, family contact, work record and legal status. Also, outpatients tended to be better educated. These differences are not surprising since social stability was used as a criterion for assigning clients to outpatient care. The assumption is that a reasonable level of community support is necessary to sustain treatment on an outpatient basis. Observe that there are no systematic age or sex differences across programmes.

4. *Intellectual Abilities and Neuropsychological Tests.* With respect to intellectual ability, the outpatient clients were clearly higher than either the inpatient or primary care groups. Also, the outpatient group performed better on the neuropsychological tests, especially of visual-motor co-ordination and response speed (WAIS Digit Symbols).

5. *Personality Characteristics.* In general there were few differences in personality characteristics across the three groups. Only impulsivity was an important discriminator, with the inpatient group reporting a greater tendency to act on the spur of the moment.

6. *Measures of Psychopathology.* The inpatient clients reported a more severe level of symptoms on several indices of psychopathology. That is, they tended to be more suspicious of others, experienced generalised symptoms of anxiety and depression, were more preoccupied with bodily functions and somatic complaints, and reported problems with cognitive functioning (memory lapses, confusion).

In summary, it is clear that clients streamed into the inpatient programmes tended to be more deviant in several domains. That is, they reported greater alcohol consumption levels and problems associated with drinking, they had fewer community supports and were less socially stable, and they tended to experience a more severe range of symptoms related to psychopathology, such as depression and anxiety. In brief, inpatient clients were more maladjusted. However, it is interesting to note that inpatients tended to be more open about admitting to symptoms and problem areas. Defence mechanisms tended to be more operative among clients streamed into the outpatient and primary care programmes. In general, the outpatient clients tended to have more favourable prognostic indicators, such as social stability and lower level of alcoholic involvement. Finally, it is important to recognise that the differences among groups are differences in degree not kind.

Client Profiles Based On The MMPI

The Minnesota Multiphasic Personality Inventory or MMPI has been the most widely used instrument in studies of personality characteristics of alcoholics.[22] This instrument has been employed to compare clients across different treatment settings,[14] to study changes within clients over the course of treatment,[23] and to identify relatively homogeneous personality types among samples of alcoholic patients.[4] Because of its extensive use, the MMPI provides a rich source of data on alcoholic clients. As a means of integrating these diverse studies, Skinner[24] has developed a model of psychopathology based on the MMPI. The integrative power of this model will be illustrated by several recent studies.

Background

This model is based on a quantitative, dimensional approach to classification, and was stimulated, in part, by a vector model of disease states in clinical medicine proposed by Sneath.[25] The model is comprised of three clinical types or syndromes: *neurotic, psychotic* and *sociopathic*, that were derived by Skinner and Jackson[26] from an empirical analysis of code types contained in the Gilberstadt and Duker[27] and Marks, Seeman and Haller[28] MMPI actuarial systems. Each type is defined empirically by a configuration of scores on the MMPI clinical scales. The neurotic type has highpoints on *Hs, D* and *Hy*, and is characterised by somatic complaints, depression symptoms and an immature or egocentric orientation. On the other hand, the psychotic type is defined by elevations on *Sc, Pt* and *Pa*. This syndrome is evidenced by unusual thought content, inappropriate affect, emotional agitation and fearfulness, and to a lesser extent by suspiciousness of others. Finally, the sociopathic type has highpoints on *Pd* and *Ma*, and represents a character disorder. These individuals tend to be rebellious and impulsive, experience family and social problems, and are outgoing and manipulative.

Similar to Sneath's[25] vector model, each superordinate type in our system defines an orthogonal axis (Figure 16.3). Given the MMPI clinical scales in T score format, one may compute the co-ordinates for individual profiles in this three dimensional space. For example, if a person has highpoints on *Hs*, *D* and *Hy*, his vector would be located near the neurotic axis. Likewise, a person with elevations on *Sc* and *Pt* would project along the psychotic axis, whereas another individual with a *Pd* and *Ma* configuration would be located near the sociopathic reference axis. Computational details are given by Skinner[24] and by Skinner and Jackson.[26]

In practice it is expected that a certain number of individuals will

Figure 16.3: A Three Dimensional Model of Psychopathology with Neurotic, Psychotic and Sociopathic Typal Axes.

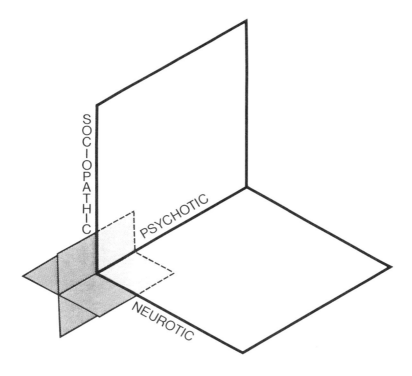

resemble primarily one type. Consequently, there will be a swarm of vectors near each reference axis in Figure 16.3. However, some persons will resemble to some extent more than one type. Their vectors will span the space between axes. In addition, other persons may not resemble any of the three types, and their vectors will be clustered near the origin. The empirical import of the model is contingent on the degree to which a reasonable number of cases have a predominant location near a single reference axis. For these cases, one may use the respective type to characterise the sub-group without great loss of information. Furthermore, one may observe loci of vectors at other locations in Figure 16.3. These cases would represent mixed types.

The location of a person's profile in Figure 16.3 is determined by MMPI profile *shape*, that is, the actual pattern of 'ups and downs' across the 13 clinical scales. Three shape parameters are generated, one describing the resemblance of the profile to each type. The three shape parameters also give the co-ordinates for plotting a vector in Figure 16.3. It is hypothesised that shape represents the clinical pattern or type of disorder[29] and that this parameter should be relatively consistent over time. Another important parameter of the model is *elevation*, which is the mean score of the individual across all 13 MMPI clinical scales. It is postulated that profile elevation provides a quantitative index of symptom severity. Elevation is hypothesised to be more situationally specific. Thus, by examining shape and elevation parameters, one may integrate various aspects of the trait (shape) and situational (elevation) approaches to the study of personality.[30,31]

Applications

In two independent samples of hospitalised alcoholics, Goldstein and Linden[4] identified and replicated four alcoholic types, labelled (1) psychopathic personality and emotional instability, (2) psychoneuroses with severe alcoholism, (3) alcoholism with secondary psychopathic personality, and (4) alcoholism with secondary drug addiction and paranoia. The MMPI profile parameters for these types are given in Skinner.[19] The first Goldstein and Linden[4] type has a moderate weighting on the psychotic axis, with a secondary correlation on the neurotic axis. Since these individuals have been described as manifesting the most severe, chronic evidence of alcoholism, it is consistent to observe that this type has the highest elevation parameter of all groups. The third Goldstein and Linden[4] type has a substantial weighting on the sociopathic axis. Individuals with this profile have been described as alcoholic with a psychopathic personality. Finally, the fourth Goldstein and Linden[4] type has a marked similarity to the sociopathic axis.

In a subsequent study, Whitelock, Overall and Patrick[5] replicated the Goldstein and Linden[4] typology. The Whitelock *et al.* analysis helps to clarify the status of Types III and IV. That is, they found that the Type III profile is predominantly characterised by the psychotic axis with a secondary weighting on the sociopathic axis. This trend is suggested by the Goldstein and Linden[4] Type III Original profile, although the weightings are not as large in magnitude. Type IV in the Whitelock *et al.*[5] replication is consistent with the Goldstein and Linden results. It is interesting to note that the elevation parameters are generally larger with the Whitelock *et al.* sample, which could reflect differences between samples employed in each study or variations in the lag between last drinking bout and time of assessment. That is, one would expect the elevation parameter to decrease as clients progress through stages of alcohol withdrawal.

English and Curtin[14] have compared the MMPI profiles of alcoholic clients at three treatment programmes: VA Hospital, state hospital and halfway house. Skinner[19] presents the profile parameters. With respect to profile shape, the three groups have a substantial weighting on the psychotic axis with a secondary weighting on the neurotic axis. This profile is quite similar to the psychoneuroses with severe alcoholism Type II of Goldstein and Linden.[4] However, the VA Hospital patients are higher on profile elevation. This suggests that these clients are experiencing a more severe level of symptoms that could result from a more chronic history of alcohol abuse.

In Skinner,[19] the results are given from two longitudinal studies. Kammeier, Hoffmann and Loper[32] compared the MMPI profiles of men when they entered college and when they first entered an alcoholism treatment facility (an average of 13 years later). There was a clear increase in profile elevation (54.8 versus 61.8) on the second testing, which indicated a rise in the degree of pathology. Also, there was an interesting shift in profile shape. While college freshmen, the clients resembled the sociopathic axis which signifies a tendency toward rebellious attitudes and high energy level. However, the level of symptoms is generally within the normal range. At the time these clients entered treatment, there is a substantial weighting on the psychotic axis as well. This could represent consequences due to alcohol abuse such as impaired concentration, hallucinations and periods of confusion. Bean and Karasievich[23] tested alcoholic clients at three stages of treatment: five days, 30 days and 60 days. As treatment progresses, there was a decrease in the elevation parameter which corresponds to a decrease in the level of symptom severity. However, the shape parameters were relatively stable.

In review, the MMPI model of psychopathology provides a common framework for examining the diverse studies on alcoholic clients. The strength of the model is evidenced by its ability to summarise various studies within a parsimonious dimensional system. Furthermore, the three superordinate types have been found to be quite persuasive among other psychiatric and normal groups.[24] These data lend support to the speculation by Skinner *et al.*[6] that aside from the manifest symptom of alcohol abuse, alcoholic patients may be little different from other patient types seen in a general psychiatric population. Given that the three superordinate types of Figure 16.3 have been found to be generalised across different alcoholic samples, an important implication is that each type may respond best to a different treatment plan.

What Have We Learned?

In retrospect, it is instructive to summarise what has been learned thus far and point out avenues for further research:

1. The client population is multivariant.[33] Distinct clinical syndromes or client types have been consistently identified. However, research is needed to evaluate whether certain client types respond best to specific interventions. This is the 'acid' test.

2. There is evidence that many clinical syndromes found among alcoholic samples are similar to patient types found in general psychiatric populations. Thus, an adequate diagnostic system may need to encompass general psychiatric syndromes (which a portion of alcoholic clients significantly resemble) plus several types unique to alcoholism. Research could examine if for certain client types it is more efficacious to focus upon the clinical syndrome (e.g. chronic anxiety) than on drinking behaviour.

3. Differences exist among clients across various treatment programmes. Nevertheless, these differences are of degree not kind. Treatment programmes may be ordered along several continua or dimensions, such as level of alcoholic involvement, social competence, social class, and degree of psychopathology. Research is needed to delineate key differences within a multi-dimensional framework.

4. Clients with more severe symptoms and problems related to drinking tend to be found in the more costly inpatient programmes.

One might question why clients with poor prognostic indications (e.g. low social stability) are given expensive care. Would lower cost basic care alternatives yield comparable treatment outcomes?

5. There are severe limitations on treatment research with most existing programmes: (a) because certain client types are often grossly under-represented in a particular programme, (b) since many treatment services offer only one approach and this is a smorgasbord of modalities, and (c) because of lack of consistency within programmes or of an explicit statement of what actually goes on. Controlled studies are needed where clients are randomly assigned to carefully specified interventions.

Although this chapter has concentrated upon clinical alcoholic samples, there are limitations on how much one can learn with clients at later stages of alcohol abuse. Equal energy should be directed toward the study of early risk factors and the natural history of alcoholism. As with much mental health research, there is a tendency to neglect normalcy, that is, to fail to understand the behavioural patterns of 'normal' drinkers.

Despite the lack of progress on alcoholism treatment, a positive outlook on research prospects is justified. The paucity of evidence to date on the effectiveness of alcoholism treatment reflects both inadequate research designs, as well as the immense practical constraints on conducting controlled studies in most treatment settings. Indeed, many studies were not 'technically feasible' of demonstrating significant results because of small sample sizes, client pre-selection, less than perfect predictor and criterion reliability, and the absence of a control group. Several real improvements in treatment methods may be staring us in the face, eagerly awaiting an opportunity to show their mettle if we would only look.

In conclusion, one may argue that some very clear and urgent research directions are known — we simply have not progressed far enough along the map. Indeed, for several directions we have rarely left the comfortable environment of our armchairs. It is most embarrassing, for example, to find that there is scant properly controlled *scientific* evidence for the therapeutic effectiveness of disulfiram,[34] a drug that we have been prescribing for over 30 years. It is important to find new research directions. But, one must use sound judgement in parsing the real contributions from a myriad will-o'-the-wisps. Otherwise, we may suffer a fate similar to Leacock's horseman, 'who flung himself from the room, flung himself upon his horse and rode madly off in all directions'.[35]

Notes

1. Pattison, E.M., Coe, R. and Rhodes, R.J. (1969), 'Evaluation of Alcoholism Treatment. A Comparison of Three Facilities', *Archives of General Psychiatry*, vol. 20, pp. 478-88.

2. Pattison, E.M. (1976), 'Non-Abstinent Drinking Goals in the Treatment of Alcoholism', *Archives of General Psychiatry*, vol. 33, pp. 923-30.

3. Foster, F.M., Horn, J.L. and Wanberg, K.W. (1972), 'Dimensions of Treatment Outcome. A Factor-analytic Study of Alcoholics' Responses to a Follow-up Questionnaire', *Quarterly Journal of Studies on Alcohol*, vol. 33, pp. 1079-98.

4. Goldstein, S.G. and Linden, J.D. (1969), 'Multivariate Classification of Alcoholics by Means of the MMPI', *Journal of Abnormal Psychology*, vol. 74, pp. 661-9.

5. Whitelock, P.R., Overall, J.E. and Patrick, J.H. (1971), 'Personality Patterns and Alcohol Abuse in a State Hospital Population', *Journal of Abnormal Psychology*, vol. 78, pp. 9-16.

6. Skinner, H.A., Jackson, D.N. and Hoffmann, H. (1974), 'Alcoholic Personality Types: Identification and Correlates', *Journal of Abnormal Psychology*, vol. 83, pp. 658-66.

7. Skinner, H.A., Reed, P.L. and Jackson, D.N. (1976), 'Toward the Objective Diagnosis of Psychopathology: Generalizability of Modal Personality Profiles', *Journal of Consulting and Clinical Psychology*, vol. 44, pp. 111-17.

8. Kern, J.C., Schmelter, W. and Fanelli, M. (1978), 'A Comparison of Three Alcoholism Treatment Populations. Implications for Treatment', *Journal of Studies on Alcohol*, vol. 39, pp. 785-92.

9. Pattison, E.M., Coe, R. and Doerr, H.O. (1973), 'Population Variation Among Alcoholism Treatment Facilities', *International Journal of the Addictions*, vol. 8, pp. 199-229.

10. Bromet, E.J., Moos, R.H. and Bliss, F. (1976), 'The Social Climate of Alcoholism Treatment Programs', *Archives of General Psychiatry*, vol. 33, pp. 910-16.

11. Cronkite, R.C. and Moos, R.H. (1978), 'Evaluating Alcoholism Treatment Programs: An Integrated Approach', *Journal of Consulting and Clinical Psychology*, vol. 46, pp. 1105-19.

12. Edwards, G., Kyle, E. and Nicholls, P. (1974), 'Alcoholics Admitted to Four Hospitals in England. I. Social Class and the Interaction of Alcoholics with the Treatment System', *Quarterly Journal of Studies on Alcohol*, vol. 35, pp. 499-522.

13. Schmidt, W., Smart, R.G. and Moss, M.K. (1968), *Social Class and the Treatment of Alcoholism; an Investigation of Social Class as a Determinant of Diagnosis, Prognosis and Therapy* (University of Toronto Press, Toronto).

14. English, G.E. and Curtin, M.E. (1975), 'Personality Differences in Patients at Three Alcoholism Treatment Agencies', *Journal of Studies on Alcohol*, vol. 36, pp. 52-61.

15. Delahaye, S. (1977), 'An Analysis of Clients Using Alcoholic Agencies within One Community Service', in Madden, J.S., Walker, R. and Kenyon, W.H. (eds.), *Alcoholism and Drug Dependence. A Multidisciplinary Approach* (Plenum Press, New York), p. 349.

16. Glaser, F.B. (1977), 'The "Average Package of Help" vs the Matching Hypothesis: A Doggerel Dialogue', *Journal of Studies on Alcohol*, vol. 38, pp. 1819-27.

17. Glaser, F.B., Greenberg, S.W. and Barrett, M. (1978), *A Systems Approach to Alcohol Treatment* (Addiction Research Foundation, Toronto).

18. Finney, J.W. and Moos, R.H. (1979), 'Treatment and Outcome for Empirical Subtypes of Alcoholic Patients', *Journal of Consulting and Clinical*

Psychology, vol. 47, pp. 25-38.

19. Skinner, H.A. (1979), 'Profiles of Treatment-Seeking Populations', Sub-study no. 1054 (Addiction Research Foundation, Toronto).

20. Glaser, F.B., Annis, H.M., Pearlman, S., Segal, R.L. and Skinner, H.A. (1979), 'The Differential Therapy of Alcoholism: A Systems Approach', in Masserman, J. (ed.), *Current Psychiatric Therapies*, vol. 10 (Grune & Stratton, New York).

21. Cooley, W.W. and Lohnes, P.R. (1971), *Multivariate Data Analysis* (Wiley, New York).

22. Clopton, J.R. (1978), 'Alcoholism and the MMPI: A Review', *Journal of Studies on Alcohol*, vol. 39, pp. 1540-58.

23. Bean, K.L. and Karasievich, G.O. (1975), 'Psychological Test Results at Three Stages of Inpatient Alcoholism Treatment', *Journal of Studies on Alcohol*, vol. 36, pp. 838-52.

24. Skinner, H.A. (1979), 'A Model of Psychopathology Based on the MMPI', in Newmark, C.S. (ed.), *MMPI: Current Clinical and Research Trends* (Praeger Publishers, New York).

25. Sneath, P.H.E. (1975), 'A Vector Model of Disease for Teaching and Diagnosis', *Medical Hypotheses*, vol. 1, pp. 12-22.

26. Skinner, H.A. and Jackson, D.N. (1978), 'A Model of Psychopathology Based on an Integration of MMPI Actuarial Systems', *Journal of Consulting and Clinical Psychology*, vol. 46, pp. 231-8.

27. Gilberstadt, H. and Duker, J. (1965), *A Handbook for Clinical and Actuarial MMPI Interpretation* (Saunders, Philadelphia).

28. Marks, P.A., Seeman, W. and Haller, D.L. (1974), *The Actuarial Use of the MMPI with Adolescents and Adults* (Williams and Wilkins, Baltimore).

29. Skinner, H.A. (1978), 'Differentiating the Contribution of Elevation, Scatter, and Shape in Profile Similiarity', *Educational and Psychological Measurement*, vol. 38, pp. 297-308.

30. Bowers, K.S. (1973), 'Situationism in Psychology: An Analysis and Critique', *Psychological Review*, vol. 80, pp. 307-36.

31. Mischel, W. (1973), 'Toward a Cognitive Social Learning Reconceptualization of Personality', *Psychological Review*, vol. 80, pp. 252-83.

32. Kammeier, M.L., Hoffmann, H. and Loper, R.G. (1973), 'Personality Characteristics of Alcoholics as College Freshmen and at Time of Treatment', *Quarterly Journal of Studies on Alcohol*, vol. 34, pp. 390-9.

33. Pattison, E.M., Sobell, M.B. and Sobell, L.C. (1977), *Emerging Concepts of Alcohol Dependence* (Springer, New York).

34. Mottin, J.L. (1973), 'Drug-induced Attenuation of Alcohol Consumption', *Quarterly Journal of Studies on Alcohol*, vol. 34, pp. 444-72.

35. Leacock, S. (1969), *Nonsense Novels* (McClelland & Stewart, Toronto; first published in 1911 by John Lane, the Bodley Head), p. 54.

17 HEALTH SERVICES PLANNING — DOES IT EVER WORK?

John M.M. Banham

Many Discontents but Hopeful Indications

In any enterprise, the purpose of planning is to bring about change. In effect, the planner is deciding how the future should be different from the past, and what needs to be done to move from the present situation to the desired future. In the context of health services, planning can take place at a number of different levels. At the national or regional level, at the local level, or at the level of planning services for individual patients, the question *'Does health planning ever work?'* is rather like that once put to George Bernard Shaw: 'Does socialism ever work?' He is said to have replied: 'I don't know — it has never been tried'. However, there is no cause for despair, for at least two of the three levels just referred to in health planning obviously do work.

At the level of planning services for individual patients, in hospitals all over the world, patients are being managed — their health problems are being diagnosed, treatment is being planned, the necessary resources allocated, action co-ordinated across a bewildering array of different professions and skills, and the results monitored.

At the national level also, planning seems to be working — at least in some jurisdictions. Consider, from an overall point of view, the position of the National Health Service in the UK. There are stories of its imminent collapse which are much exaggerated, and mask some real achievements. There are in fact very few organisations in Britain which can boast the combination of major (and continuing) improvements in productivity, smooth and rapid adaptation to technological change, aggressive rationalisation of resources, and remarkably effective (by international standards) control over costs. And this is a nationwide organisation employing almost one million people. Any business enterprise with a record like this would have a (justified) reputation for good management — and effective planning.

Yet dissatisfaction with the planning of health services at regional and local levels remains. In the United States, in Canada, on the Continent as well as in the UK, those involved in the planning and delivery of health care complain that planning has become a huge and unproductive exercise in paper generation, benefiting no one other than Rank Xerox – and certainly not the quality of care provided to patients. Why is this? Does health services planning ever really work? If it is any comfort, business leaders are asking the same question, as they find traditional planning and budgeting approaches inadequate for coping with an increasingly risky, unpredictable and competitive future. In their case, as for health services, the experience of McKinsey suggests that planning can and does work, provided that three apparently simple (but difficult to meet) conditions exist:

1. An environment conducive to planning;
2. realistic expectations of what planning can achieve;
3. simplicity: over-complication is the bane of all planning systems.

These requirements will now be considered in turn, and suggestions made as to how individual jurisdictions can help to ensure that each of them is met.

Securing an Environment Conducive to Planning

McKinsey's has worked on the problems of health planning for individual health maintenance organisations, for major hospitals, for districts, areas, regions or provinces and indeed, in some instances, at the national level. When a number of partners sat down recently to define 'an environment conducive to planning' they concluded that for planning to stand a chance of taking hold four conditions need to be met.

1. *Clear Goals for the Health Care System.* Planning without a clear sense of objectives is inevitably going to be a frustrating process. All the most successful organisations have some clearly defined goals – 'Victory', in the case of the British armed forces in 1940; 'to take a man to the moon and bring him back safely before the decade is out' in the case of NASA. We are at present investing massive public resources in Britain in our National Health Service – the proportion of the gross national product devoted to health care has risen from 3.5 per cent in 1960 to 6.5 per cent today. This difference alone represents approaching £4 billion a year in additional taxation, more than five times the amount necessary to reduce the top marginal tax rate in Britain to 50 per cent.

As astonishing as it may seem, this investment has been made without any agreement of what that health service is required to achieve. Care of outstanding quality for all who need it regardless of ability to pay? Healthier people? Longer life? Happier taxpayers? Contented employees? If you were to go into any hospital in Britain, and ask the first five people that you met how they would judge whether or not the National Health Service as a whole and their particular part of it is doing well, indifferently, or badly, it is extremely doubtful that they would even understand what you were talking about. In one sense, perhaps it is just as well. No indicators suggest that today the British public is any healthier than it was in 1960. Indeed there are substantial indications that the reverse is true. And the British public is a lot less satisfied with the health service today than it was in 1960, and so, judging by the distressing labour relations problems, are those working within it. On the other hand, without clear objectives, planning for health services must remain at best a frustrating exercise.

2. *Clear Limits to the Available Resources.* In many jurisdictions, both in Europe and North America, there are no real limits to expenditures on health care. In the United States, for example, a planning and regulatory strategy has been pursued that presumes no limits on resources devoted to health care, and concentrates on trying to ensure that only 'needed' services are provided, by application of a range of planning and control processes. Planning in such circumstances is doomed to failure. Almost all improvements to health services can be demonstrated to be 'needed'. The difficulty is to distinguish between services which are 'more needed' from those which are 'less needed'. Unless there is a limit to potential expenditure, there are simply no reasons for people to go through this rather painful priority setting exercise.

3. *Top Management Commitments.* In any enterprise, the success or failure of planning approaches depends critically on the attitude and commitment of top management. In those companies where planning works and produces real benefits, the chairman himself will devote a very substantial amount of his time to the planning process. Managers at all levels know that planning is important, that failure to produce sound plans and implement them will have unfortunate consequences for their career prospects, and that imaginative and thorough plans will enhance their chances of promotion.

By contrast, it is unknown to find evidence of any health service administrator whose career has been advanced, or (even more likely) the health of his bank account improved, by his demonstrated skill at coming up with imaginative solutions to health service problems. Too often, as is the case in many business enterprises, planning simply degenerates into an exercise in paper shuffling and form filling because the man at the top – be he Minister, Chairman of the Board, or hospital administrator – simply does not devote enough time and public attention to establishing clear and explicit guidelines, reviewing planning detail, insisting that agreed plans are reflected in budgets, and monitoring performance against plan as well as budget.

4. *Incentives.* Crude though it sounds, one must reluctantly come to the conclusion that the old combination of the carrot and the stick works. Of course, the nature of the carrot, and the type of stick and the way in which it is applied and by whom will need to reflect the nature and traditions of the organisation in question. But it is unlikely that health planning will ever take hold in a jurisdiction where there are (a) no incentives to reward good or even outstanding planning effort for those whose efforts will make the differences between success and failure, and (b) no sanctions to be applied if a performance is unsatisfactory.

Establishing Realistic Expectations for Planning

There are some miracles that health services planning, however imaginative, will never be able to perform. It will not generate accurate predictions of the future. It will not induce sudden rational behaviour on the part of people and professions who are competing for scarce resources. It will not prevent sudden changes in national policy. Neither will it avoid the need to adapt quickly to technological advances. If a cure for some hitherto incurable disease affecting a large number of people emerges from the laboratories, existing priorities and plans are simply going to have to be rewritten. On the other hand there are some important benefits that health planning can provide.

1. *Understanding the Main Health-related Problems or Managerial Weaknesses that Need to be Tackled.* It is a mark of any well-managed organisation that people at all levels within it have a sure sense both of the most important problems that the organisation as a whole is trying to tackle (or opportunities that it is trying to realise) and of their own

part in this effort.

Within a health service jurisdiction, the same should apply. Experience suggests that the task of developing reasonably detailed statements for an individual jurisdiction of the main problems and opportunities is not as impossible as it might at first sight seem. Such an effort usually involves:

Comparing standardised mortality and morbidity rates with neighbouring or similar jurisdictions, to identify any major differences. The exhibit shows an example which immediately prompts some questions.

Comparing existing provision of services with other jurisdictions.

Assessing the importance of the problems that emerge, both in terms of their severity and prevalence.

Evaluating the likely efficiency of any investment in tackling the problem.

2. *Providing a Consistent Framework for Establishing Priorities Among Competing Claims for Resources.* Once there is general agreement, or at least a decision committed to writing, on which problems are to have priority attention because they are both important and susceptible to treatment, a constructive debate can take place on the relative merits of different projects, taking into account the resources that are available and viable goals of the systems.

3. *Providing a Forum for Deciding Specific Action Steps, and for Co-ordinating Implementation.* It is almost invariably a mistake to separate the responsibility for planning a particular service from the possibility for its management. Just by requiring all those that are principally concerned to sit down around the same table, look at the same pieces of paper, hear the same arguments and conclusions, planning performs very useful functions. A sense of urgency and commitment to action is (or can be) injected, and implementation can be co-ordinated. The National Health Service provides some excellent examples of just these benefits in action, in the form of health care planning teams which were one of the features of the 1974 reorganisation. Here, at local level, doctors, nurses, administrators, and others involved sit down to agree on what needs to be done differently to improve health care locally for particular groups or patients. This is an example of planning in action.

Avoiding Over Complication

A health service — even a hospital — is an extraordinarily complex organisation, far more so than most commercial enterprises. A planning system that attempts to mirror the complexity of the service with which it is concerned, is doomed to be buried under the weight of its own paper. 'Keep it simple' should be a watchword for all designers of health services planning systems. All too often, it seems to have been ignored.

Attempts to Forecast the Future. As we all know, population trends, availability of funds, changes in social attitudes (not least to alcoholism) and the implications of a technical change simply cannot be assessed with any accuracy. As commercial enterprises have found, one can only be confident of one thing in forecasting the future — that you will be wrong. In the commercial world, the most sophisticated and successful planners have abandoned the fruitless attempt to project the future, in favour of identifying and seeking to resolve strategic issues. Yet health planners persist in putting forward Five Year Plans showing funds available — to the nearest £'000 with single point estimates of demand. Sadly, the world is no longer so conveniently predictable.

The Passion for Comprehensiveness. The very term 'comprehensive health planning' carries within it the seeds of its own destruction. By attempting to be comprehensive, any planning system will be unnecessarily complex. Planning needs to concentrate on what is going to change and on what is important. Some things cannot change. Others do not need to. Some problems are important, others more marginal. Planning efforts should concentrate on important problems or issues where pressure for action exists, when doing nothing is unacceptable, and when there are opportunities for constructive change within the available resource constraints.

Concern for Decimal Point Accuracy. This is a particular curse for government. There was the case of an official within the DHSS in London who was asked for some estimate of the number of people with a serious alcohol abuse problem within a particular area. Five hundred and sixty-three, he replied. The numbers tended to confer a spurious plausibility to plans. Yet too often, as in this case, the quality of the underlying assumptions is insufficient to support the apparent accuracy of the figures. Order-of-magnitude would have been far more useful.

Very often to be within ten per cent of the real numbers is quite accurate enough. Indeed, sometimes apparently crude estimates are more useful than more sophisticated approaches. For instance, a US state agency proposed to set prospective budgets for hospitals on the basis of detailed case budgets for 388 different types of cases. The number of cases in each category will be forecast, and multiplied by the 'standard' cost per case. The effort is designed to come up with a budget for an individual hospital. The benefits of such a detailed evaluation, compared to a more simplistic approach, seem negligible.

Distinction Between Revenue and Capital. In a labour intensive environment, managers must necessarily be concerned to make sure that the scarce human resources are being as productively employed as possible. Moreover, as the willingness of people working within health services to put up with what they regard as unacceptably low wages decreases, opportunities to improve labour productivity must be aggressively pursued. At present, it is often difficult at the local level to substitute capital for labour or indeed the other way around. In the NHS, revenue and capital are looked at separately — 'investing in people not buildings'. In the USA, a certificate of need (CON) is required for items of equipment or buildings — but not for the people who really control costs of health care.

Surely it would be much more sensible to plan health services on a cash basis. This would make it much more possible for health planners to deal, for example, with the implications of introduction of CT scanners into a neurological and neurosurgical service.

How then can the requirement for simplicity be more readily met?

Separate thinking is needed about the physical structure of health services over the long-term from planning for near-term action. It makes more sense for each jurisdiction to have what one might call a long-term structure plan, with a horizon of perhaps 15-20 years which sets out, where in an ideal world the major health facilities (hospitals, clinics, etc.) would be located. The pace at which the jurisdiction could move towards the desired fixture will depend on the usual factors: availability of funds, local pressures and so forth. Near-term planning should be an entirely separate effort, simply using the structure plan as a backdrop. Within this broad scheme the planner should then:

Be Selective. Near-term planning efforts should be concentrated on important problems. Once the major problems and opportunities facing the service locally have been identified, planning effort can focus on them — to the near exclusion of other services. This concept is quite familiar to many of the better business planners. In a multi-product business, planners (and management) concentrate their efforts on those businesses that are (a) important, and (b) in trouble. The same should apply to health planning.

Concentrate on Action. The idea of planning is to induce change. Change implies action. Thus, any worthwhile plan should set out what is going to happen, who is going to do it, how long it is going to take, what is likely to result, what resources are required and what milestones will flash by on the way.

Limit the Space for Verbiage. It was again George Bernard Shaw who claimed that whenever he did not have enough time to write a letter, he wrote a postcard. Health planners suffer from the same difficulties. The discipline of brevity cannot be overrated.

Agree in Advance Some Indicators of Success. These should be in terms of what you hope would happen to patients, and to the process, as well as to the available effectiveness of the service in question. In other words, how will the observer know whether or not the effort has been worthwhile?

Limit the Size of the Central Bureaucracy. Civil servants are never idle. They are perennial complicators and revisionists. One requirement for simplicity is to limit the number of civil servants involved. All health planning regulation for the population of Ontario is carried out by no more than 385 individuals. By contrast, today in the Department of Health in London there are over 5,000 people. Total administrative staff at area and local levels in the NHS amount to over 15,000. A simple planning approach under these circumstances, is, to say the least, unlikely.

Conclusion

The requirements for an effective health planning system then are through a supportive environment, realistic expectations, and simplicity. What does this mean for the treatment of alcoholism? Simply this: in every local jurisdiction there should be written down, a statement of (1) how many people there are locally suffering from alcohol abuse, why that is important to a local community, what sort of people they are, (2) what is happening now in each segment of the market, (3) what those responsible for the treatment of this scourge propose should be done differently in the next 24 months in each market segment and who is going to do it, (4) what it would cost, and (5) how we would know it has all been worthwhile. Two sides of a sheet of paper should do for each jurisdiction.

That, in a nutshell would be planning. Only if something happened would it be worthwhile. It sounds simplistic and it is. In the UK, with perhaps 200 districts, we are talking about perhaps 400 pages — one per 5,000 alcoholics, or one page per £7.5 million lost to industry due to alcohol abuse each year. A reasonable investment for any country, if it really wants to manage this difficult problem effectively.

Part Five

MODELS IN TRANSITION

18 SCIENCES IN TRANSITION

Rom Harré

A necessary preliminary for understanding and perhaps remedying a science in a state of crisis is to find a suitable schema for analysing the intellectual products that form that science. One might suppose that philosophers were in possession of morally, logically and intellectually acceptable schema which could be applied to any case, revealing the inward structure of the material one is working with. However, this is far from being so. In recent years philosophers have been guilty of a particularly perverse caricature of the natural sciences in pursuit of an ideal reduction of all forms of language and symbolisation to the structures provided by formal logic. We must begin by setting aside two tempting, but thoroughly unsatisfactory, schemata, created within the assumptions of logicism.

Two Unsatisfactory Schemata

The Inductive Plan

The inductive idea presumes that scientists can describe identifiable and particular matters of fact and the correlates that are usually found with them. The act of induction is to generalise descriptions of the patterns of correlation that have been observed, into laws of nature, which have the typical 'if a occurs then b follows' form. Statistical methods may make the mathematics of induction more sophisticated but the underlying plan is just the same. The difficulty with this way of conceiving of the job of the scientist, i.e. seeing him as identifying correlations and generalising them to laws, is that this confines the science to consideration of only those matters which can be observed. Furthermore, if one thinks it through, the use of the inductive plan confines the content of science to the actual rather than the possible or the hidden. But most real laws of nature in real sciences do not have to do with observables at all, but with the action of unobservable tendencies. The law of gravity, for example, is not a gigantic summary of all the gravitational events that have ever taken place or ever will, but rather a succinct description of the tendencies of bodies to fall when placed at certain points in the gravitational field. Now tendencies and fields — the subject matter of the laws of gravity — are quite unobservable. And the same goes for chemical valencies, for the process of natural selection, and so on. These objections that have just been raised are not those with which philosophers usually trouble themselves when considering the inductive schema. They are usually concerned with the domestic issue of the failure of that plan to reflect a legitimate mode of logical inference.

The Hypothetico-deductive Plan

The traditional philosophical objection to the inductive plan is that it requires one to infer from some cases to all similar cases of a certain pattern. And this inference pattern is invalid. The hypothetico-deductive method does not require that inference. It supposes that we simply hypothesise, or perhaps even guess, what is the law for a certain field of phenomena. Assuming the law we draw some conclusions by deduction, and see if they are realised in nature. If not, the hypothesis and/or whatever else may be required to make the inference, must be rejected. If they are realised, the hypothesis will tend to be accepted. Furthermore, the hypothetico-deductive plan seems able to deal with the difficulties that have been pointed out about the inductive method, namely the way it confines the content of science to the actual and the observable. Unfortunately, the hypothetico-deductive method too has serious defects. It says nothing about how hypotheses are formed; whether there are good or bad ways of making guesses about natural regularities, whether some hypotheses are more plausible than others. These are central considerations for anyone who is actually at work trying to create explanations and so to be in a position to formulate policies for action in any given field. Furthermore, the structure of most explanations in the natural sciences does not reflect a strict logical ordering of the deductive kind. Instead most explanations are internally organised through relations of analogy. They are characterised not so much by their logical structure as by their peculiar subject-matter. They have to do with imagined generative processes, created on the analogy of some real process which a scientist has already studied, or knows about from his ordinary, everyday experience of the world.

To remedy the defects of the traditional plans, a more realistic scheme will be proposed here which catches the main features of the sciences as they involve theorising more precisely, more accurately and more comprehensively. We shall find that with the help of this schema we are able to give a much better account of the way models function in any kind of theorising, whether it is concerned with the diagnosis and treatment of alcoholics or the explanations of black holes.

Figure 18.1: The Realist Plan

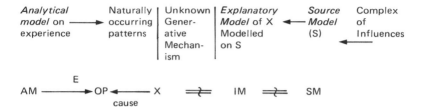

The Realist Plan

The realist plan illustrated in Figure 18.1 is a way of analysing the content of a theory. There will be parallel distinctions in the discourse — the language in which that theory is couched and its content expressed. However, if one examines only the linguistic aspect of the theory, without considering the content, then one is likely to miss two most important features. Since the generative mechanism which really produces a natural pattern is usually unknown (represented by 'X' in the schema) there can be no sentences describing it in the linguistic formulation of the theory. And since the source model, SM, is usually agreed by everyone who is competent in a science at some period, it is not usually mentioned explicitly either. So, by looking simply at the logical structure of the theory — that is analysing the discourse in which the theory is expressed — one is quite likely to overlook two very important components.

A word or two must be said about the way the schema above is organised. First of all, in the vertical dimension, if we were to express our knowledge and beliefs about the items mentioned in each column in a discourse, then it would be perfectly proper to attempt to make a deductive, logical ordering of the items in each column. We would not expect there to be deductive principles linking columns which are side by side. This can be made clear by looking at a very simple example, taken from the physical sciences. Suppose the observed pattern which we have identified (out of all the things that happen in the world) is the behaviour of gases when confined in narrow tubes. We find the most convenient way of describing this is '$PV = RT$'. This formulation can be represented as the deductive consequence of sentences representing the two experimentally discovered patterns, $PV = K_1$ and

$P/T = K_2$. Looked at in that way the laws form a deductive pattern. How to explain these laws? The real structure of gases and the nature of their inner constituents were quite unknown. Physicists were required to imagine an internal constitution by conceiving of a gas as a swarm of molecules. From whence came the idea of the molecule? Molecules and their behaviour were a model *of* the unknown causal process X. It was modelled on the unknown behaviour of particles of Matter (SM). Now these relationships of modelling are not deductive relationships. We can say only that the swarm of molecules is *like* a gas and that a molecule is *like* a Newtonian particle. Horizontal relationships in the schema are then likely to be analogical. There are two important analogue relations:

(i)   The pattern P is the way gases of unknown internal constitution behave. (In saying this we rule out the move of putting the patterning of behaviour down to external influences, though the existence of an instance of that pattern is clearly caused by the imposition of an external force on the gas.) For IM, the (iconic) model of X to be an adequate model, it must behave in a way which is analogous to the behaviour of X, i.e. it must produce, or be imagined to produce, patterns analogous to the patterns described in the formula PV = RT. We could call this the behavioural analogy. The more the explanatory model IM behaves, i.e. the more its imagined behaviour simulates the real behaviour of X — the unknown generative mechanism — the more acceptable it is as the basis of a theory of those observed patterns.

(ii)   But that is not sufficient. It is very easy to imagine models of X which will simulate its behaviour. Most of these can be rejected out of hand as absurd. They involve entities which could not, according to our general principles of science (our metaphysics) and in accordance with our historically-situated social consensus as to what the world is like, be causal mechanisms. For example, one could equally well explain the evolution of new species by supposing that the psychological phenomenon of striving can produce inheritable change in the gametes. But such a view, though not absurd, does not chime in with our idea of what the world is like. So the complex of influences entered at the right-hand end of the schema is an important control on what source-models are available upon which to model the hypothetical generative mechanisms which stand in for the unknown productive processes of nature. It is customary to call this relationship between IM and SM a material analogy.

Another Example of the Realist Schema

Just in case it seems as if this theory is too closely associated with a particular kind of theorising in the physical sciences, it is easy to show that the same structure is exemplified in Darwin's own Theory of Evolution. Darwin took as his source-model the process of selection as accomplished by a breeder. He did not know what was the real causal mechanism which produced the patterns in the palaeontological record and in the geographical distribution of animal and plant forms. So he proposed a model of that unknown mechanism, namely natural selection, consciously created as an analogue of the domestic selection which he had observed in the breeding practices of pigeon-fanciers, gardeners, cattle-breeders and so on. It was an analogue because, of course, in natural selection the role of the breeder is occupied by differential reproduction rates, adverted to in Spenser's unsatisfactory metaphor 'the struggle for existence'. The realist schema has hardly been better set out than in the first two chapters of Darwin's *Origin of Species*, a classical example of how important it is to get one's philosophy of science right before one begins the process of the construction of theories.

The value of a theory, its total worth so to speak, is determined by the balance between behavioural analogy – the degree to which the model of the unknown mechanism simulates the form of the behaviour in question – and the material analogy – the degree to which the imagined processes and their physical supports are viable as things in the world, analogues of the appropriate source-models. In many cases observation and experiment alter accepted ideas as to what the observed patterns really are. In consequence, modifications are made to the iconic model, IM, to restore its ability to stimulate the real observed pattern of events. Now in altering an iconic explanatory model there must be a change in its relation to the source-model. For example, in making the molecule model more able to serve as the basic explanatory notion in dealing with more refined knowledge of the behaviour of gases, the original point-molecule had to be elaborated by borrowing the notion of molecular volume from the source-model, a notion ultimately deriving from our ordinary notion of a material particle. In the case of the kinetic theory of gases, the efforts to improve the model to continue to match the behaviour of the world, led to borrowings of the source-model which enriched the iconic or explanatory model, in just the way that makes physicists more and more confident that molecules really exist. In other cases the efforts to preserve the power of an explanatory model are bought at the cost of more and more tenuous analogies with the source-model and consequently a loss of intelligibility and plausibility. Finally, it is sometimes necessary to draw upon more than one source-model to construct a theory for some particularly puzzling field of phenomena. The physical sciences used to be thought to be immune from this necessity, but the need to draw on concepts from particle-theory and from wave-physics to develop the new theory of quantum mechanics has shown that sometimes the only way forward may be by the bringing together of an irreducible ensemble of source-models to generate a theory. And this, of course, raises very grave difficulties about the plausibility of that model as a picture of a possible productive mechanism in the real world.

These examples have been explained in some detail since the physical and biological sciences drawn on here are generally regarded as uncontroversial now and in a healthy state.

The Third Model: The Source of Analytical Concepts

The analytical model which is required to help us identify the patterns in nature which we want to explain has not been discussed here at any length. The world of experience is enigmatic, diverse, and in many ways unyielding. We need a set of concepts to begin the process of separating patterns from the complexity with which the world is presented to us. In the case of evolutionary theory the analytical model that Darwin, and later Mendel, applied to identifying the patterns they wished to explain, was roughly that of the family; that is the properties of plants and animals were looked at in relation to minute similarities to and differences from corresponding attributes of their parents. Drawing analytical concepts from that model helped reveal a radically different system of relationships from those picked out by the use of the analytical model common in the middle ages, when plants were seen to form groups to be patterned in their relations with respect to their supposed medicinal properties. The order perceived in the biological world by herbalists was radically different from the order that Darwin, Mendel and others in the nineteenth century perceived. This kind of difference can be partly explained by the difference between the analytical models which they brought to bear. In the second half of this chapter consideration will be given to the way in which we can use the realist schema to understand crises in science. The cases which are to be considered are social sciences, and there more than in the natural sciences, the role of the analytical model is central. We cannot reach a proper understanding of a crisis in the development of a field unless we pay close attention to the relation between the three kinds of models at work in a scientific explanation – the analytic, the explanatory and the source-models.

The Crisis in Social Psychology

The study of alcoholism is not the only field of sociopsychological science which is presently in disarray. Oxford continues to perform its traditional role as a convalescent centre for ailing sciences. Lately social psychology sickened, passed through a crisis, and is now on the road to recovery.[1] There are some important lessons to be learned from contemplating the nature of the crisis which affected that science and the steps needed to effect a cure. Essentially, the crisis involved loss of confidence in two aspects of method. Doubts first emerged as to whether causal patterns are best revealed by making statistical analyses of simplified and controlled treatments in a large number of cases (the extensive design). Confidence then also declined in the use of unexamined common sense as a source of analytical concepts for revealing the texture of interactions, and in the use of a simple automaton as a source-model for explanatory models. The result was predictable: crisis.

The cure for that crisis can then be described in terms of two 'transitions' from old assumptions to new principles.

The First Transition: The Study of Individuals

There has been a shift in empirical work from the *ex*tensive design based upon the assumption of a given extension or set of members of a class. In this design a psychologist studies a representative sample of members and from the properties which the members of that sample have in common relative to the whole extension, an *in*tension or type, is derived. The trouble with this sort of design is that though a wide application – as wide as the given extension – is guaranteed, the generalisations that emerge nearly always seem to be disappointingly thin. So variable, it seems, are the individuals which form the extension of most human groups, that most of the features which seem most germane to understanding action, such as actors' interpretations, are eliminated in the formal process of creating a common intension. As Wittgenstein pointed out, in human affairs groupings more often than not are held together by 'family resemblance', so that though any pair of members are similar, remote members may have little or nothing in common. In response to these difficulties there has been a shift to the intensive design.[2] A few individuals are selected as typical, and are then subjected to detailed investigation. Instead of studying every group of football hooligans in the country and then looking for common features, one group was studied in great depth. Very complex structure emerged from this study. *With this knowledge* in hand similar structures could be looked for in other similar clubs. Respectable sciences do not generally use the extensive design. One must know what one is looking for if one is to find or fail to find it.

The effect of moving to the intensive design is to bring individuals to the centre of the empirical stage, so to speak. But individuals appear in the natural sciences in two radically different ways. The basic reason for turning to a study of individuals is that causal mechanisms exist and operate only in individuals, but one might study an individual as the bearer of a type, in trying to get a line on the type of causal mechanisms present in all (or most) of the members of the group of similar cases one is trying to construct. One might study an individual as the bearer of a type. This is the role of individuals as objects of study in the intensive design. But one might study an individual as a mini-universe. Each individual would be thought of as having its own laws of development, change and causation. Studying individuals under these assumptions, we should rather call the idiographic design. The moment one considers the possibility of an idiographic design for investigating certain human affairs, one is struck immediately by the need for biography. Individual human beings do not come to their life-events as if newly-minted, but with the weight of their past lives and their present conceptions of those past lives upon them. Not only is the biographical dimension quite crucial to the idiographic design, but it must also play an important part in the intensive design — that is, individuals as type-bearers are not sprung fully-formed from the subject-panel or the criminal courts, or referred by a general practitioner, but have biographies which may or may not be similar to others who are superficially of the same kind. To identify a typical event or process in human affairs one must examine the intersection of synchronic patterning of present conditions, and diachronic patterning of the assumed past and the contemplated future.

The Second Transition: Improving the Models

We must return to a consideration of the use of the realist schema in looking at a social science. Hopefully the importance has been made clear of identifying and critically examining three kinds of models — the analytic, the explanatory, and the source-models — and controlling the relations between them. A dramatic transformation has been wrought in social psychology by the use of alternative analytical models. Previously, if any analytical models were used at all, other than unexamined common sense assumptions, the most naive form of behaviour identification was usually involved. For example, such matters as frequency of interaction, distance of interactors one from another, and so on, were used as the main analytical concepts for identifying the textures and structures of life events. The most clearly discernible feature of the development of a new form of social psychology in recent years has been the use of much more sophisticated analytical models, in particular the dramaturgical model. Adopting that model for controlling the creation of the *a priori* concepts necessary to a scientific study of the events of social life leads one to look on such events *as if* they were performances by actors taking place on a stage in distinctive settings with appropriate props, before an audience and critics, and under the direction of an experienced producer. With the help of such a powerful analytical model a great many aspects of social events, which has previously been unattended, came to the fore.[3] In particular, it became possible to discern and so to bring under scrutiny as an object of study, the powerful effect of the settings of social life, the important differences between the presentations of self in accordance with different conventions as to proper persona, in different kinds of events with different kinds of people. Elaborations of this model have led to a taxonomy of life-events based upon a distinction between informal rituals and agonistic or game-like events.

Analytic and Explanatory Models: a Crucial Relation

A glance at the schema for an analysis and prescription of the content of a scientific theory shows that the analytical and explanatory models are theoretically independent of one another. There is no particular reason why the best mode of analysis of some field of phenomena should involve the same conceptual system as the best kind of explanation requires. Indeed, in those sciences which invoke an underlying structure of hidden levels of operation to explain the observed patterns, such as chemistry and physiology, it is very unlikely that analytic and explanatory models will be identical. But generally, in times of the successful development of a science, they are strongly co-ordinated.

The transitional character of social psychology in its present phase is evident in the sharp disconnection between analytic and explanatory models noticeable in even the most advanced work. In the days when a simple behaviourist or even ethological model was in use, very simplistic models of human functioning were employed to generate theories. Decline-in-response competition as an explanation of liking is a notorious case. The dramaturgical model has proved powerful and successful in identifying a much more complex and interesting range of phenomena than could have been identified with the more simplistic models which it has displaced. But its success does not entail that the actions which it analyses should be assumed to be produced in the same way as the performances of a play are produced by a company of actors. For example, it is not at all clear that the modes of consciousness of most competent people in the events of everyday life are much like those of actors when they are rehearsing and performing a play. There are similarities, of course, but there are also differences. In most cases ordinary life does not depend upon an explicit script, though one must note that there are now forms of experimental theatre in which there is no script either. An explanatory model has begun to develop in social psychology but it is derived not from a microsociological source, like the dramaturgical model, but rather from philosophical analysis of common sense explanatory concepts such as intentions and motives. The development of the explanatory model is as yet far from complete, but it is likely to be a specific form of a generic class of models based upon the source-model of agents following rules for the realisation of projects of one sort or another. It is co-ordinate with but not a species of the dramaturgical model currently used for the analysis of episodes.

Sciences in Crisis: the Transition to New Forms

We are now in a position to characterise periods of crisis and transition more precisely. In such periods analytical and explanatory models become disconnected. Once disconnected they may change out of phase. For example, in social psychology there has been a change of analytical model from ethological to ethogenic, co-ordinate with a change in the explanatory model from roughly stimulus-response to approximately rule-following. In the case of football hooliganism, the change of analytical model was shared by all those interested in the phenomenon, and the events were seen as if they were rituals conducive to the creation and maintenance of a male-status hierarchy. But the explanatory model appropriate to accounting for these events is still disputed. Peter Marsh is inclined to favour some form of sociobiological explanation, while I am much more inclined to a cultural-historical account which draws upon other kinds of social events and social structures as models.[4] Once the disconnection has occurred and the events are analysed in a way distinctive from the manner in which they are explained, the science is clearly in a state of disorder. A superficial impression of the scene in the scientific study of alcoholism suggests that the separation of analytical from explanatory models is fairly complete.

How, then, to recreate the co-ordination, to return a science from a transitory phase to a settled and constructive development? There is no recipe that history can teach us. In the human sciences it may be too much to expect that the final co-ordination can be completed with one generic model serving both analytic and explanatory purposes. For example, it seems likely that an ensemble of distinct sources is required for both the analytical and the explanatory task. On the analytical side it seems that a useful distinction can be drawn between our analysis of the influences which create problems for human beings and our analysis of the way those human beings create solutions for dealing with the problems. It seems obvious that one range of problems is set by our biological nature. (It would be wrong, of course, to speak of our *common* biological nature because, of course, many of the problems we set ourselves are products not so much of what our biological nature actually is, but what we take it to be and this is historically and socially conditioned.) On the other hand, it seems clear that our ways of dealing with the problems posed by our biological nature as we conceive of it are frequently ethogenic, involving interpretations, negotiations of meanings, rituals for the creation of status, conventions for the presentation of self, and so on. The biologically-based genetic difference between different colours of the skin is a good example of a feature of human life, the variety of ways of dealing with which are culturally determined. The same goes, of course, for the difference between the sexes, the young and the old, and so on.

A second major phenomenon observable in sciences in transition is the explicit reversion to what one may call the moral and political indexing of the intermediate models which we use in explanation and analysis. This indexing occurs because in such a condition of transition we are brought to contemplate explicitly formulated source-models. Another aspect of the crisis in contemporary social psychology, and indeed in psychology generally, has been the possibility of looking squarely at the underlying model of man in general use as a source of explanatory models. The old psychology seemed to be working with a general picture of human beings as automata. Placed in stimulus conditions the automata showed, it was supposed, various levels of automatic functioning. If nodded to, gazed at for 60 per cent of the time etc., they kept on talking and gazed back 20 per cent of the time. If ordered to electrocute other automata 63 per cent did so. The patterns in life of such beings could be no more than reflections or products of natural laws of some kind. Reflective judgements of consequences, Machiavellian projects and so on, could have no part in the social behaviour of beings like this. Only on such an assumed source-model could the experimental phase of empirical work in social psychology make any sense. A new source-model seems to be appearing in various places, marking the emergence of a more sensitive phase in work in this field. It is based on an image of human beings as agents generally responsible for their actions and capable of being reasoned with. Patterns of life are seen as creations of autonomous actors following rules for their own purposes and projects.[5]

The moral and political distinctions between these two source-models are very much clearer than the moral and political distinctions between theories formulated at one remove from them. On the automatic model external treatments designed to promote reprogramming of the automaton's mechanisms would be the appropriate response to behaviour perceived as disorderly. The views, perceptions, interpretations and theories of the actors would be largely irrelevant and safely ignored, i.e. treated with contempt. But if the actor-model is adopted as a source of explanatory models of action then judgements as to the quality of that action, for instance rational or irrational, orderly or disorderly, must take the views of the actors entirely seriously. One must take the explanatory theories of football hooligans as seriously as those of anyone else in trying to understand acts of aggro. It may be that there are parallels in the study of 'alcoholism', and indeed some of the chapters in this book suggest that very strongly.

Notes

1. Brenner, M. and Marsh, P. (1978), *The Social Contexts of Method* (Croom Helm, London).
2. De Waele, J.P. (1976), 'The Personality of Individuals', in Harré, R. (ed.), *Personality* (Blackwell, Oxford).
3. Goffman, E. (1974), *Frame Analysis* (Harper, New York).
4. Marsh, P., Rosser, E. and Harré, R. (1978), *The Rules of Disorder* (Routledge & Kegan Paul, London).
5. Shotter, J. (1975), *Images of Man in Psychological Research* (Methuen, London).

19 IS THERE A LEADING THEORY?

David L. Davies

The leading theory about any phenomenon is that which explains most of the facts and fails to explain least of them.

The phenomenon in this case is not drunkenness, since a great many drugs in high dosage produce similar effects of acute intoxication, nor harm (such as cirrhosis of the liver or break-up of marriage) since every substance if ingested for long periods in high dosage is capable of damaging tissues, and social damage can obviously follow drug use of that order.

What we are concerned with is the *long-term use of alcohol which is associated with dependency and harm.* The theory which best accounts for this runs something as follows.

The Theory

Every society has its own ethic for alcohol usage, varying from the total abstinence of some Muslim groups, for example, to endorsement of a relatively high alcohol intake in others (e.g. France). Additional to its uses as a condiment, for social, and for religious purposes, alcohol ingestion in our own culture becomes the mark of the grown-up person, witness our legislation for sale and supply of drink. In our formative years we most of us drink to some extent, and this in response to sociocultural pressures which reflect in the main parental attitudes as perceived by young people, and peer group pressures. The sex differences in drinking behaviour are probably only culturally determined at this stage.

So begun, drinking behaviour becomes subject to the laws of learning, which apply to a great many other repeated acts which we perform. All the factors which behavioural psychology teaches as important in learning, such as imitation, practice, setting, mental set, and reward, affect this aspect of behaviour too, so the act of drinking becomes a piece of learned behaviour – in short, a habit. Habits are powerful bits of mental organisation so that the continuation of drinking, once begun under social pressures, may later continue for quite different reasons, in this case psychological.

Alcohol is one of that class of drugs which, on repeated use, induces some change in the individual so that he responds to it later in a different way from that in which he did initially. It is a drug of dependence. Below a certain quantity/frequency of intake no dependence will develop (just as two or three injections of morphine pre- and post-operatively will fail to induce morphine dependence). However, after perhaps months, more likely years, a daily intake of about six centilitres of absolute alcohol is enough to induce this dependence, manifest on withdrawal at this level not by physical symptoms but by some awareness of not being quite oneself (let us call this psychic discomfort or psychological dependence). It is on all fours with the feeling of the habitual smoker that he needs another cigarette. This level is that provided by an average daily intake of about two double whiskies or its equivalent in beer — say two pints. At this level then, the habit factor (psychological) is reinforced by the drug factor (pharmacological). The more alcohol taken, on daily average, from six centilitres up to about fifteen centilitres, the stronger both factors will be without evidence of harm necessarily developing.

The extent to which drinking is practised will be affected by widely operating general factors of availability, which can be measured in terms of price of alcoholic beverages, for example, and by opening hours, to mention two obvious ones. Occupation will also be an important aspect of availability so that more alcohol is available say to the publican than to the farmer and more alcohol is drunk by the one than the other. Free availability will promote drinking and the habit will tend on the mere ground of frequent repetition alone, to put the matter at its simplest, to become more strongly established.

These general factors may increase with time, and drink may become cheaper in real terms. This may happen not just to the man himself, but to his friends, resulting in an increased social pressure on him to drink more. Again, having become conditioned to associating a removal of psychic discomfort with taking more alcohol, he may respond to a variety of life events causing psychic discomfort by increased drinking. The man who is dependent is specially vulnerable to responding to everyday pressures by more drinking than a man not so dependent. Such escalation would carry in its train the risk that a threshold, at about 15 centilitres of absolute alcohol daily, will be exceeded and the stage is then set for tissue damage, in response to the chemical effect of alcohol in quantity, and social damage because of that, and because of the social implications of his actions — for example, the effect on his economic circumstances, or his relationships with others.

This theory of the development of alcoholism accounts for the vast majority of sufferers. Some excessive harmful drinking, however, develops differently in that the drinking behaviour is a symptom of identifiable illness – dementia, schizophrenia, mania, to mention only some. Clinically, the differentiation of this tiny fraction of the whole population of alcoholics is straightforward. Such alcoholism stands to alcoholism as generally conceived in much the same way as symptomatic epilepsy stands to idiopathic epilepsy.

The Evidence

Epidemiological

It is not possible here to do much more than indicate the factual evidence on which the general theory outlined rests. Most important and central is the view that drinking behaviour is a continuum. The positive evidence for this is the clinical observation that most alcoholics present for help after many years of apparently harmless drinking. Furthermore, the general characteristics of the Ledermann Curve[1] support this view, and even without recourse to sophisticated mathematical considerations there is a great deal of evidence that the number of alcoholics in a population increases with *per capita* alcohol intake.

Because drinking behaviour is a continuum, the mechanisms of the development of such are appropriate to the development of excessive drinking. The fact that different ethnic groups have different vulnerability to alcoholism is a hard fact which has been known and discussed for a very long time. There are various possibilities to account for such differences, but the recent work by Joyce O'Connor[2] who studied normal drinking in young people of differing ethnic groups has demonstrated very clearly that the basic difference is cultural, and, more precisely, that the drinking of young people in these groups is moulded by the attitudes of parents as seen by young people and by the peer group pressures to which these young are exposed.

For the opposite view that alcoholics are in some way marked out from an early age to manifest their incapacity there is little or no support from biochemical or psychological research. Of course, there are individual differences which will interact with the factors already considered, which will account to some extent for individual differences in quantity/frequency of alcohol intake, and no doubt some of these are related to genetic constitution as with all drugs. This factor is not to be overlooked when approach is made to the drinking behaviour of any one person, but from the point of view of the phenomenon we are considering, it is of minimal importance since it hardly shows up, if at all, in the epidemiological facts. Such individual variance is not to be equated with genetic differences without further evidence. It is evident with all drugs and not just with humans, witness the techniques for determining minimum lethal dose.

The relationship of consumption to availability is well established, and is a cornerstone of the theory, and the different alcoholism rates by occupation become explicable on the theory. It seems from the work of Plant[3] on recruits to the brewing industry that conditions of employment compound a tendency to higher levels of drinking already evident at recruitment, and that the effect of this employment factor ceases in some who later give up this work. These people were in no sense alcoholics when recruited, so that his research lends no support to the view that alcoholics are particularly attracted to the drink industry, whilst providing clear evidence of how multiple factors (the personal and the occupational) reinforce each other.

Pharmacological

Drug dependence is a general phenomenon. It is not incumbent on those who advocate the theory outlined here that they should be able to explain all that is involved in that phenomenon. It is sufficient to say that there is most likely a chemical basis for it, which aligns phenomena relevant to all drugs of dependency. Recent discoveries about the role of endorphins in opiate dependency are cited as evidence of the chemical basis for drug dependence in general.

The present day tendency to decry even the existence of what has been called psychological dependence on drugs is misconceived, based as it is largely on a semantic confusion between the word dependency as so qualified, and non-drug states where a man describes himself as dependent on his secretary or his motor car. Drug dependence is very widespread in the majority of the world population, and relates to a great variety of drugs, as Seevers[4] pointed out, adding that possibly 70 per cent of the US adult population voluntarily use alcohol in moderation, even to the point of strong psychological dependence, with minimal personal injury and social consequence.

Although inspection of the Ledermann Curve[1] indicates that there must be a great many people who are just short of the threshold beyond which harm develops from their drinking, and who are therefore likely to be psychologically dependent on alcohol, it has not been feasible hitherto to estimate with any confidence the size of this group, and attempts have been open to objections. However, the recent work of Whitehead, Clarke and Whitfield[5] has thrown new light on the size of this group. What these workers did was to examine the records of more than 2,000 healthy men having annual physical checks and they found that those who were taking more than two drinks a day showed a raised serum level of gamma glutamyl transpeptidase (γ GT), and that the more the man drank on a daily basis the higher was this level, so that everyone taking four drinks a day showed a positive response. The characteristics of this group of regular moderately heavy drinkers who are not showing harm over a period of time are indeed the characteristics which the theory lays down as attaching to those who are merely psychologically dependent. Thus it is not too much of a leap to equate the two populations, and if we take 'a drink' as being three centilitres of alcohol, then the area of the curve from six centilitres to twelve centilitres is the area covered by these workers. Their estimate was that this group was ten times greater than the estimated number of alcoholics in England and Wales, that is to say five million as against 500,000.

Psychological

Turning to the psychological factors referred to in the theory, it should not be necessary here to do more than mention the learning theory itself. It is clearly relevant to drinking. It has one minor aspect which to some people might seem of crucial significance, in that it explains very well the widely observed phenomenon in animal learning that initial exposure to the relevant drug of dependence, before relearning extinguished behavioural responses to that drug, can shorten dramatically the number of trials necessary to re-establish such behaviour.[6] Thus a laboratory animal, which has learned in 30 trials to perform certain tasks to receive a drug reward, might then unlearn this piece of behaviour possibly by ceasing to be rewarded. At a later date it would relearn the same tasks to obtain the drug reward in perhaps 15 trials instead of the initial 30, because of traces of learning left behind. If, however, before starting to relearn, it received a dose of the rewarding drug, then the number of trials to relearn could drop to say three or four.

This 'priming dose' is not exclusive to alcohol or man and most of the conclusions built on the corresponding phenomenon in abstinent alcoholics relating their subsequent behaviour to the first drink initiating relapse, need not worry those people any longer.

Learning theory also explains very fully how important are cues, state of mind, setting of the action, practice and reward in reacquiring *unlearned* behaviour responses so that all the phenomena seen after successfully treating alcoholics can be explained on that theory, just as it will explain why 'forgotten' shorthand speeds may be reacquired or not according to the extent of the practice, and of course of the state of the individual's mind in that regard.

Recovery to a stabilised dependent state, or to a drinking non-dependent state, thus explained, as well as abstinence. Relapse may be triggered by cues, for example, while the individual is still dependent, or by a reduced amount of relearning while non-dependent, or not at all if the setting of the drinking as well as the restricted frequency of practice are insufficient to re-establish the pattern afresh.

The Implications

This theory has a positive value. It encourages a new approach to *history taking*, in which the quantity/frequency of intake is noted at key points in the patient's life, and the relation of this to life events. It enables a judgement to be made of the differing strengths of various factors — cultural, occupational, psychological — at different times, the point of onset of dependency, and then of harm. In short, it gives a dynamic aspect to formulation.

It opens up a *preventive approach* to alcoholism, by focussing on dependence, indicating those most at risk, and providing a role for education, in the broadest sense, to enable the individual to monitor his own drinking. It also provides for environmental measures of a legislative and fiscal kind to play a part in relation to control of consumption. It suggests that if treatment is failing to halt the growth of the problem, as it clearly is, then a shift to prevention in greater degree than hitherto is worth a trial.

It also has a lot to say about further preparing, for this preventive role, the many helping agents now involved almost wholly in treatment and aftercare. Most important, it specifies quite different drinking goals for prevention, goals which have nothing to do with abstinence, and so might be acceptable in the way prohibition was not.

In relation to *treatment*, it provides a rational basis for an educative approach, using some knowledge of pharmacology and behaviour therapy. This latter is by no means synonymous with formal measures to that end — it may be enough simply to explain these mechanisms and counsel appropriate changes in lifestyle in accord with the principles which govern the learning and unlearning of habits.

In *aftercare* it recognises the contribution of lifestyle to the earlier established drinking pattern, and points to the importance of a changed lifestyle if that pattern is not to be repeated. Above all, it makes us question the vague religious or psychodynamic approaches common to most treatment programmes now in vogue, and to shift to dealing with the here and now of everyday life.

It is necessarily tentative and incomplete as a theory. Without doing violence to the known facts it is good enough to provide a rational framework for all who work with alcoholics, enabling them to order their own observations constructively, and it leads to the formulation of questions which are capable of being answered by further enquiry. If there are better theories, their proponents should argue them rationally, to show that they accord more closely with the known facts.

Notes

1. The Ledermann Curve (1977), Report of a Conference (Alcohol Education Centre, London).
2. O'Connor, J. (1978), *The Young Drinkers* (Tavistock Publications, London).
3. Plant, M.A. (1979), 'Occupations, Drinking Patterns and Alcohol-Related Problems: Conclusions from a Follow-up Study', *British Journal of Addictions* (in press).
4. Seevers, M.H. (1968), 'Psychopharmacological Elements of Drug Dependence', *Journal of American Medical Association*, vol. 206, pp. 1263-6.
5. Whitehead, T.P., Clarke, C.A. and Whitfield, A.G.W. (1978), 'Biochemical and Haematological Markers of Alcohol Intake', *Lancet*, vol. I, pp. 978-81.
6. Thompson, T., Griffiths, R. and Pickens, R. (1973), 'Behavioural Variables Influencing Drug Self-Administration by Animals: Implications for Controlling Human Drug Use', in Bayer-Symposium, IV, *Psychic Dependence* (Springer-Verlag, Berlin and New York), pp. 88-103.

20 RELAPSE IN ALCOHOLISM: TRADITIONAL AND CURRENT APPROACHES

Gloria K. Litman

One of the few statements that can safely be made about alcoholism is that it is a relapsing condition. While in the short term treatment may be effective, it is the high rate of relapse subsequent to treatment that is of ultimate concern. Depending on the criteria for outcome, the fact that from 33 per cent to 66 per cent of patients will relapse is well recognised. Yet, as an area of research, this phenomenon has been surprisingly neglected until recently. This chapter will focus on the reasons for this neglect and then go on to examine current approaches to the problems. The basic premise is that shifting the focus from treatment success to precipitants of relapse raises a multitude of theoretical and practical questions about the nature of dependency disorders.

Relapse and the Disease Concept: Loss of Control and Craving

Alcoholic relapse attributed to 'loss of control' was first described by Jellinek[1] in 1946. The empirical data on which Jellinek's conclusions were based actually came from a questionnaire designed by members of Alcoholics Anonymous and circulated through their official organ, the *AA Grapevine*. Based on the 98 responses he received, Jellinek concluded:

> Loss of control means that as soon as a small quantity of alcohol enters the organism a demand for more alcohol is set up which is felt as a physical demand by the drinker . . . The drinker has lost the ability to control the quantity once he has started, but he can still control whether he will drink on any given occasion or not.

'Loss of control' was seen as 'the critical symptom of alcohol addiction'. It was thus that the disease model of alcoholism and the notion that relapse is inevitable once alcohol is ingested in any amount became irrevocably entwined. 'Loss of control' from Jellinek's point of view was a clear-cut model where the first drink acts as a signal to 'the metabolism of nervous tissue cells' so that a strong and compulsive desire is set up for more alcohol. This implies that there is no volition on the part of the alcoholic, that once this metabolic triggering has been set off, relapse is automatic, inevitable and beyond control. Because of the beginnings of research that seemed to indicate that some alcoholics could learn to control their drinking, particularly the laboratory work of Mello and Mendelson,[2,3] Keller[4] attempted to clarify and define the issue of loss of control. First of all, Keller points out that the medical model which Jellinek postulated was in fact a capitulation of the medical profession to a lay organisation, Alcoholics Anonymous. Keller's paper may be seen both as an attempt to re-conceptualise 'loss of control' and to wrest the concept from the layman and put it back in the hands of the medical profession, where he clearly thought it belonged. The centrality of the loss of control notion to the disease model of alcoholism was confirmed: 'Loss of control is pathognomonic of alcoholism . . . there is no room for an alcoholism without loss of control. Without loss of control, there is only a pre-alcoholismic phase.'

Keller reformulated the 'loss of control' concept to argue that the essence of addiction is that the alcoholic does not always have the choice of whether he will take that first drink or not, or whether when he does take that first drink, he will be able to stop. The automatic nature of the phenomenon was maintained, but the inevitability gave way to unpredictability. The concept of addiction was extended so that it was seen as a learned or conditioned response, which was an attempt to take the loss of control phenomenon out of the realm of primitive impulses and psychic pressures. The alcoholic had learned to respond to subtle and complex cues in his environment by drinking. If he has responded to 'critical' cues in the environment, he will not be able to stop. If the cues are not critical, then he can regain control over his drinking. To explain the fact that alcoholism was more common in men than in women, Keller advocated a genetic predis-position explanation.

Before we can discuss the implications of the 'loss of control' model for research on relapse, there is another concept that needs to be introduced, that of 'craving'.

In 1954, the World Health Organisation set up a meeting of experts to discuss physical dependence on alcohol. The concept of 'craving' was stressed as an important factor. Isbell[5] postulated that there were essentially two types of craving. First, there was 'non-symbolic' or physical craving which occurs in alcoholics who have consumed excessive amounts of alcohol over a protracted period of time. This type of craving is manifested by certain symptoms when alcohol is withdrawn. The cause of this craving was attributed to physiological alterations, although the mechanisms by which this took place were not understood. Isbell also postulated that there was another type of craving, 'symbolic' craving, which was psychological in origin, to account for relapse after a period of abstinence. Craving was also defined in such terms as 'urgent and overpowering desire', and 'irresistible urge' by Mardones.[6]

'Loss of control' and 'craving' are intimately related in Jellinek's[7] view. 'Non-symbolic' craving is responsible not for the actual ingestion of alcohol, which may be viewed by the alcoholic with 'distress and disgust', but to the expected relief from painful withdrawal symptoms. 'Symbolic' craving reflects the obsessive belief that if a sufficient amount of alcohol is consumed there will be reduction in tension. Before loss of control sets in, the alcoholic could reduce tension quite easily. After loss of control sets in, tension reduction could be achieved only through resumption of drinking.

Although Mello[8] pointed out that the constructs of 'craving' and 'loss of control' had little clinical or scientific utility because they were logical tautologies defined in terms of subsequent drinking behaviour, Ludwig and his colleagues[9] concluded that craving may be a determinant of relapse. When examined closely, the data they present fail to support this conclusion. Other work[10] which explored the relationships between stress, affect and craving concluded that craving may relate to other emotional states in some patients, but not in others.

But according to the disease model of alcoholism, relapse is determined by two constructs, 'craving' and 'loss of control'. As Marlatt[11] points out in his excellent review, 'craving' became reified to explain relapse, as 'will-power' became reified to explain abstinence. The scientific naiveté of this approach is regrettable. However, and more importantly, if craving explains the first drink and if loss of control is the explanation for subsequent drinking, then we can persuade ourselves that we already understand what is going on, and relapse is not a pressing subject for systematic investigation. It is not surprising that this crucial area has been neglected until fairly recently.

Psychological Approaches to Craving

Although 'psychological' aspects of relapse were acknowledged by both

Jellinek and Keller, there was no attempt to specify or operationalise what these aspects were. In this section, we shall examine three models of relapse which are psychologically based.

Relapse as 'Decay of Extinction'

A seminal attempt to formulate a psychological model of relapse was made by Hunt and his colleagues.[12,13,14] According to this model, the treatment of smoking, alcoholism and other dependent behaviours requires the removal of a previously well established behaviour pattern and/or the substitution of newer patterns. Therefore, they conceptualise treatment as the extinction of dependent behaviour and relapse as the 'decay of extinction' so that behaviour prior to treatment re-emerges. They also suggest that the underlying mechanism in nicotine, alcohol and heroin dependence may be similar.

The empirical data from which this model was derived demonstrated that when relapse over time was tabulated for a group of smokers who had successfully completed a treatment programme, the result was a downward sloping, negatively accelerated curve. This sort of decay process was seen to be similar to the typical 'extinction' or 'forgetting' curve which has been described in the literature on learning. Similar curves were found for alcoholics and heroin addicts.

This is an interesting formulation, both theoretically and in practical clinical terms. It would suggest that treatment, to be successful, would have to be restructured so that extinction or forgetting would not take place. However, as Litman, Eiser and Taylor[15] have shown, this attempt to reduce complex relapse behaviour to a simple curve does not take into account the fact that relapse is an individual process and cannot adequately be described by group data. Moreover, the data on which Hunt's model was based were calculated in such a way that the kind of curves they obtained were inevitable. Whether there is some underlying mechanism of relapse common to nicotine, alcohol and heroin remains an open question. What Hunt and his colleagues have actually shown is that cumulative curves calculated in similar fashion will show similar shapes.

Furthermore, Litman *et al.*[15] have analysed data which indicates that there are marked individual variations in relapse, both as to the period of time following treatment when alcoholics first relapse and to the patterns of drinking they resume following that initial relapse.

These data do not support a model of relapse which assumes that once an individual begins to drink heavily again, this heavy drinking will continue unabated, which is the essence of the 'loss of control' notion. In their data, the highest frequency of heavy drinking during the year following relapse was achieved by those individuals who showed erratic variation in their drinking. These findings suggest that those individuals whose relapse pattern is characterised by bouts of heavy drinking followed by short periods of complete abstinence were more likely to spend more days drinking heavily than those who were able to maintain a more stable drinking pattern. In other words, contrary to what traditional wisdom would suggest, those individuals who cut down on their drinking between bouts of heavy drinking, rather than cut out drinking completely, actually spent less days in heavy drinking and more days in 'acceptable' drinking during the year than did those who cut out drinking altogether between bouts of heavy drinking.

A Cognitive-behavioural Approach to Relapse

In a continuing series of careful experimental investigations into the determinants of relapse, Marlatt[11,16] has evolved what he has called a 'cognitive-behavioural' analysis. From this analysis, he has concluded that the most important determinants of relapse are environmental/situational factors and the individual's emotional and cognitive reactions to them. Central to this formulation is that regardless of what the actual effects of alcohol may be, it is the alcoholic's subjective experience and expectations of these effects that are crucial. They have postulated a common cognitive denominator, the Abstinence Violation Effect, which is based on cognitive dissonance theory and attribution theory, to account for the loss of control phenomenon in other than physiological terms.

Briefly then, relapse is seen to occur when the individual is in a high-risk situation with which he or she cannot cope except by drinking alcohol. These high-risk situations were: frustration and anger, social pressure, intrapersonal temptation and negative emotional states. Once this high-risk situation has been encountered and alcohol consumed, cognitive factors, particularly the perception of the self, come into play. Alcoholics may then modify their self-image to make it consonant with their drinking behaviour ('I haven't fully recovered, the disease has got me again') and will continue drinking. If the alcoholic has achieved a sufficient period of sobriety and is gaining confidence and personal control, a lapse would be self-attributed to personal weakness and shortcomings, rather than to environmental stressors and the individual's expectancy for continued failure will increase as a result. Thus the probability of continued drinking markedly increases. To overcome these attributions and expectancies of failure, Marlatt[16] suggests that a 'programmed relapse' could be incorporated into a treatment programme to demonstrate that one drink doesn't necessarily make one drunk. Skill training with alcoholics to teach them to cope with high-risk situations was carried out by Chaney, O'Leary and Marlatt.[17] The results indicated that the group who were trained in certain skills, particularly social skills, showed a significant decrease in the duration and severity of relapse episodes compared with individuals who participated in a discussion group or patients who received conventional inpatient treatment. However, these differences fell off sharply after three months.

The Interactional Model of Relapse

Litman and her colleagues[18,19] have postulated that relapse in alcoholics is an interaction between: (1) situations seen as dangerous in precipitating relapse; (2) the behaviours available in the individual's repertoire to cope with these situations; (3) the perceived effectiveness of these coping behaviours; and (4) the degree of self-attributed alcohol dependence.

Analysis of a questionnaire sent to a heterogeneous population of alcoholics indicated that relapse precipitants could be categorised as: (1) unpleasant mood states such as anxiety and depression; (2) external situations and euphoric feelings (e.g. 'When I pass a pub or off-licence'); (3) social anxiety ('When I have to meet people and feel afraid'); and (4) lessened cognitive vigilance and rationalisation (e.g. 'When I start thinking that one drink would do no harm').

Four different types of coping behaviours were found: (1) positive thinking (e.g. 'Stopping to examine my motives'); (2) distraction/substitution ('Doing some work around the house'); (3) avoidance ('Keeping away from friends who drink'); and (4) negative thinking ('Remembering the mess I've gotten myself in through drinking').

Effective coping behaviours were: (1) cognitive control (which combined both positive and negative thinking); (2) avoidance; and (3) distraction/substitution.

When it was first put forward, the interactional model suggested that there might be specific coping behaviours for specific dangerous situations. However, data on the differences between relapsers and survivors indicated that while cognitive control was the most effective coping strategy for survival, it was the flexibility of coping behaviour that seemed to determine survival. Relapsers saw more situations as dangerous than did survivors. The most dangerous situations were unpleasant mood states and external events. Contrary to what was expected, survivors saw themselves as more severely dependent than did relapsers.

From data gathered in intensive interviews with individuals who had not relapsed for a minimum of one year, Litman and Oppenheim[20] formulated a 'Model for Alcoholism Survival' which indicates that different coping strategies may have to be introduced at different times, ranging from simple avoidance to more complex cognitive strategies. If true, this may explain Chaney *et al.*'s[17] finding that skill training was effective in the short term in decreasing the duration and severity of relapse episodes, but not in the long term.

Psychological Models of Relapse: An Overview

Although conceived independently, there are similarities between the cognitive-behavioural model and the interactional model of relapse in that they both consider the relationship between environmental events and coping strategies. The major differences between the two appear to lie in the emphasis of social skills training in the cognitive-behavioural model on the one hand and on the other hand the emphasis on flexibility of coping skills, cognitive control and the gradual acquisition of coping behaviours in hierarchical fashion in the interactional model.

However, psychological approaches to the prevention of relapse, while promising, are still at an early stage. If charges of reification of 'craving' and 'loss of control' are hurled at the disease model, equally these charges could be thrown at psychological models which seem to reify 'cognitive control' without specifying the conditions and mechanisms of the underlying processes. One can compare the present status of psychological work on relapse with the situation in research on psychotherapy several years ago. There it was realised that the 'non-specifics' of the treatment situation were crucial factors and the laborious task began of specifying and measuring these factors.

As we have seen from Hunt's[12,13,14] work, complex behaviours such as relapse do not lend themselves readily to simple models. If the emphasis now is on cognitive factors, then these factors have to be operationalised and measured. Such concepts as motivation, self-efficacy,[21] learned helplessness[22] and locus of control[23] which may serve as mediators between environmental circumstances and subsequent relapse behaviour should be examined experimentally. Retrospective accounts may be used in model-building. But the crucial test of any theory is whether it will predict with accuracy subsequent behaviour, without the tautology inherent in the medical model approach.

At this point, we can begin to speculate about the implications for treatment in the psychological approaches to the problem of relapse in alcoholism. There are two main areas in which current treatment practices would need to be altered quite radically.

The first is the actual structure of the treatment situation itself. If the focus is shifted from the treatment of alcoholism to the prevention of relapse, then the intensive hospitalisation of patients followed by the occasional outpatient appointment would have to be changed. If we examine the concept underlying this type of structure, it becomes apparent that this was developed directly from the medical model for treatment of many acute illnesses. The patient is hospitalised, the 'disease' is treated, and post-hospitalisation appointments are seen primarily as 'check-ups'. It is assumed that the major part of the treatment has already been carried out in the hospital setting. However, restructuring would mean that initial hospitalisation, if necessary at all, is seen as only the first step in treatment, with subsequent appointments geared intensively towards the prevention of relapse. In practical terms, this would mean that resources would have to be extended over a longer period of time.

This brings us to the second way in which treatment would have to be altered. For many years now, the cry has been for individualised treatment rather than large scale treatment programmes. But, with few notable exceptions very little work has been done to specify how this could be carried out effectively. Current work would suggest that a gradient of coping strategies over time may be a productive method. This would mean that for a given patient, different forms of coping skills could be taught at different times, depending on the individual's life situation and psychological readiness and preparedness to learn and utilise such skills.

At first glance, the cost of this approach may seem high. However, if we consider this in terms of cost-effectiveness, it may be far more economical in the long run to design systematic treatment programmes to prevent relapse than to continue with intervention which in theory is geared to handle acute phases, but which in practice can mean that treatment is extended over many years, with discouraging results.

Notes

1. Jellinek, E.M. (1952), 'The Phases of Alcohol Addiction', *Quarterly Journal of Studies on Alcohol*, vol. 13, pp. 673-84.
2. Mello, N.K., McNamee, H.B. and Mendelson, J.H. (1968), 'Drinking Patterns of Chronic Alcoholics: Gambling and Motivation for Alcohol', in Cole, O.J. (ed.), *Clinical Research in Alcoholism*, Psychiatric Research Reports, no. 24 (American Psychiatric Association, Washington, D.C.).
3. Mendelson, J.H., Mello, N.K. and Soloman, P. (1968), 'Small Group Drinking Behavior: An Experimental Study of Chronic Alcoholics', in Wikler, A. (ed.), *The Addictive States*, Proceedings of the Association for Research in Nervous and Mental Disease (Plenum Press, New York).
4. Keller, M. (1972), 'On the Loss of Control Phenomenon in Alcoholism', *British Journal of Addiction*, vol. 67, pp. 153-66.
5. Isbell, H. (1955), 'Craving for Alcohol', *Quarterly Journal of Studies on Alcohol*, vol. 16, pp. 38-42.
6. Mardones, R.J. (1955), ' "Craving" for Alcohol', *Quarterly Journal of Studies on Alcohol*, vol. 16, pp. 51-3.
7. Jellinek, E.M. (1960), *The Disease Concept of Alcoholism* (Hillhouse Press, Highland Park, New Jersey).
8. Mello, N.K. (1975), 'A Semantic Aspect of Alcoholism', in Cappell, H.D. and LeBlanc, A.E. (eds.), *Biological and Behavioural Approaches to Drug Dependence* (The Addiction Research Foundation, Toronto).
9. Ludwig, A.M. and Wikler, A. (1974), ' "Craving" and Relapse to Drink', *Quarterly Journal of Studies on Alcohol*, vol. 35, pp. 108-30.
10. Litman, G.K. (1974), 'Stress, Affect and Craving: The Single Case as a Research Strategy', *Quarterly Journal of Studies on Alcohol*, vol. 35, pp. 131-46.
11. Marlatt, G.A. (1978), 'Craving for Alcohol, Loss of Control and Relapse: A Cognitive-behavioural Analysis', in Nathan, P.E., Marlatt, G.A. and Løberg, T. (eds.), *Alcoholism: New Directions in Behavioural Research* (Plenum Press, New York).
12. Hunt, W.A., Barnett, L.W. and Branch, L.G. (1971), 'Relapse Rates in Addiction Programs', *Journal of Clinical Psychology*, vol. 27, pp. 455-6.
13. Hunt, W.A. and Matarazzo, J.D. (1970), 'Habit Mechanisms in Smoking', in Hunt, W.A. (ed.), *Learning Mechanisms in Smoking* (Aldine, Chicago).
14. Hunt, W.A. and Matarazzo, J.D. (1973), 'Three Years Later: Recent Developments in the Experimental Modification of Smoking Behavior', *Journal of Abnormal Psychology*, vol. 81, pp. 107-14.
15. Litman, G.K., Eiser, J.R. and Taylor, C. (1979), 'Dependence, Relapse and Extinction: A Theoretical Critique and Behavioral Examination', *Journal of Clinical Psychology*, vol. 35, pp. 192-9.
16. Marlatt, G.A. and Gordon, J.R. (1978), 'Determinants of Relapse', in Davidson, P. (ed.), *Behavioural Medicine, Changing Health Lifestyle* (Bruner-Mazel, New York).
17. Chaney, E.P., O'Leary, M.R. and Marlatt, G.A. (1979), 'Skill Training with Alcoholics', *Journal of Consulting and Clinical Psychology*, vol. 46, no. 5, pp. 1092-1104.
18. Litman, G.K., Eiser, J.R., Rawson, N.S.B. and Oppenheim, A.N. (1977), 'Towards a Typology of Relapse: A Preliminary Report', *Drug and Alcohol Dependence*, vol. 2, pp. 157-62.
19. Litman, G.K., Eiser, J.R., Rawson, N.S.B. and Oppenheim, A.N. (1979), 'Differences in Relapse Precipitants and Coping Behaviours Between Alcoholic Relapsers and Survivors', *Behaviour Research and Therapy*, vol. 17, pp. 89-94.
20. Litman, G.K. and Oppenheim, A.N. (1980), 'A Model for Alcoholism Survival' (in preparation).

21. Bandura, A. (1977), 'Self-efficacy: Toward a Unifying Theory of Behavior Change', *Psychological Review*, vol. 84, pp. 191-215.
22. Abramson, L.Y., Seligman, M.E.P. and Teasdale, J.D. (1978), 'Learned Helplessness in Humans: Critique and Reformulation', *Journal of Abnormal Psychology*, vol. 87, pp. 49-74.
23. Rotter, J.B. (1966), 'Generalized Expectancies for Internal Versus External Control of Reinforcement', *Psychological Monographs*, vol. 8 (whole no. 609).

Part Six

ALCOHOL AGENDAS

21 ALCOHOLISM TREATMENT: BETWEEN GUESSWORK AND CERTAINTY

Griffith Edwards

There is nothing disreputable about guesswork. If a difference of opinion is what makes a horse race, the backing of a good guess is what leads to productive research, an astute and helpful therapeutic intervention, a bold and constructive policy decision, a new model of understanding. Neither is there anything improper about certainty. We need to hold on to the certainty that our fellow human beings who have fallen foul of alcohol must not be demeaned or rejected or thrown on any scrap heap, but are given such succour as is within our power, and Vaillant's chapter in this book is a resounding affirmation of this position. Scientific certainties are also very important. It is important to identify and hold on to what we certainly know, and to determine how this knowledge is to be applied and exploited.

Both guesswork and certainty also have their dangers, especially when the two categories are confused. A guess rather easily becomes a received wisdom — it was never more than an imperfectly informed guess that no alcoholic could ever return to normal drinking. Once the guess had been elevated to received wisdom no one cared or dared to look for evidence which might refute the conjecture. Moral postures, institutional and professional positions, political expedients, self-comfort, fears and fantasies, all frequently invite premature closure of useful questioning. But there is also the danger of losing touch with our few certainties, of gaining and holding no ground. We can be certain that many people who have been vastly beset by drinking have shown themselves capable of dealing with their problems, although we may at present only be able to guess their reasons for recovery.

Anyone interested in alcoholism treatment and in contributing to its advance has therefore to come to terms with how he is to navigate an area which is inevitably characterised by many perplexities, and discover how he is to find a way through without running on to the rocks on either side, without wrecking himself on the gloom-washed reefs of nihilism or running on to the dazzling but treacherous rocks of blind and premature certainty. It is not an easy course to chart, as the report by Grant and Clare (Chapter 3) so vividly demonstrates.

How do we find our way through the rich, varied, usefully

contentious and unusually thought-provoking material which the contributors to this book have provided? The purpose of this final chapter is to examine in practical manner what we might today best do about treatment in the light of what these authors tell us. And any position taken today must of necessity be provisional and a holding operation.

The form of this chapter will be to examine under a number of headings what is and what is not known about alcoholism treatment and what actions might be recommended as the interim 'best buy', while at the same time seeking to identify the gaps and guesses which could profitably be made the subject of research.

What Is It That We Are Treating?

We are at present lacking any well worked out and validated model which explains the nature of the condition with which we are dealing. Someone should take Harré's challenge (Chapter 18) and attempt a formal analysis of the models which are at present latent in our thinking, and see whether a model can now be proposed which is likely to serve us better. Indeed, Davies (Chapter 19) makes a bold and useful start.

Medicine has often got on quite well with effective treatment of conditions where neither the nature of the condition being treated nor the nature of the treatment being employed are understood — depression and its treatment by ECT provide a familiar example. But with alcoholism the situation has not been one of agnosticism: we have believed that we know the nature of the condition being treated and have therefore believed that our treatments are rationally founded. A faulty model with guesswork enshrined as certainty is much less to be preferred than out-and-out pragmatism.

Let us look at a proposition as to the nature of abnormal drinking which is now rather coming to the fore. A recent WHO report[1] has proposed that differentiation should be made between the *alcohol dependence syndrome* and *alcohol-related disabilities*. Alcohol dependence is then seen as graded, rather than all-or-none. The implications of this formulation have been discussed elsewhere.[2] Some of the work which is published in this volume begins to confirm the usefulness of the dependence idea — the experimental work on response to a challenge dose of alcohol discussed by Hodgson (Chapter 10) and the predictive power of dependence in a four year outcome study reported by Polich (Chapter 6). Things become interesting when the same idea is found to be of use in two very different types of research. Some other reports have also recently been published bearing on the utility of the dependence concept,[3,4] and Hodgson has offered an up-to-date review of evidence and arguments[5] while Shaw[6] has taken a usefully critical stance.

Here then let us risk a guess. We may guess that somewhere within the range of behaviours that go by the name of alcoholism, there lies a condition which is not to be understood simply in terms of variation but rather in terms of state. We try today to catch its image descriptively in terms of the dependence syndrome while others before us have certainly been trying to perceive its outline in terms of 'alcoholism as disease'. We are guessing though that somewhere in that landscape there is a real beast to be described rather than an arbitrary cut on a continuum, a label, an abominable and mythical medicalisation.

How far can this guesswork be edged toward certainty? This is a question to be watched closely over the next few years and it may before long be possible to take a much less tentative position. If there really is a dependence syndrome of the kind which WHO describes, the significance for the future of treatment and of related researches may be profound. A new dimension is introduced for the description of any case series, and no control group can then be constructed without reference to this dimension. In terms of Glaser's 'matching hypothesis' (Chapter 11) we are then immediately faced with the question of 'What treatments for what degrees of dependence?' Outcome studies may look at progression or regression of dependence as a measurable outcome variable. Different degrees of dependence may propose different drinking goals. And if one finds that this descriptive concept has such a range of useful predictive powers it then becomes mandatory to invest in the effort to get behind the description, to understanding the psychobiological nature of the syndrome.

In focussing this amount of attention on the recent WHO formulation we should not forget that there are also many other ideas in circulation as to the nature of the condition being treated: these ideas are not necessarily mutually exclusive or contradictory, and they may ultimately be brought together within a more comprehensive model. For instance, there is the essential premise that the drinking behaviour does not exist in disembodied state, but is manifested by an *individual*. Properties of the individual may therefore be presumed to be relevant to a range of concerns — to the origins and perpetuation of the behaviour in question, the response to treatment intervention and to the course of natural history. Too much attention has previously perhaps been given to whether and to what extent people with drinking problems differ from the generality of the population, and to the search for the uniquely differentiating 'alcoholic personality', for instance. The question of how people with drinking problems differ from people without such problems may be of far less importance than analysis of the between-individual variations in the problem population. Skinner's work (Chapter 16) bears on this issue.

There are though many other postulates of psychological or social as well as biological nature, which would have to be built into any comprehensive model as to 'the nature of the condition', with all the pointers toward heterogeneity rather than any monolithic concept of 'the' alcoholic. Ultimately such analysis of the individual and his social attributes must speak to the person-specific approach to treatment, and to refinement of 'the matching hypothesis'.

Natural History and Career

Here we have very few certainties but the story is to an extent unfolding as evidenced in the work reported by Vaillant (Chapter 1), Polich (Chapter 6) and Armor (Chapter 5). We are beginning to know the outlines of what happens to a clinical population of alcoholics over time, and to know a little of the strategies that may be related to their attainment and maintenance of sobriety. Although Vaillant's work offers us some insights into the fate of the untreated alcoholic, there is still difficulty in building up the full picture of 'the two worlds' with a danger that the clinic-centred view of things will overshadow our understanding (Room, Chapter 13).

Apart from further descriptive longitudinal studies we also stand in need of certain conceptual clarifications if any sense is to be made of the material of such studies. We need to separate out the ideas of *natural history* and *career*. Those two terms sometimes seem to be employed as if they were equivalent, whereas they in fact carry very different messages. 'Natural history' is an idea borrowed from medicine, and underlies such concepts as Jellinek's 'phases of alcoholism' – it implies a biological condition with a tendency once established toward a march of symptoms and progression, but with possibilities of fluctuation and 'spontaneous regression' not excluded. Social scientists are however usually very aware that the two concepts are not identical, and are today rather likely to stigmatise natural history as carrying ideas which are out-dated and much embedded in the now unpopular disease theory. To discard the natural history formulation would though be premature, and the possibility of the dependence syndrome having a natural history cannot be dismissed. Once tolerance has been established and withdrawal symptoms experienced there may be biological processes at work which in the presence of further drinking will show further developments which are biologically determined and in those circumstances inevitable: by the same token once drinking has been cued to withdrawal relief and avoidance, the reinforcement and elaboration of this learning process may be predictable if the person continues to drink. At present we know far too little about the pace, progress, variation and significance of such progressions, the co-variance of variables, and the psychobiological basis of such progression.

The medically or psychobiologically rooted concept of natural history should in no way be seen as inimical to the social concept of career. The two ideas are supplementary. What in totality happens to the individual must be determined by his individuality, and by all manner of social processes and the perceptions and reactions of those around him, by ideas as to the nature of his condition which society offers him, and by routings in and out of difficulty which are as much socially determined pathways as any highways and byways. But having stressed the importance of the social perspective to understanding what happens to the drinker, one must hold in view the likelihood that those social processes may here be bearing on an individual who is not in a naive and pristine state as regards his response to alcohol: the natural history of his dependence (in psychobiological terms) may be more or less narrowing his drinking options, and to greater or lesser degree negating or defeating the social influences. As witness to a modifiable, slowly working and sometimes dormant psychobiological determinism, natural history speaks to the influence of the rather sinister joker in the pack of career. The idea of natural history if taken in isolation will lead to a mechanistic and hopelessly insensitive analysis of the unfolding story of the individual's life, while the idea of career will be self-handicapping if it rejects the relevance of the natural history of dependence for fear of the hegemony of medical thinking. We need to put our guesses together.

Coming for Help

We have too little understanding of why it is that people with drinking

problems come for help. The conventional approach which attempts
to analyse this matter in terms only of the immediate pressures and
motivations is inadequate, for there must surely be a *process* which
leads up to this point, a sequence of events, actions and reactions,
self-appraisals and appraisals by others. The immediate crisis may in a
proportion of instances be overwhelmingly important, but that crisis
only has its meaning in the context of what has gone before. What is
the nature of the ripe moment?

This moment often has within it enormous potential for change.
In the controlled trial which compared 'treatment' and 'advice',[7,8]
despite the lack of outcome difference between the two modalities
there was considerable before-and-after difference for each group.
The twelve months after seeking help were on a number of criteria
greatly improved when compared with reconstruction of the twelve
months before treatment. We may guess that whatever the impact of
treatment, it is interacting with a special state of preparedness for
change.

How essential in fact is treatment intervention to the full
realisation of that moment? No doubt the answer to this question must
vary from patient to patient. At one extreme there may be the case
where treatment is mere epiphenomenon, while in other instances
treatment may be essential to hold and develop that moment, and
where this is the case one must wonder what are the essential and
immediate elements in treatment that work this alliance with the
moment. How much is it a matter of offering transition into the social
role of 'patient in treatment', how much depends on some immediate
clarification and redefinition of the problem or the goal, what weight
is to be given to the immediate encouragement? A more precise analysis
of the nature of this moment might allow us to understand the *interaction* between treatment and career at an important juncture, and thus
lead to the design of immediate interventions intelligently to maximise
the possibilities for change. At present we may often be failing fully to
exploit this moment, or at worst our immediate reception of the
patient may be such as to damage possibilities.

The argument has often been heard that we should 'get patients into
treatment earlier'. With uncertainties as to what treatment will actually
give benefit to whom, it seems premature to search the streets and bring
in great numbers of 'early cases'. But in principle there are again here
questions susceptible to research. If we accept the idea that the
moment of help-seeking is often a point for potential change but that
what has to be understood is the antecedent process, there is then a

conceptual difference between pulling people into treatment earlier (which may be useless), and accelerating the process of preparation for change (which may be valuable).

In Chapter 13 of this book Robin Room considers the relationship between clinical alcoholic populations and the total pool of the community's drinking problems and the matters with which he deals are close to those which we have just been discussing, as is Mäkelä's discussion of what medicine can properly take on (Chapter 14). Apart from analysis of the general process of help-seeking and the way in which cultural expectations, public health messages, and professional activism select this or that category of problem drinker out of the general pool as being 'the suitable case for treatment', there are interesting ancillary questions as to why some people who are seeking help route themselves in one direction while others find a different route. Why do some people turn to AA rather than to formal treatment services? Why do some patients predominantly seek help through the services of physical illness hospitals and with self-presentation which emphasises the physical problems, while others are far more inclined to route themselves toward psychiatric help, despite physical disabilities? Some patients present themselves to special alcoholism agencies, while others receive their help through more general agencies which do not define the drinking problem as central. Is all this to be seen as evidence of informed self-matching, or are people often routing themselves in inappropriate directions?

Both treatment staff and treatment researchers have over recent years been rather neglectful of help-seeking as an important and complex process. We have too easily wrapped it up with some glib phrase about 'motivation', too easily categorised our patients as 'court referred or self-referred', while failing to be sufficiently surprised by the extraordinary and central fact that another patient has decided to come for help.

Assessment

That patients should be assessed is implicit in any discussion of treatment — we could scarcely dispute that we need to know with what and with whom we are dealing as a prelude to any formulation of an individual treatment plan. Given current uncertainties as to how best to carry out treatment there must then also be parallel uncertainty as to what sort of knowledge about that patient is relevant to treatment planning. In such a situation an honest appraisal of our case notes may suggest that we are sometimes routinely collecting a lot of information that we never put to any very certain use, or alternatively a little reflection may suggest that the current scope of our intake assessment fails adequately to deal with issues which we have begun to sense as being of importance.

Besides what must be retained in traditional areas of assessment, here are some of the issues which discussions in this book point toward as being important in any total assessment. The aim is to identify some of the areas which need attention rather than to tackle questions of how in each instance measurements are to be made. There is much work to be done in designing instruments and procedures.

This list may start with the plea that *degree of dependence* should now always be routinely measured as part of the intake procedure. As already argued, it is a reasonable guess that assessment of dependence must be related to goal setting. Here Hodgson and his colleagues have designed a standardised instrument.[9] Ideas which Orford puts forward in Chapter 9 of this book suggest that assessment of what might be called *the patient's cognitive mapping* may be very important. In general terms what is being focussed on under that heading is the need to understand under a number of sub-headings the way in which the patient himself is appraising his situation — the need to get beyond and behind the objective facts of the case to the patient's interpretation and internalisation of the objective facts. We need for instance to develop more precise ways of defining and measuring the dimensions and substance of his ambivalences (the good and bad pay-offs from further drinking), and the point he has reached in decision-making. This is vital to assessment if one of the aims of treatment is to aid the decision-making process and edge people toward resolution of their ambivalence. Another sub-heading must deal with the patient's sense of autonomy and resourcefulness as opposed to his sense of helplessness.

A further important area for assessment is opened by Litman (Chapter 20), when she discusses work on coping strategies and precipitants of relapse. Assessment of these factors must be the preliminary to any attempt to apply these ideas in treatment. For instance, it seems possible that patients may be repeatedly passing before our eyes who are grossly deficient in coping repertoire. They may have made all the right decisions, but are lacking in the skills to transform resolve into successful action. Analysis of precipitants of relapse must be similarly important.

This book has not dealt to any extent with drinking and family interactions, but it would seem necessary in any comprehensive assessment to find ways in which we can describe the place of the excessive drinking within the family nexus. For example, what are the wife's coping styles, and how productive or counter-productive do they appear to be? What are the gains or losses resulting from the alcoholic's drinking, so far as the non-alcoholic partner is concerned?

And implicit in Glaser's plea for more accurate matching (Chapter 11) is the reminder that we need to give sharper attention to screening for possible underlying conditions. Here we are touching on a sector of the traditional agenda of assessment. This aspect of the work is though by no means always carried out with thoroughness when specialism has resulted in too exclusive focus on drinking at the cost of wider awarenesses. Assessment of the many presentations of affective disturbance requires a high level of practised clinical skill. Phobic states or pathological jealousy are easily overlooked if they are not routinely screened.

Turning then from these notes on the re-thinking which may be needed on the content of assessment, there is a related question which requires attention. What is the impact of any assessment procedure on the person being assessed? What vision of his situation and definition of his problem is being covertly implied by the questions we ask, or do not ask? To see assessment and treatment as sharply demarcated is false. Assessment can and should be the initiation of treatment, and a powerful influence for self re-appraisal and change. We need to seek much better understanding of the nature of the processes which are involved.

It could be argued that the ideas put forward in this section are liittle more than an elaboration of the obvious, a plea for elaboration of what we would all today do anyhow in a competent clinical assessment. The plea is in fact that we should build on what we are doing but with the coupled belief that there really is quite a lot of building to be done. The data-bank which could be built up by more systematic and imaginative assessment would be of great value. We need an approach to assessment which goes more beneath the surface.

Treatment in Transition

The alcoholism treatment field may over recent years sometimes have looked rather like a smoking battle-field, littered with the smashed remains of previous beliefs and practices. Who today can believe in abstinence as the only treatment goal? What has happened to apomorphine aversion, to lysergic acid, to metronidazole? Who can really believe that the long inpatient stay or intensive involvement in analytically oriented groups holds the answers? In simple terms the bulk of recent treatment research challenges rather than confirms conventional treatment approaches.

Yet some of the figures on that battle-ground have the appearance of being dead but unwilling to lie down. It is easy enough for a sharp-shooter or a neat controlled trial to pick off such a peripheral figure as metronidazole, but it is far more difficult to knock over a central and pervasive assumption such that in alcoholism treatment 'more means better'. Whatever the research may show, whatever the barrage of facts laid down, there when the smoke clears sits the great survivor still running 'his' programme, with ten weeks' inpatient stay as recommended minimum, a group therapy session every day, classes and blackboard lectures, busy OT workshops, the team approach and a visiting padre, bussing-out of patients to AA around the district, all this and more and at great expense. One must plead that Jaffe's contrasting of prodigal and parsimonious treatment (Chapter 2) be taken to heart. How does the prodigal model of treatment relate to any currently supportable model as to the nature of the condition being treated?

The only research evidence which might be interpreted as supporting intensive interventions comes from Costello's re-analysis of previously published series (Chapter 7). This elegant work should though be interpreted cautiously, for the material analysed is data which may in many ways be subject to selection bias and artifact. For instance, the more prestigious and richly endowed treatment facility may be in a position selectively to recruit a more motivated clientele, while the centre with poor facilities becomes the dumping-ground for the less hopeful case.

To insist on the need radically to revise old certainties on what counts as good treatment is not to be destructive for the sake of destruction. We cannot though hope to advance, or free time and resources to tackle the needed investigations of the next wave of good guesses if too great a proportion of our energies is tied to old ways of doing things.

What on present evidence and in the light of present uncertainties can indeed be offered as the interim outlines of a 'best buy' treatment approach? This is the question which will be asked by the clinician who is close to the demands of daily realities, and who is constitutionally suspicious of research discussion if it drifts too far from these realities. He is the person whose position Vaillant (Chapter 1) understands so well. Taking both Jaffe's and Schuckit's reviews as important starting points, synthesising what has been argued by different authors in this book and adding some more personal guesswork, the answer to such an enquiring clinician might be set out under the following headings:

1. *Different patients require different types of help*, and alcoholic populations are not homogeneous. To run a programme by a rule-book is not sensible.

2. *Assessment of patients matters very much*, and is a clinical responsibility which must be scrupulously met. Time at present allocated to treatments of unnecessary intensity should be re-allocated to more thorough initial assessment.

3. *Underlying and accompanying conditions* must be identified and treated. Staff must therefore have within the team a high level of general medical and psychiatric competence.

4. *The moment of help seeking* has to be sympathetically understood in terms of its meaning for patient and family. Everything possible must be done to confirm the potential of this moment.

5. *Goals* have to be agreed on rather than imposed, and this implies due attention to the process of *decision-making*. The goals should be explicit and should be worked out practically and in detail, both for the long and the short term. Short-term goals should be attainable and immediately rewarding. Once a decision has been made by the patient, an invitation to firm commitment may aid the keeping of the commitment.

6. *The therapist matters*. He should be positively encouraging and willing to show his warmth and convey a message of hope and possibility.

7. *Self-determination and self-responsibility* should be emphasised, not only in terms of the spoken message but in the content of the programme leaving much to the patient once goals and methods have been identified. The therapist must not teach or reinforce helplessness.

8. *Methods for working toward agreed goals* should include review and discussion of the patient's coping repertoire, and encouragement of substitute activities. Relapse precipitants should be identified and plans made as to how they are to be better met, or avoided.

9. *Self-monitoring* should be encouraged, by note-keeping or diary. This information should be reported back to the therapist and used in further planning.

10. *The spouse* should be involved in the initial assessment, goal setting, and the whole follow-through.

11. *The treatment setting* should be outpatient care except for

detoxification, or where necessary for treatment of underlying or accompanying conditions, or where indicated as life-saving intervention.

12. *The intensity of treatment* should be kept to a sensible minimum with emphasis on facilitating the patient's own exploitation of his natural resources, on clarification of his own working methods, with treatment an aid to monitoring rather than its being a massive or escalating intervention.

13. *The social dimension of treatment* in terms of the patient's dealing with external realities is of importance and goals and methods in this area will require clarification, but this is a prime area for the rewarding exercise of self-determination.

14. *AA referral* should routinely be put on offer where an abstinence goal has been chosen. It is freely available, but not to be forced.

15. *The cost of treatment* should be monitored with constant willingness to revise deployment of resources so as to maximise the benefits.

So much for an outline which is intended more as a check list for discussion than as anything definitive. It must be evident that a great deal here is guesswork. And if we are to talk about special needs of individual people and special sub-groups, Annis (Chapter 8) reminds us of the need further to investigate the extent to which women with drinking problems may have special needs.

The Treatment Programme as Case in its Own Right

Those who give treatment and who organise treatment services familiarly see their patients as subject for study. The focus of analysis is in fact nearly always exclusively upon the determinants of the patient's drinking rather than the determinants of the therapist's treatment, the patient's rather than the treatment service's motivation, the patient's failure rather than the clinic's, the personality of the alcoholic rather than the image of the institution. However, institutional self-scrutiny far from being an introspective luxury is a necessity if we are to understand why we run our services in a particular way, and the extent to which the choice is made rationally or alternatively by fad or fashion or political pressure. Analysis of these matters is necessary if we are to enjoy true freedom of choice rather than be the play-thing of processes we choose to ignore.

The study of the evolution, organisation, function and ideology of alcoholism treatment services must therefore be seen as having become a matter of practical urgency. Room (Chapter 13) produces evidence of the extraordinary and burgeoning growth in American alcoholism treatment facilities over recent years, and the work by Robinson and Ettorre (Chapter 15) begins to sketch out the evolution of services in the UK. As Hawks emphasises (Chapter 12) the Third World has to resist any invitation to follow unthinkingly in Western ways of treatment design. We need studies not only of national and local organisation, but case studies of individual treatment enterprises taken as social institutions in their own right. Ground-rules for sensible and practical planning are discussed by Banham (Chapter 17), who also exemplifies the advantage of bringing outside thinking to bear on a specialised field.

What Future for Guesswork?

The whole alcoholism treatment field now has about it a great sense of potential for change and movement. In terms of analogy with our patients, we might though be seen as having reached a stage of discontent with our old ways and a sensed need for change, rather than as yet showing any firm evidence of committed decision-making, or of having arrived at any absolute clarification of goals and methods. Somewhat confusedly we have reached a help-seeking moment and we at least agree that the potential and meaning of what is in many ways a crisis, should not be lost.

If we look at the past error of our ways, it might be seen in terms of our having too often confused guesswork with certainty. For the future what is needed is sharper distinction between knowledge and assumption, coupled with the freshness and daring which will generate new and better guesses.

Notes

1. Edwards, G., Gross, M.M., Keller, M., Moser, J. and Room, R. (1977), *Alcohol-Related Disabilities*, WHO Offset Publication no. 32 (WHO, Geneva).
2. Edwards, G. (1977), 'The Alcohol Dependence Syndrome: Usefulness of an Idea', in Edwards, G. and Grant, M. (eds.), *New Knowledge and New Responses* (Croom Helm, London; University Park Press, Baltimore).
3. Chick, J. (1980), 'Is There a Unidimensional Alcohol Dependence Syndrome?' *British Journal of Addiction* (in press).
4. Saunders, W.M. and Kershaw, B.W. (1979), 'Spontaneous Remission From Alcoholism − A Community Study', *British Journal of Addiction*, vol. 74, pp. 251-66.

5. Hodgson, R. (1980), 'The Alcohol Dependence Syndrome: A Psychological Perspective', *British Journal of Addiction* (forthcoming).

6. Shaw, S. (1979), 'A Critique of the Concept of the Alcohol Dependence Syndrome', *British Journal of Addiction,* vol. 74, pp. 339-48.

7. Edwards, G., Orford, J., Egert, S., Guthrie, S., Hawker, A., Hensman, C., Mitcheson, M., Oppenheimer, E. and Taylor, C. (1977), 'Alcoholism: A Controlled Trial of "Treatment" and "Advice" ', *Journal of Studies on Alcohol,* vol. 38, pp. 1004-31.

8. Orford, G. and Edwards, G. (1977), *Alcoholism,* Maudsley Monograph (Oxford University Press, Oxford).

9. Stockwell, R., Hodgson, R., Edwards, G., Taylor, C. and Rankin, R. (1979), 'The Development of a Questionnaire to Measure Severity of Alcohol Dependence', *British Journal of Addiction,* vol. 74, pp. 79-87.

NOTES ON CONTRIBUTORS

Helen M. Annis: Addiction Research Foundation, Toronto, Ontario.

David J. Armor: Rand Corporation, California.

John M.M. Banham: McKinsey & Co. Inc., London.

Anthony Clare: Institute of Psychiatry, University of London.

Raymond M. Costello: University of Texas.

David L. Davies: Alcohol Education Centre, London.

Griffith Edwards: Addiction Research Unit, Institute of Psychiatry, University of London.

Betsy Ettorre: Addiction Research Unit, Institute of Psychiatry, University of London.

Frederick B. Glaser: Addiction Research Foundation, Toronto, Ontario.

Marcus Grant: Alcohol Education Centre, London.

Rom Harré: University of Oxford.

David V. Hawks: World Health Organization, Geneva.

Ray J. Hodgson: Addiction Research Unit, Institute of Psychiatry, University of London.

Jerome H. Jaffe: New York State Psychiatric Hospital.

Gloria K. Litman: Addiction Research Unit, Institute of Psychiatry, University of London.

Klaus Mäkelä: Finnish Foundation for Alcohol Studies, Helsinki.

Jim Orford: University of Exeter.

J. Michael Polich: Rand Corporation, California.

David Robinson: Addiction Research Unit, Institute of Psychiatry, University of London.

Robin Room: School of Public Health, Berkeley, California.

Marc A. Schuckit: UCSD School of Medicine, California.

Harvey A. Skinner: Addiction Research Foundation, Toronto, Ontario.

George E. Vaillant: Harvard Medical School, Boston.

INDEX

abstinence: abstention theories of
dependence 82-3, 92; abstinence
violation effect 298; as outcome
criterion 150; as treatment goal
16, 34, 54, 67, 82-4, 91-3, 103,
158, 165; associated with relapse
rate 81, 87-9, 92; following
treatment 16; follow-up study
data of remission 101-2; maintained without treatment 20,
35, 38; one day at a time 15,
170; reinstatement of drinking
after 162; results of Alcoholics
Anonymous study 28; short-
term abstinent prognosis 86,
92, 108-9; *see also* treatment
goals
accidents, alcohol-related death rate
99, *see also* drunken driving
offenders
addiction, alcohol *see* alcohol
dependence syndrome
Addiction Research Foundation,
Ontario 128, 135, 181, 191, 252
Addiction Research Unit, London
143
'advice versus treatment' study 65,
143-4, 154, 186, 312
age, relation to relapse rates 90; *see
also* young alcoholics
Al-Anon 13, 27
alcohol abuse, contrasted with
dependence 21; *see also* problem
drinking
alcohol consumption figures 100
alcohol dependence syndrome:
abstention theory (Jellinek) 82;
contrasted with alcohol-related
disabilities 308; description of
syndrome 162, importance as
prognostic factor 107; integrity
of concept 309, research criteria
101; subdivision of 38-40
alcoholic beverage industry 62
Alcoholics Anonymous (AA) 14, 20,
26, 32, 63, 65; abstinence as sole
goal 181; assists natural recovery
forces 21; attitude to 'controlled

drinking' 68, 294-5; compared
with aversion therapies 24; in
North America 34; influence on
planning policy 239; medical
referral to 28, 318; women in AA
131
Alcoholism Treatment Units (ATUs):
current planning policy 235;
development, historical 236-8
America, North: fashions in treatment
style 34-5; social changes 61
Antabuse (Disulfiram) 20-1, 24-5,
53-5, 113, 115, 184
antidepressant drugs 41, 42
apomorphine 70, *see also* aversion
techniques
arrest: as compulsion to treatment
219; criterion for relapse 97, 101;
drunkenness offenders 229-30;
see also drunken driving offenders
aversion techniques 24, *see also*
Antabuse

Beck depression Inventory 187-8
behaviour modification techniques:
associated with treatment
outcome 20, 113; aversion
techniques 24; caused by natural
forces 21; changing attitudes to
63, 70; cognitive-behavioural
approach to relapse 298-9;
controlled drinking as goal 166;
coping skills training 300-1; cue
exposure 175; decay of extinction
theory 297
binge drinking 82
blackouts 85, 101
bleeding, gastro-intestinal 99
blood alcohol concentration (BAC)
97
brain damage 198

Cambridge-Somerville (CASPAR)
Programme 14, 27-8
chronicity of alcoholism 18, 110
cirrhosis: alcohol-related cause of
death 90; criterion for problem
drinking 101; mortality rate 99